# GH💀STBUSTERS™
## GHOST BUSTED

### GHOSTBUSTERS: Ghost Busted
#### Stories by Nathan Johnson and Matt Yamashita
#### Art by Chrissy Delk, Maximo V. Lorenzo, Michael Shelfer & Nate Watson

Copy Editor - Ao Ringo
Layout and Lettering - Michael Paolilli & Lucas Rivera
Cover Design - James Lee
Original Cover Art - Hans Steinbach

Editors - Luis Reyes & Bryce P. Coleman
Pre-Production Supervisor - Vicente Rivera, Jr.
Print-Production Specialist - Lucas Rivera
Managing Editor - Vy Nguyen
Senior Designer - Louis Csontos
Senior Designer - James Lee
Associate Publisher - Marco F. Pavia
President and C.O.O. - John Parker
C.E.O. and Chief Creative Officer - Stu Levy

A  Manga

TOKYOPOP and 👁 are trademarks or registered trademarks of TOKYOPOP Inc.

TOKYOPOP Inc.
5900 Wilshire Blvd. Suite 2000
Los Angeles, CA 90036

E-mail: info@TOKYOPOP.com
Come visit us online at www.TOKYOPOP.com

ISBN: 978-1-4278-1459-3

First TOKYOPOP printing: October 2008
10 9 8 7 6 5 4 3 2 1
Printed in the USA

# GH🍥STBUSTERS™

## GHOST BUSTED

**STORIES BY**
**NATHAN JOHNSON AND MATT YAMASHITA**

**ART BY**
**CHRISSY DELK, MAXIMO V. LORENZO,**
**MICHAEL SHELFER & NATE WATSON**

**TOKYOPOP®**

HAMBURG // LONDON // LOS ANGELES // TOKYO

# GHOSTBUSTERS
## Ghost Busted

## Table of Contents

# WHO YA GONNA CALL?

# GHOSTBUSTERS

IN THOSE HALCYON DAYS OF THE MID-1980'S THE PHANTASTIC GHOSTBUSTERS – RAY, EGON, PETER AND WINSTON – ARRIVED ON THE SCENE TO SAVE ALL OF NEW YORK CITY FROM THE EVIL SUMERIAN GOD OF DESTRUCTION, GOZER. SURE, MANHATTAN WAS LEFT COVERED IN MOLTEN MARSHMALLOW, THANKS TO THE TEAM'S IMMOLATION OF A GIGANTIC MANIFESTATION OF RAY'S BELOVED STAY PUFT MARSHMALLOW MAN, BUT AT LEAST THE CITY WAS SAFE. THE GHOSTBUSTERS WERE HEROES, NOW, RIGHT?

THAT IS, UNTIL A LAWSUIT FROM THE CITY FORCED THE BOYS TO CLOSE UP SHOP AND PERFORM THE MOST DEMEANING OF TASKS TO MAKE ENDS MEET. BUT WHEN NEW YORK'S OWN PENT-UP ANGER BEGAN TO FEED AN UNDERGROUND RIVER OF PURE CONCENTRATED EVIL, WHO DO YOU THINK THE MAYOR CALLED? YOU KNOW IT! AND ONCE AGAIN, WITH THE HELP OF LOVELY LADY LIBERTY, THE BIG APPLE WAS SAVED, AND THE BOYS WERE BACK ON TOP.

WHAT HAVE THE GHOSTBUSTERS BEEN UP TO SINCE THEN, YOU MAY ASK? WELL, PARANORMAL DISTURBANCES CONTINUE TO POP UP ALL AROUND THE CITY – FROM A HAUNTED BROADWAY MUSICAL TO A HIGH-FASHION PHANTASM – BUSINESS IS GOOD! MAYBE TOO GOOD, IN FACT, BECAUSE A PEST FROM THE PAST HAS DECIDED TO MAKE THINGS PERSONAL...

# GHOSTBUSTERS™

# CHAPTER I

# THE THEATER OF PAIN

### STORY BY
### MATT YAMASHITA

### ART BY
### MAXIMO V. LORENZO

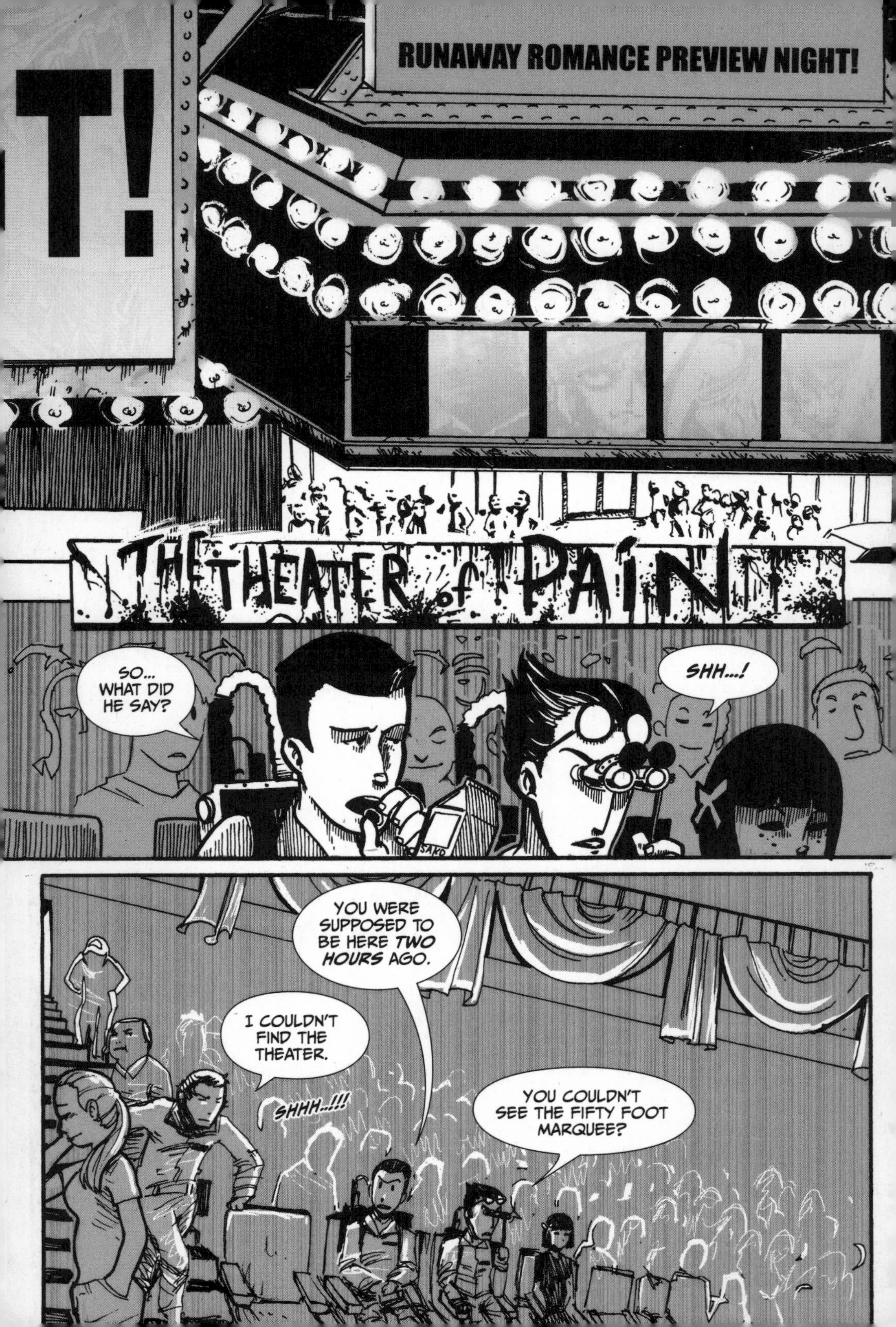
RUNAWAY ROMANCE PREVIEW NIGHT!
T!
THE THEATER of PAIN
SO... WHAT DID HE SAY?
SHH...!
YOU WERE SUPPOSED TO BE HERE TWO HOURS AGO.
I COULDN'T FIND THE THEATER.
SHHH...!!!
YOU COULDN'T SEE THE FIFTY FOOT MARQUEE?

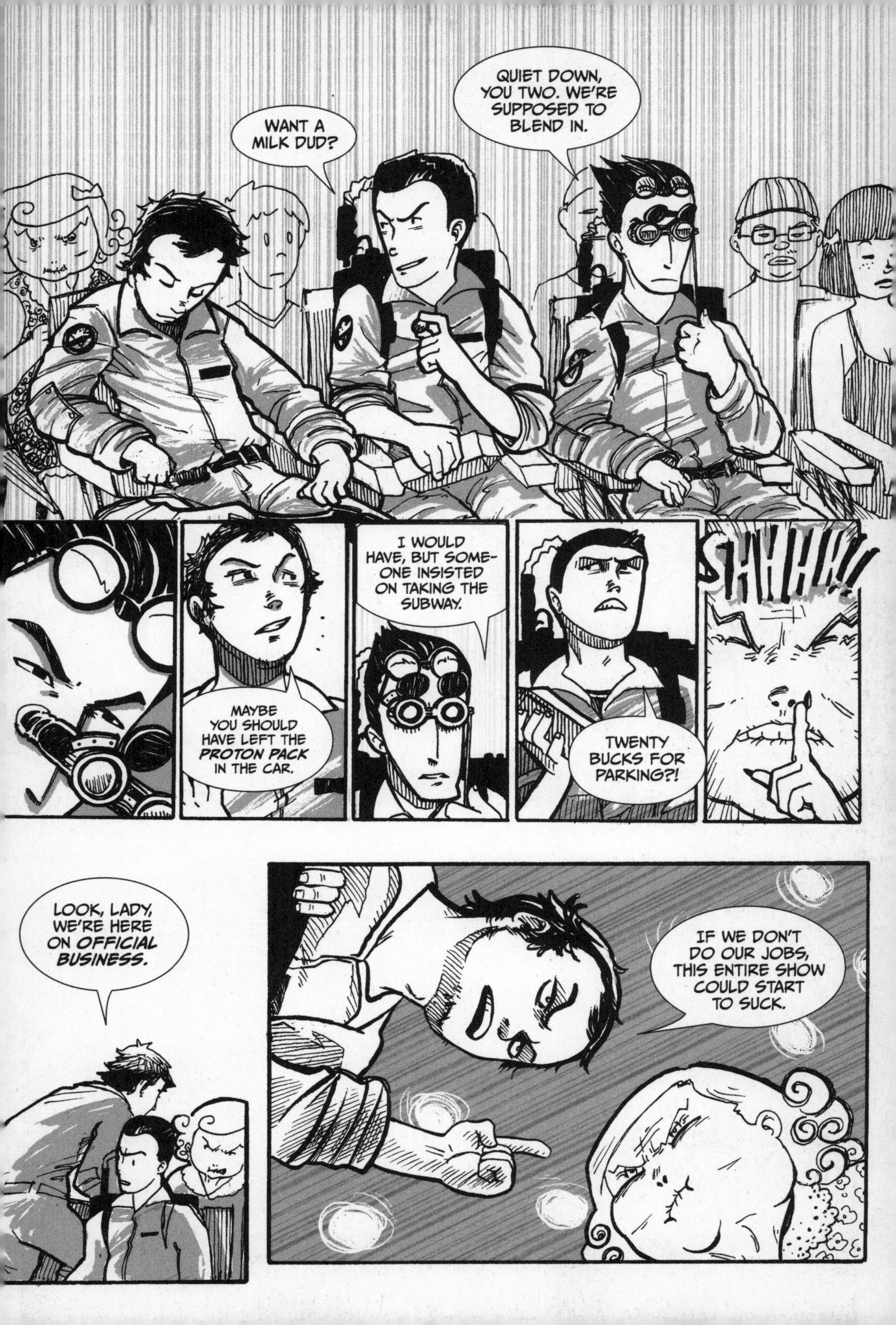

WANT A MILK DUD?
QUIET DOWN, YOU TWO. WE'RE SUPPOSED TO BLEND IN.
MAYBE YOU SHOULD HAVE LEFT THE *PROTON PACK* IN THE CAR.
I WOULD HAVE, BUT SOME-ONE INSISTED ON TAKING THE SUBWAY.
TWENTY BUCKS FOR PARKING?!
SHHHH!!
LOOK, LADY, WE'RE HERE ON *OFFICIAL BUSINESS*.
IF WE DON'T DO OUR JOBS, THIS ENTIRE SHOW COULD START TO SUCK.

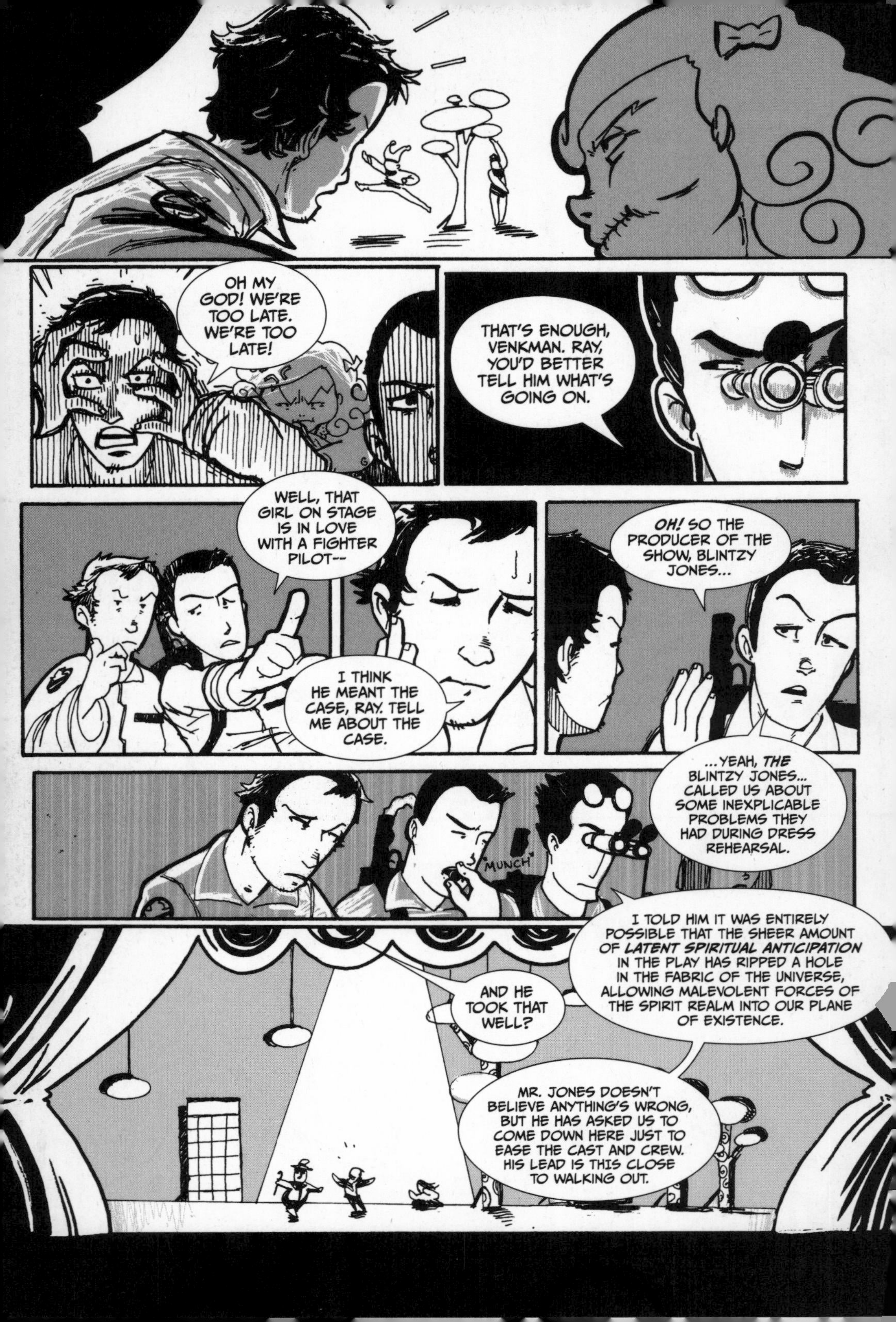
OH MY GOD! WE'RE TOO LATE. WE'RE TOO LATE!
THAT'S ENOUGH, VENKMAN. RAY, YOU'D BETTER TELL HIM WHAT'S GOING ON.
WELL, THAT GIRL ON STAGE IS IN LOVE WITH A FIGHTER PILOT--
I THINK HE MEANT THE CASE, RAY. TELL ME ABOUT THE CASE.
*OH!* SO THE PRODUCER OF THE SHOW, BLINTZY JONES...
...YEAH, *THE* BLINTZY JONES... CALLED US ABOUT SOME INEXPLICABLE PROBLEMS THEY HAD DURING DRESS REHEARSAL.
MUNCH
I TOLD HIM IT WAS ENTIRELY POSSIBLE THAT THE SHEER AMOUNT OF *LATENT SPIRITUAL ANTICIPATION* IN THE PLAY HAS RIPPED A HOLE IN THE FABRIC OF THE UNIVERSE, ALLOWING MALEVOLENT FORCES OF THE SPIRIT REALM INTO OUR PLANE OF EXISTENCE.
AND HE TOOK THAT WELL?
MR. JONES DOESN'T BELIEVE ANYTHING'S WRONG, BUT HE HAS ASKED US TO COME DOWN HERE JUST TO EASE THE CAST AND CREW. HIS LEAD IS THIS CLOSE TO WALKING OUT.

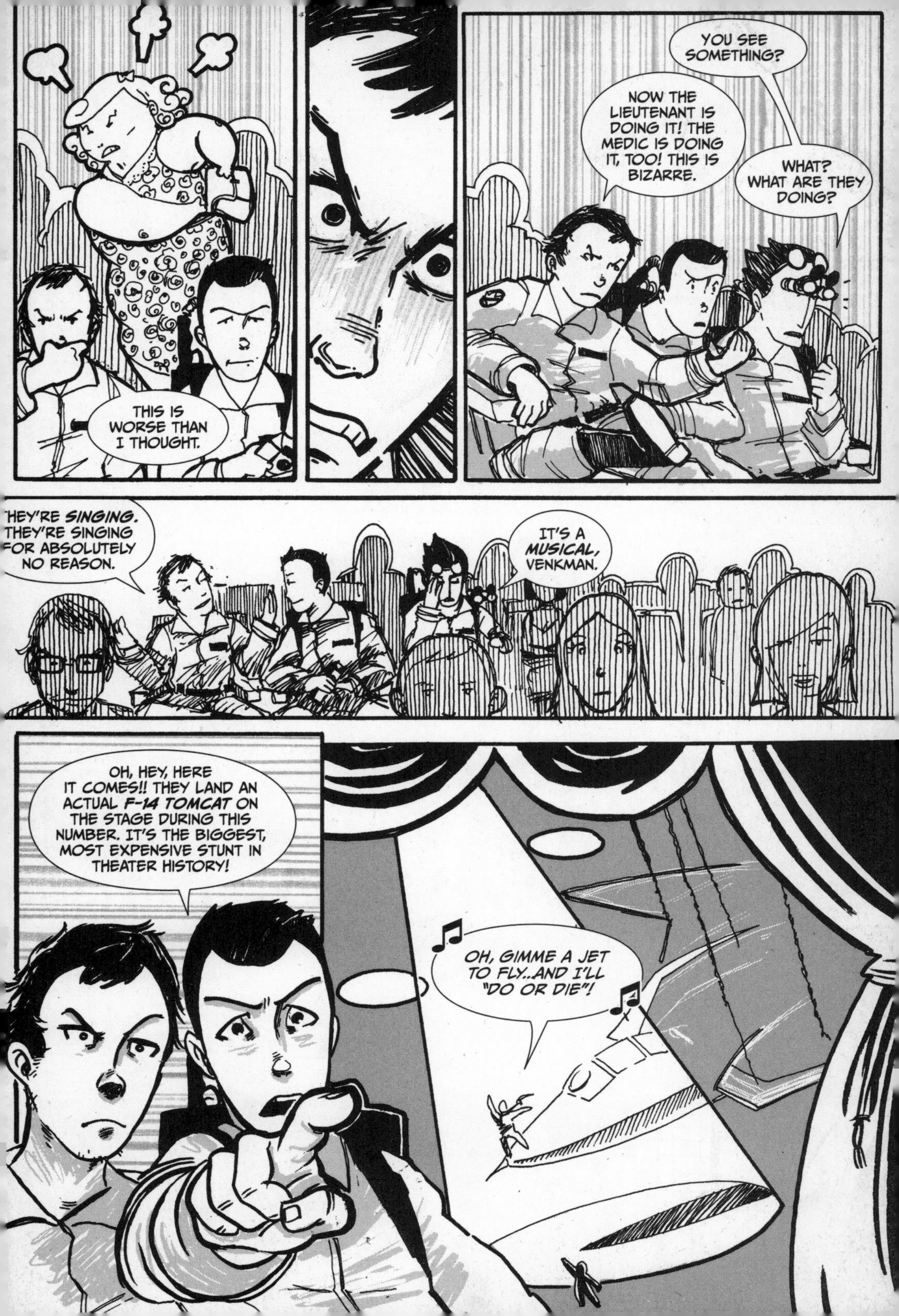
THIS IS WORSE THAN I THOUGHT.
YOU SEE SOMETHING?
NOW THE LIEUTENANT IS DOING IT! THE MEDIC IS DOING IT, TOO! THIS IS BIZARRE.
WHAT? WHAT ARE THEY DOING?
THEY'RE *SINGING*. THEY'RE SINGING FOR ABSOLUTELY NO REASON.
IT'S A *MUSICAL*, VENKMAN.
OH, HEY, HERE IT COMES!! THEY LAND AN ACTUAL *F-14 TOMCAT* ON THE STAGE DURING THIS NUMBER. IT'S THE BIGGEST, MOST EXPENSIVE STUNT IN THEATER HISTORY!
*OH, GIMME A JET TO FLY...AND I'LL "DO OR DIE"!*

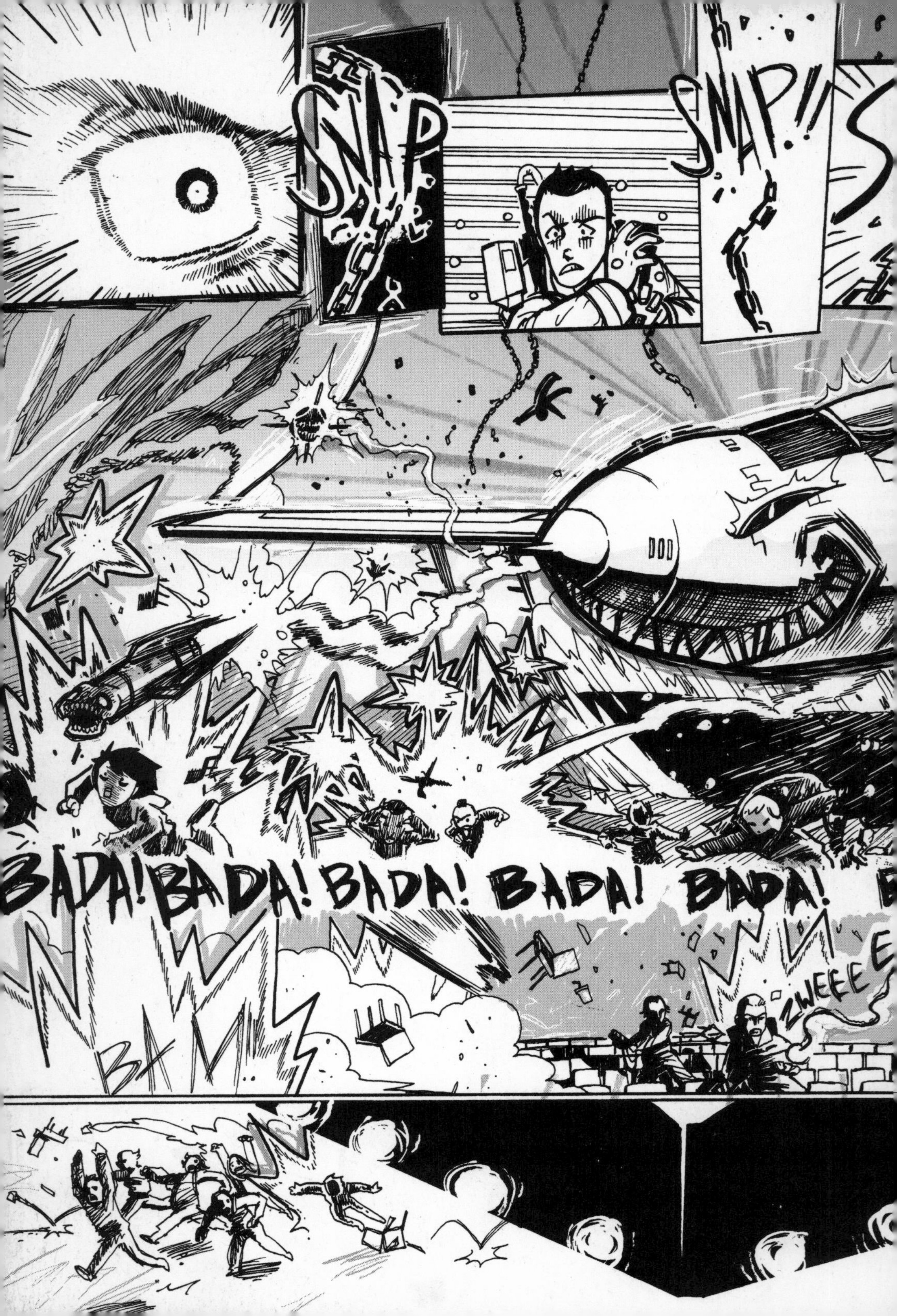
SNAP
SNAP!!
BADA! BADA! BADA! BADA! BADA!
BAM
ZWEEEE

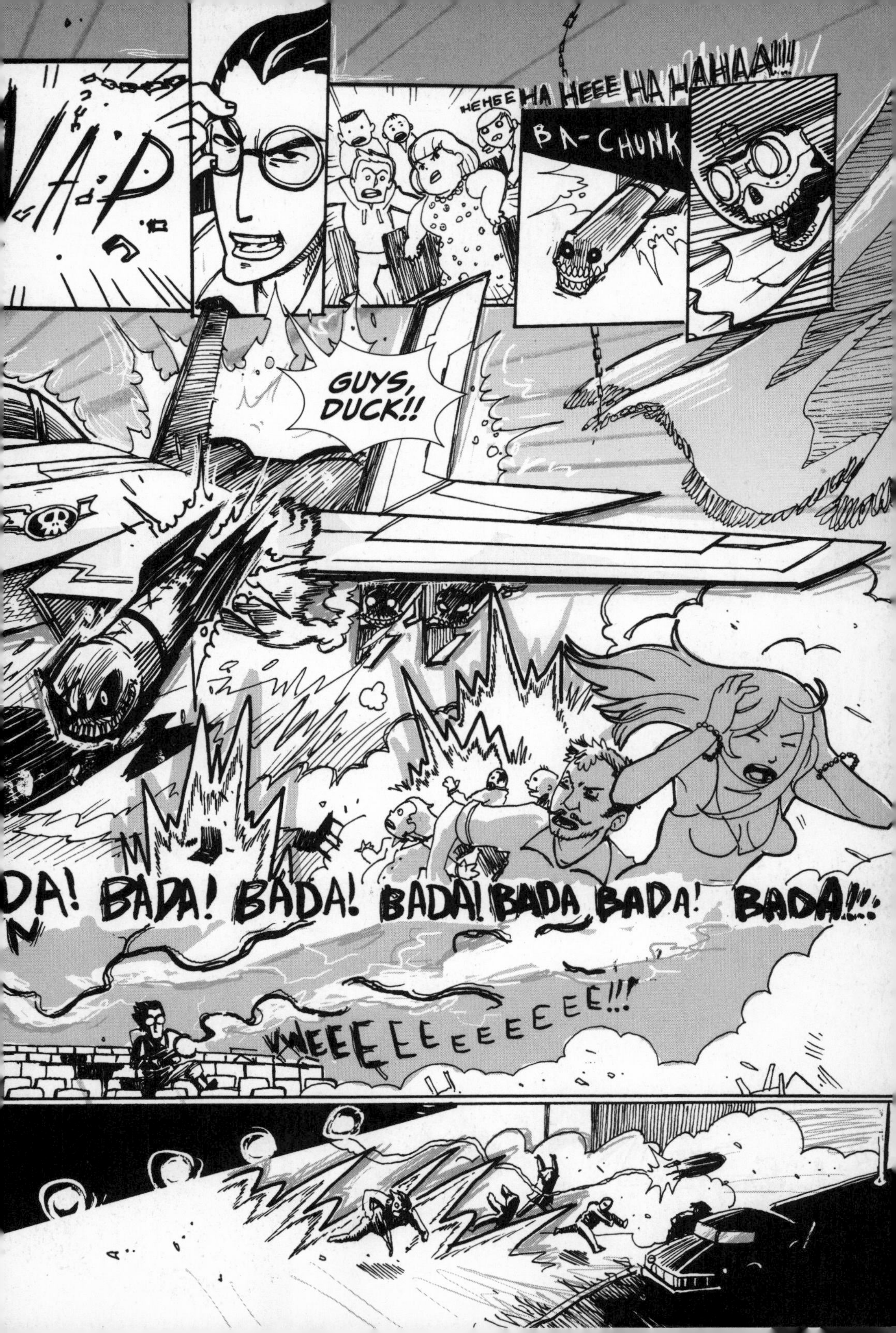

VA:P
HEHEE HA HEEE HA HAHAA!!!
BA-CHUNK
GUYS, DUCK!!
DA! BADA! BADA! BADA! BADA BADA! BADA!!!
WEEEEEEEEEEEE!!!

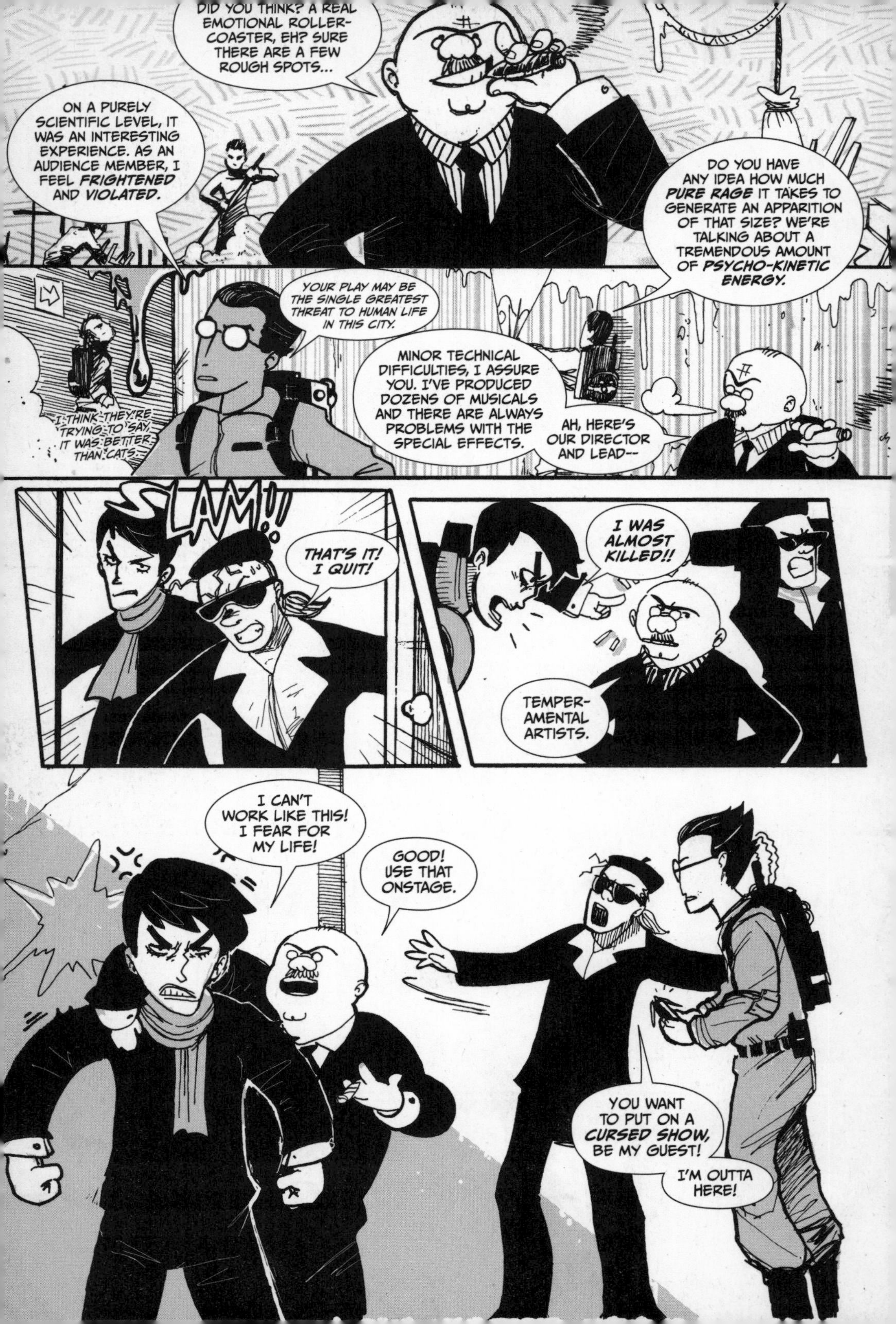

DID YOU THINK? A REAL EMOTIONAL ROLLER-COASTER, EH? SURE THERE ARE A FEW ROUGH SPOTS...
ON A PURELY SCIENTIFIC LEVEL, IT WAS AN INTERESTING EXPERIENCE. AS AN AUDIENCE MEMBER, I FEEL FRIGHTENED AND VIOLATED.
DO YOU HAVE ANY IDEA HOW MUCH PURE RAGE IT TAKES TO GENERATE AN APPARITION OF THAT SIZE? WE'RE TALKING ABOUT A TREMENDOUS AMOUNT OF PSYCHO-KINETIC ENERGY.
YOUR PLAY MAY BE THE SINGLE GREATEST THREAT TO HUMAN LIFE IN THIS CITY.
I THINK THEY'RE TRYING TO SAY, IT WAS BETTER THAN CATS.
MINOR TECHNICAL DIFFICULTIES, I ASSURE YOU. I'VE PRODUCED DOZENS OF MUSICALS AND THERE ARE ALWAYS PROBLEMS WITH THE SPECIAL EFFECTS.
AH, HERE'S OUR DIRECTOR AND LEAD--
SLAM!!
THAT'S IT! I QUIT!
I WAS ALMOST KILLED!!
TEMPER-AMENTAL ARTISTS.
I CAN'T WORK LIKE THIS! I FEAR FOR MY LIFE!
GOOD! USE THAT ONSTAGE.
YOU WANT TO PUT ON A CURSED SHOW, BE MY GUEST!
I'M OUTTA HERE!

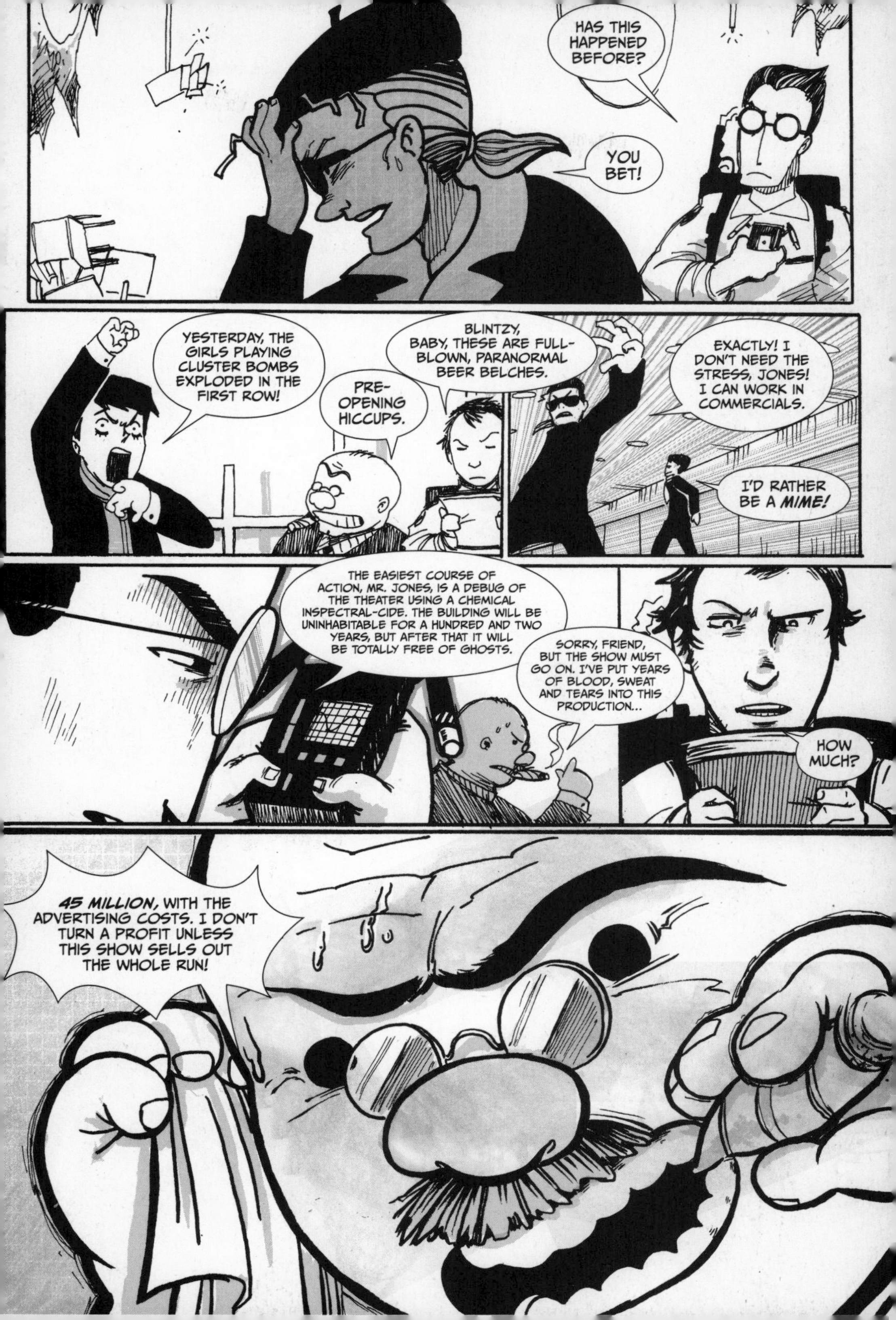
HAS THIS HAPPENED BEFORE?
YOU BET!
YESTERDAY, THE GIRLS PLAYING CLUSTER BOMBS EXPLODED IN THE FIRST ROW!
PRE-OPENING HICCUPS.
BLINTZY, BABY, THESE ARE FULL-BLOWN, PARANORMAL BEER BELCHES.
EXACTLY! I DON'T NEED THE STRESS, JONES! I CAN WORK IN COMMERCIALS.
I'D RATHER BE A *MIME!*
THE EASIEST COURSE OF ACTION, MR. JONES, IS A DEBUG OF THE THEATER USING A CHEMICAL INSPECTRAL-CIDE. THE BUILDING WILL BE UNINHABITABLE FOR A HUNDRED AND TWO YEARS, BUT AFTER THAT IT WILL BE TOTALLY FREE OF GHOSTS.
SORRY, FRIEND, BUT THE SHOW MUST GO ON. I'VE PUT YEARS OF BLOOD, SWEAT AND TEARS INTO THIS PRODUCTION...
HOW MUCH?
***45 MILLION,*** WITH THE ADVERTISING COSTS. I DON'T TURN A PROFIT UNLESS THIS SHOW SELLS OUT THE WHOLE RUN!

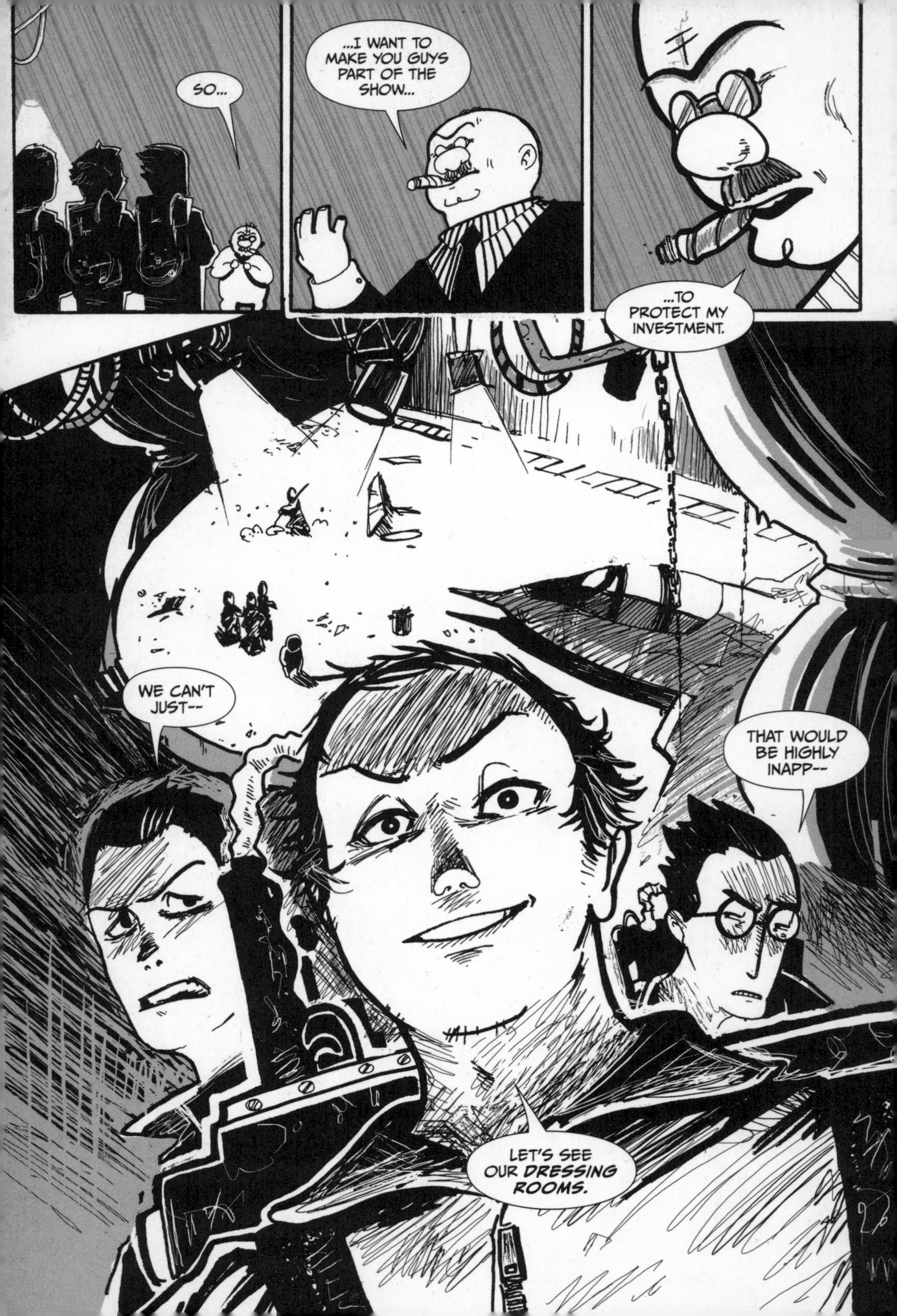
SO...
...I WANT TO MAKE YOU GUYS PART OF THE SHOW...
...TO PROTECT MY INVESTMENT.
WE CAN'T JUST--
THAT WOULD BE HIGHLY INAPP--
LET'S SEE OUR *DRESSING ROOMS.*

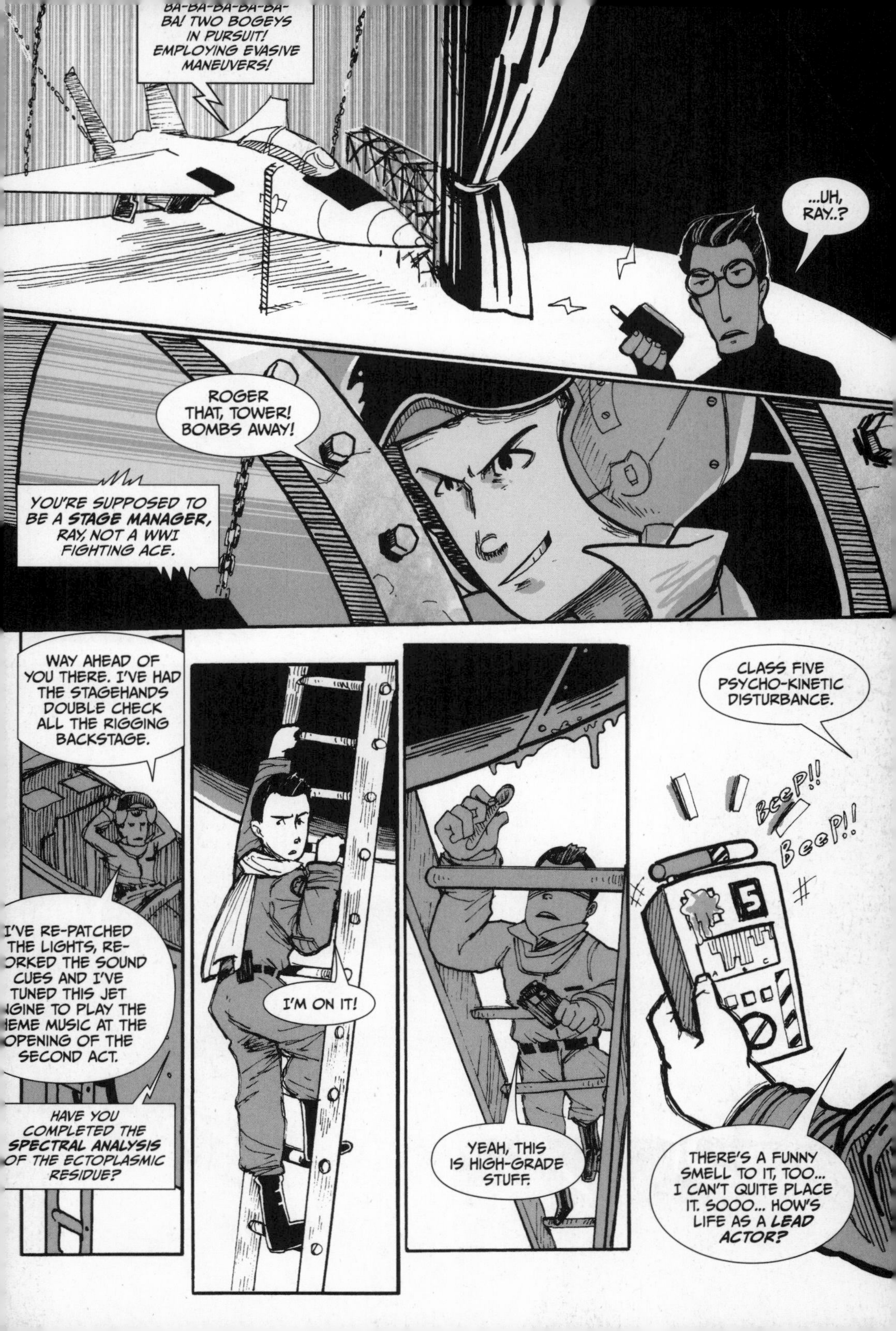
BA-BA-BA-BA-BA-BA! TWO BOGEYS IN PURSUIT! EMPLOYING EVASIVE MANEUVERS!
...UH, RAY..?
ROGER THAT, TOWER! BOMBS AWAY!
YOU'RE SUPPOSED TO BE A STAGE MANAGER, RAY, NOT A WWI FIGHTING ACE.
WAY AHEAD OF YOU THERE. I'VE HAD THE STAGEHANDS DOUBLE CHECK ALL THE RIGGING BACKSTAGE.
I'VE RE-PATCHED THE LIGHTS, RE-ORKED THE SOUND CUES AND I'VE TUNED THIS JET IGINE TO PLAY THE HEME MUSIC AT THE OPENING OF THE SECOND ACT.
HAVE YOU COMPLETED THE SPECTRAL ANALYSIS OF THE ECTOPLASMIC RESIDUE?
I'M ON IT!
YEAH, THIS IS HIGH-GRADE STUFF.
CLASS FIVE PSYCHO-KINETIC DISTURBANCE.
BEEP!! BEEP!!
5
THERE'S A FUNNY SMELL TO IT, TOO... I CAN'T QUITE PLACE IT. SOOO... HOW'S LIFE AS A LEAD ACTOR?

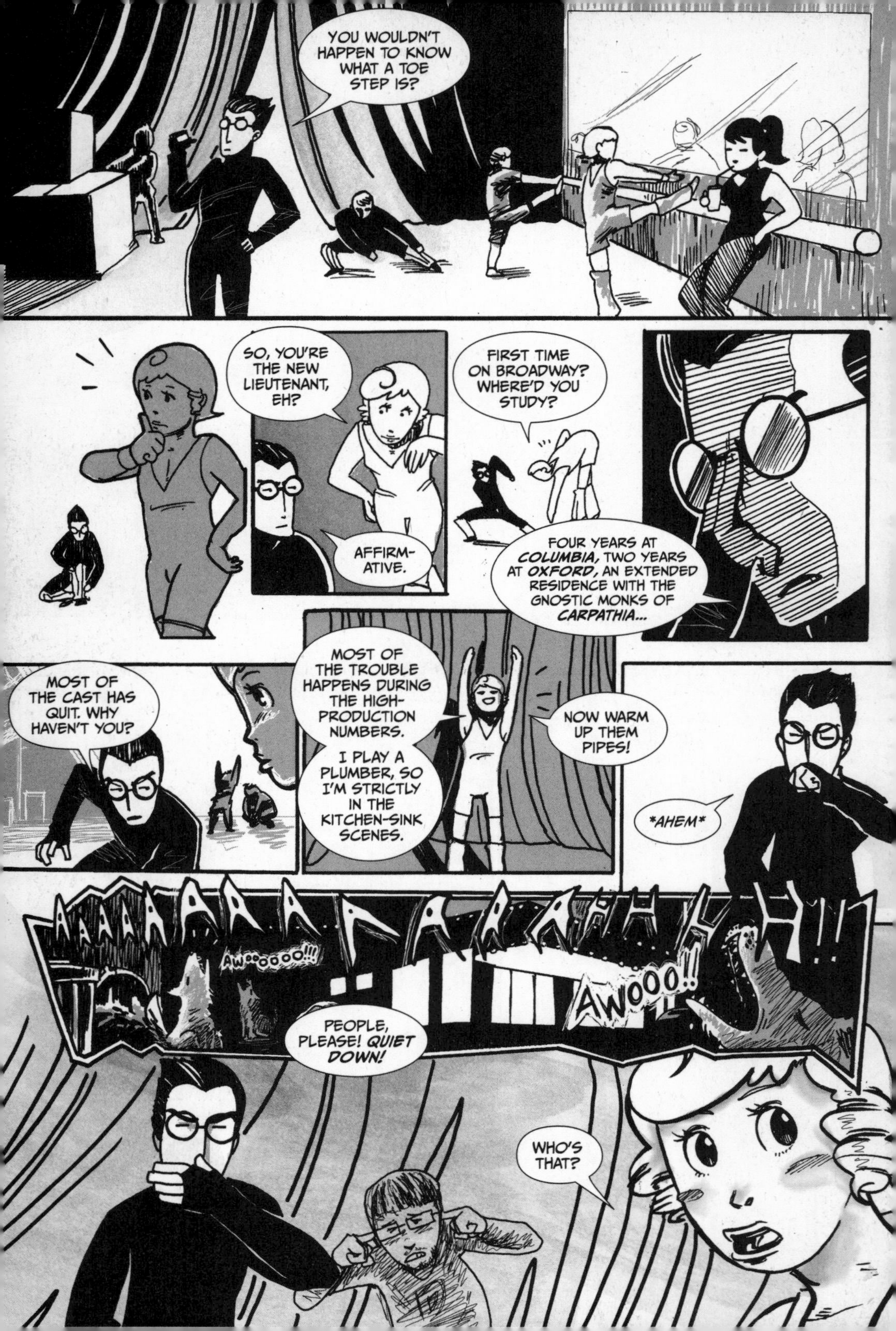
YOU WOULDN'T HAPPEN TO KNOW WHAT A TOE STEP IS?
SO, YOU'RE THE NEW LIEUTENANT, EH?
AFFIRM- ATIVE.
FIRST TIME ON BROADWAY? WHERE'D YOU STUDY?
FOUR YEARS AT COLUMBIA, TWO YEARS AT OXFORD, AN EXTENDED RESIDENCE WITH THE GNOSTIC MONKS OF CARPATHIA...
MOST OF THE CAST HAS QUIT. WHY HAVEN'T YOU?
MOST OF THE TROUBLE HAPPENS DURING THE HIGH-PRODUCTION NUMBERS.
I PLAY A PLUMBER, SO I'M STRICTLY IN THE KITCHEN-SINK SCENES.
NOW WARM UP THEM PIPES!
*AHEM*
AAAAAAAAAAAAAAHHHHH!!
AWOOOOOO!!!
AWOOO!!
PEOPLE, PLEASE! QUIET DOWN!
WHO'S THAT?

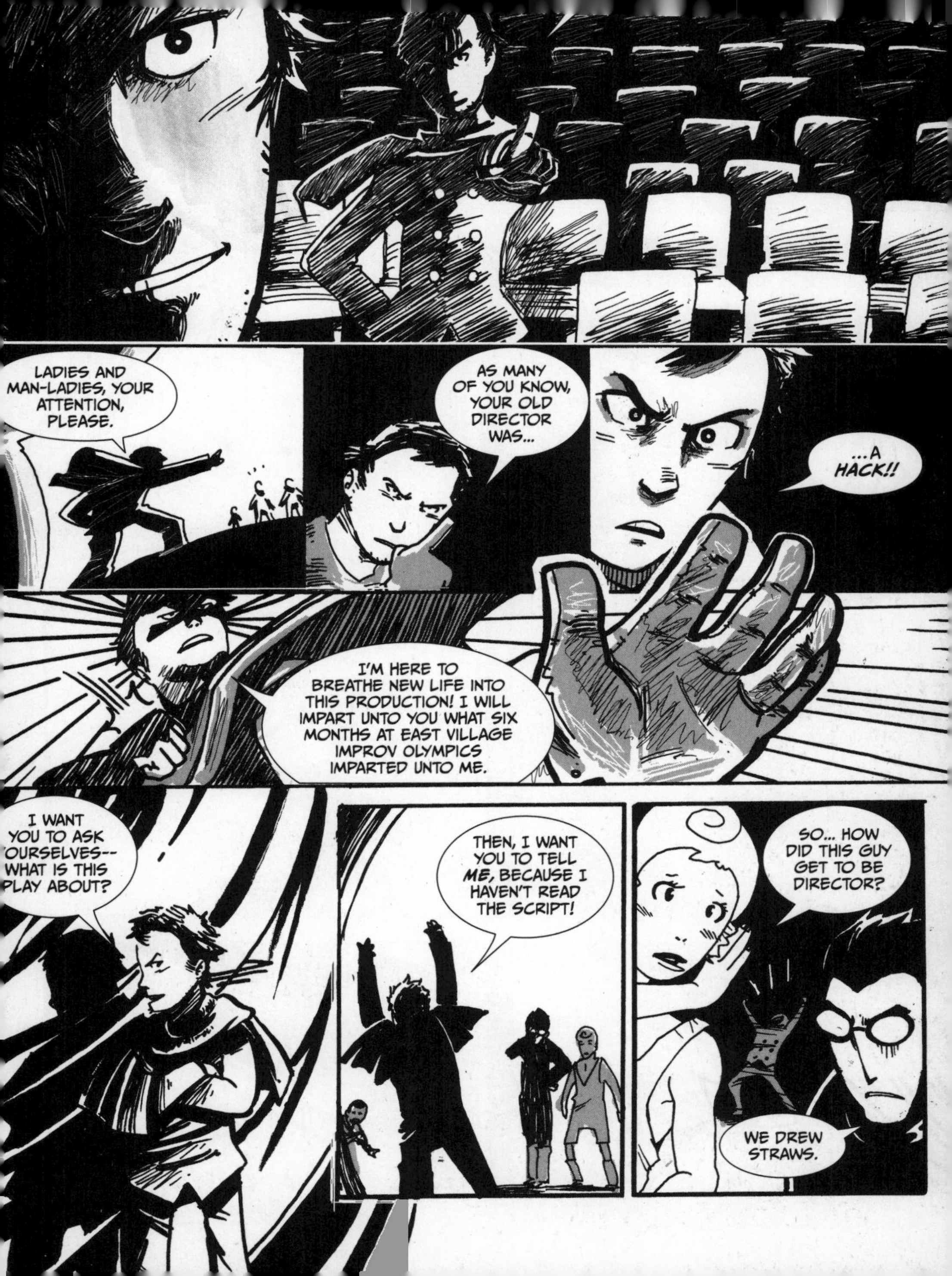
LADIES AND MAN-LADIES, YOUR ATTENTION, PLEASE.
AS MANY OF YOU KNOW, YOUR OLD DIRECTOR WAS...
...A HACK!!
I'M HERE TO BREATHE NEW LIFE INTO THIS PRODUCTION! I WILL IMPART UNTO YOU WHAT SIX MONTHS AT EAST VILLAGE IMPROV OLYMPICS IMPARTED UNTO ME.
I WANT YOU TO ASK OURSELVES-- WHAT IS THIS PLAY ABOUT?
THEN, I WANT YOU TO TELL *ME*, BECAUSE I HAVEN'T READ THE SCRIPT!
SO... HOW DID THIS GUY GET TO BE DIRECTOR?
WE DREW STRAWS.

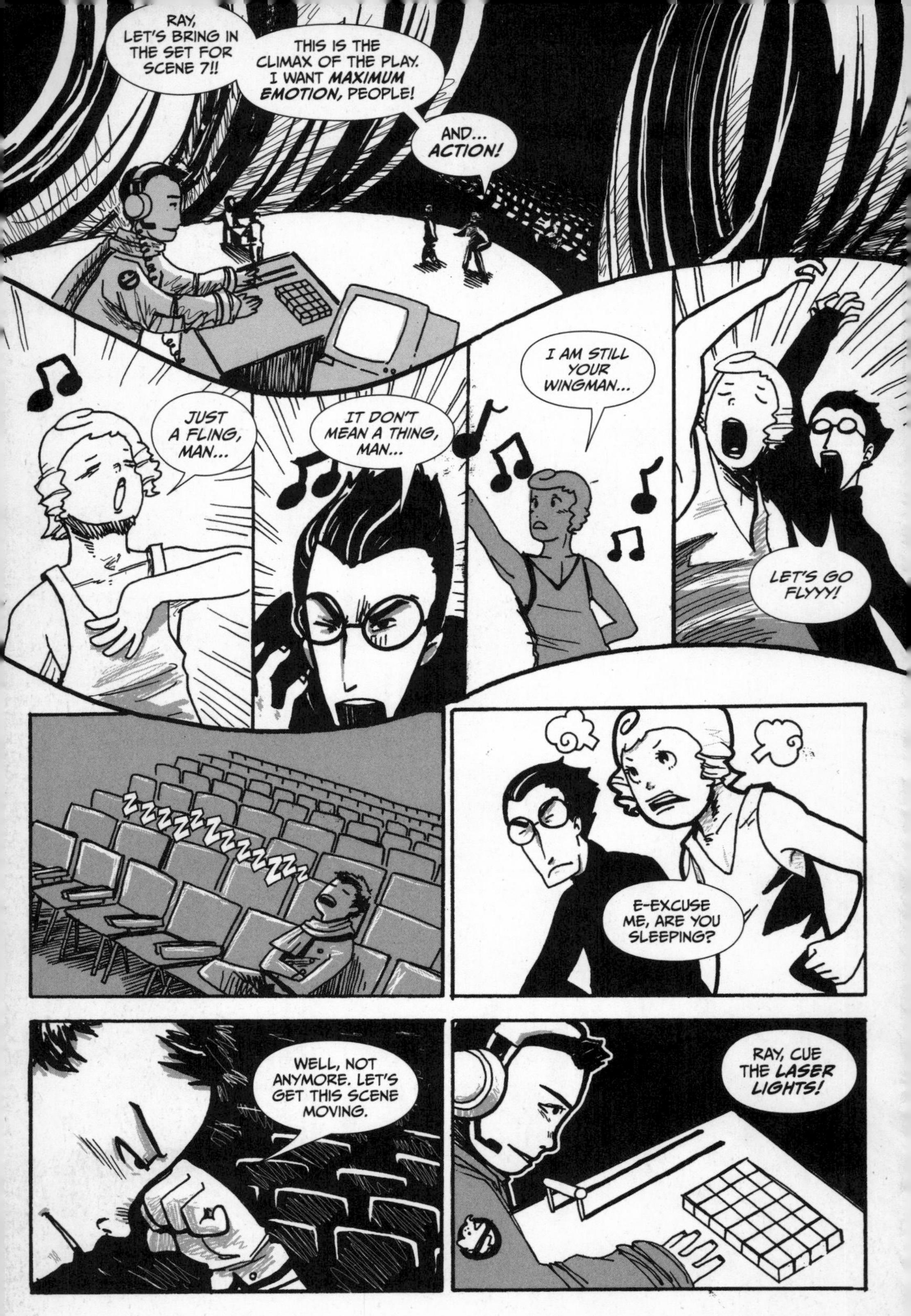
RAY, LET'S BRING IN THE SET FOR SCENE 7!!
THIS IS THE CLIMAX OF THE PLAY. I WANT *MAXIMUM EMOTION*, PEOPLE!
AND... *ACTION!*
JUST A FLING, MAN...
IT DON'T MEAN A THING, MAN...
I AM STILL YOUR WINGMAN...
LET'S GO FLYYY!
ZZZZZZZZZZZZZ
E-EXCUSE ME, ARE YOU SLEEPING?
WELL, NOT ANYMORE. LET'S GET THIS SCENE MOVING.
RAY, CUE THE *LASER LIGHTS!*

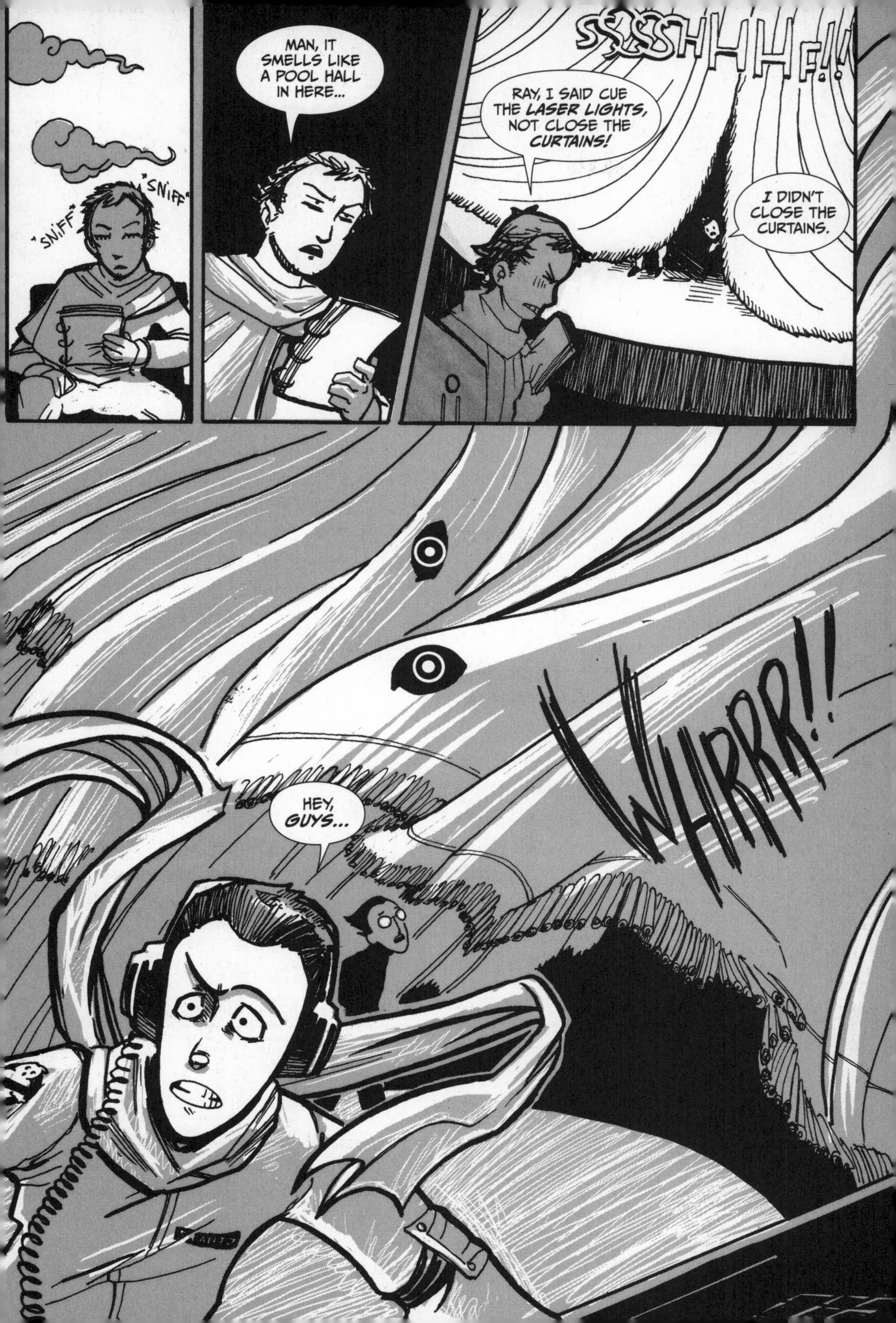
"SNIFF"
"SNIFF"
MAN, IT SMELLS LIKE A POOL HALL IN HERE...
SSSSHHHF!!
RAY, I SAID CUE THE LASER LIGHTS, NOT CLOSE THE CURTAINS!
I DIDN'T CLOSE THE CURTAINS.
WHRRR!!
HEY, GUYS...

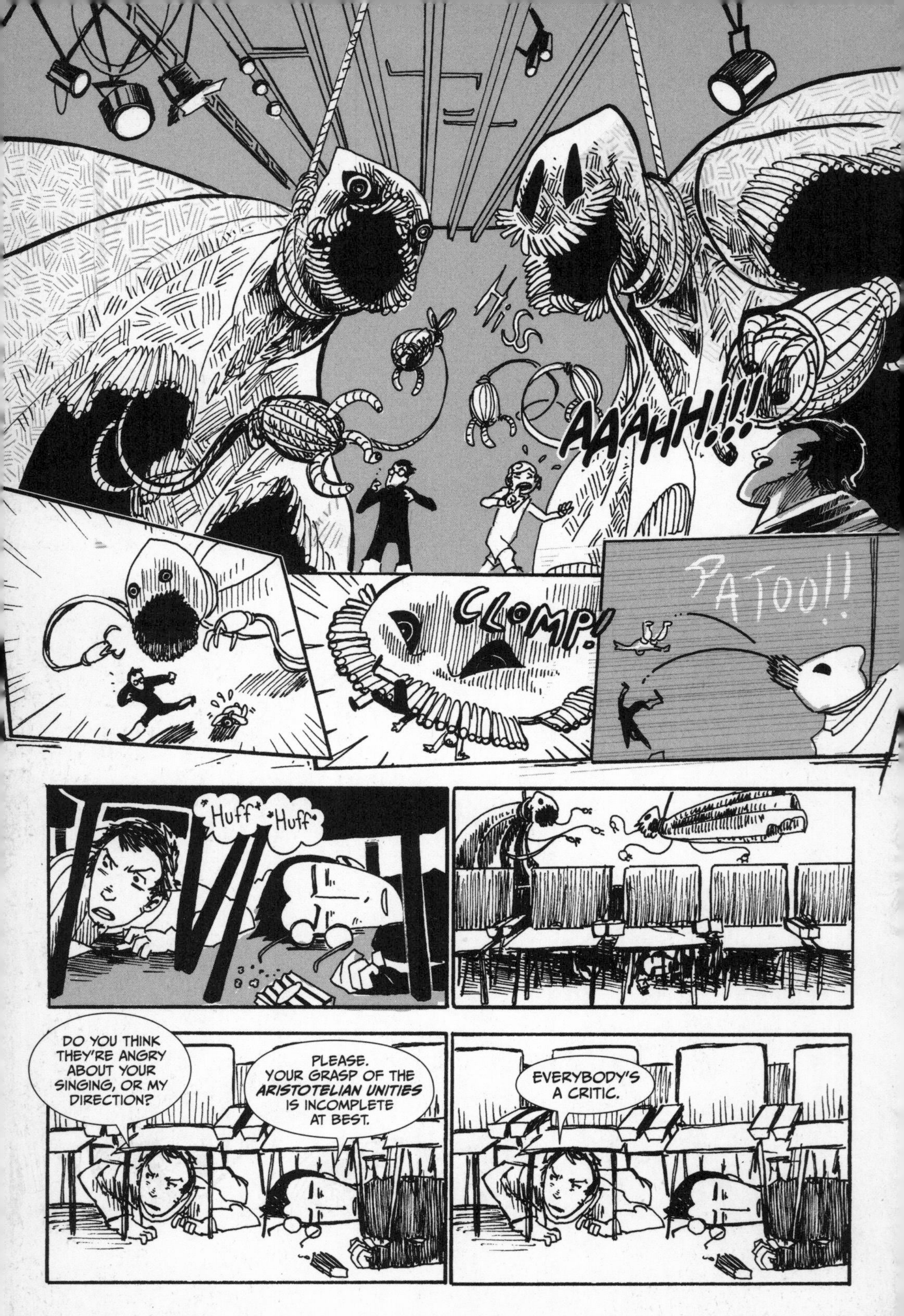
HISS
AAAHH!!!!
CLOMP!
PATOO!!
*Huff* *Huff*
DO YOU THINK THEY'RE ANGRY ABOUT YOUR SINGING, OR MY DIRECTION?
PLEASE. YOUR GRASP OF THE *ARISTOTELIAN UNITIES* IS INCOMPLETE AT BEST.
EVERYBODY'S A CRITIC.

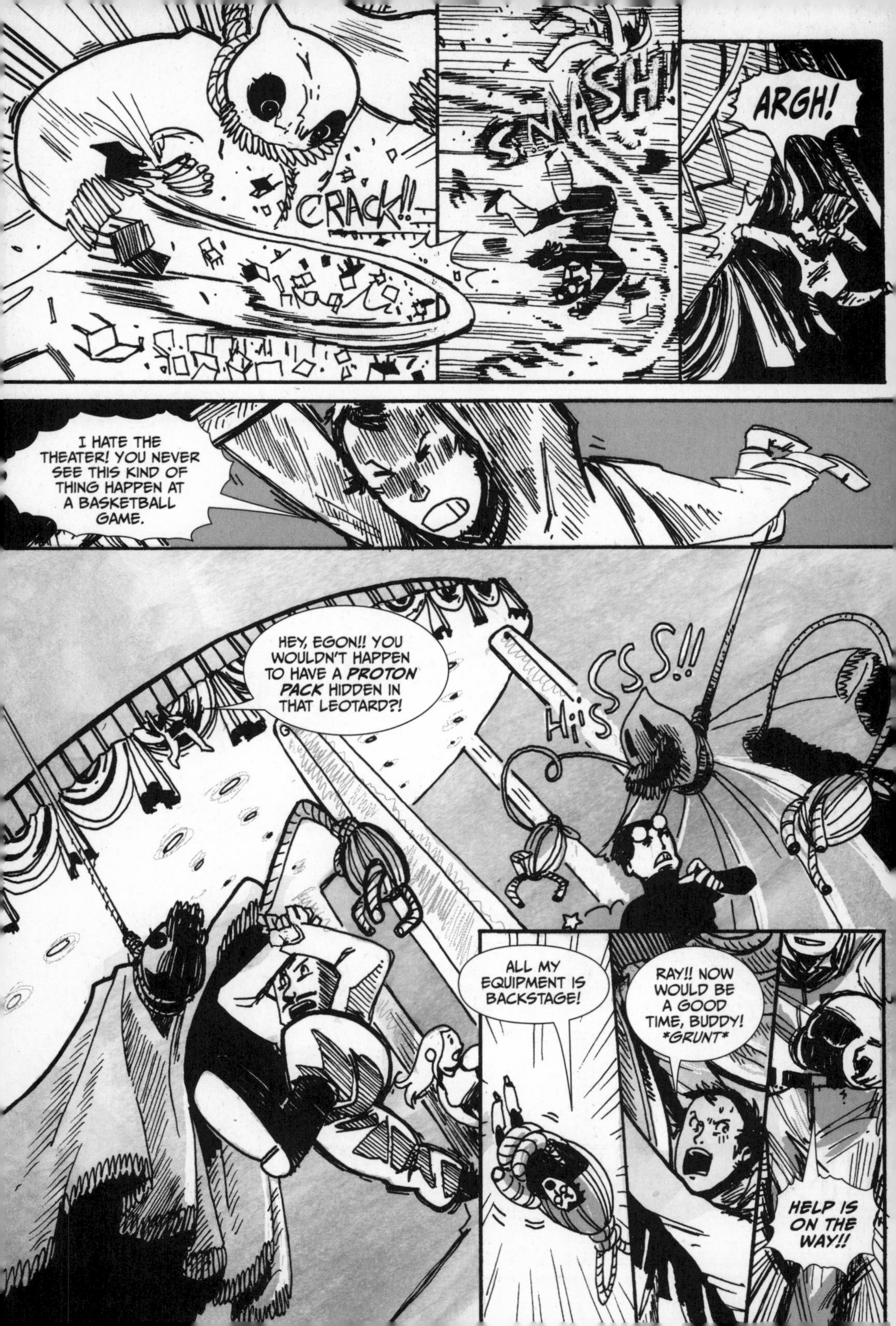
CRACK!!
SMASH!
ARGH!
I HATE THE THEATER! YOU NEVER SEE THIS KIND OF THING HAPPEN AT A BASKETBALL GAME.
HEY, EGON!! YOU WOULDN'T HAPPEN TO HAVE A *PROTON PACK* HIDDEN IN THAT LEOTARD?!
HiSSS!!
ALL MY EQUIPMENT IS BACKSTAGE!
RAY!! NOW WOULD BE A GOOD TIME, BUDDY! *GRUNT*
HELP IS ON THE WAY!!

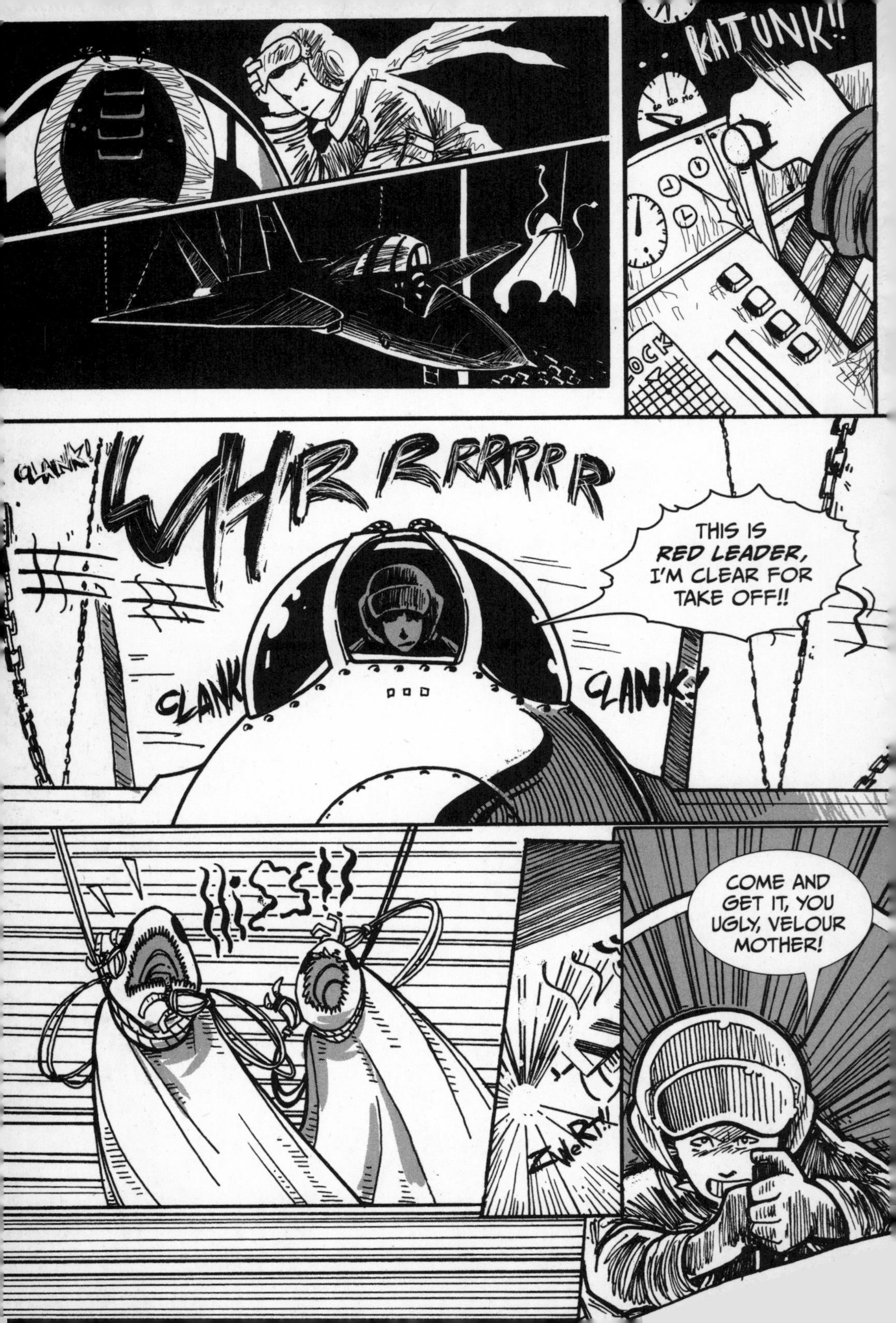
KATUNK!!
LOCK
CLANK!
WHR RRRRRR
THIS IS RED LEADER, I'M CLEAR FOR TAKE OFF!!
CLANK
CLANK!
HISS!!
COME AND GET IT, YOU UGLY, VELOUR MOTHER!
ZWERT!!

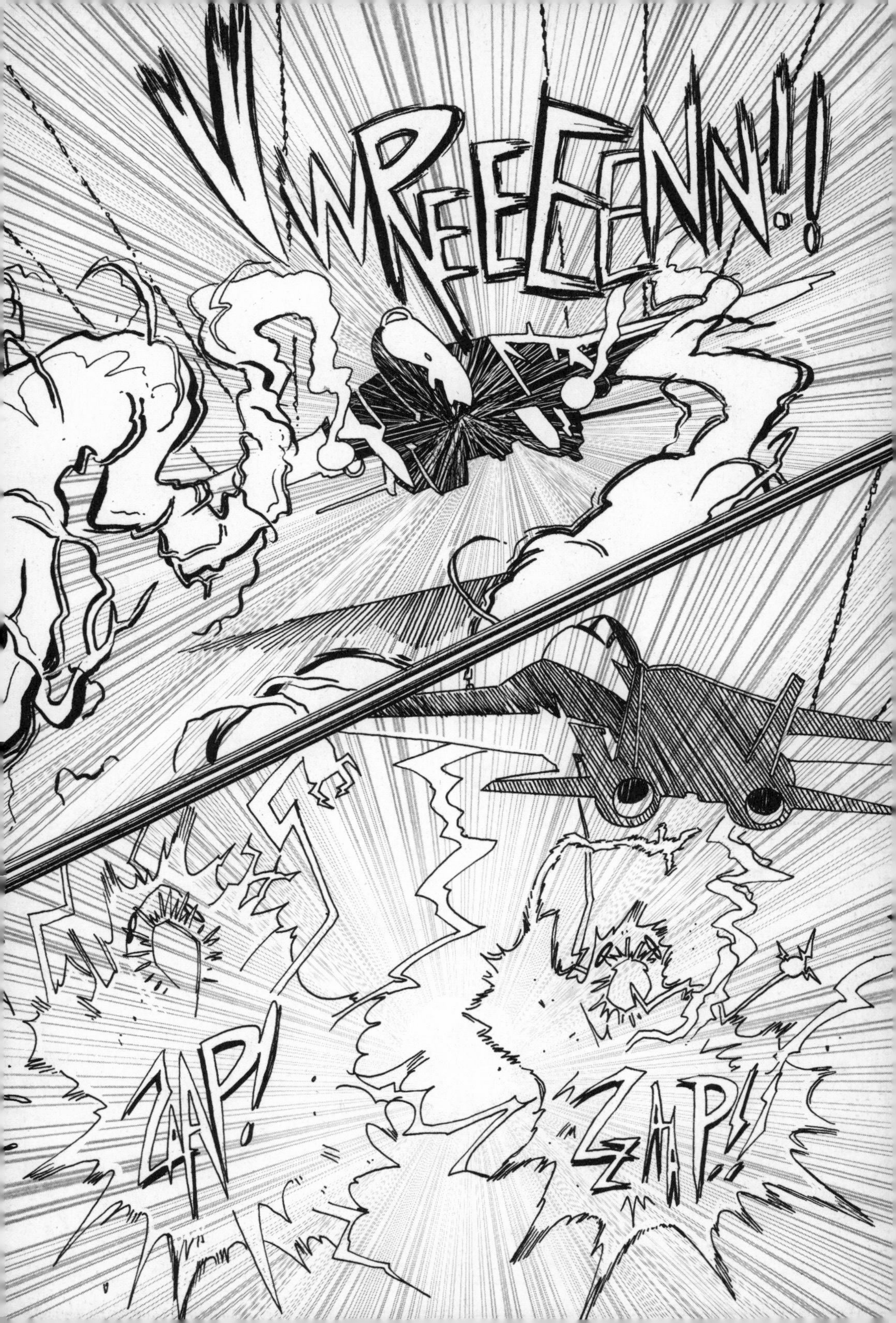
VWREEEENN!!
ZAP!
ZAP!

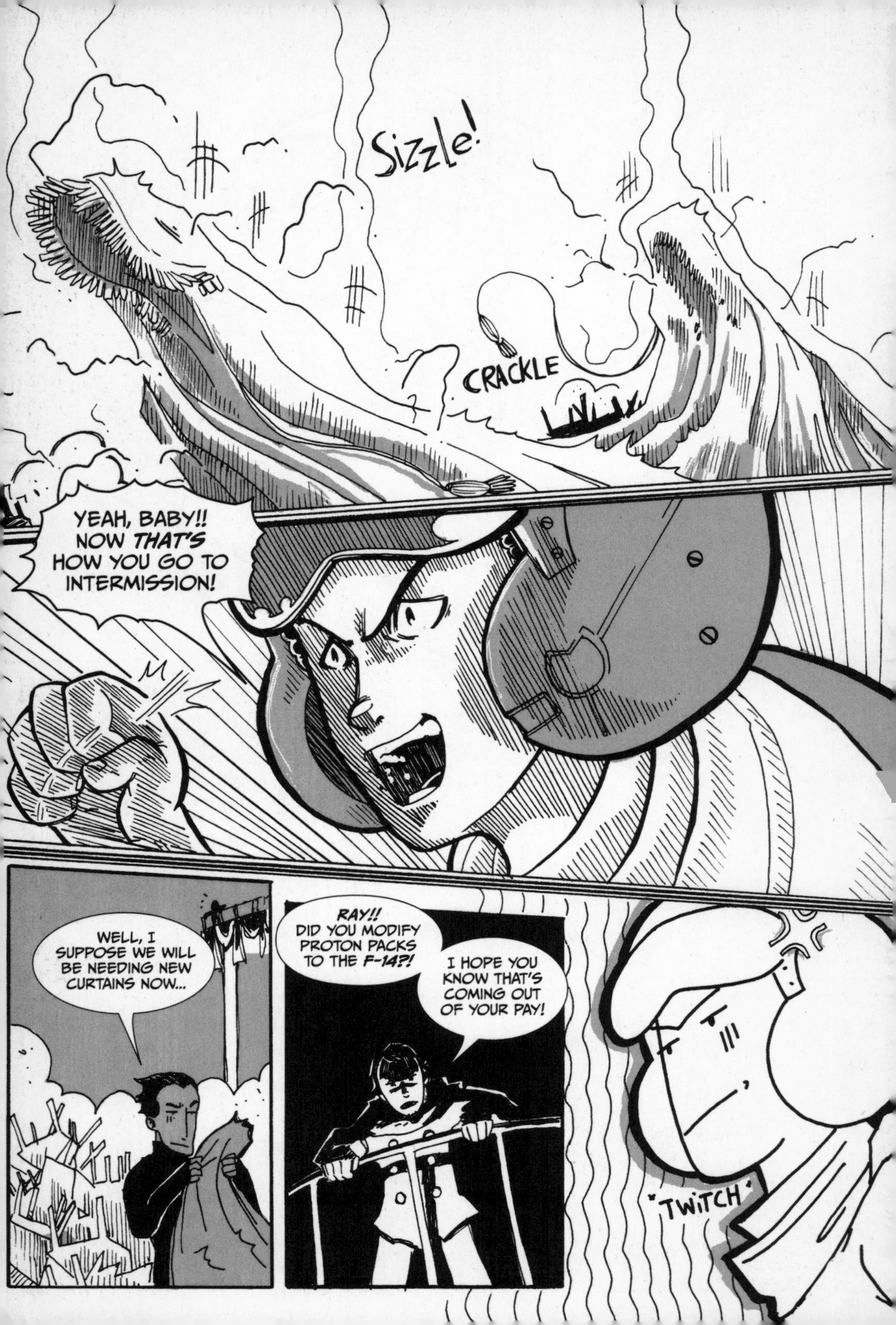
Sizzle!
CRACKLE
YEAH, BABY!! NOW THAT'S HOW YOU GO TO INTERMISSION!
WELL, I SUPPOSE WE WILL BE NEEDING NEW CURTAINS NOW...
RAY!! DID YOU MODIFY PROTON PACKS TO THE F-14?!
I HOPE YOU KNOW THAT'S COMING OUT OF YOUR PAY!
*TWITCH*

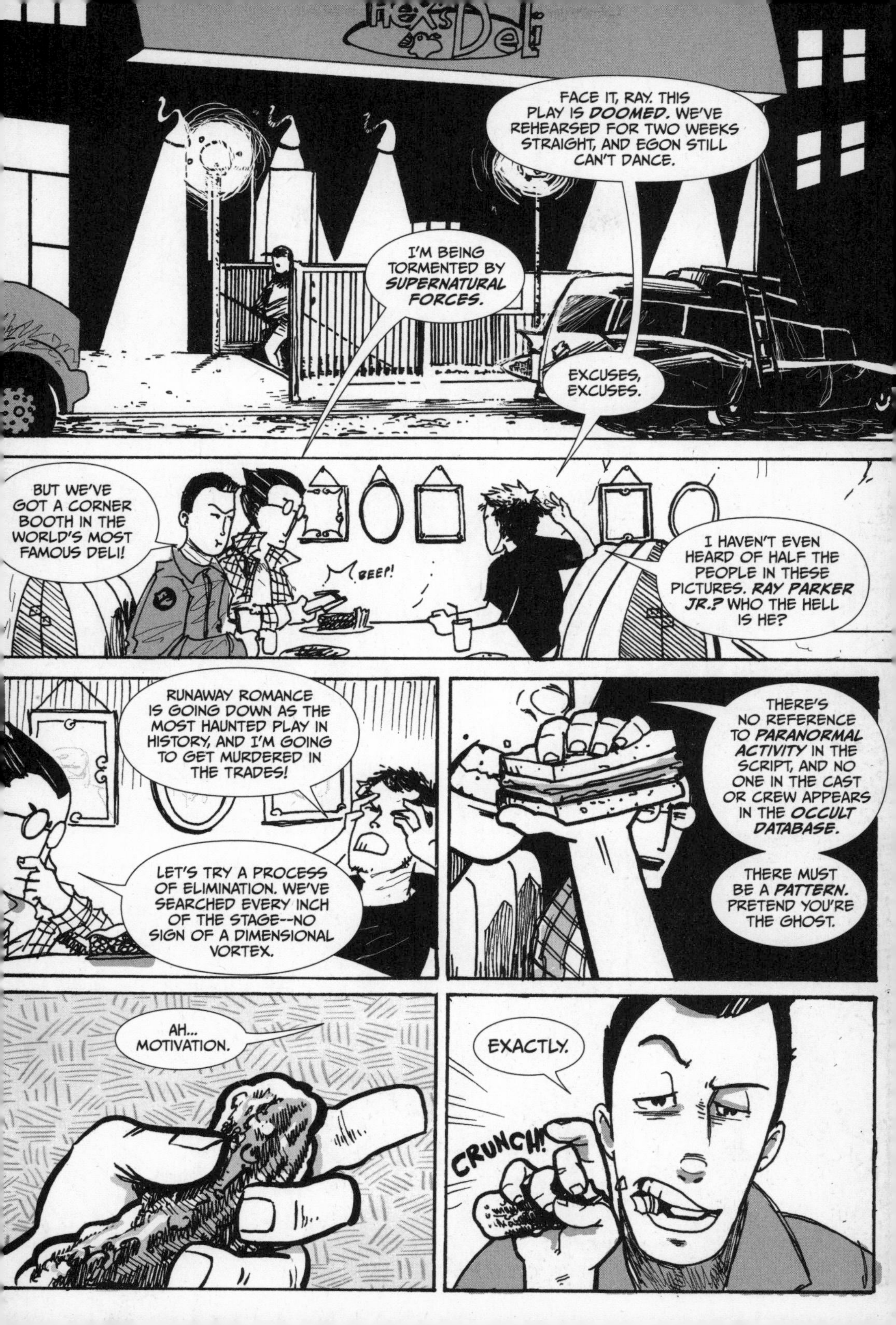

Rex's Deli
FACE IT, RAY. THIS PLAY IS DOOMED. WE'VE REHEARSED FOR TWO WEEKS STRAIGHT, AND EGON STILL CAN'T DANCE.
I'M BEING TORMENTED BY SUPERNATURAL FORCES.
EXCUSES, EXCUSES.
BUT WE'VE GOT A CORNER BOOTH IN THE WORLD'S MOST FAMOUS DELI!
BEEP!
I HAVEN'T EVEN HEARD OF HALF THE PEOPLE IN THESE PICTURES. RAY PARKER JR.? WHO THE HELL IS HE?
RUNAWAY ROMANCE IS GOING DOWN AS THE MOST HAUNTED PLAY IN HISTORY, AND I'M GOING TO GET MURDERED IN THE TRADES!
LET'S TRY A PROCESS OF ELIMINATION. WE'VE SEARCHED EVERY INCH OF THE STAGE--NO SIGN OF A DIMENSIONAL VORTEX.
THERE'S NO REFERENCE TO PARANORMAL ACTIVITY IN THE SCRIPT, AND NO ONE IN THE CAST OR CREW APPEARS IN THE OCCULT DATABASE.
THERE MUST BE A PATTERN. PRETEND YOU'RE THE GHOST.
AH... MOTIVATION.
EXACTLY.
CRUNCH!

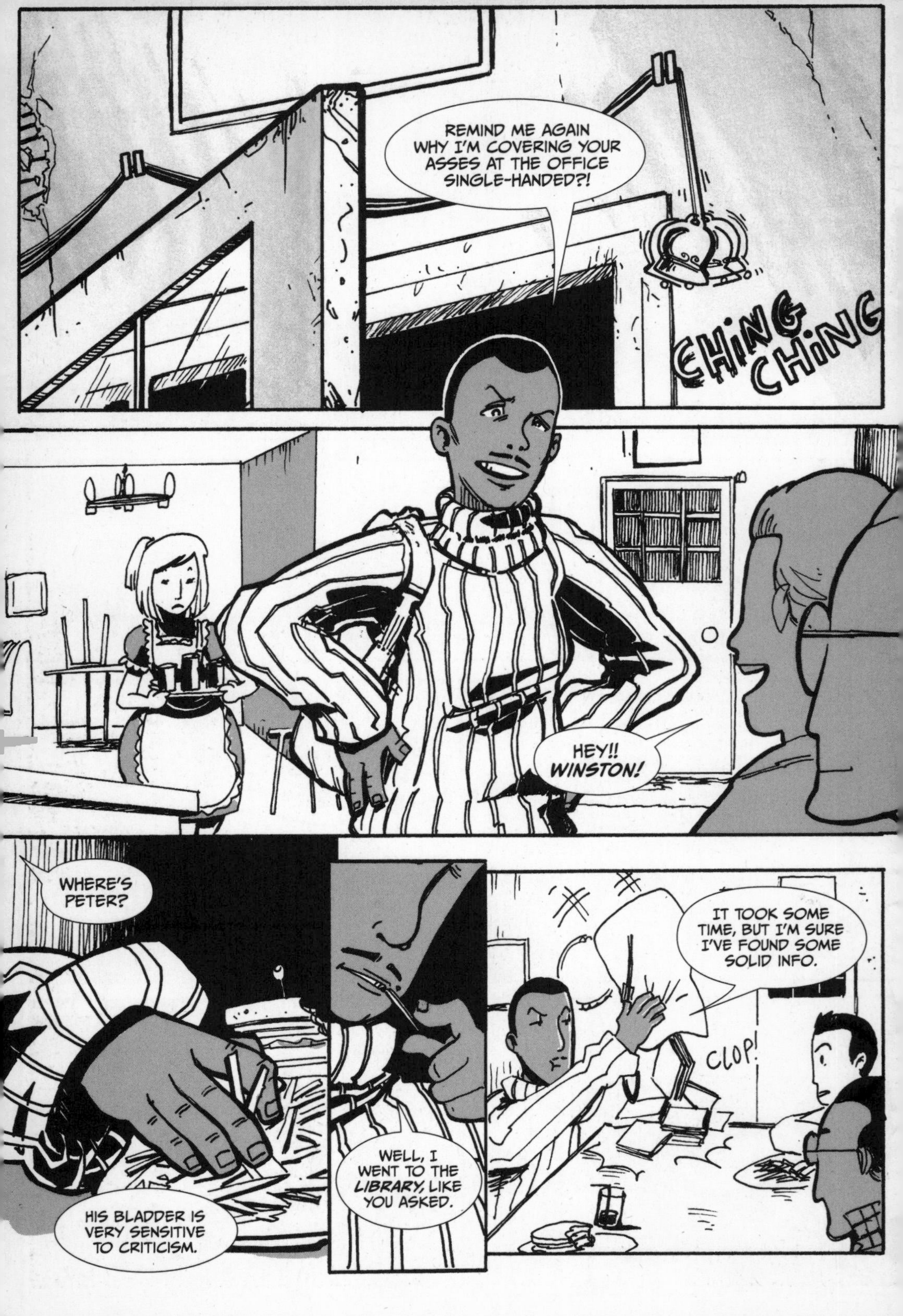
REMIND ME AGAIN WHY I'M COVERING YOUR ASSES AT THE OFFICE SINGLE-HANDED?!
CHING CHING
HEY!! *WINSTON!*
WHERE'S PETER?
HIS BLADDER IS VERY SENSITIVE TO CRITICISM.
WELL, I WENT TO THE *LIBRARY,* LIKE YOU ASKED.
IT TOOK SOME TIME, BUT I'M SURE I'VE FOUND SOME SOLID INFO.
CLOP!

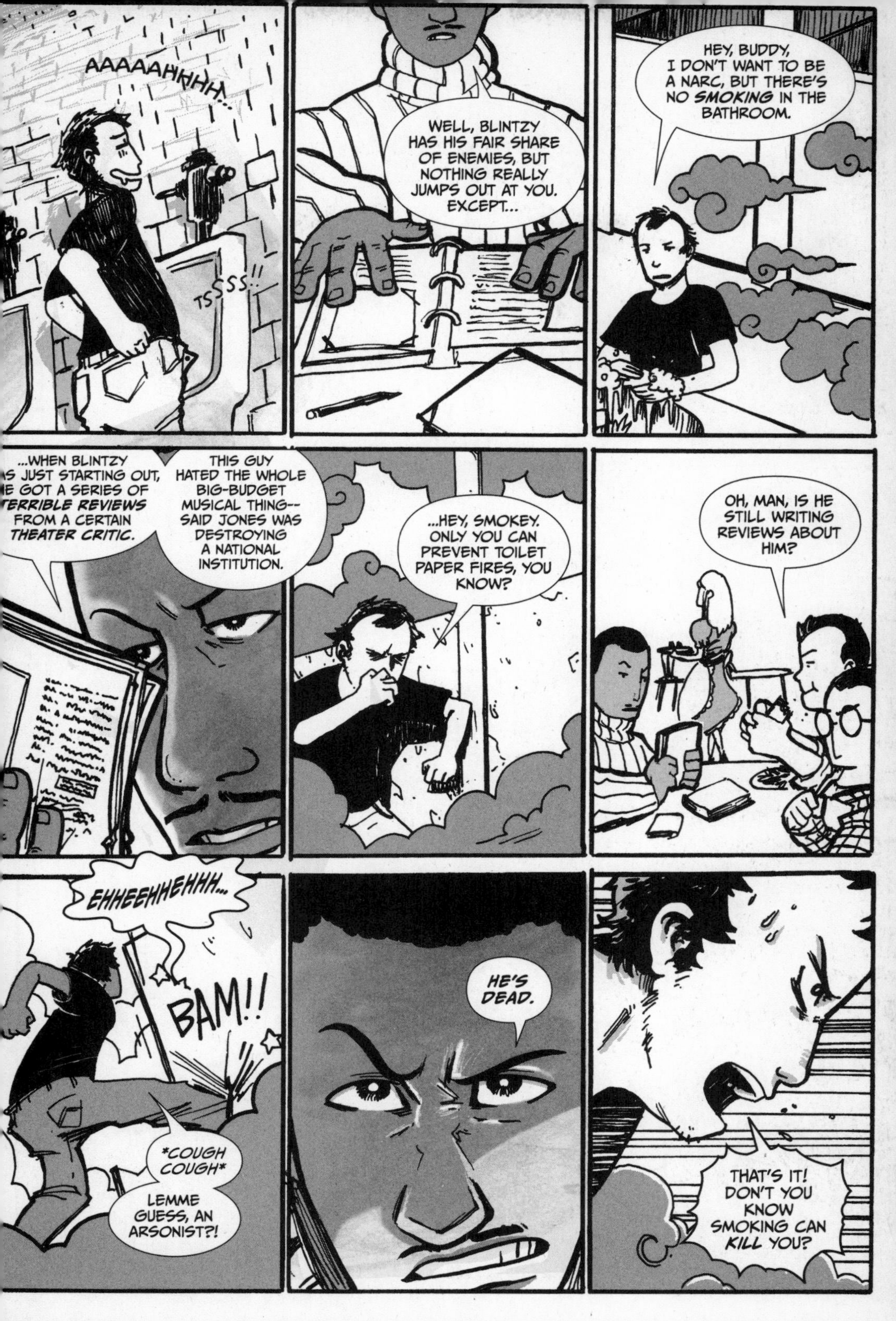
AAAAAHHHH...
TSSSS!!
WELL, BLINTZY HAS HIS FAIR SHARE OF ENEMIES, BUT NOTHING REALLY JUMPS OUT AT YOU. EXCEPT...
HEY, BUDDY, I DON'T WANT TO BE A NARC, BUT THERE'S NO *SMOKING* IN THE BATHROOM.
...WHEN BLINTZY AS JUST STARTING OUT, E GOT A SERIES OF *TERRIBLE REVIEWS* FROM A CERTAIN *THEATER CRITIC*.
THIS GUY HATED THE WHOLE BIG-BUDGET MUSICAL THING-- SAID JONES WAS DESTROYING A NATIONAL INSTITUTION.
...HEY, SMOKEY. ONLY YOU CAN PREVENT TOILET PAPER FIRES, YOU KNOW?
OH, MAN, IS HE STILL WRITING REVIEWS ABOUT HIM?
EHHEEHHEHHH...
BAM!!
*COUGH COUGH*
LEMME GUESS, AN ARSONIST?!
*HE'S DEAD.*
THAT'S IT! DON'T YOU KNOW SMOKING CAN *KILL* YOU?

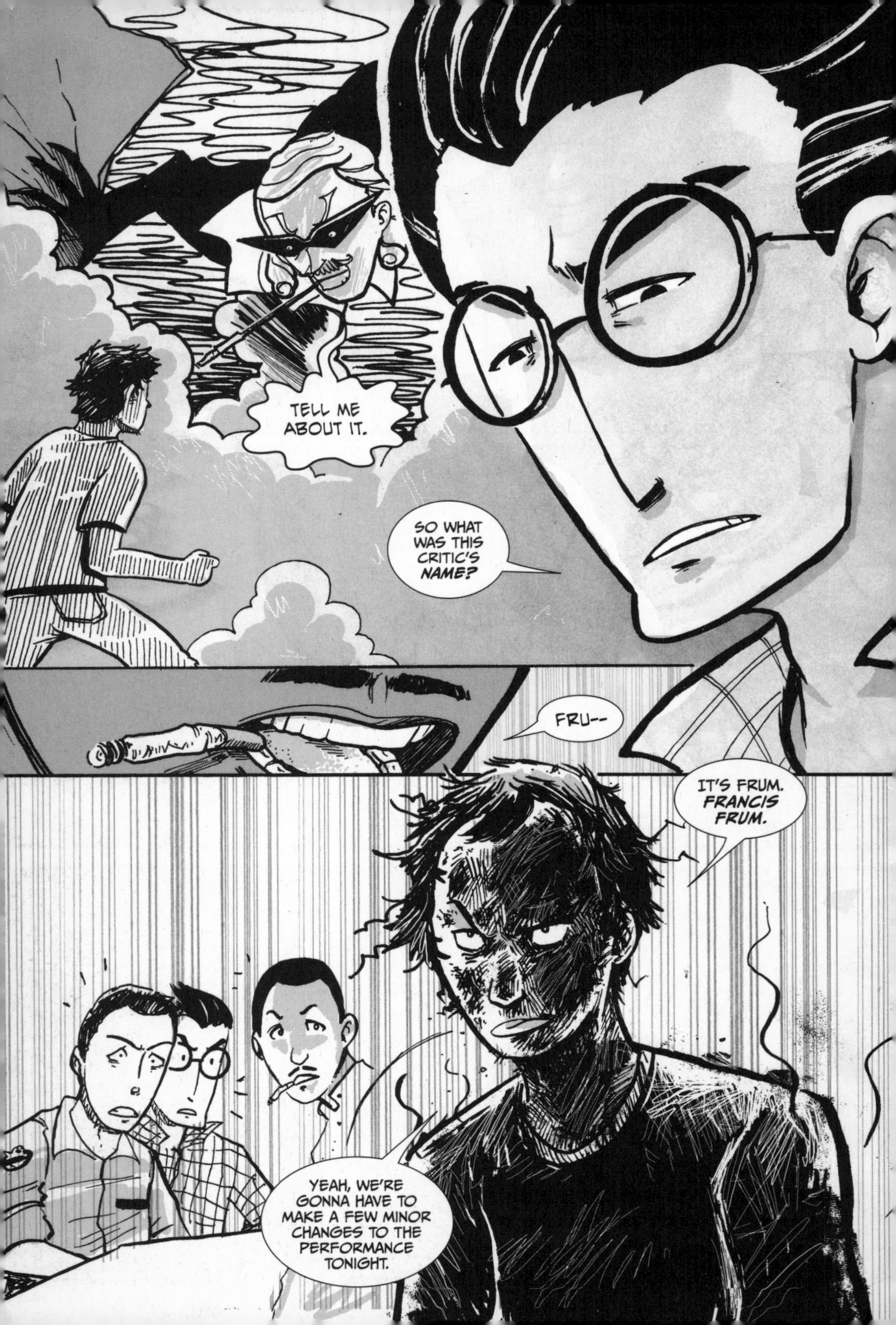
TELL ME ABOUT IT.
SO WHAT WAS THIS CRITIC'S *NAME?*
FRU--
IT'S FRUM. *FRANCIS FRUM.*
YEAH, WE'RE GONNA HAVE TO MAKE A FEW MINOR CHANGES TO THE PERFORMANCE TONIGHT.

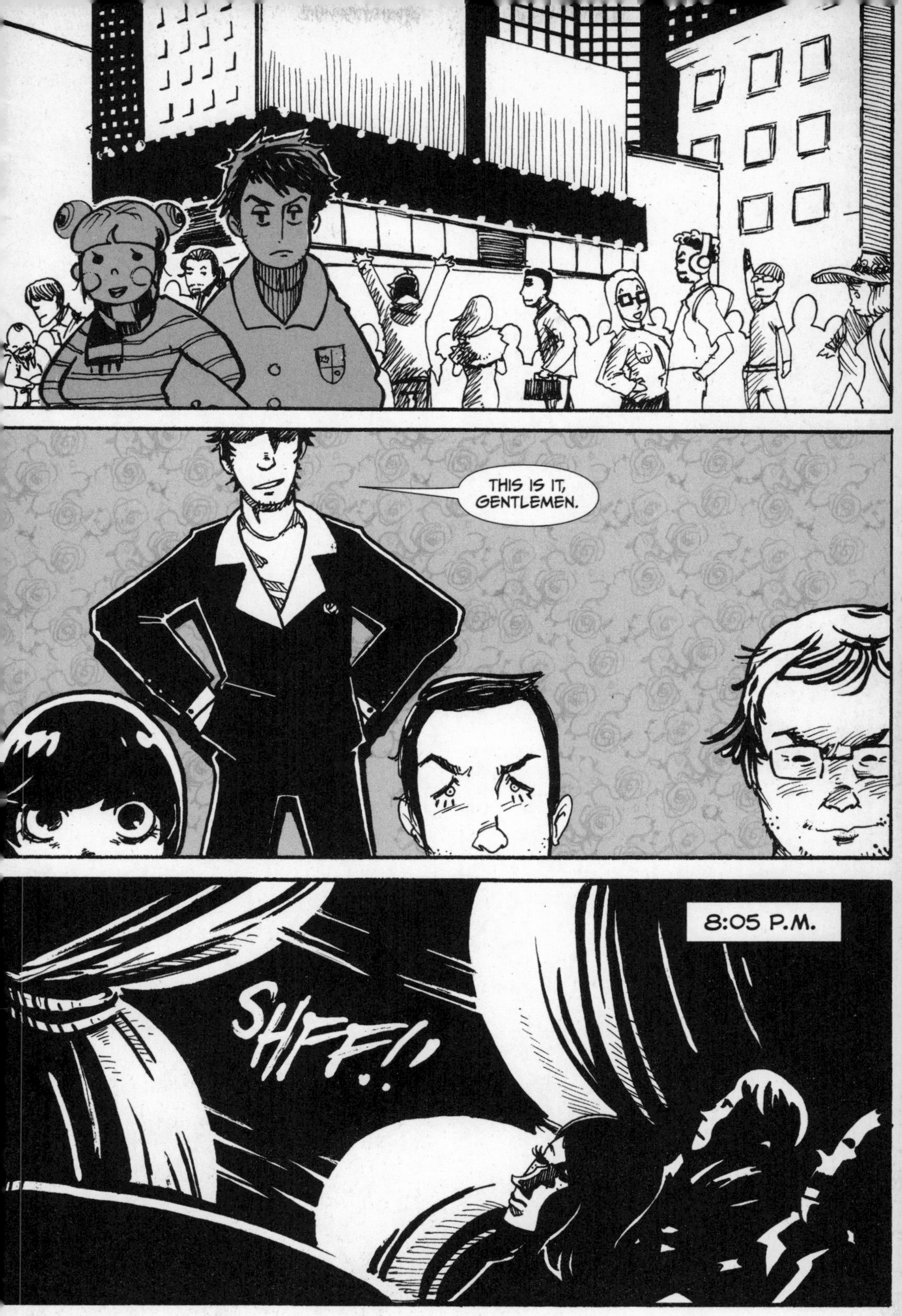
THIS IS IT, GENTLEMEN.
8:05 P.M.
SHFF!!

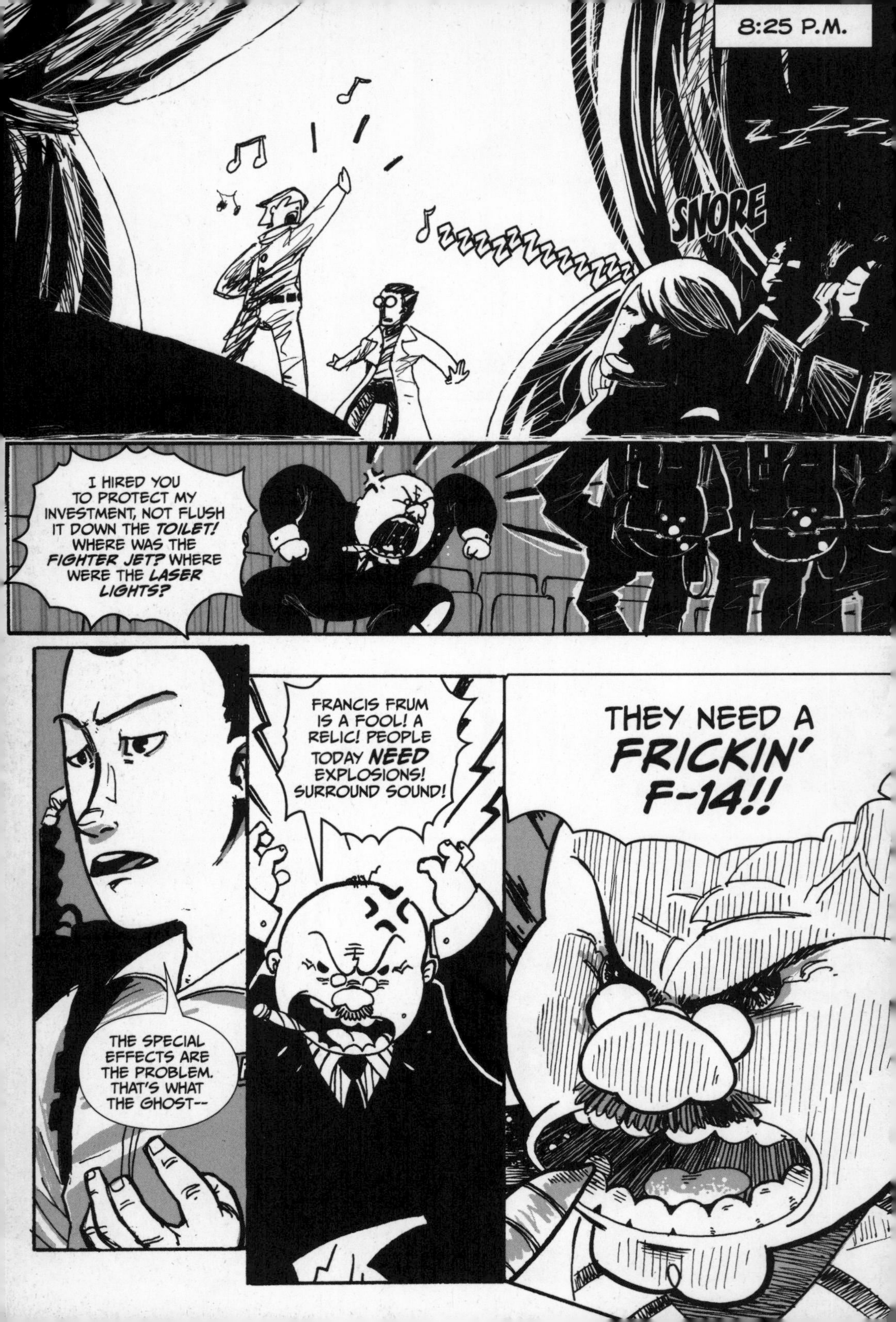
8:25 P.M.
SNORE
I HIRED YOU TO PROTECT MY INVESTMENT, NOT FLUSH IT DOWN THE TOILET! WHERE WAS THE FIGHTER JET? WHERE WERE THE LASER LIGHTS?
THE SPECIAL EFFECTS ARE THE PROBLEM. THAT'S WHAT THE GHOST--
FRANCIS FRUM IS A FOOL! A RELIC! PEOPLE TODAY NEED EXPLOSIONS! SURROUND SOUND!
THEY NEED A FRICKIN' F-14!!

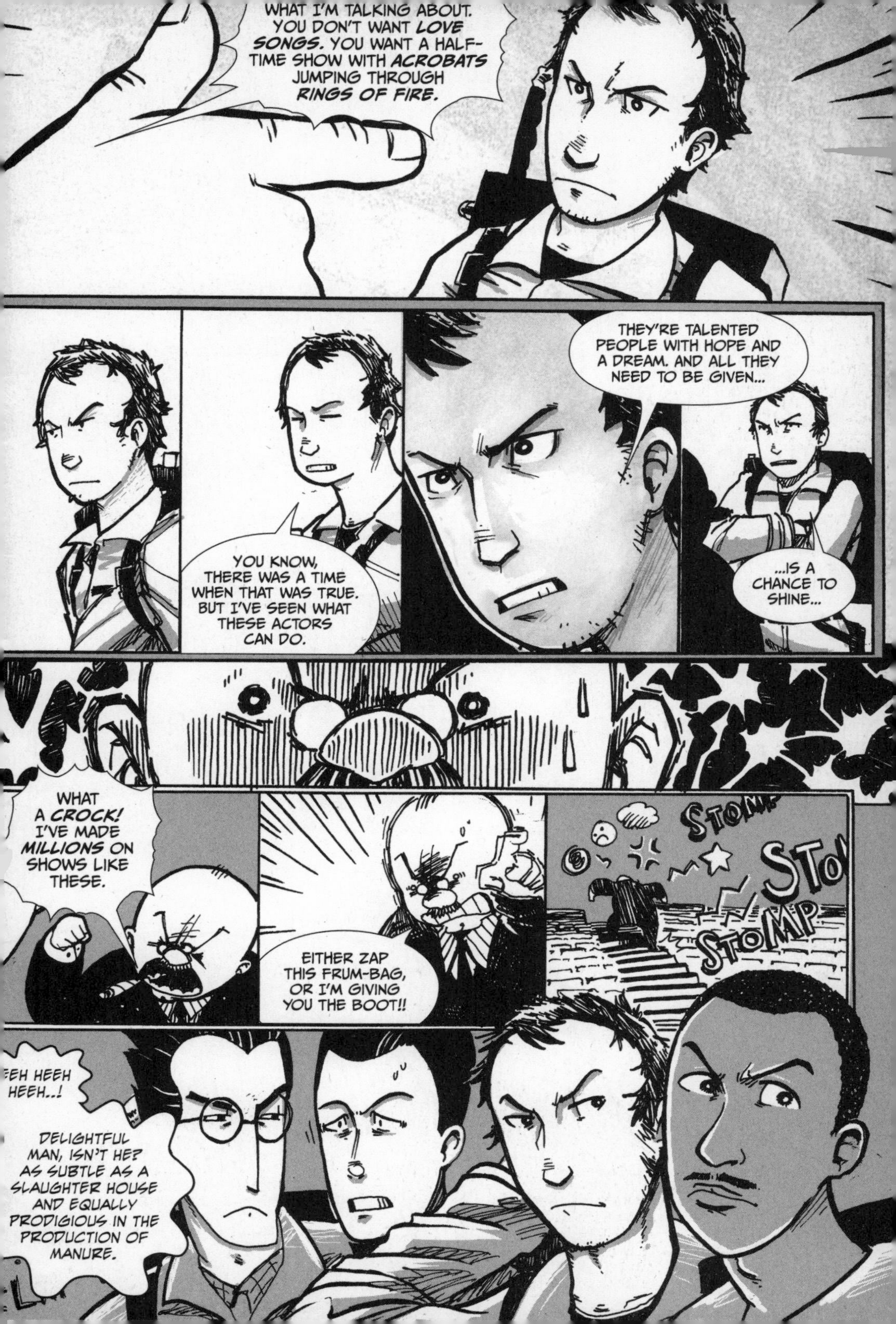
WHAT I'M TALKING ABOUT. YOU DON'T WANT LOVE SONGS. YOU WANT A HALF-TIME SHOW WITH ACROBATS JUMPING THROUGH RINGS OF FIRE.
YOU KNOW, THERE WAS A TIME WHEN THAT WAS TRUE. BUT I'VE SEEN WHAT THESE ACTORS CAN DO.
THEY'RE TALENTED PEOPLE WITH HOPE AND A DREAM. AND ALL THEY NEED TO BE GIVEN...
...IS A CHANCE TO SHINE...
WHAT A CROCK! I'VE MADE MILLIONS ON SHOWS LIKE THESE.
EITHER ZAP THIS FRUM-BAG, OR I'M GIVING YOU THE BOOT!!
STOMP
STOMP
STOMP
EEH HEEH HEEH..!
DELIGHTFUL MAN, ISN'T HE? AS SUBTLE AS A SLAUGHTER HOUSE AND EQUALLY PRODIGIOUS IN THE PRODUCTION OF MANURE.

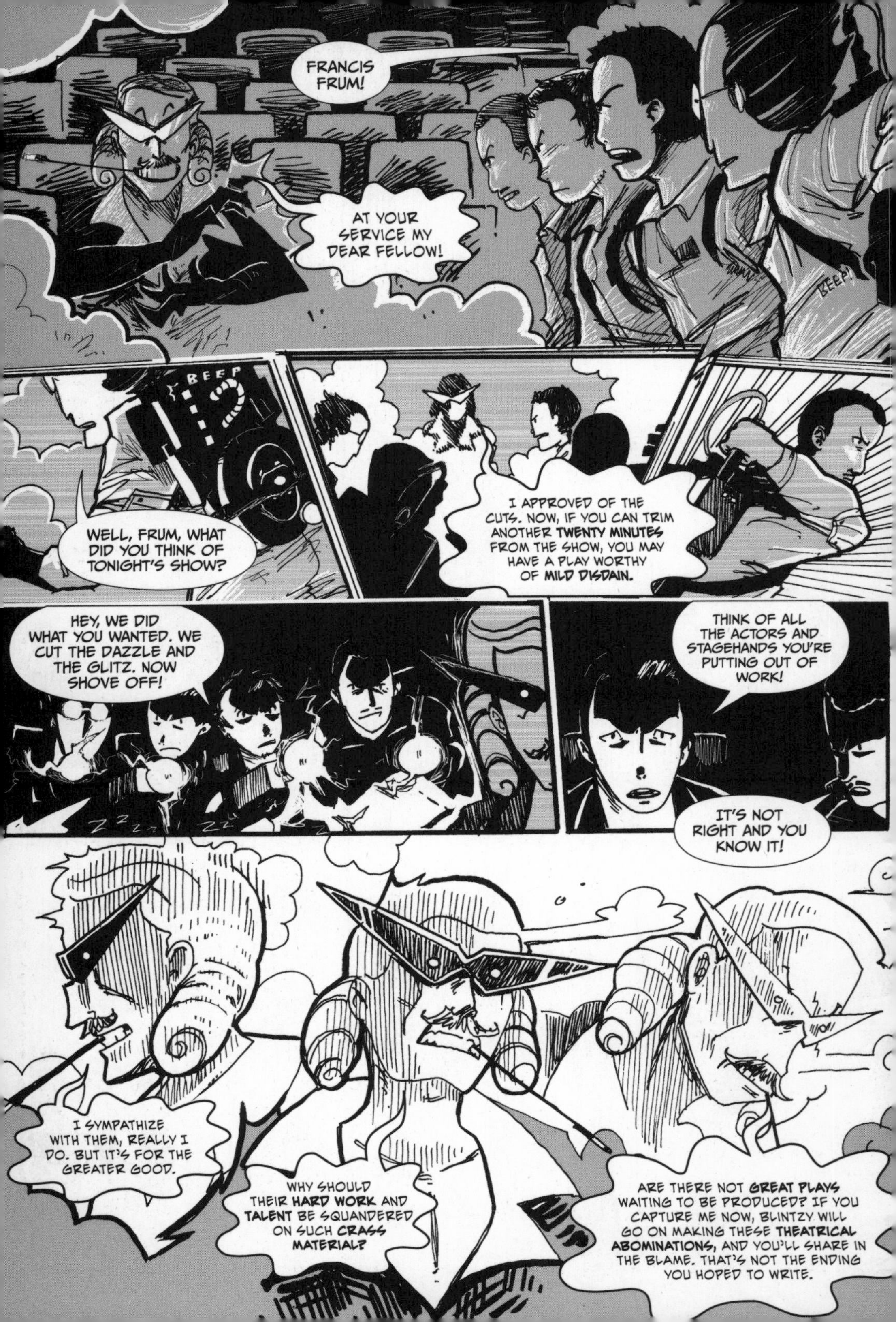

FRANCIS FRUM!
AT YOUR SERVICE MY DEAR FELLOW!
BEEP!
BEEP
WELL, FRUM, WHAT DID YOU THINK OF TONIGHT'S SHOW?
I APPROVED OF THE CUTS. NOW, IF YOU CAN TRIM ANOTHER TWENTY MINUTES FROM THE SHOW, YOU MAY HAVE A PLAY WORTHY OF MILD DISDAIN.
HEY, WE DID WHAT YOU WANTED. WE CUT THE DAZZLE AND THE GLITZ. NOW SHOVE OFF!
THINK OF ALL THE ACTORS AND STAGEHANDS YOU'RE PUTTING OUT OF WORK!
IT'S NOT RIGHT AND YOU KNOW IT!
I SYMPATHIZE WITH THEM, REALLY I DO. BUT IT'S FOR THE GREATER GOOD.
WHY SHOULD THEIR HARD WORK AND TALENT BE SQUANDERED ON SUCH CRASS MATERIAL?
ARE THERE NOT GREAT PLAYS WAITING TO BE PRODUCED? IF YOU CAPTURE ME NOW, BLINTZY WILL GO ON MAKING THESE THEATRICAL ABOMINATIONS, AND YOU'LL SHARE IN THE BLAME. THAT'S NOT THE ENDING YOU HOPED TO WRITE.

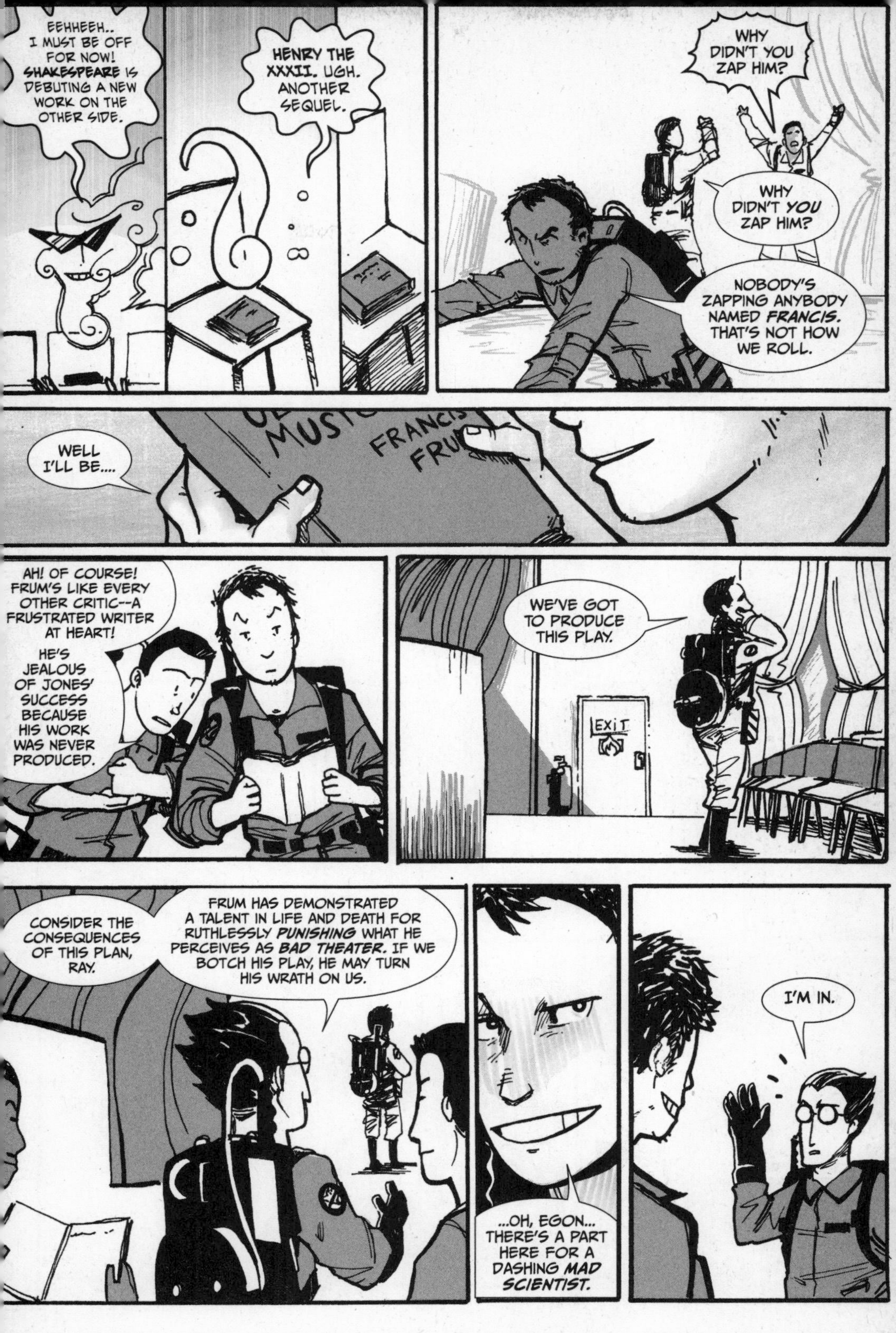
EEHHEEH.. I MUST BE OFF FOR NOW! SHAKESPEARE IS DEBUTING A NEW WORK ON THE OTHER SIDE.
HENRY THE XXXII. UGH. ANOTHER SEQUEL.
WHY DIDN'T YOU ZAP HIM?
WHY DIDN'T YOU ZAP HIM?
NOBODY'S ZAPPING ANYBODY NAMED FRANCIS. THAT'S NOT HOW WE ROLL.
WELL I'LL BE....
FRANCIS FRU
AH! OF COURSE! FRUM'S LIKE EVERY OTHER CRITIC--A FRUSTRATED WRITER AT HEART!
HE'S JEALOUS OF JONES' SUCCESS BECAUSE HIS WORK WAS NEVER PRODUCED.
WE'VE GOT TO PRODUCE THIS PLAY.
EXIT
CONSIDER THE CONSEQUENCES OF THIS PLAN, RAY.
FRUM HAS DEMONSTRATED A TALENT IN LIFE AND DEATH FOR RUTHLESSLY PUNISHING WHAT HE PERCEIVES AS BAD THEATER. IF WE BOTCH HIS PLAY, HE MAY TURN HIS WRATH ON US.
...OH, EGON... THERE'S A PART HERE FOR A DASHING MAD SCIENTIST.
I'M IN.

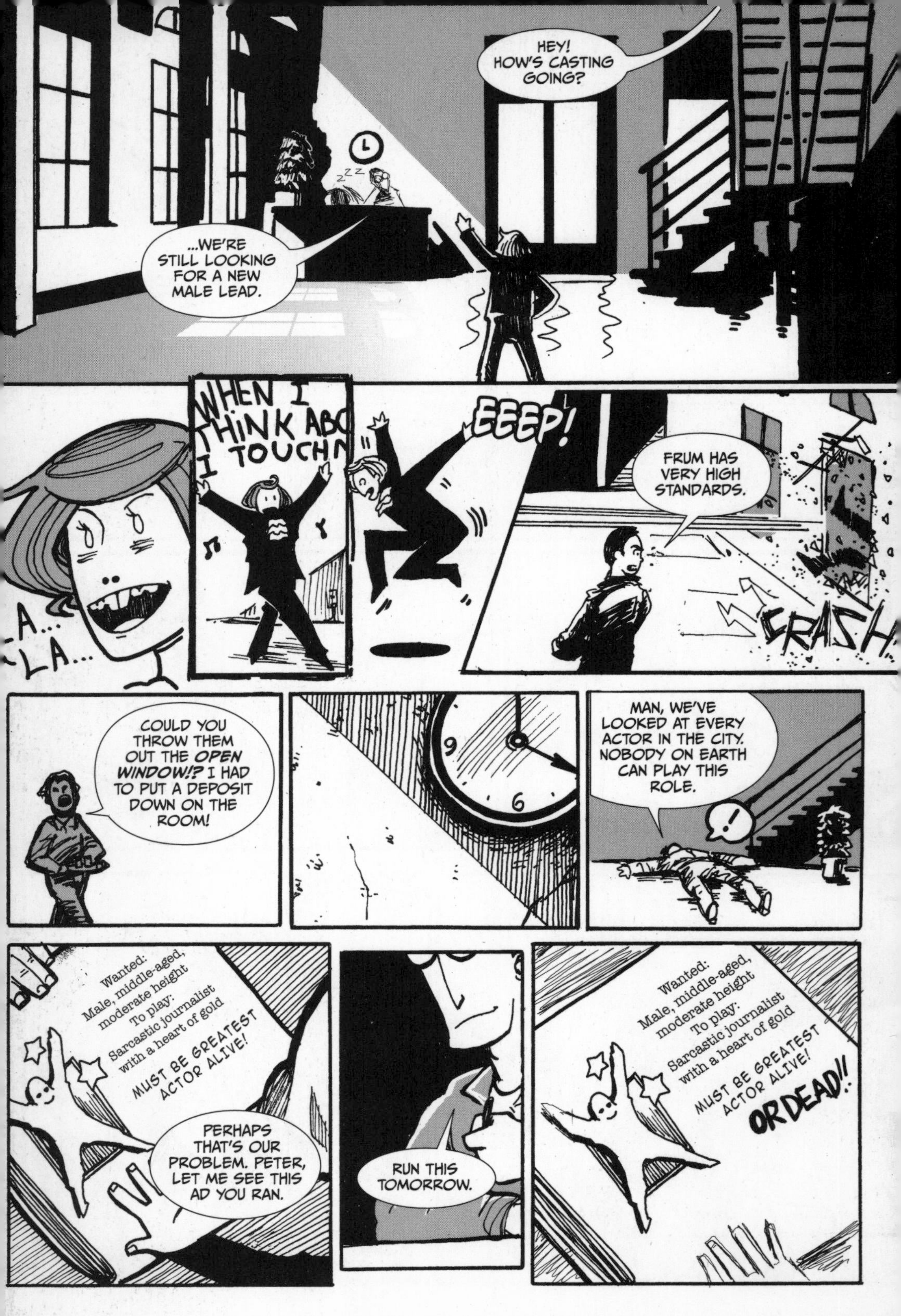
HEY! HOW'S CASTING GOING?
...WE'RE STILL LOOKING FOR A NEW MALE LEAD.
-A... -LA...
WHEN I THINK ABO I TOUCH
EEEP!
FRUM HAS VERY HIGH STANDARDS.
CRASH
COULD YOU THROW THEM OUT THE *OPEN WINDOW!?* I HAD TO PUT A DEPOSIT DOWN ON THE ROOM!
MAN, WE'VE LOOKED AT EVERY ACTOR IN THE CITY. NOBODY ON EARTH CAN PLAY THIS ROLE.
!
Wanted: Male, middle-aged, moderate height To play: Sarcastic journalist with a heart of gold
MUST BE GREATEST ACTOR ALIVE!
PERHAPS THAT'S OUR PROBLEM. PETER, LET ME SEE THIS AD YOU RAN.
RUN THIS TOMORROW.
Wanted: Male, middle-aged, moderate height To play: Sarcastic journalist with a heart of gold
MUST BE GREATEST ACTOR ALIVE!
OR DEAD!!

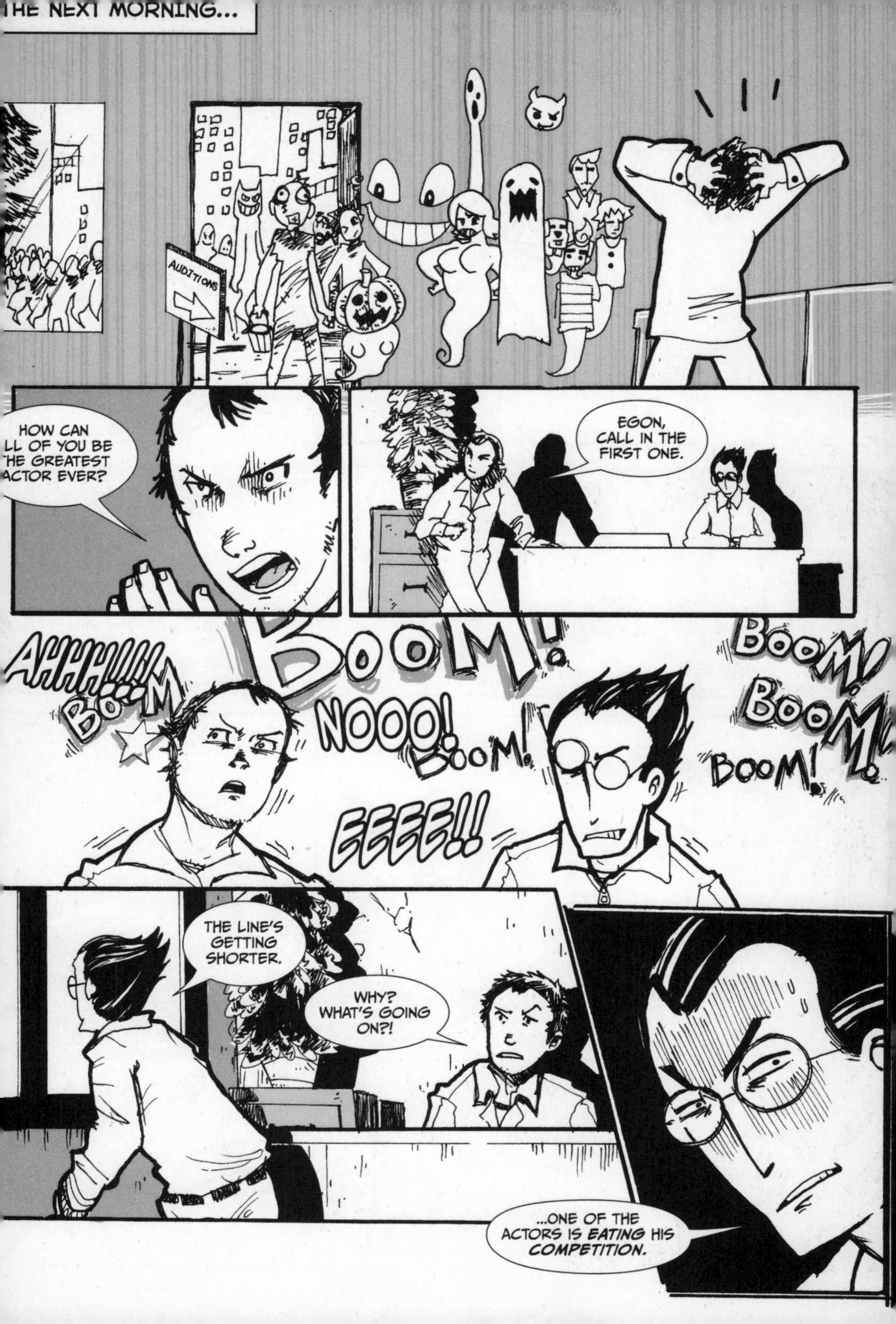
THE NEXT MORNING...
AUDITIONS
HOW CAN ALL OF YOU BE THE GREATEST ACTOR EVER?
EGON, CALL IN THE FIRST ONE.
BOOM!
AHHH!!!!
BOOM
NOOO!
BOOM!
BOOM!
BOOM!
BOOM!
EEEE!!
THE LINE'S GETTING SHORTER.
WHY? WHAT'S GOING ON?!
...ONE OF THE ACTORS IS *EATING* HIS *COMPETITION*.

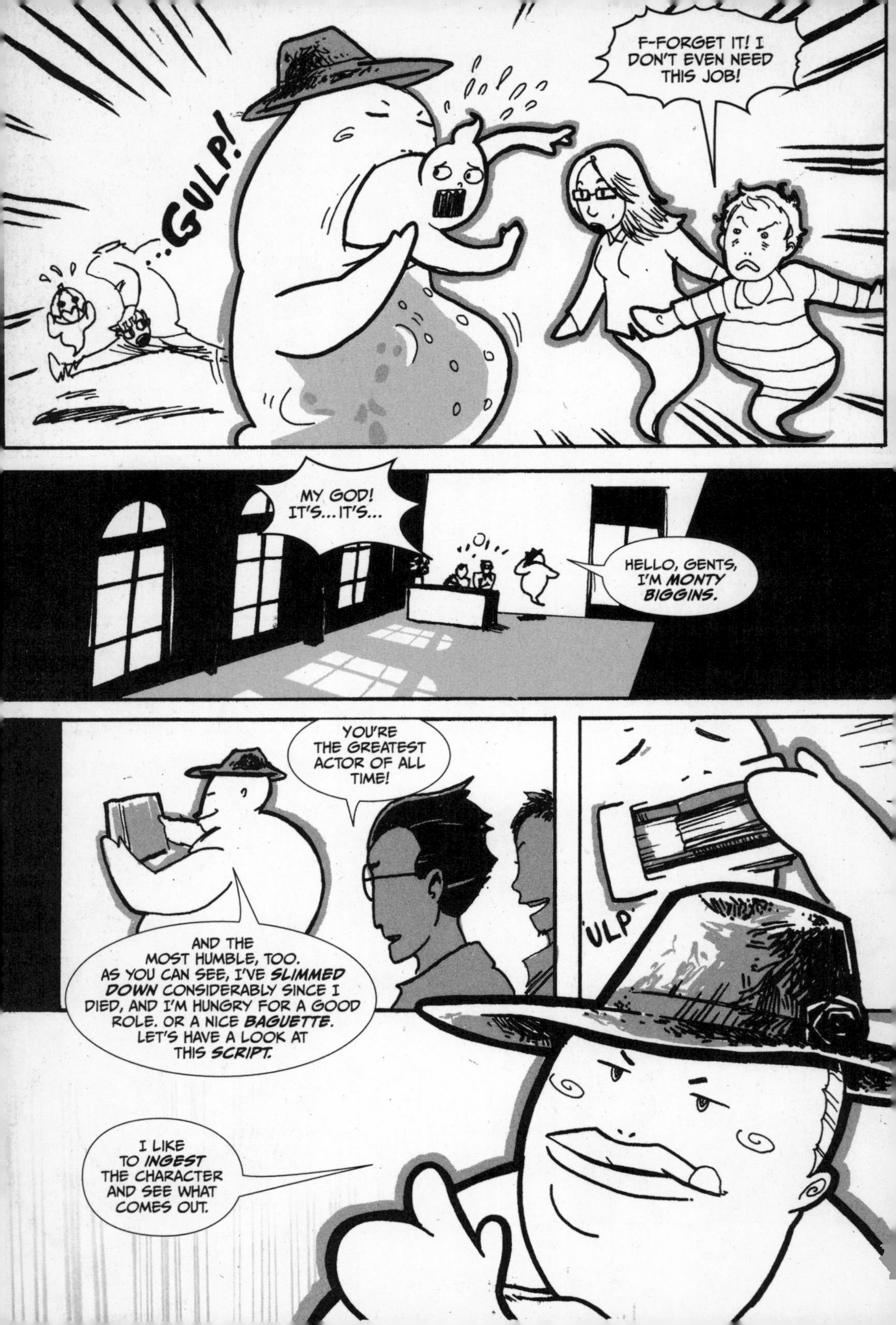
F-FORGET IT! I DON'T EVEN NEED THIS JOB!
GULP!
MY GOD! IT'S... IT'S...
HELLO, GENTS, I'M MONTY BIGGINS.
YOU'RE THE GREATEST ACTOR OF ALL TIME!
AND THE MOST HUMBLE, TOO. AS YOU CAN SEE, I'VE SLIMMED DOWN CONSIDERABLY SINCE I DIED, AND I'M HUNGRY FOR A GOOD ROLE. OR A NICE BAGUETTE. LET'S HAVE A LOOK AT THIS SCRIPT.
ULP
I LIKE TO INGEST THE CHARACTER AND SEE WHAT COMES OUT.

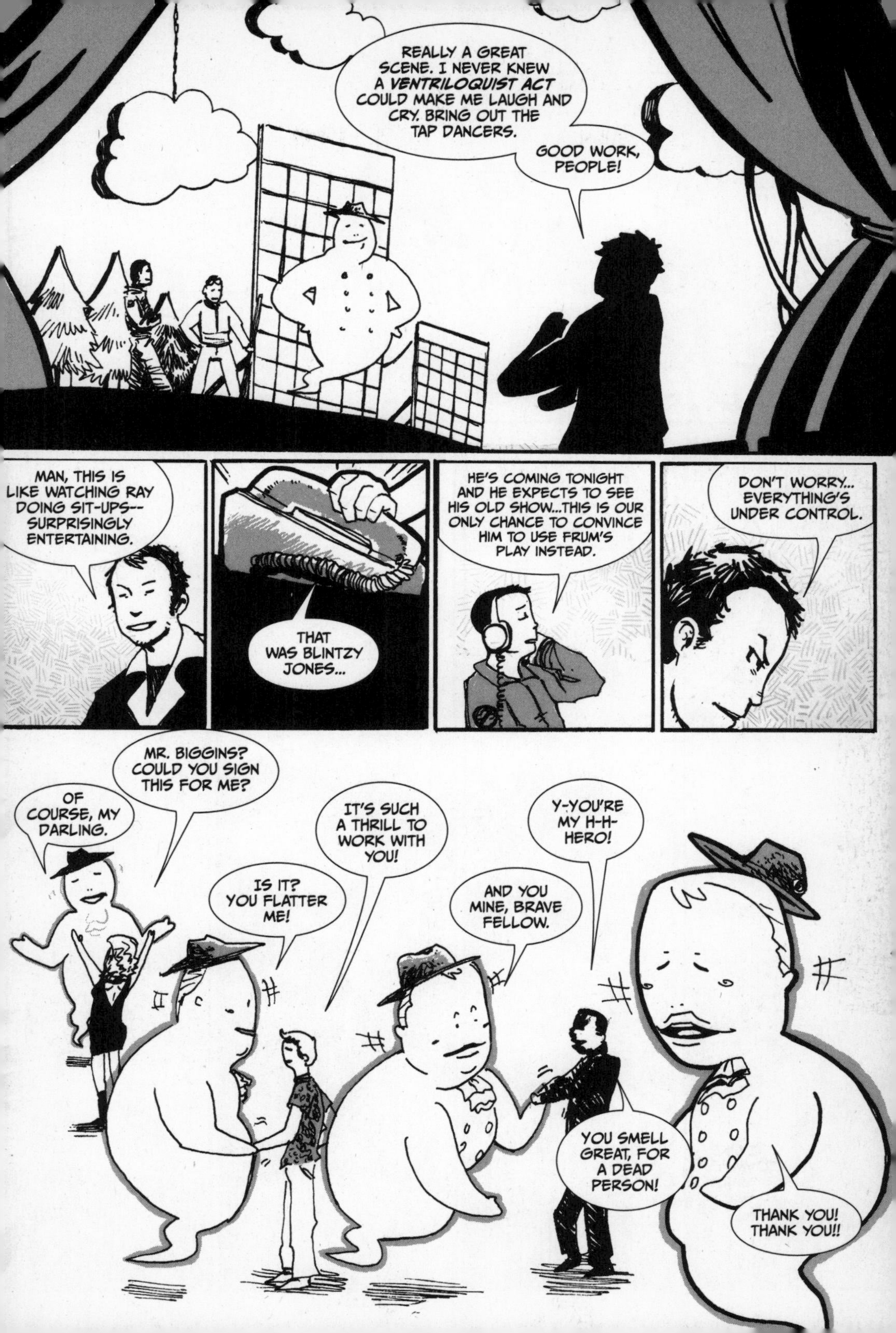
REALLY A GREAT SCENE. I NEVER KNEW A *VENTRILOQUIST ACT* COULD MAKE ME LAUGH AND CRY. BRING OUT THE TAP DANCERS.
GOOD WORK, PEOPLE!
MAN, THIS IS LIKE WATCHING RAY DOING SIT-UPS-- SURPRISINGLY ENTERTAINING.
THAT WAS BLINTZY JONES...
HE'S COMING TONIGHT AND HE EXPECTS TO SEE HIS OLD SHOW...THIS IS OUR ONLY CHANCE TO CONVINCE HIM TO USE FRUM'S PLAY INSTEAD.
DON'T WORRY... EVERYTHING'S UNDER CONTROL.
MR. BIGGINS? COULD YOU SIGN THIS FOR ME?
OF COURSE, MY DARLING.
IT'S SUCH A THRILL TO WORK WITH YOU!
IS IT? YOU FLATTER ME!
Y-YOU'RE MY H-H-HERO!
AND YOU MINE, BRAVE FELLOW.
YOU SMELL GREAT, FOR A DEAD PERSON!
THANK YOU! THANK YOU!!

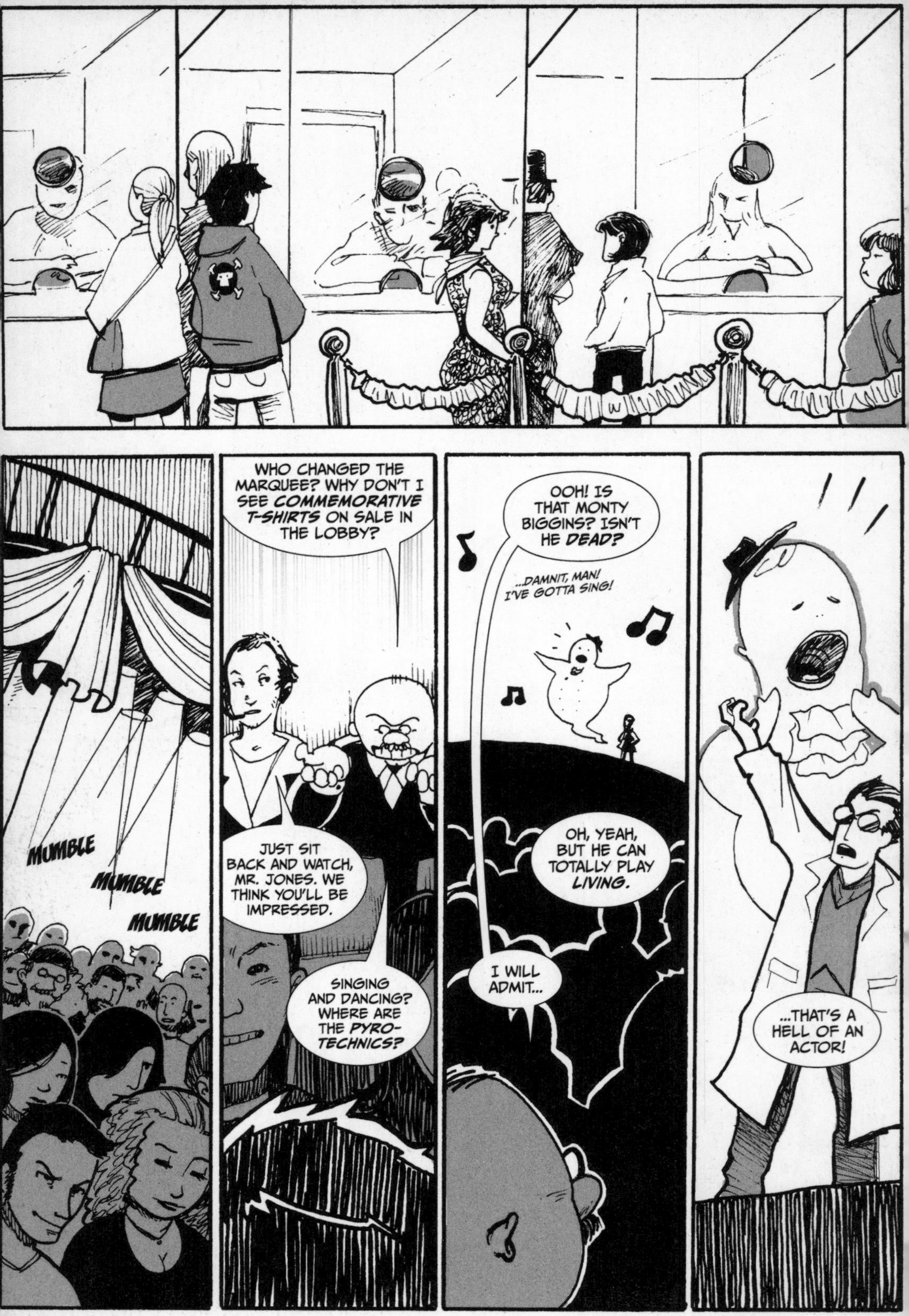
MUMBLE
MUMBLE
MUMBLE
WHO CHANGED THE MARQUEE? WHY DON'T I SEE COMMEMORATIVE T-SHIRTS ON SALE IN THE LOBBY?
JUST SIT BACK AND WATCH, MR. JONES. WE THINK YOU'LL BE IMPRESSED.
SINGING AND DANCING? WHERE ARE THE PYRO-TECHNICS?
OOH! IS THAT MONTY BIGGINS? ISN'T HE DEAD?
...DAMNIT, MAN! I'VE GOTTA SING!
OH, YEAH, BUT HE CAN TOTALLY PLAY LIVING.
I WILL ADMIT...
...THAT'S A HELL OF AN ACTOR!

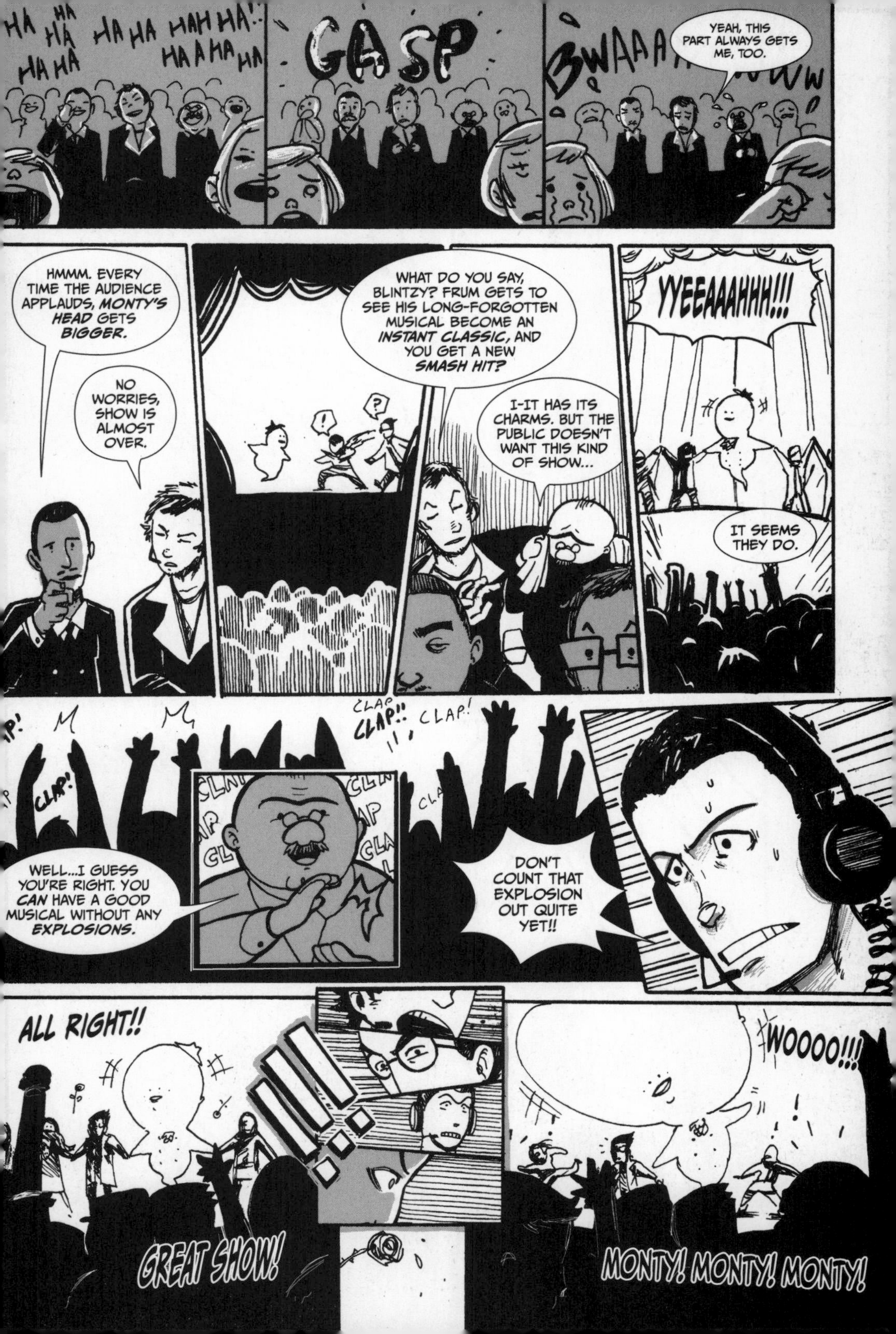
HA HA HA HA HA HA HA HA HAH HA!.. HA A HA HA HA
GASP
BWAAAAA...WW
YEAH, THIS PART ALWAYS GETS ME, TOO.
HMMM. EVERY TIME THE AUDIENCE APPLAUDS, MONTY'S HEAD GETS BIGGER.
NO WORRIES, SHOW IS ALMOST OVER.
WHAT DO YOU SAY, BLINTZY? FRUM GETS TO SEE HIS LONG-FORGOTTEN MUSICAL BECOME AN INSTANT CLASSIC, AND YOU GET A NEW SMASH HIT?
I-IT HAS ITS CHARMS. BUT THE PUBLIC DOESN'T WANT THIS KIND OF SHOW...
YYEEAAAHHH!!!
IT SEEMS THEY DO.
CLAP!
CLAP CLAP!! CLAP!
WELL...I GUESS YOU'RE RIGHT. YOU CAN HAVE A GOOD MUSICAL WITHOUT ANY EXPLOSIONS.
DON'T COUNT THAT EXPLOSION OUT QUITE YET!!
ALL RIGHT!!
WOOOO!!!
GREAT SHOW!
MONTY! MONTY! MONTY!

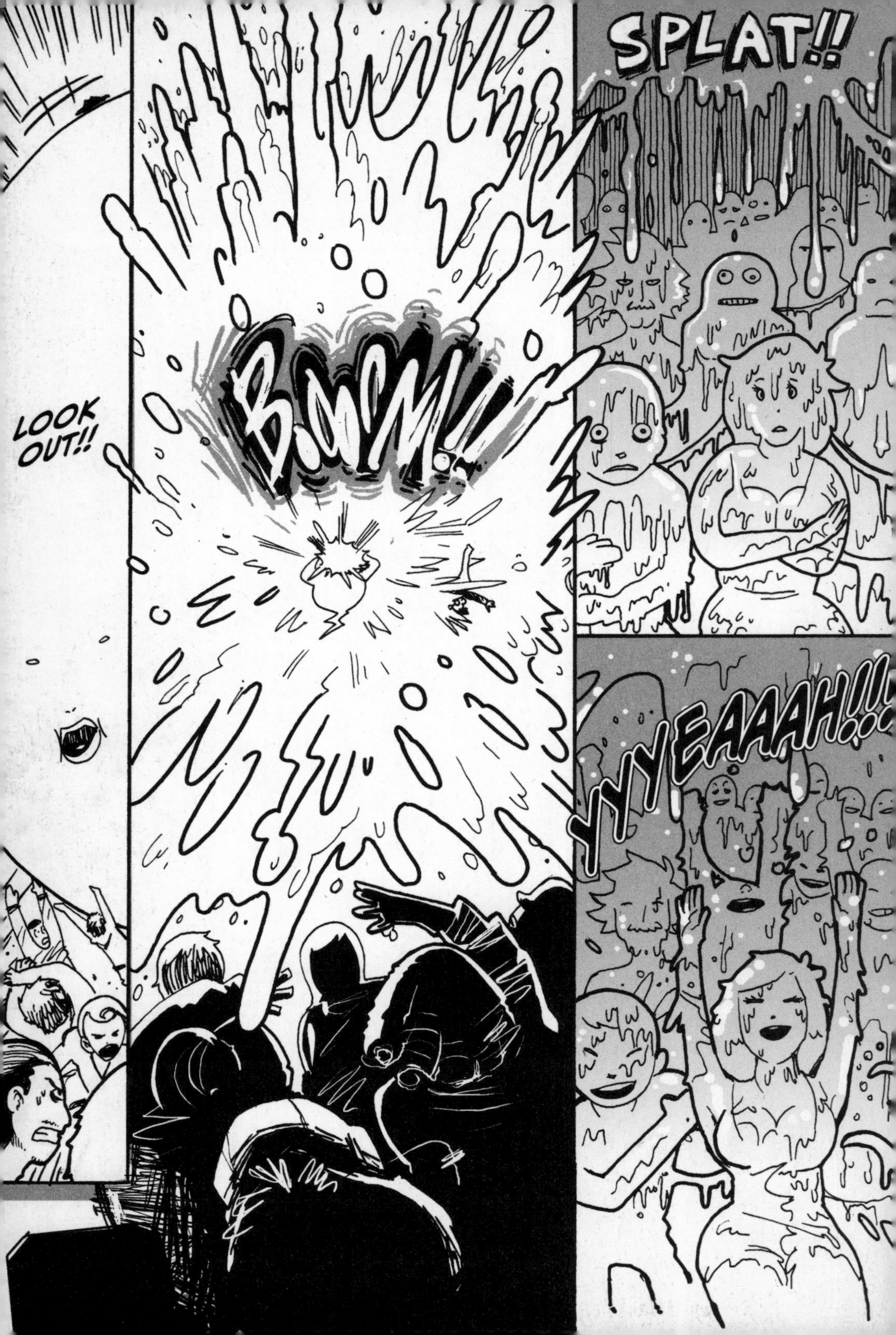
LOOK OUT!!
BOOM!!
SPLAT!!
YYYEAAAH!!!

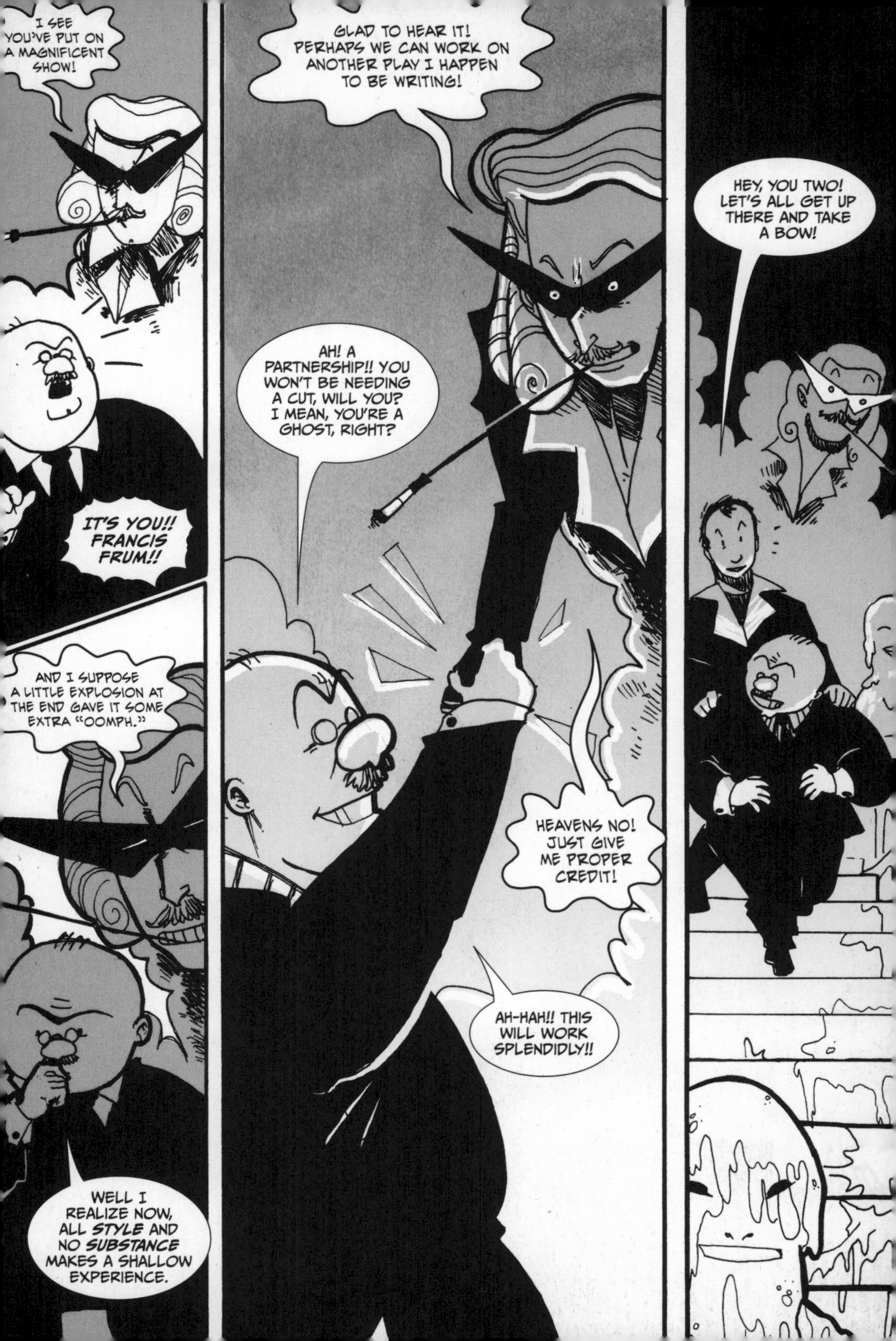
I SEE YOU'VE PUT ON A MAGNIFICENT SHOW!
IT'S YOU!! FRANCIS FRUM!!
AND I SUPPOSE A LITTLE EXPLOSION AT THE END GAVE IT SOME EXTRA "OOMPH."
WELL I REALIZE NOW, ALL STYLE AND NO SUBSTANCE MAKES A SHALLOW EXPERIENCE.
GLAD TO HEAR IT! PERHAPS WE CAN WORK ON ANOTHER PLAY I HAPPEN TO BE WRITING!
AH! A PARTNERSHIP!! YOU WON'T BE NEEDING A CUT, WILL YOU? I MEAN, YOU'RE A GHOST, RIGHT?
HEAVENS NO! JUST GIVE ME PROPER CREDIT!
AH-HAH!! THIS WILL WORK SPLENDIDLY!!
HEY, YOU TWO! LET'S ALL GET UP THERE AND TAKE A BOW!

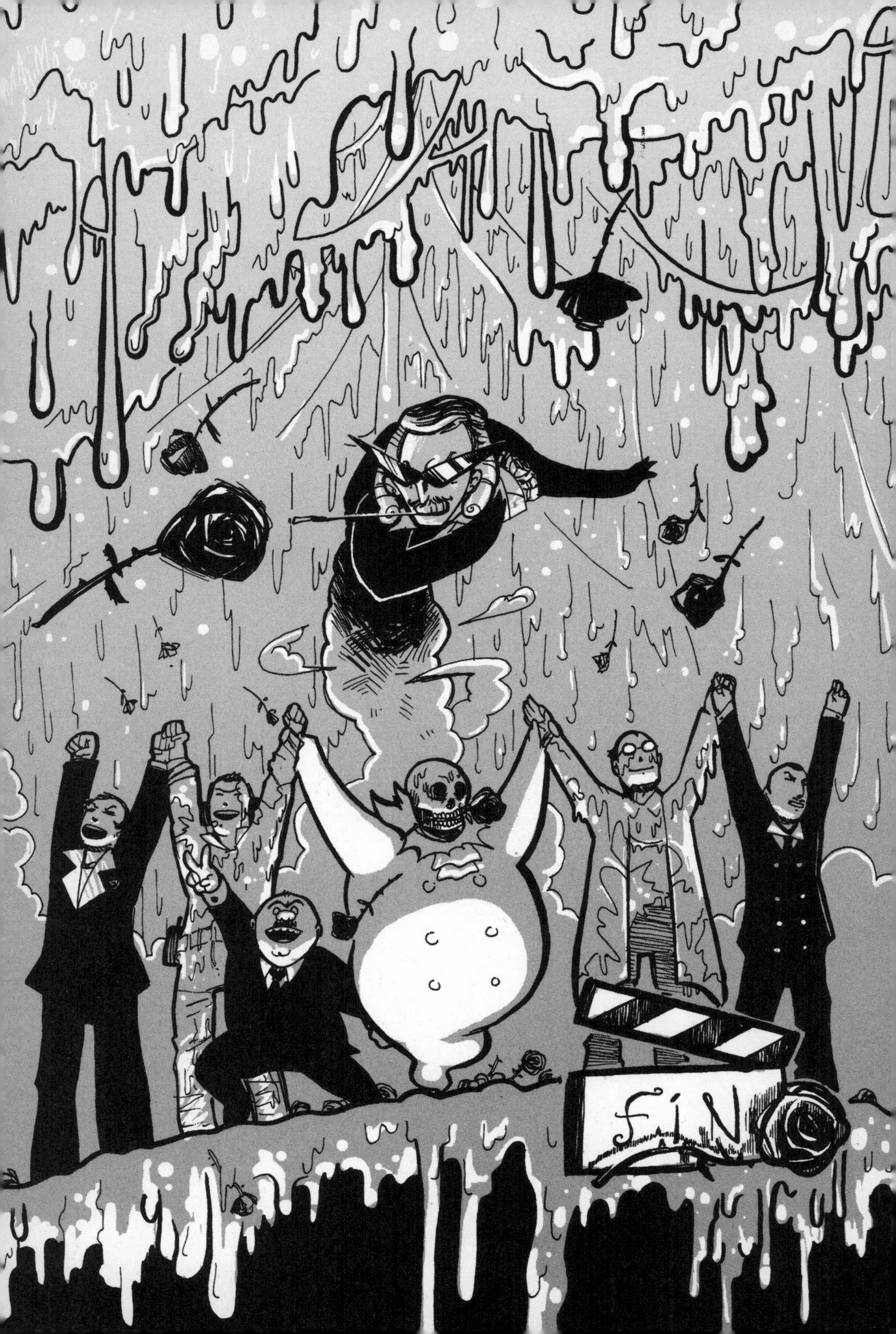
fin

# GHOSTBUSTERS

# CHAPTER II

# WORM IN THE APPLE

## STORY BY
## NATHAN JOHNSON

## ART BY
## MICHAEL SHELFER

## INKS & TONES BY
## MAXIMO V. LORENZO

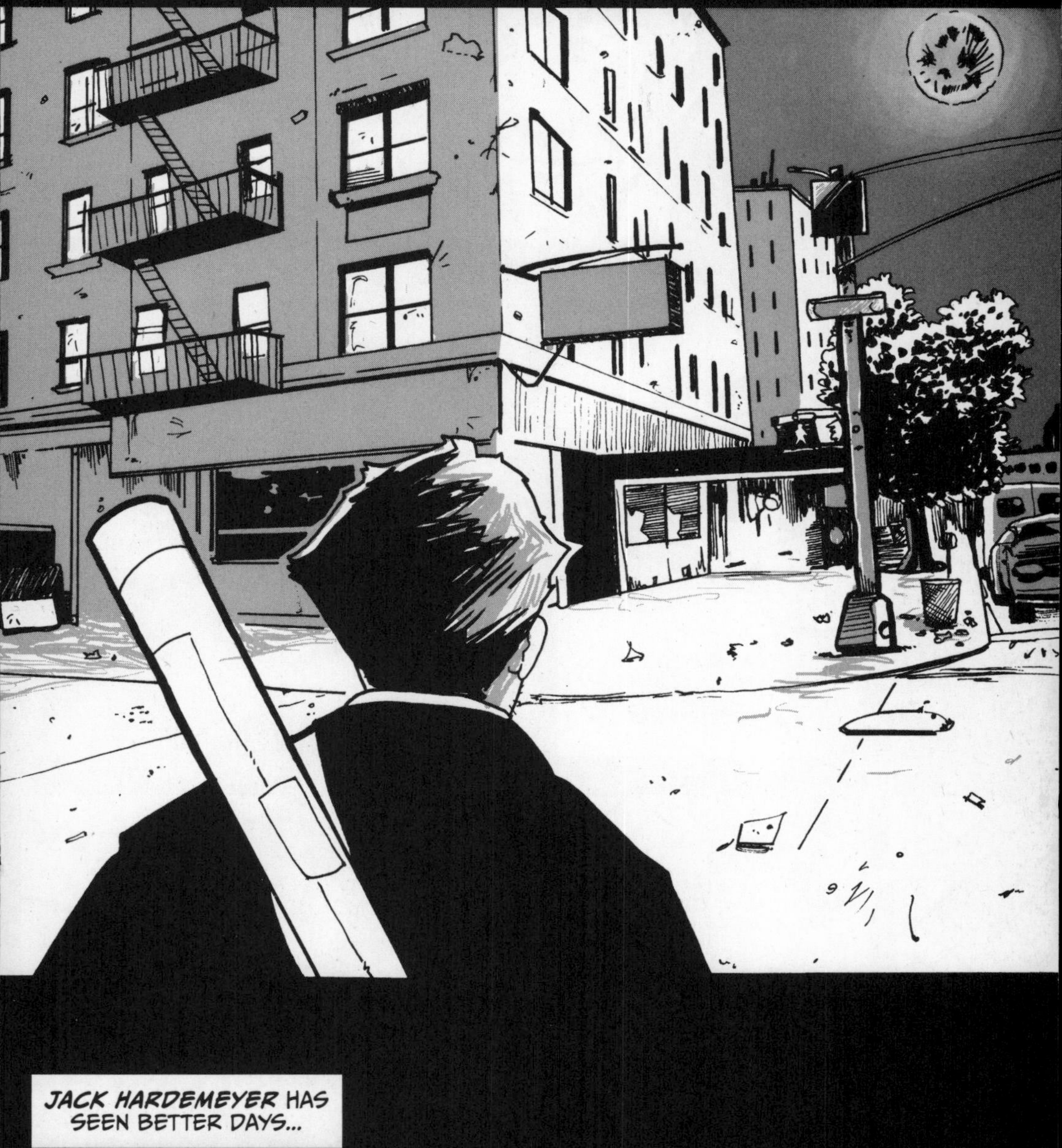
JACK HARDEMEYER HAS SEEN BETTER DAYS...

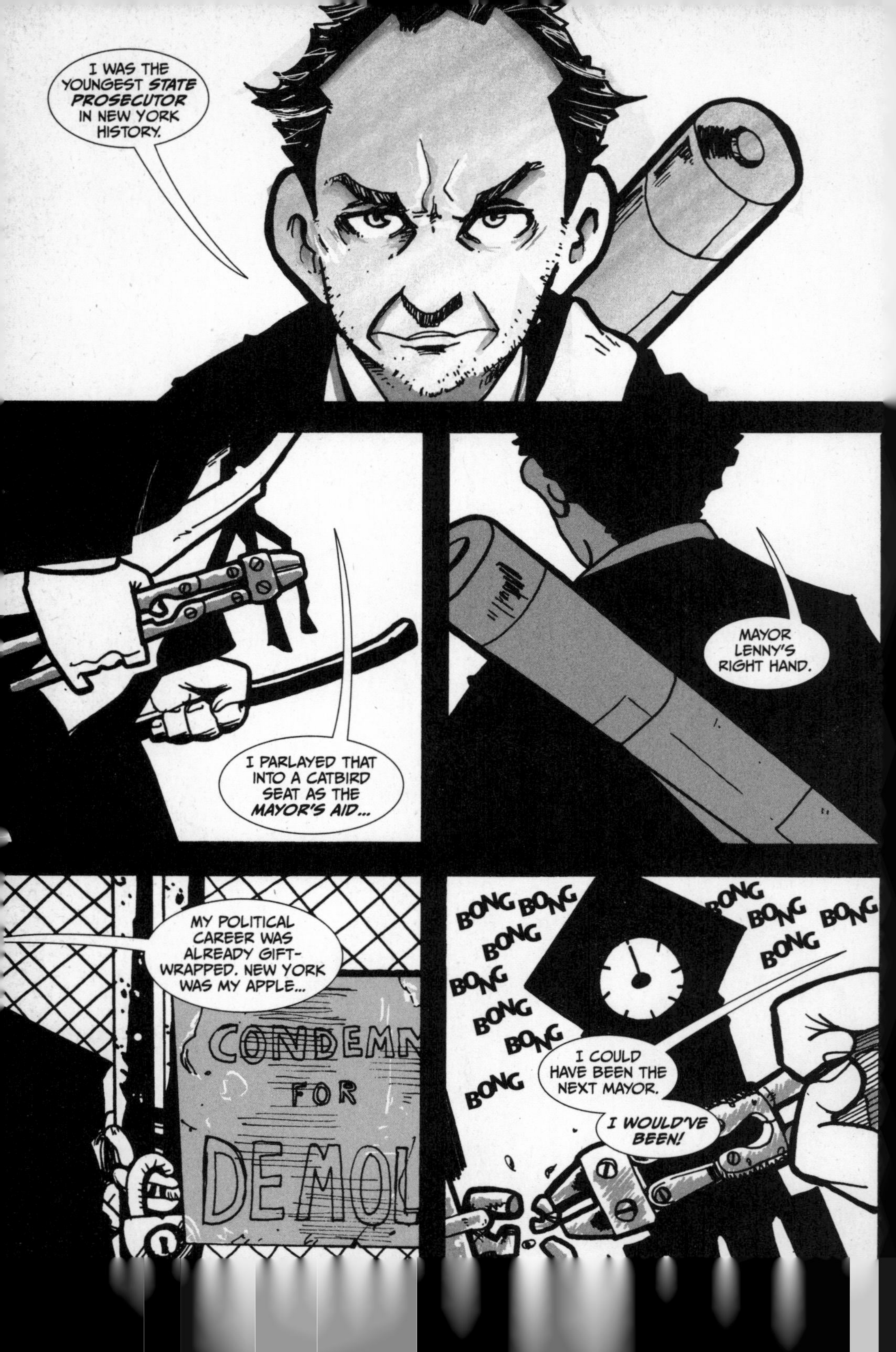

I WAS THE YOUNGEST STATE PROSECUTOR IN NEW YORK HISTORY.
I PARLAYED THAT INTO A CATBIRD SEAT AS THE MAYOR'S AID...
MAYOR LENNY'S RIGHT HAND.
MY POLITICAL CAREER WAS ALREADY GIFT-WRAPPED. NEW YORK WAS MY APPLE...
CONDEMN
FOR
DEMOL
BONG BONG BONG BONG BONG BONG BONG BONG BONG BONG BONG
I COULD HAVE BEEN THE NEXT MAYOR.
I WOULD'VE BEEN!

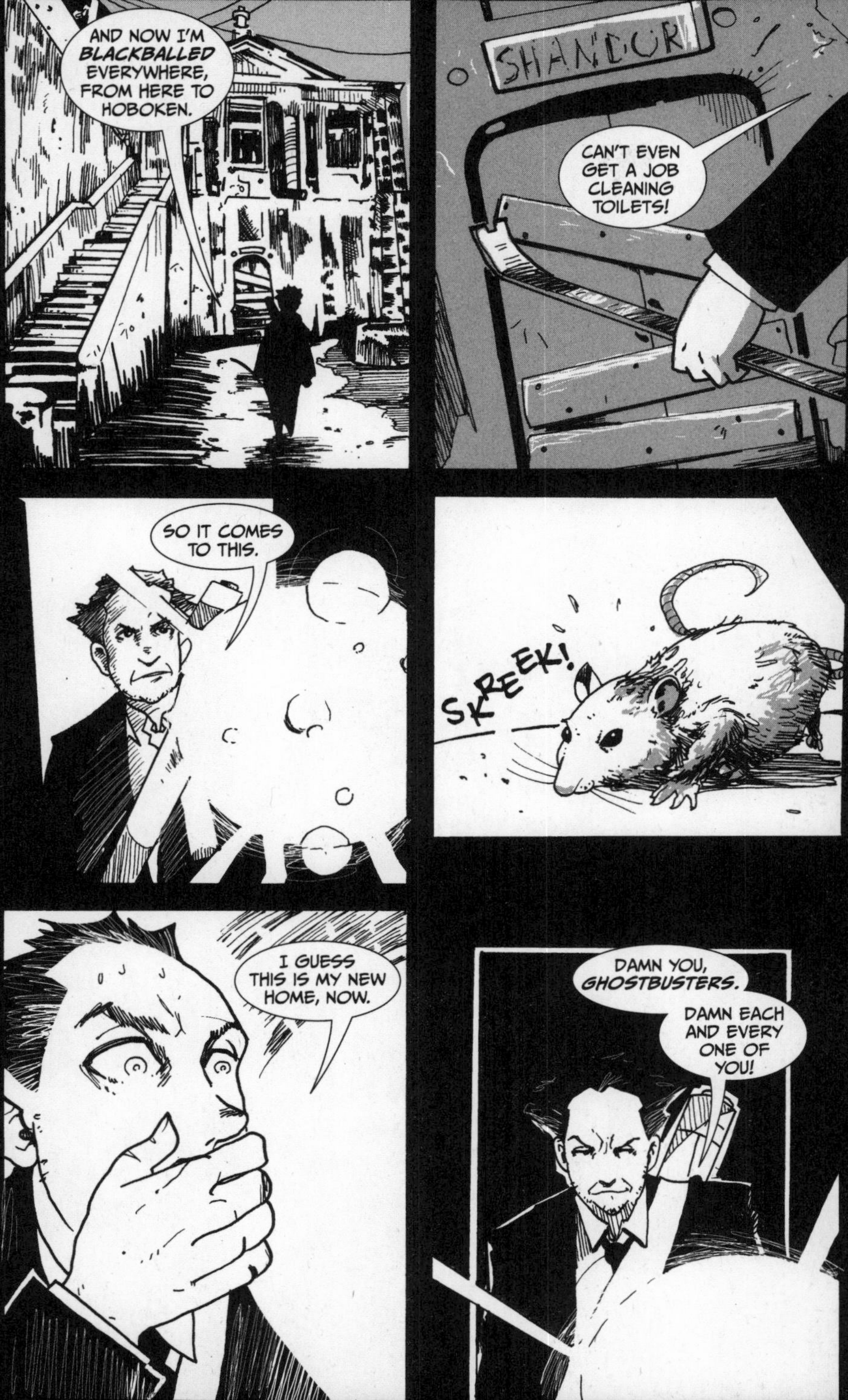
AND NOW I'M *BLACKBALLED* EVERYWHERE, FROM HERE TO HOBOKEN.
SHANDOR
CAN'T EVEN GET A JOB CLEANING TOILETS!
SO IT COMES TO THIS.
SKREEK!
I GUESS THIS IS MY NEW HOME, NOW.
DAMN YOU, *GHOSTBUSTERS.*
DAMN EACH AND EVERY ONE OF YOU!

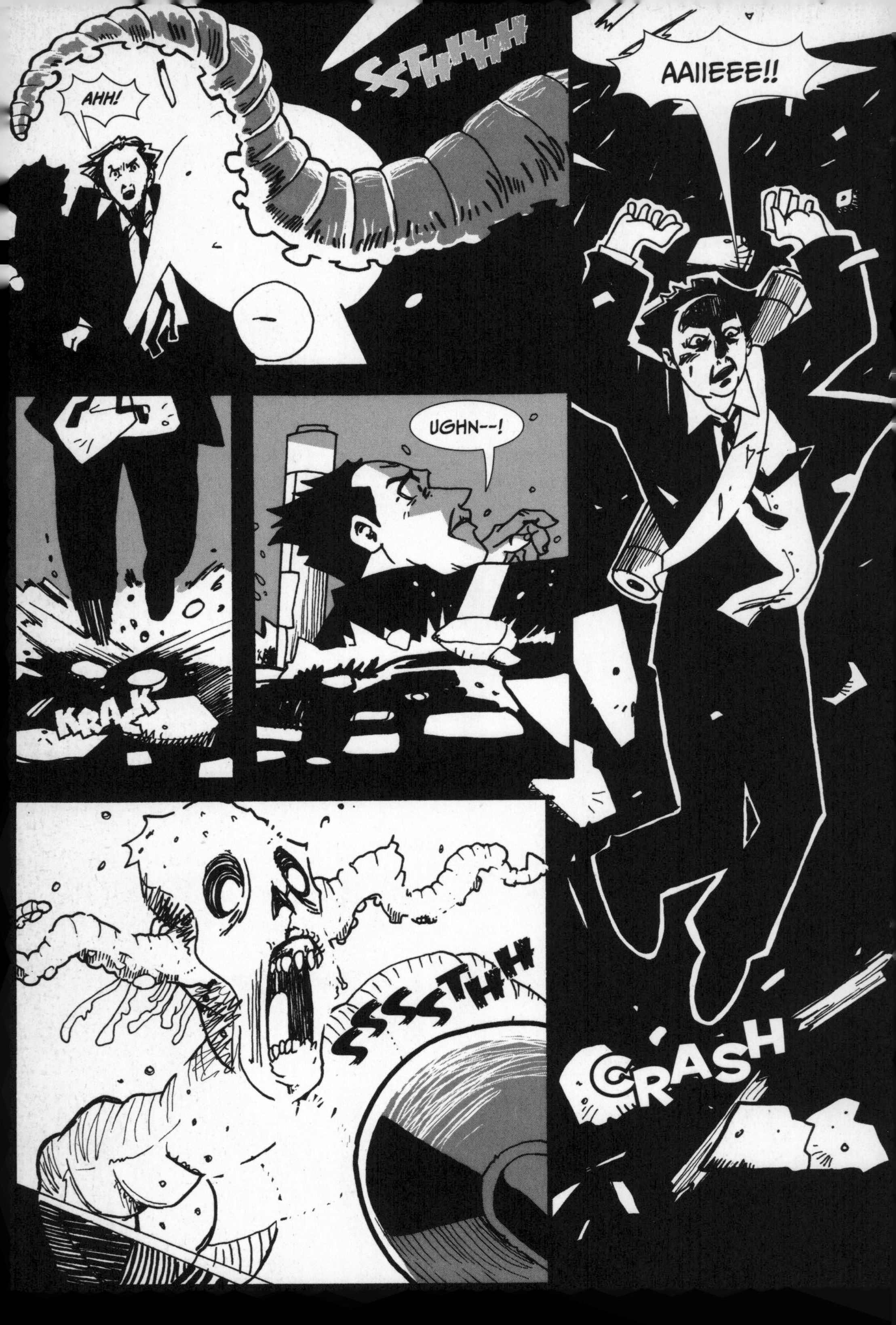
AHH!
SSTHHHHH
AAIIEEE!!
KRAK
UGHN--!
SSSTHH
CRASH

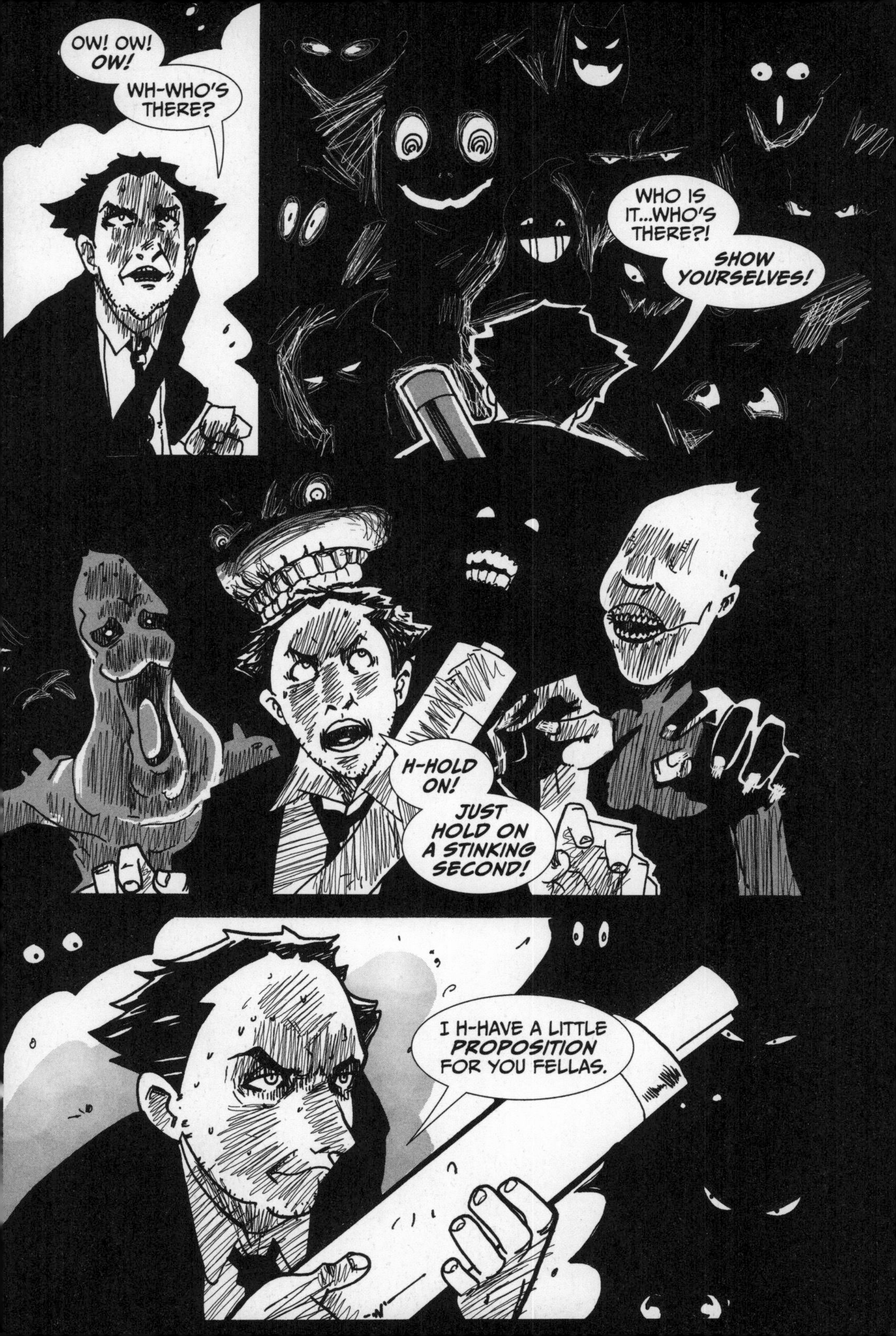
OW! OW! *OW!*
WH-WHO'S THERE?
WHO IS IT...WHO'S THERE?!
*SHOW YOURSELVES!*
*H-HOLD ON!*
*JUST HOLD ON A STINKING SECOND!*
I H-HAVE A LITTLE *PROPOSITION* FOR YOU FELLAS.

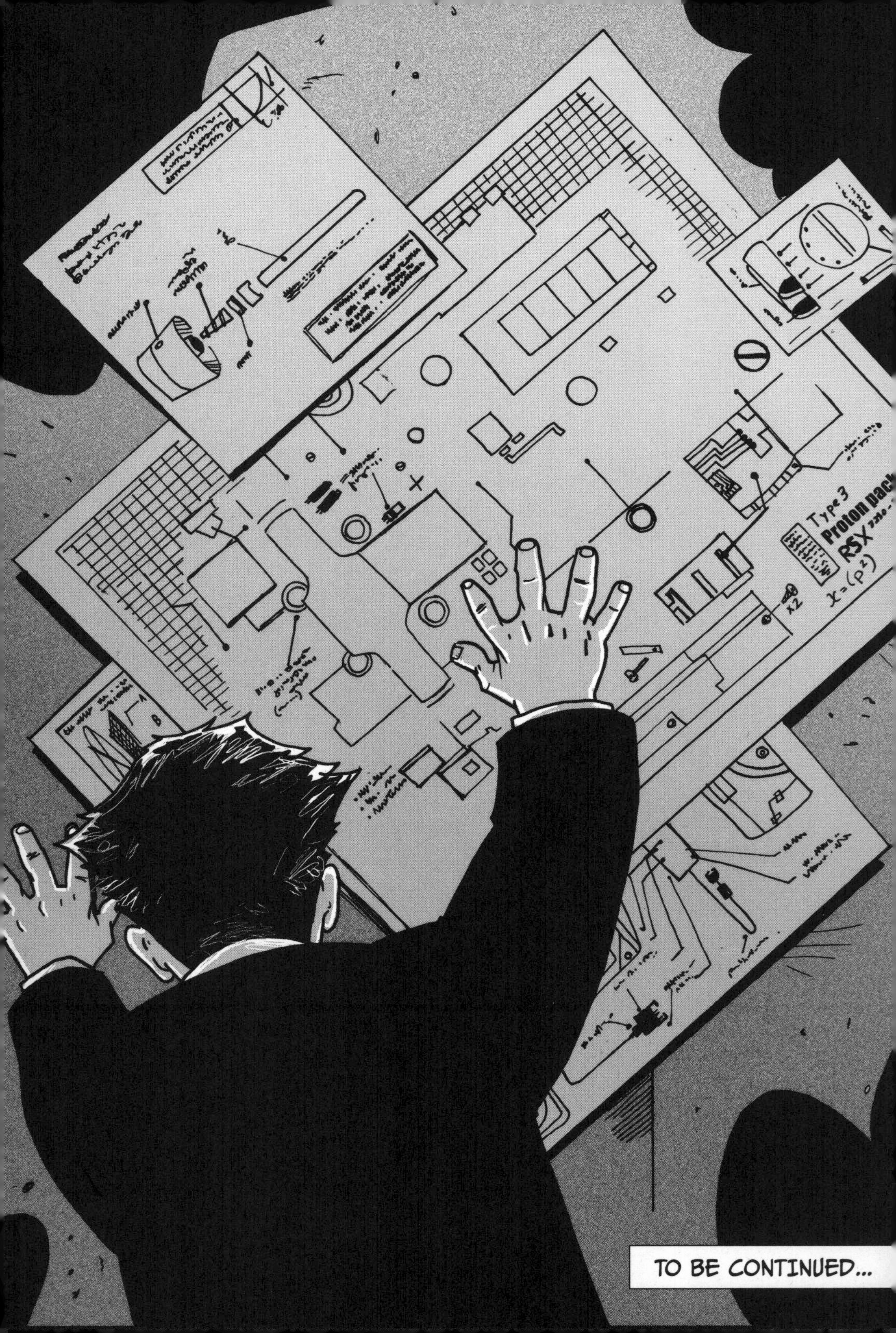
Type 3
Proton pack
RSX
x2
TO BE CONTINUED...

# GHOSTBUSTERS™

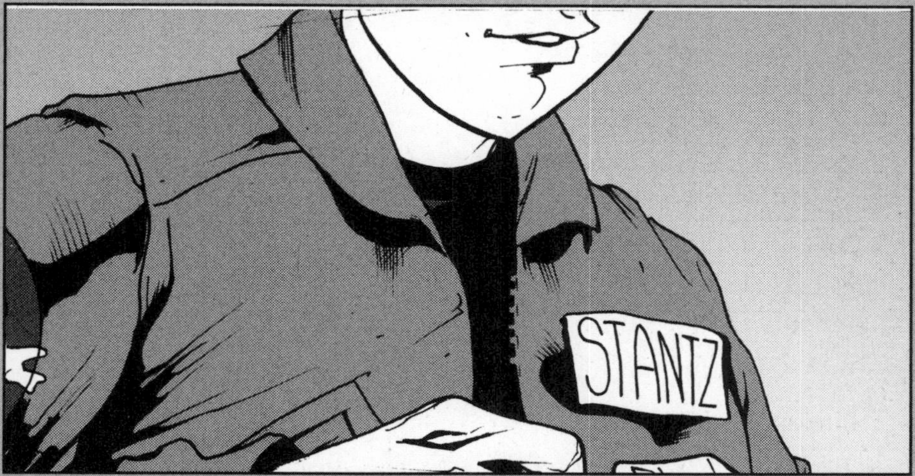
STANTZ

# CHAPTER III

# WE'RE READY TO BELIEVE YOU!

STORY BY
NATHAN JOHNSON

ART BY
NATE WATSON

TONES BY
CHI WANG

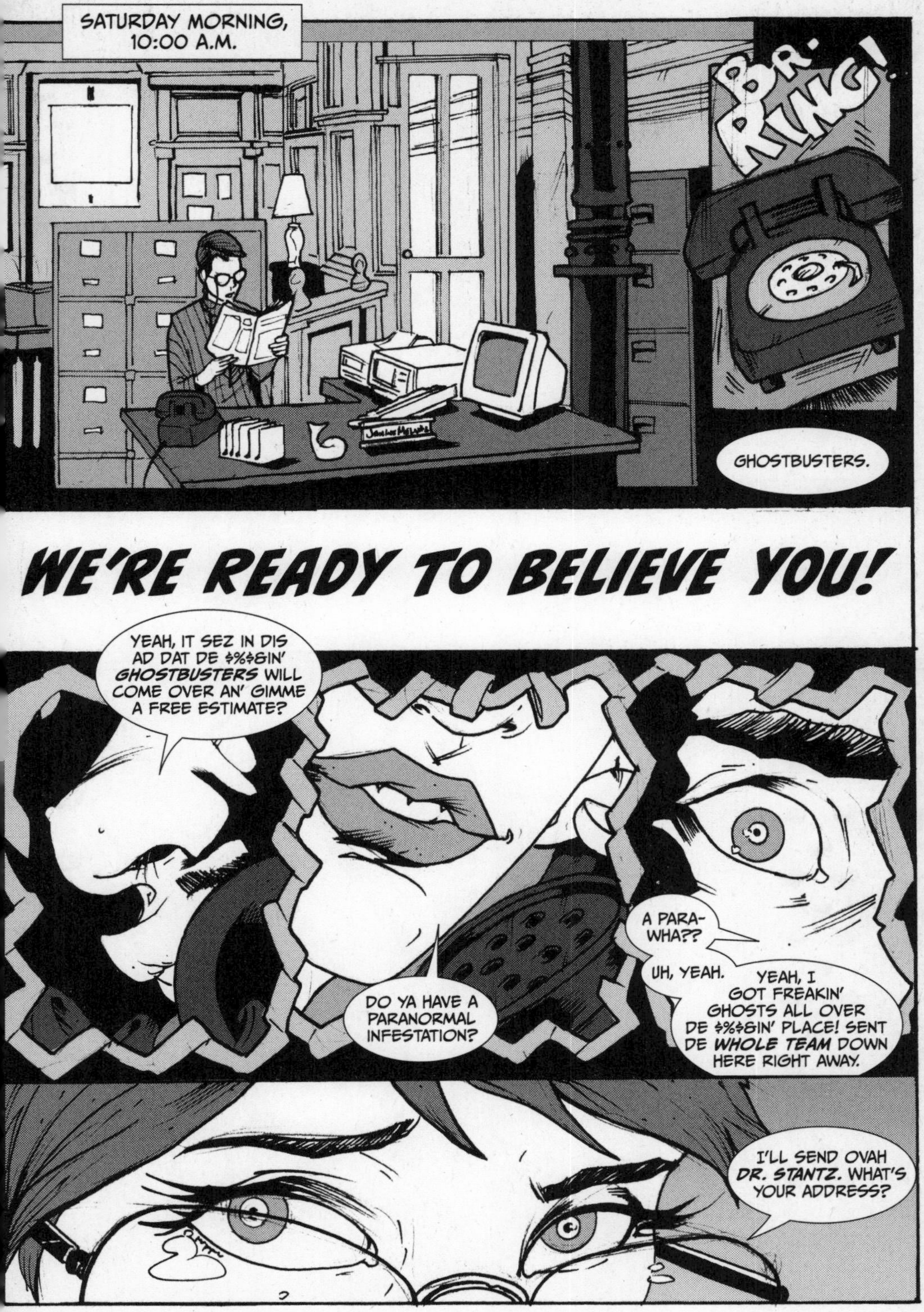

SATURDAY MORNING, 10:00 A.M.
BR-RING!
GHOSTBUSTERS.
WE'RE READY TO BELIEVE YOU!
YEAH, IT SEZ IN DIS AD DAT DE $%$&IN' GHOSTBUSTERS WILL COME OVER AN' GIMME A FREE ESTIMATE?
DO YA HAVE A PARANORMAL INFESTATION?
A PARA-WHA??
UH, YEAH.
YEAH, I GOT FREAKIN' GHOSTS ALL OVER DE $%$&IN' PLACE! SENT DE WHOLE TEAM DOWN HERE RIGHT AWAY.
I'LL SEND OVAH DR. STANTZ. WHAT'S YOUR ADDRESS?

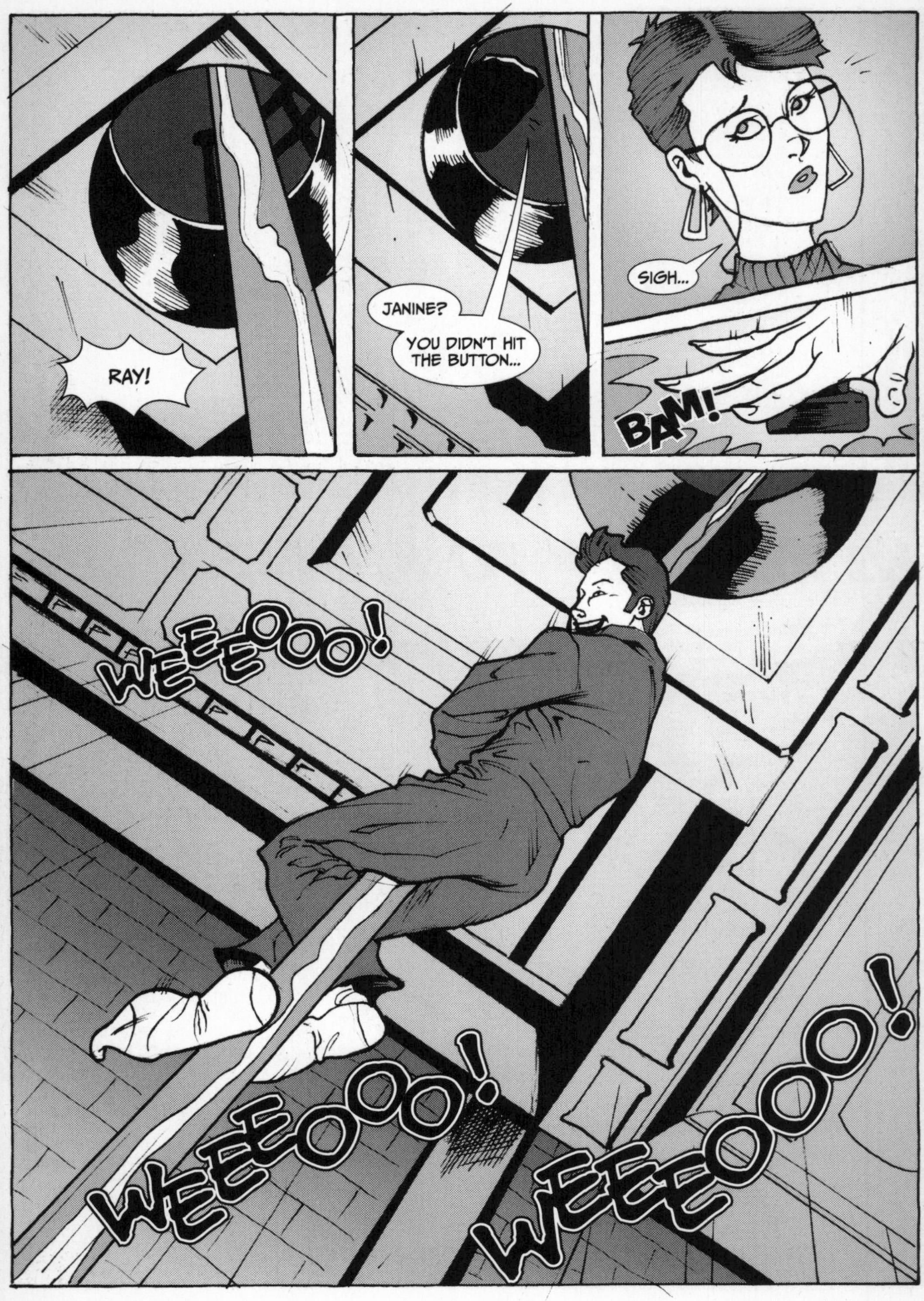

RAY!
JANINE?
YOU DIDN'T HIT THE BUTTON...
SIGH...
BAM!
WEEEOOO!
WEEEOOO!
WEEEOOO!

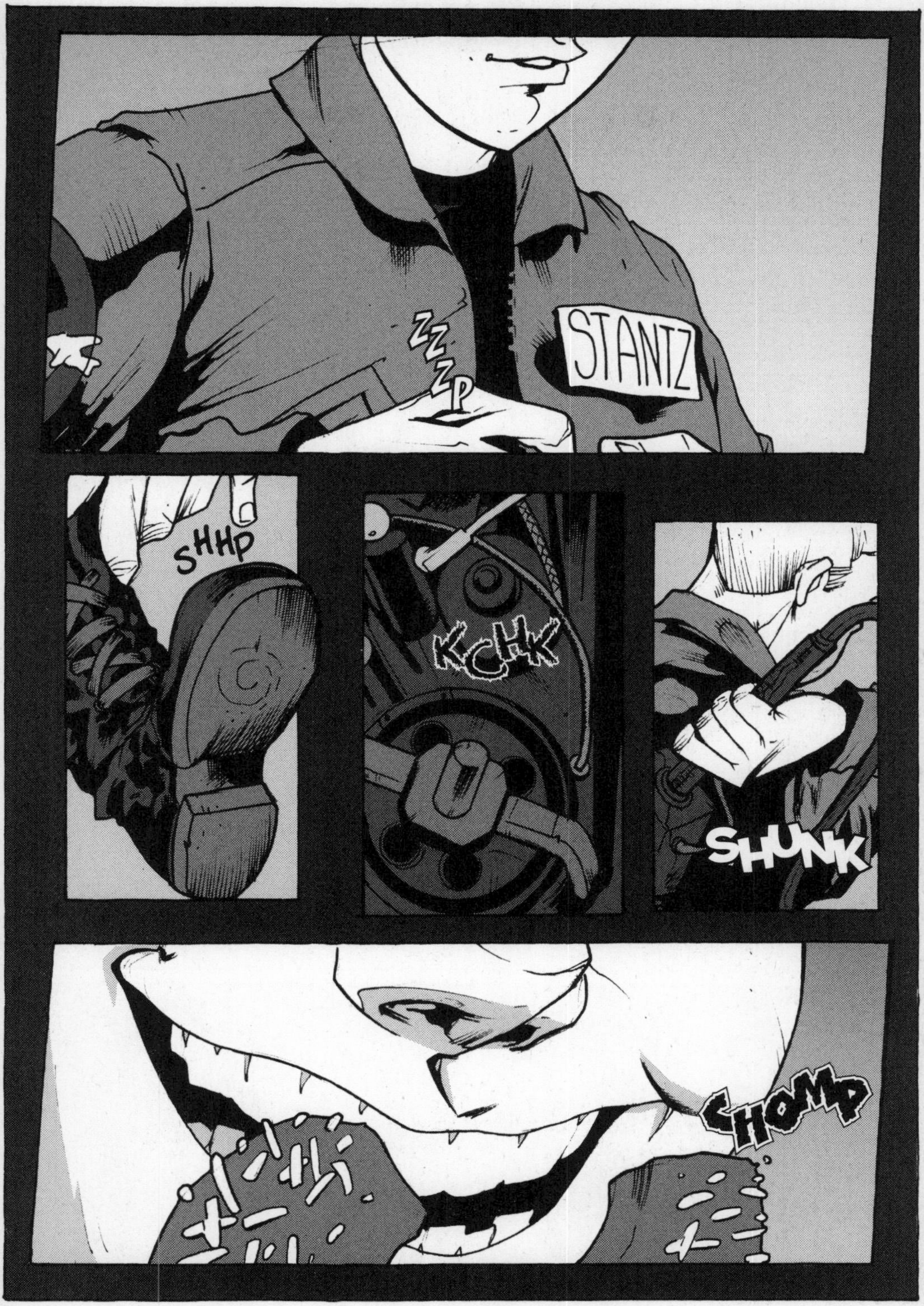
ZZZP
STANTZ
SHHP
KCHK
SHUNK
CHOMP

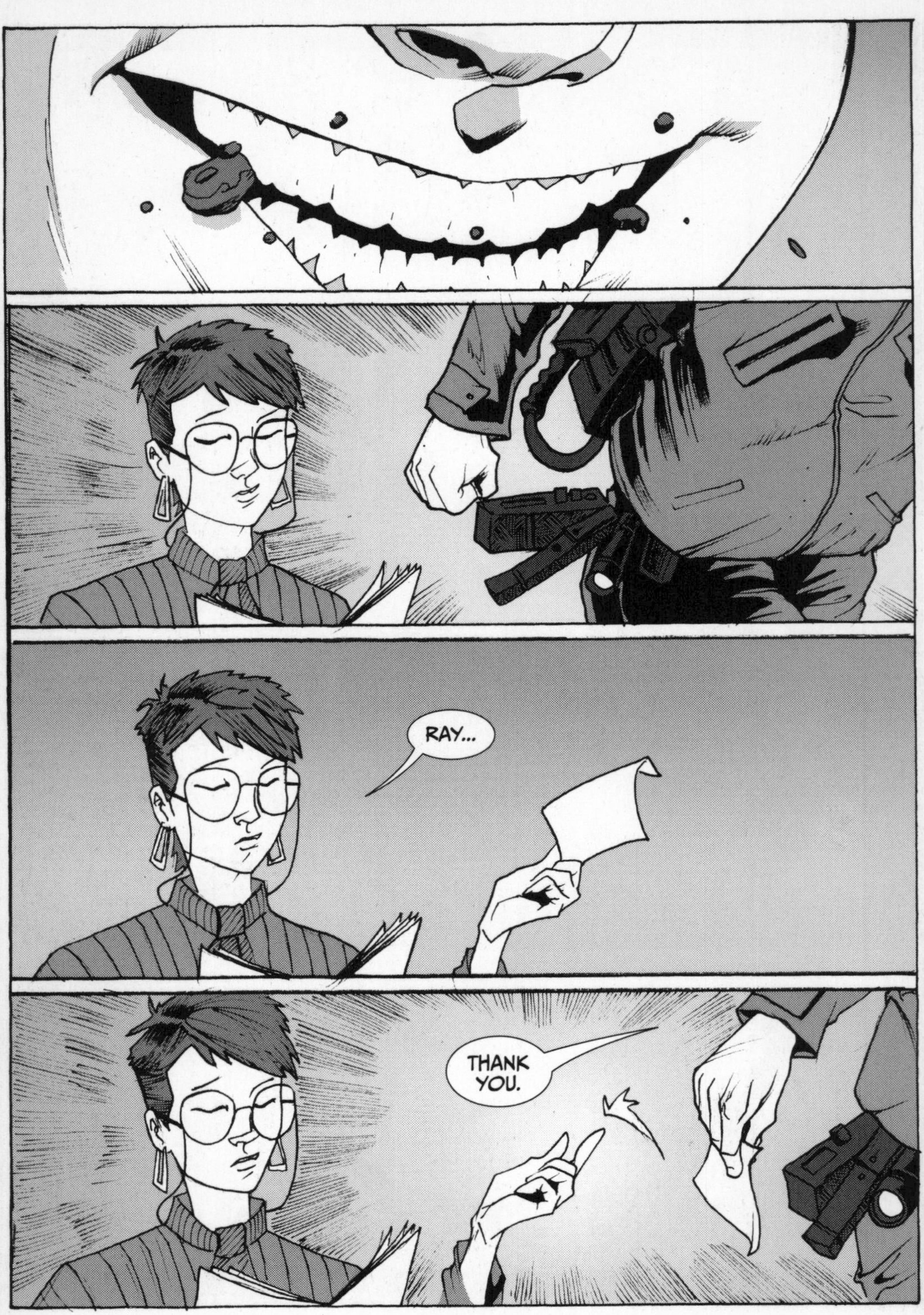
RAY...
THANK YOU.

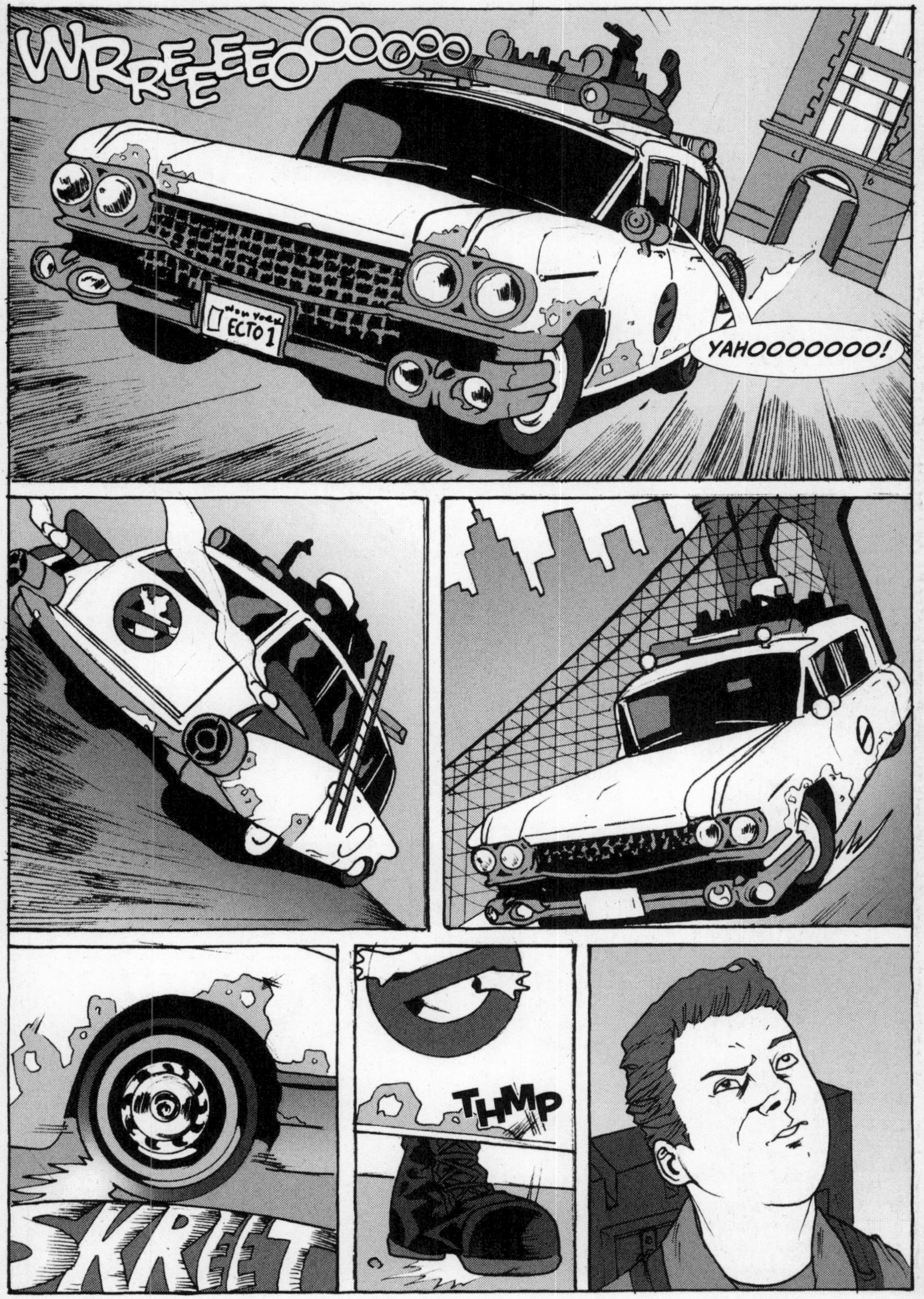
WRREEEEOOOOOOO
New York
ECTO 1
YAHOOOOOOOO!
SKREET
THMP

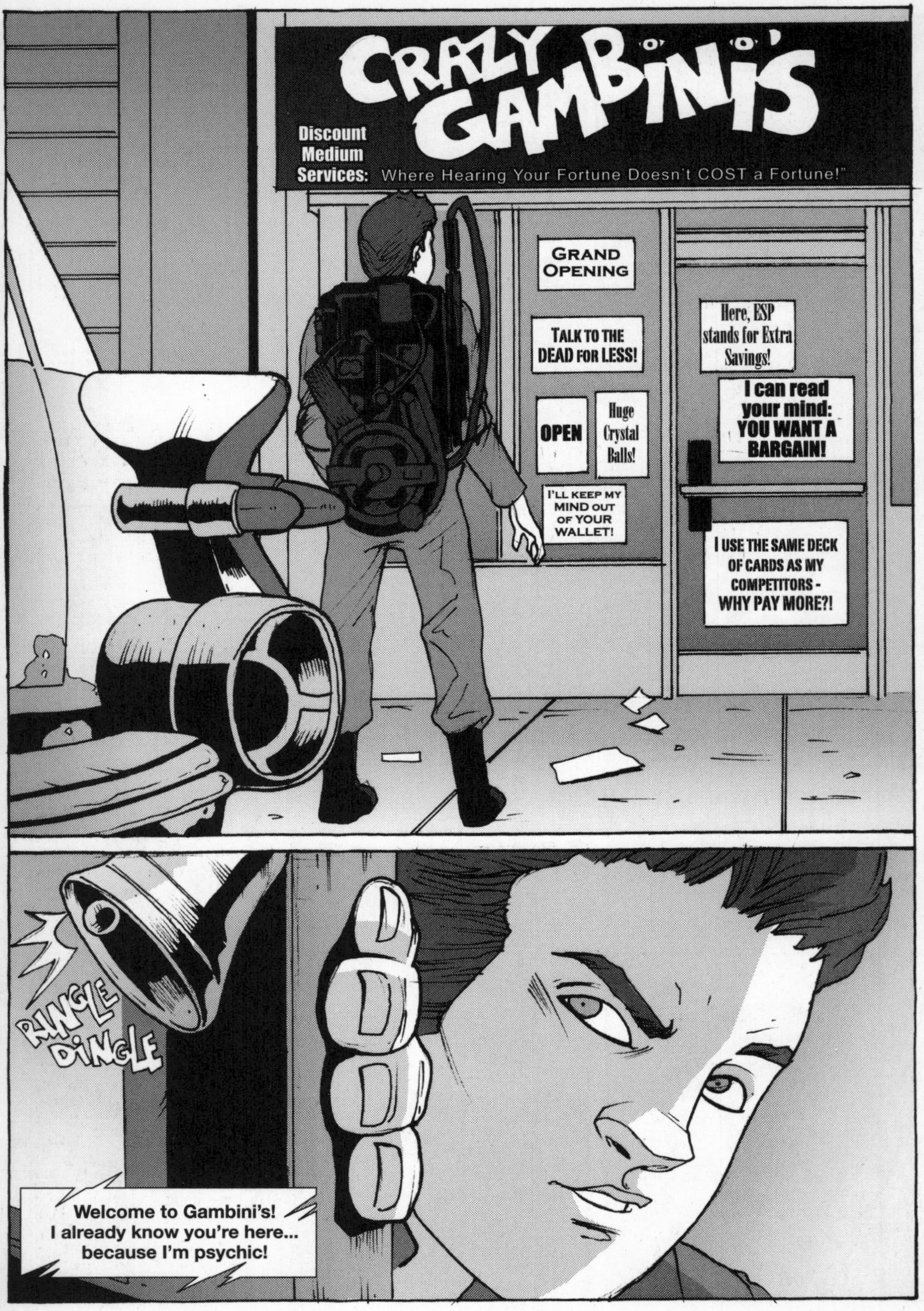
CRAZY GAMBINI'S
Discount Medium Services: Where Hearing Your Fortune Doesn't COST a Fortune!"
GRAND OPENING
TALK TO THE DEAD FOR LESS!
OPEN
Huge Crystal Balls!
I'LL KEEP MY MIND OUT OF YOUR WALLET!
Here, ESP stands for Extra Savings!
I can read your mind: YOU WANT A BARGAIN!
I USE THE SAME DECK OF CARDS AS MY COMPETITORS - WHY PAY MORE?!
RINGLE DINGLE
Welcome to Gambini's! I already know you're here... because I'm psychic!

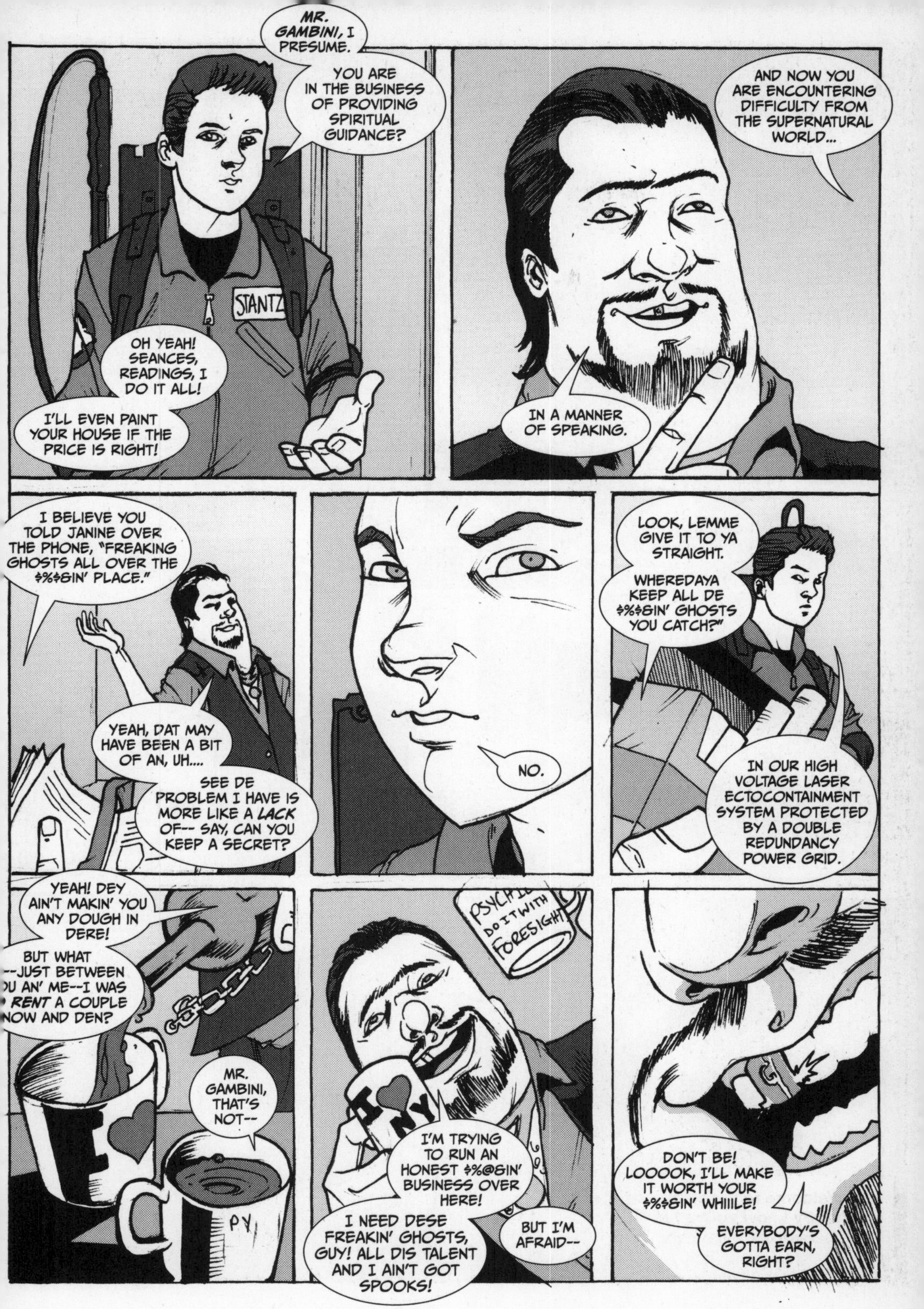
MR. GAMBINI, I PRESUME.
YOU ARE IN THE BUSINESS OF PROVIDING SPIRITUAL GUIDANCE?
OH YEAH! SEANCES, READINGS, I DO IT ALL!
I'LL EVEN PAINT YOUR HOUSE IF THE PRICE IS RIGHT!
STANTZ
AND NOW YOU ARE ENCOUNTERING DIFFICULTY FROM THE SUPERNATURAL WORLD...
IN A MANNER OF SPEAKING.
I BELIEVE YOU TOLD JANINE OVER THE PHONE, "FREAKING GHOSTS ALL OVER THE $%$&IN' PLACE."
YEAH, DAT MAY HAVE BEEN A BIT OF AN, UH....
SEE DE PROBLEM I HAVE IS MORE LIKE A *LACK* OF-- SAY, CAN YOU KEEP A SECRET?
NO.
LOOK, LEMME GIVE IT TO YA STRAIGHT.
WHEREDAYA KEEP ALL DE $%$&IN' GHOSTS YOU CATCH?"
IN OUR HIGH VOLTAGE LASER ECTOCONTAINMENT SYSTEM PROTECTED BY A DOUBLE REDUNDANCY POWER GRID.
YEAH! DEY AIN'T MAKIN' YOU ANY DOUGH IN DERE!
BUT WHAT --JUST BETWEEN OU AN' ME--I WAS RENT A COUPLE NOW AND DEN?
MR. GAMBINI, THAT'S NOT--
PSYCHICS DO IT WITH FORESIGHT
I'M TRYING TO RUN AN HONEST $%@&IN' BUSINESS OVER HERE!
I NEED DESE FREAKIN' GHOSTS, GUY! ALL DIS TALENT AND I AIN'T GOT SPOOKS!
BUT I'M AFRAID--
DON'T BE! LOOOOK, I'LL MAKE IT WORTH YOUR $%$&IN' WHIIILE!
EVERYBODY'S GOTTA EARN, RIGHT?

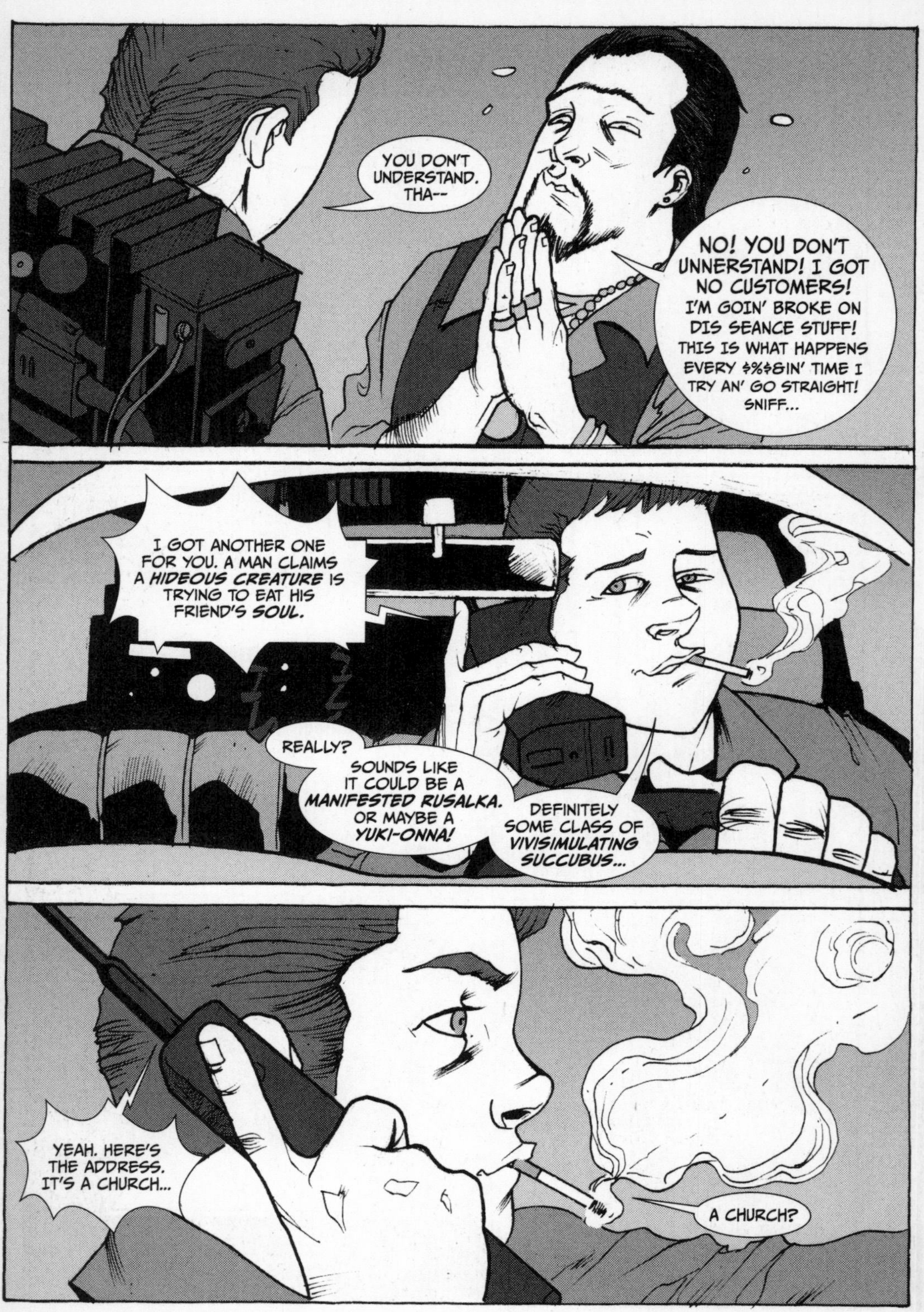
YOU DON'T UNDERSTAND. THA--
NO! YOU DON'T UNNERSTAND! I GOT NO CUSTOMERS! I'M GOIN' BROKE ON DIS SEANCE STUFF! THIS IS WHAT HAPPENS EVERY $%$&IN' TIME I TRY AN' GO STRAIGHT! SNIFF...
I GOT ANOTHER ONE FOR YOU. A MAN CLAIMS A *HIDEOUS CREATURE* IS TRYING TO EAT HIS FRIEND'S *SOUL.*
REALLY?
SOUNDS LIKE IT COULD BE A *MANIFESTED RUSALKA.* OR MAYBE A *YUKI-ONNA!*
DEFINITELY SOME CLASS OF *VIVISIMULATING SUCCUBUS...*
YEAH. HERE'S THE ADDRESS. IT'S A CHURCH...
A CHURCH?

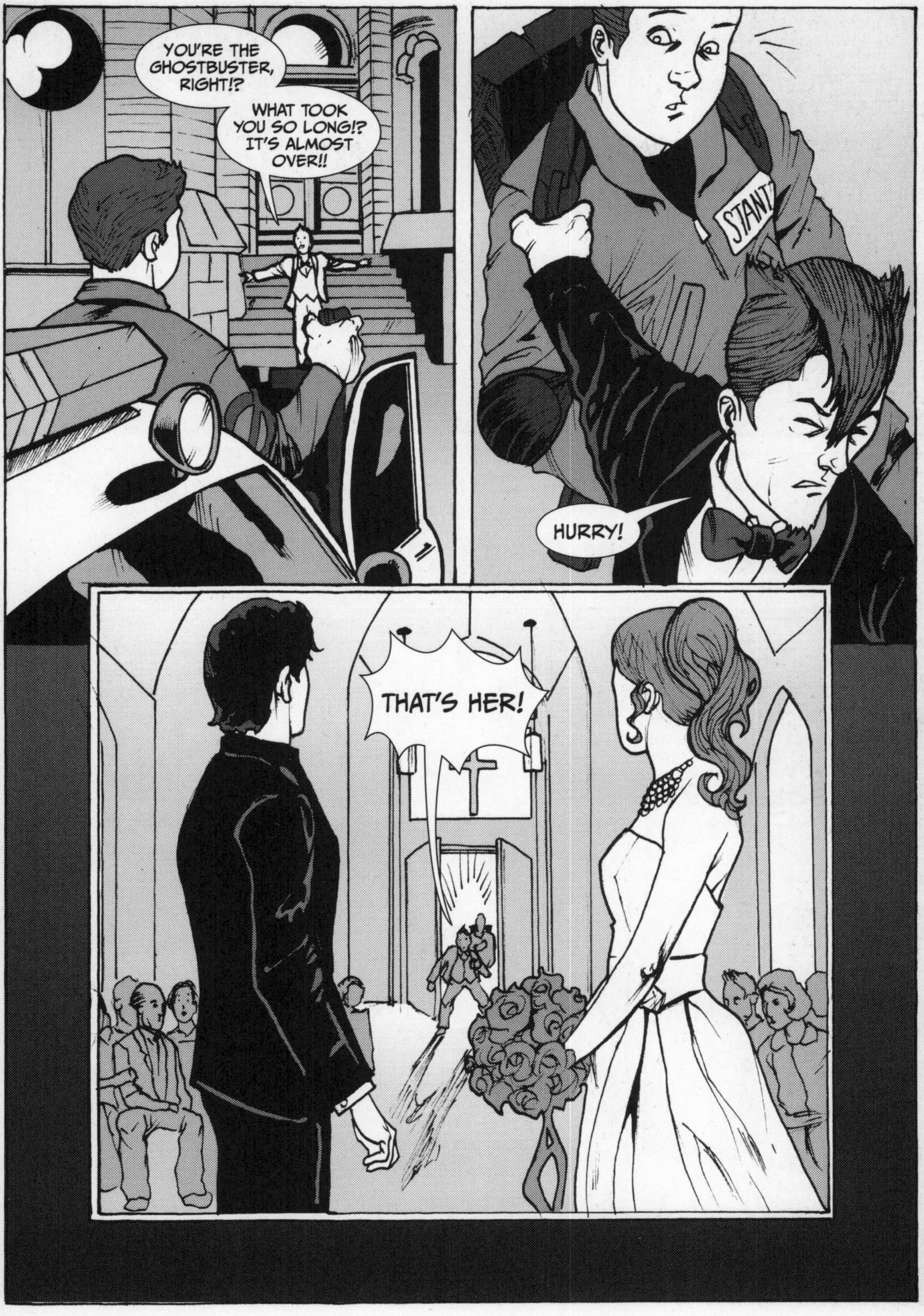
YOU'RE THE GHOSTBUSTER, RIGHT!?
WHAT TOOK YOU SO LONG!? IT'S ALMOST OVER!!
STANTZ
HURRY!
THAT'S HER!

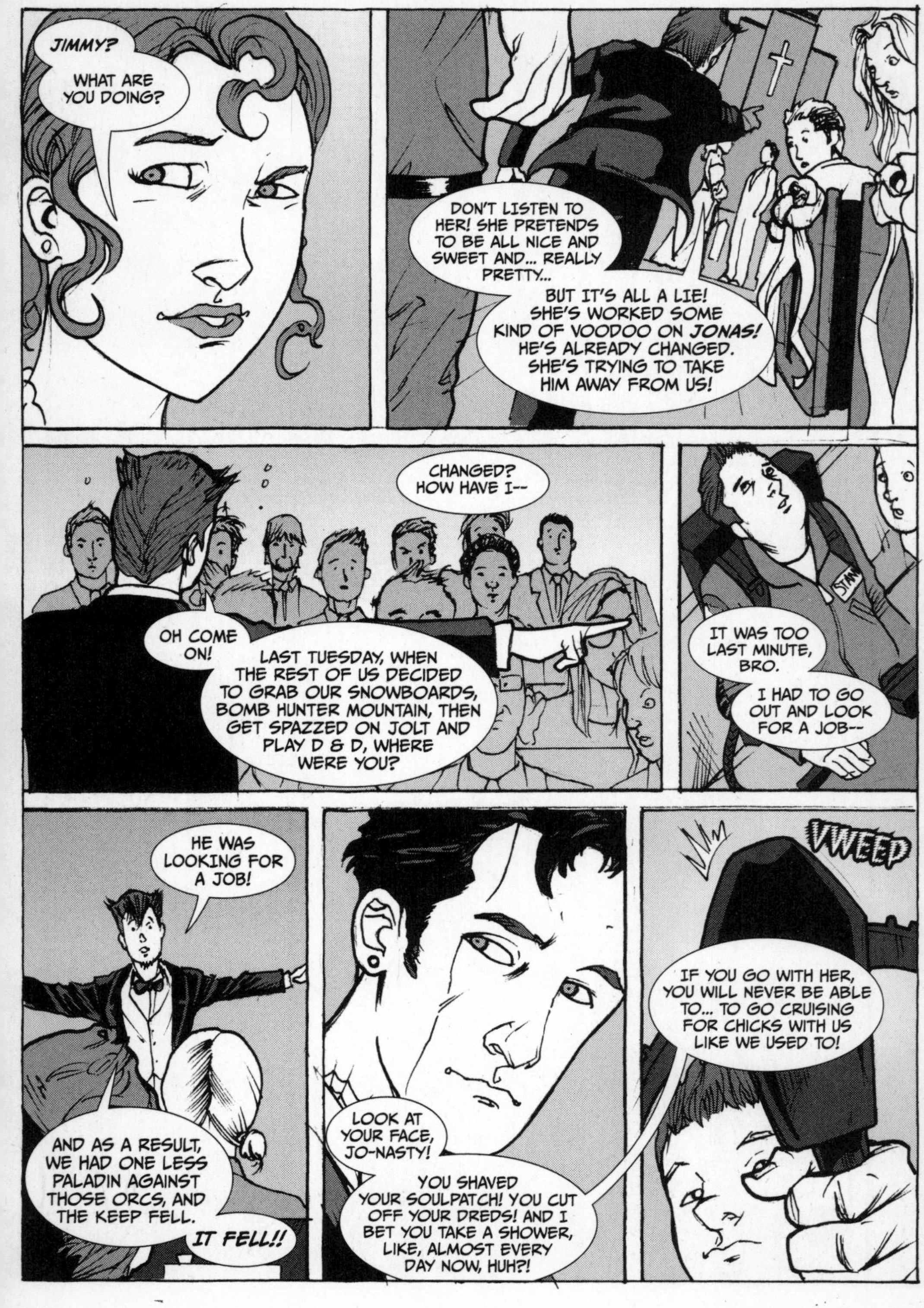
JIMMY?
WHAT ARE YOU DOING?
DON'T LISTEN TO HER! SHE PRETENDS TO BE ALL NICE AND SWEET AND... REALLY PRETTY...
BUT IT'S ALL A LIE! SHE'S WORKED SOME KIND OF VOODOO ON JONAS! HE'S ALREADY CHANGED. SHE'S TRYING TO TAKE HIM AWAY FROM US!
CHANGED? HOW HAVE I--
OH COME ON!
LAST TUESDAY, WHEN THE REST OF US DECIDED TO GRAB OUR SNOWBOARDS, BOMB HUNTER MOUNTAIN, THEN GET SPAZZED ON JOLT AND PLAY D & D, WHERE WERE YOU?
IT WAS TOO LAST MINUTE, BRO.
I HAD TO GO OUT AND LOOK FOR A JOB--
HE WAS LOOKING FOR A JOB!
AND AS A RESULT, WE HAD ONE LESS PALADIN AGAINST THOSE ORCS, AND THE KEEP FELL.
IT FELL!!
LOOK AT YOUR FACE, JO-NASTY!
YOU SHAVED YOUR SOULPATCH! YOU CUT OFF YOUR DREDS! AND I BET YOU TAKE A SHOWER, LIKE, ALMOST EVERY DAY NOW, HUH?!
VWEEP
IF YOU GO WITH HER, YOU WILL NEVER BE ABLE TO... TO GO CRUISING FOR CHICKS WITH US LIKE WE USED TO!

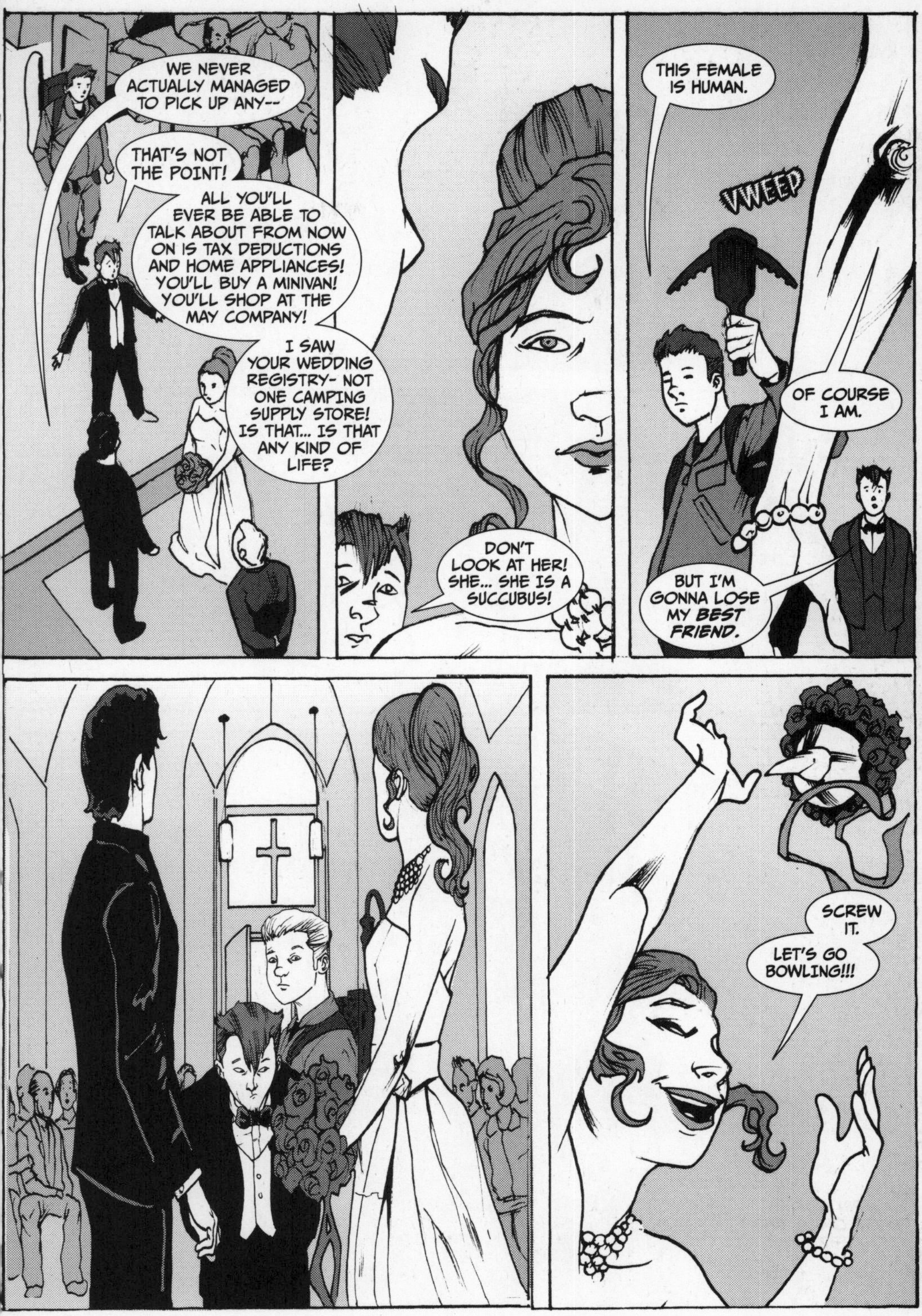
WE NEVER ACTUALLY MANAGED TO PICK UP ANY--
THAT'S NOT THE POINT!
ALL YOU'LL EVER BE ABLE TO TALK ABOUT FROM NOW ON IS TAX DEDUCTIONS AND HOME APPLIANCES! YOU'LL BUY A MINIVAN! YOU'LL SHOP AT THE MAY COMPANY!
I SAW YOUR WEDDING REGISTRY- NOT ONE CAMPING SUPPLY STORE! IS THAT... IS THAT ANY KIND OF LIFE?
DON'T LOOK AT HER! SHE... SHE IS A SUCCUBUS!
THIS FEMALE IS HUMAN.
VWEEP
OF COURSE I AM.
BUT I'M GONNA LOSE MY *BEST FRIEND.*
SCREW IT.
LET'S GO BOWLING!!!

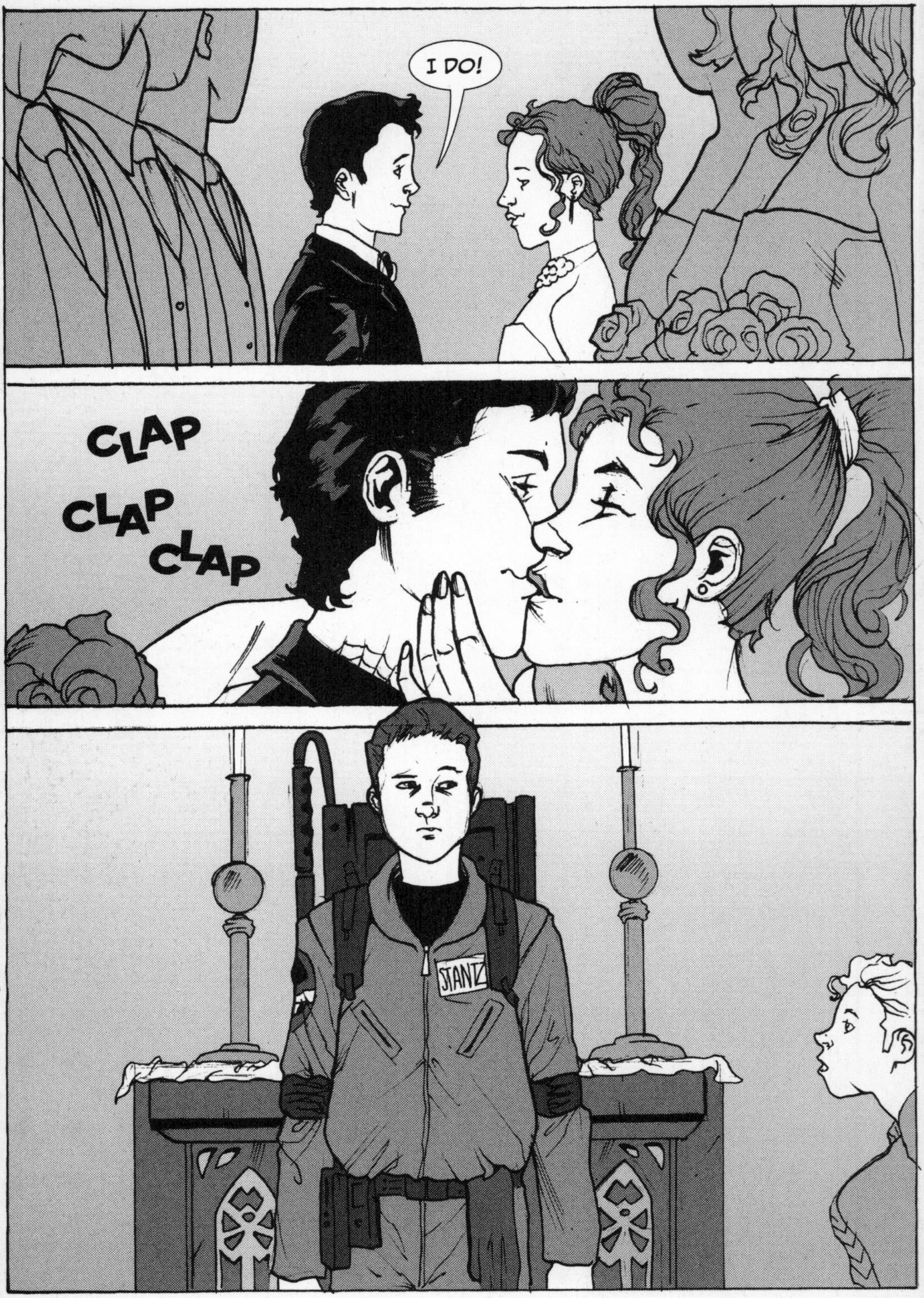
I DO!
CLAP
CLAP
CLAP
STANTZ

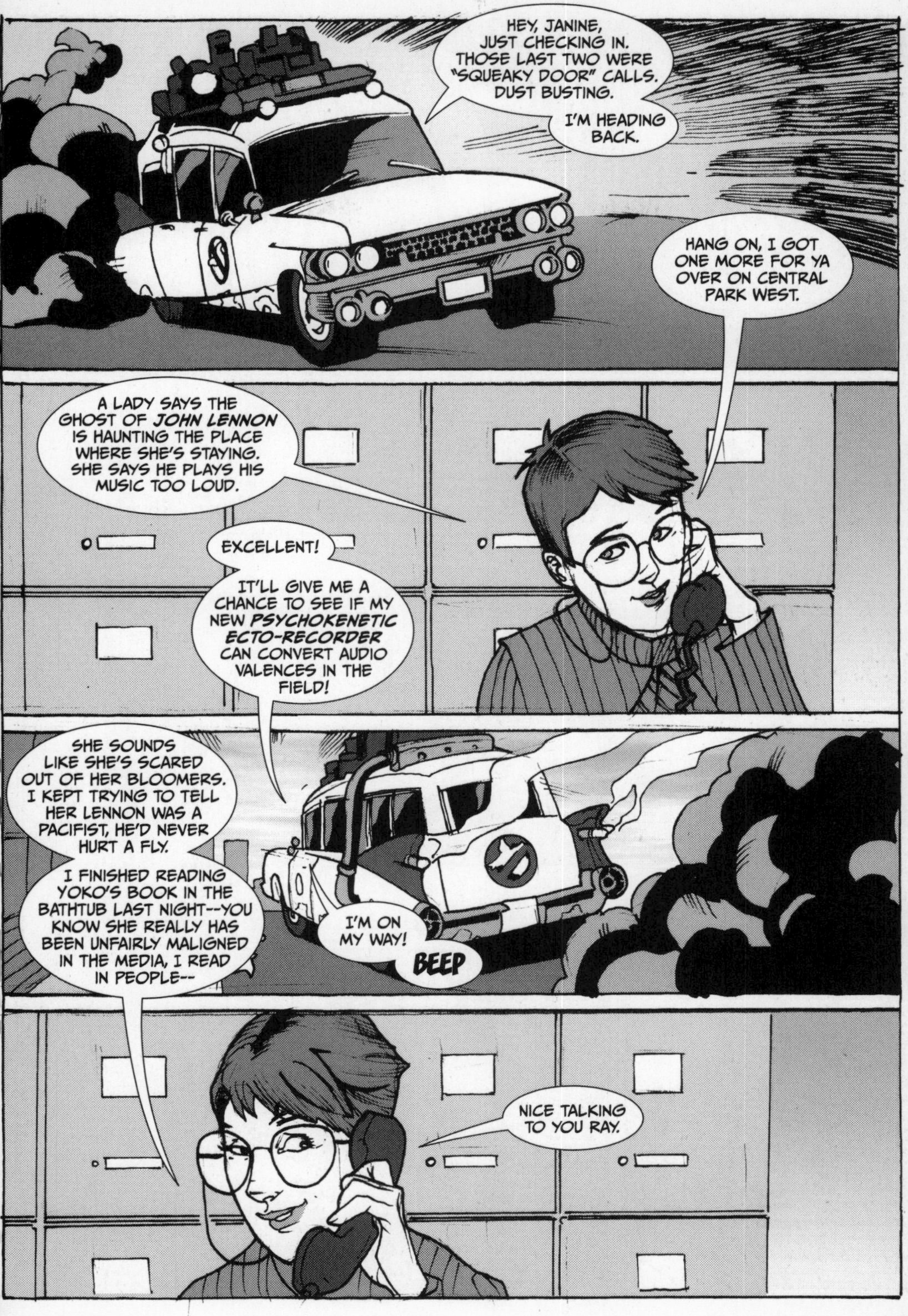
HEY, JANINE, JUST CHECKING IN. THOSE LAST TWO WERE "SQUEAKY DOOR" CALLS. DUST BUSTING.
I'M HEADING BACK.
HANG ON, I GOT ONE MORE FOR YA OVER ON CENTRAL PARK WEST.
A LADY SAYS THE GHOST OF *JOHN LENNON* IS HAUNTING THE PLACE WHERE SHE'S STAYING. SHE SAYS HE PLAYS HIS MUSIC TOO LOUD.
EXCELLENT!
IT'LL GIVE ME A CHANCE TO SEE IF MY NEW *PSYCHOKENETIC ECTO-RECORDER* CAN CONVERT AUDIO VALENCES IN THE FIELD!
SHE SOUNDS LIKE SHE'S SCARED OUT OF HER BLOOMERS. I KEPT TRYING TO TELL HER LENNON WAS A PACIFIST, HE'D NEVER HURT A FLY.
I FINISHED READING YOKO'S BOOK IN THE BATHTUB LAST NIGHT--YOU KNOW SHE REALLY HAS BEEN UNFAIRLY MALIGNED IN THE MEDIA, I READ IN PEOPLE--
I'M ON MY WAY!
BEEP
NICE TALKING TO YOU RAY.

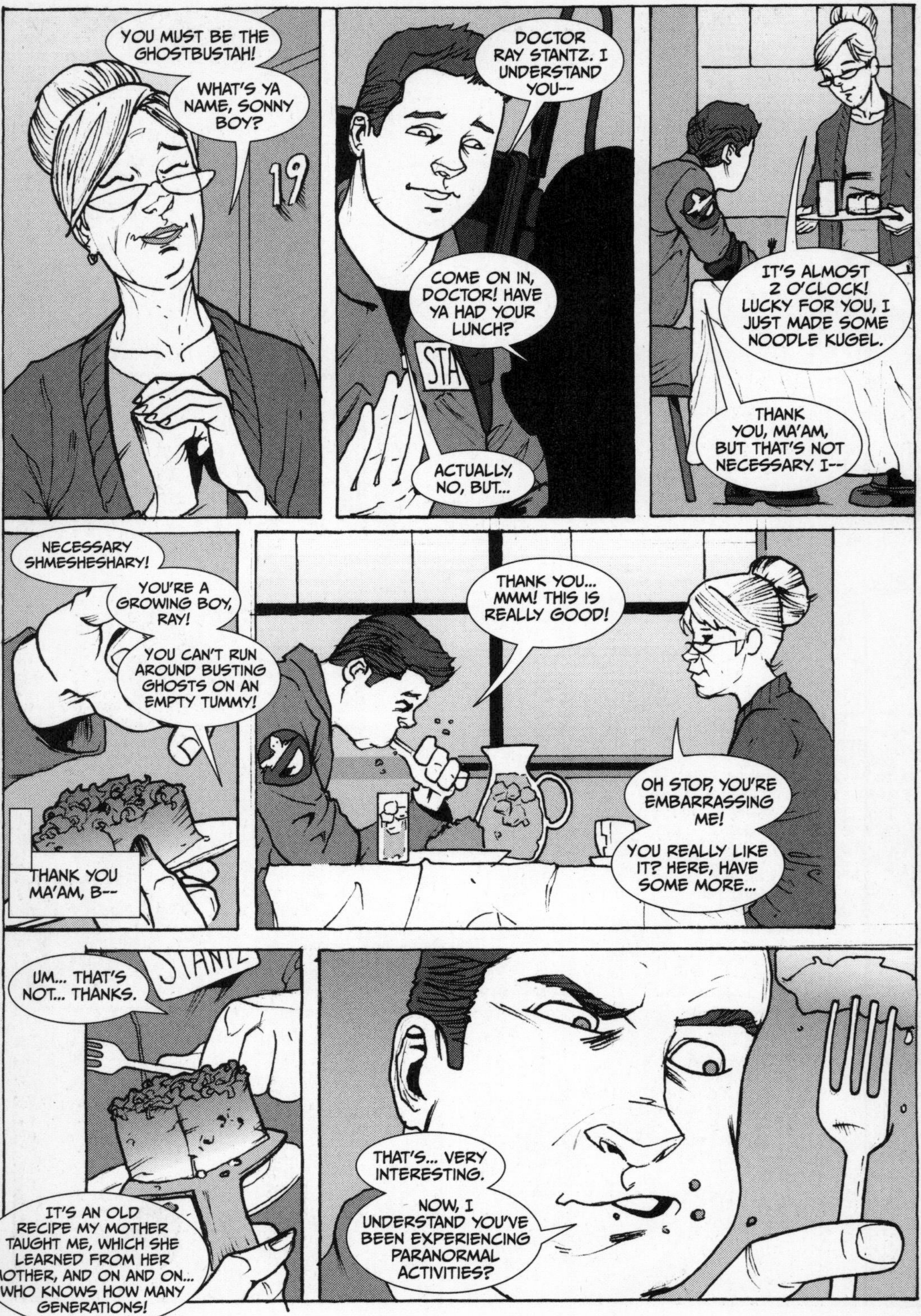
YOU MUST BE THE GHOSTBUSTAH!
WHAT'S YA NAME, SONNY BOY?
DOCTOR RAY STANTZ. I UNDERSTAND YOU--
COME ON IN, DOCTOR! HAVE YA HAD YOUR LUNCH?
ACTUALLY, NO, BUT...
IT'S ALMOST 2 O'CLOCK! LUCKY FOR YOU, I JUST MADE SOME NOODLE KUGEL.
THANK YOU, MA'AM, BUT THAT'S NOT NECESSARY. I--
NECESSARY SHMESHESHARY!
YOU'RE A GROWING BOY, RAY!
YOU CAN'T RUN AROUND BUSTING GHOSTS ON AN EMPTY TUMMY!
THANK YOU MA'AM, B--
THANK YOU... MMM! THIS IS REALLY GOOD!
OH STOP, YOU'RE EMBARRASSING ME!
YOU REALLY LIKE IT? HERE, HAVE SOME MORE...
UM... THAT'S NOT... THANKS.
IT'S AN OLD RECIPE MY MOTHER TAUGHT ME, WHICH SHE LEARNED FROM HER MOTHER, AND ON AND ON... WHO KNOWS HOW MANY GENERATIONS!
THAT'S... VERY INTERESTING.
NOW, I UNDERSTAND YOU'VE BEEN EXPERIENCING PARANORMAL ACTIVITIES?

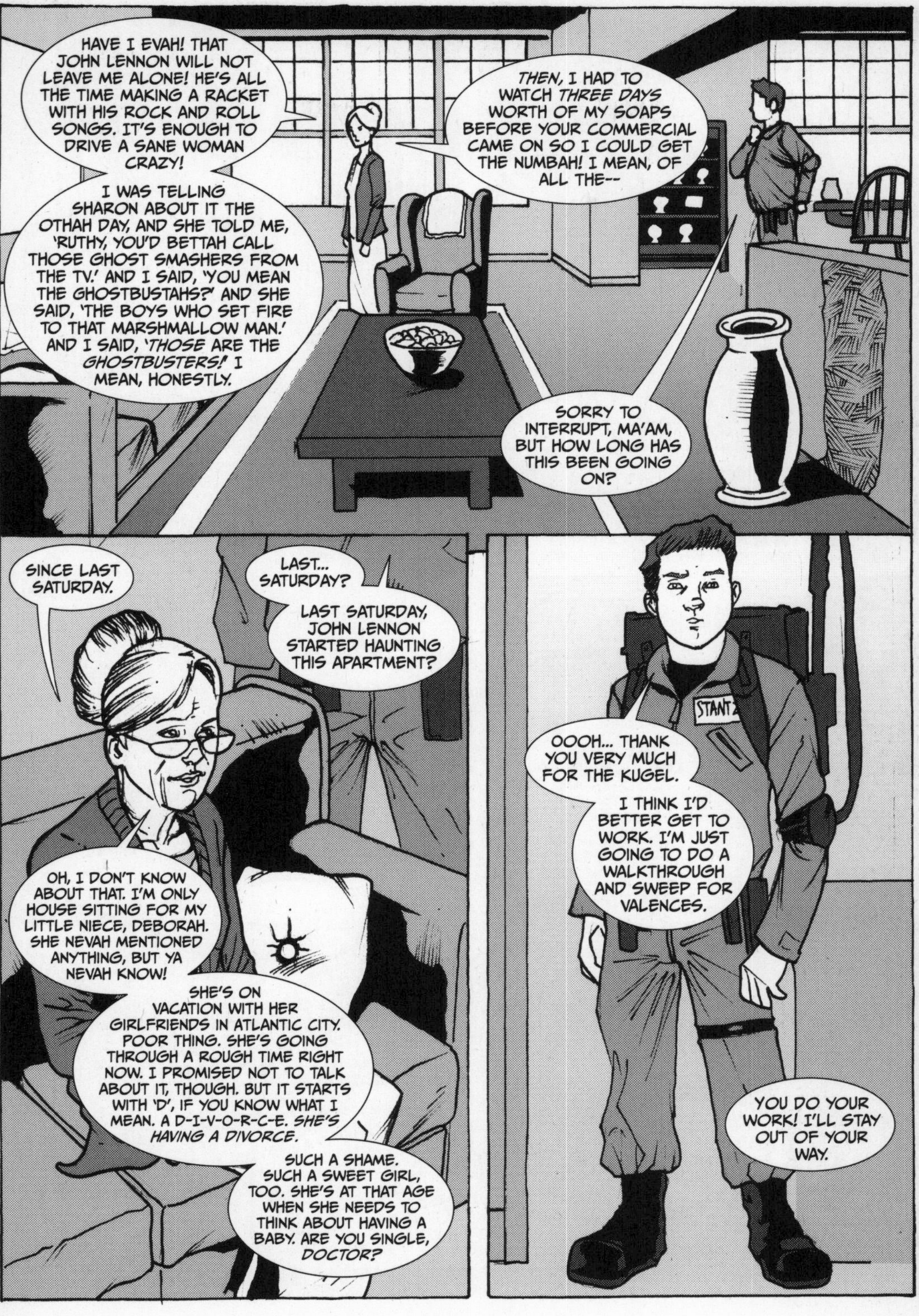
HAVE I EVAH! THAT JOHN LENNON WILL NOT LEAVE ME ALONE! HE'S ALL THE TIME MAKING A RACKET WITH HIS ROCK AND ROLL SONGS. IT'S ENOUGH TO DRIVE A SANE WOMAN CRAZY!
I WAS TELLING SHARON ABOUT IT THE OTHAH DAY, AND SHE TOLD ME, 'RUTHY, YOU'D BETTAH CALL THOSE GHOST SMASHERS FROM THE TV.' AND I SAID, 'YOU MEAN THE GHOSTBUSTAHS?' AND SHE SAID, 'THE BOYS WHO SET FIRE TO THAT MARSHMALLOW MAN.' AND I SAID, '*THOSE* ARE THE *GHOSTBUSTERS!*' I MEAN, HONESTLY.
*THEN*, I HAD TO WATCH *THREE DAYS* WORTH OF MY SOAPS BEFORE YOUR COMMERCIAL CAME ON SO I COULD GET THE NUMBAH! I MEAN, OF ALL THE--
SORRY TO INTERRUPT, MA'AM, BUT HOW LONG HAS THIS BEEN GOING ON?
SINCE LAST SATURDAY.
LAST... SATURDAY?
LAST SATURDAY, JOHN LENNON STARTED HAUNTING THIS APARTMENT?
OH, I DON'T KNOW ABOUT THAT. I'M ONLY HOUSE SITTING FOR MY LITTLE NIECE, DEBORAH. SHE NEVAH MENTIONED ANYTHING, BUT YA NEVAH KNOW!
SHE'S ON VACATION WITH HER GIRLFRIENDS IN ATLANTIC CITY. POOR THING. SHE'S GOING THROUGH A ROUGH TIME RIGHT NOW. I PROMISED NOT TO TALK ABOUT IT, THOUGH. BUT IT STARTS WITH 'D', IF YOU KNOW WHAT I MEAN. A D-I-V-O-R-C-E. *SHE'S HAVING A DIVORCE.*
SUCH A SHAME. SUCH A SWEET GIRL, TOO. SHE'S AT THAT AGE WHEN SHE NEEDS TO THINK ABOUT HAVING A BABY. ARE YOU SINGLE, *DOCTOR?*
STANTZ
OOOH... THANK YOU VERY MUCH FOR THE KUGEL.
I THINK I'D BETTER GET TO WORK. I'M JUST GOING TO DO A WALKTHROUGH AND SWEEP FOR VALENCES.
YOU DO YOUR WORK! I'LL STAY OUT OF YOUR WAY.

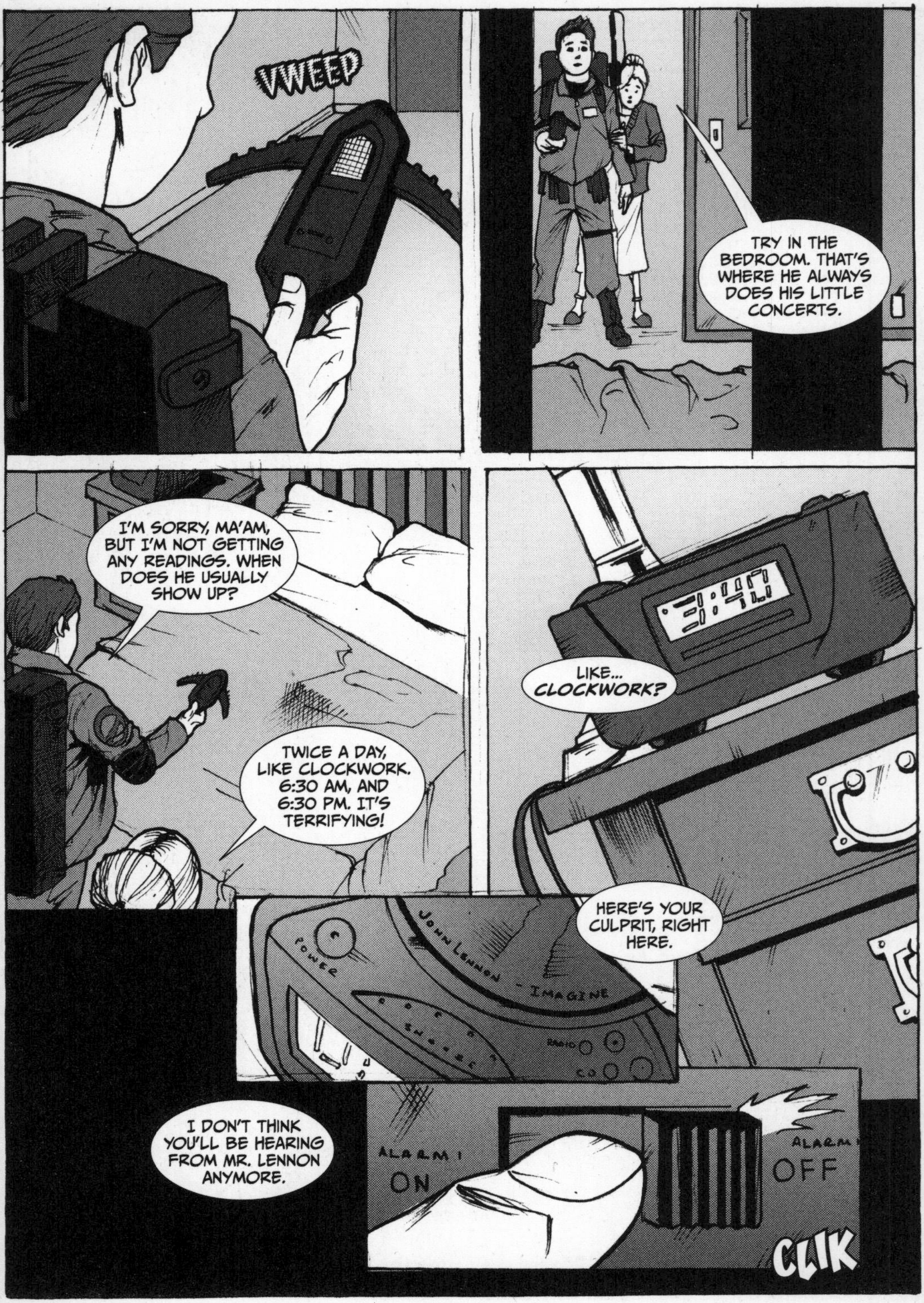
VWEEP
TRY IN THE BEDROOM. THAT'S WHERE HE ALWAYS DOES HIS LITTLE CONCERTS.
I'M SORRY, MA'AM, BUT I'M NOT GETTING ANY READINGS. WHEN DOES HE USUALLY SHOW UP?
TWICE A DAY, LIKE CLOCKWORK. 6:30 AM, AND 6:30 PM. IT'S TERRIFYING!
LIKE... CLOCKWORK?
HERE'S YOUR CULPRIT, RIGHT HERE.
JOHN LENNON - IMAGINE
POWER
RADIO
CD
I DON'T THINK YOU'LL BE HEARING FROM MR. LENNON ANYMORE.
ALARM 1
ON
ALARM 1
OFF
CLIK

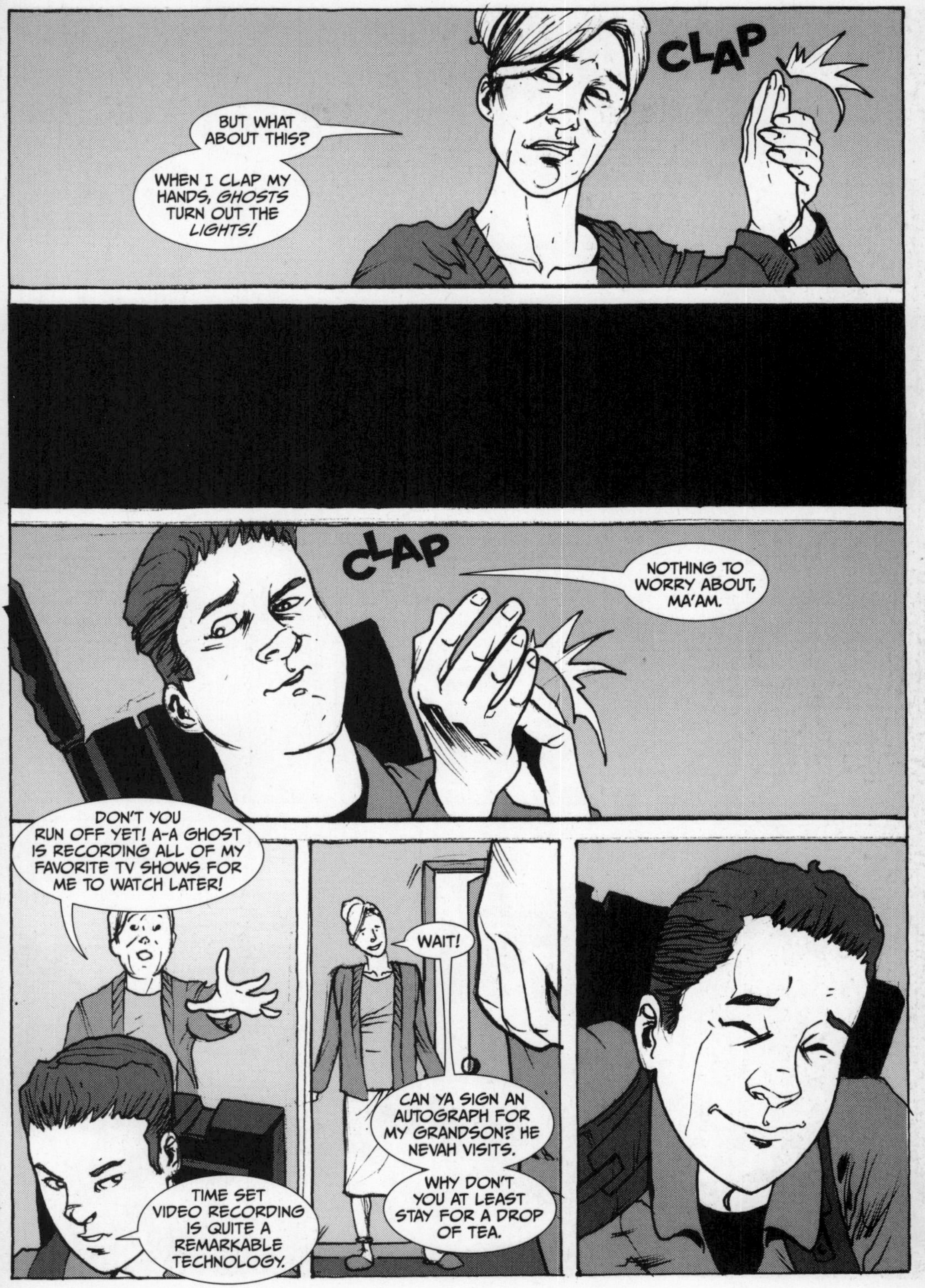
CLAP
BUT WHAT ABOUT THIS?
WHEN I CLAP MY HANDS, *GHOSTS* TURN OUT THE *LIGHTS!*
CLAP
NOTHING TO WORRY ABOUT, MA'AM.
DON'T YOU RUN OFF YET! A-A GHOST IS RECORDING ALL OF MY FAVORITE TV SHOWS FOR ME TO WATCH LATER!
TIME SET VIDEO RECORDING IS QUITE A REMARKABLE TECHNOLOGY.
WAIT!
CAN YA SIGN AN AUTOGRAPH FOR MY GRANDSON? HE NEVAH VISITS.
WHY DON'T YOU AT LEAST STAY FOR A DROP OF TEA.

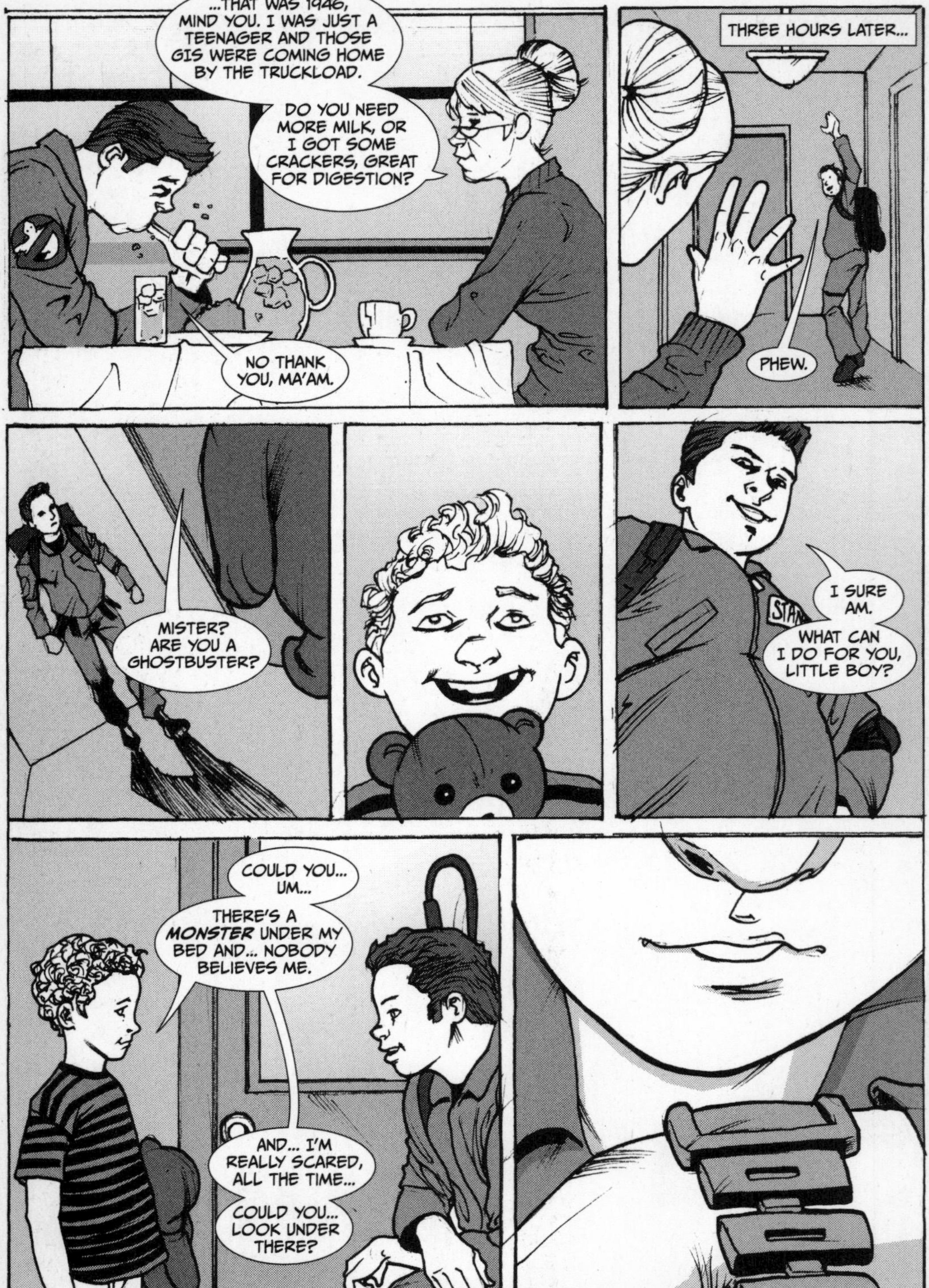
...THAT WAS 1946, MIND YOU. I WAS JUST A TEENAGER AND THOSE GIS WERE COMING HOME BY THE TRUCKLOAD.
DO YOU NEED MORE MILK, OR I GOT SOME CRACKERS, GREAT FOR DIGESTION?
NO THANK YOU, MA'AM.
THREE HOURS LATER...
PHEW.
MISTER? ARE YOU A GHOSTBUSTER?
STAN
I SURE AM.
WHAT CAN I DO FOR YOU, LITTLE BOY?
COULD YOU... UM...
THERE'S A *MONSTER* UNDER MY BED AND... NOBODY BELIEVES ME.
AND... I'M REALLY SCARED, ALL THE TIME...
COULD YOU... LOOK UNDER THERE?

IT'S IN HERE.

SO, YOU LIKE SCIENCE, KID?

YEAH, I WANT TO BE A SCIENTIST WHEN I GROW UP.

IT'S ONE OF THE FEW GREAT NOBLE PROFESSIONS LEFT.

WELL, IT LOOKS LIKE YOU'RE ALL CLEAR. THERE ARE NO MONST--

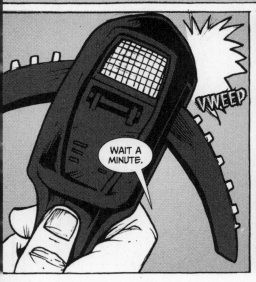

VWEEP

WAIT A MINUTE.

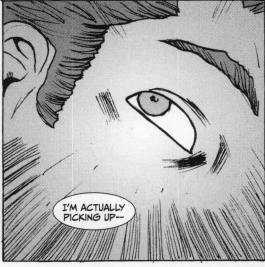

I'M ACTUALLY PICKING UP--

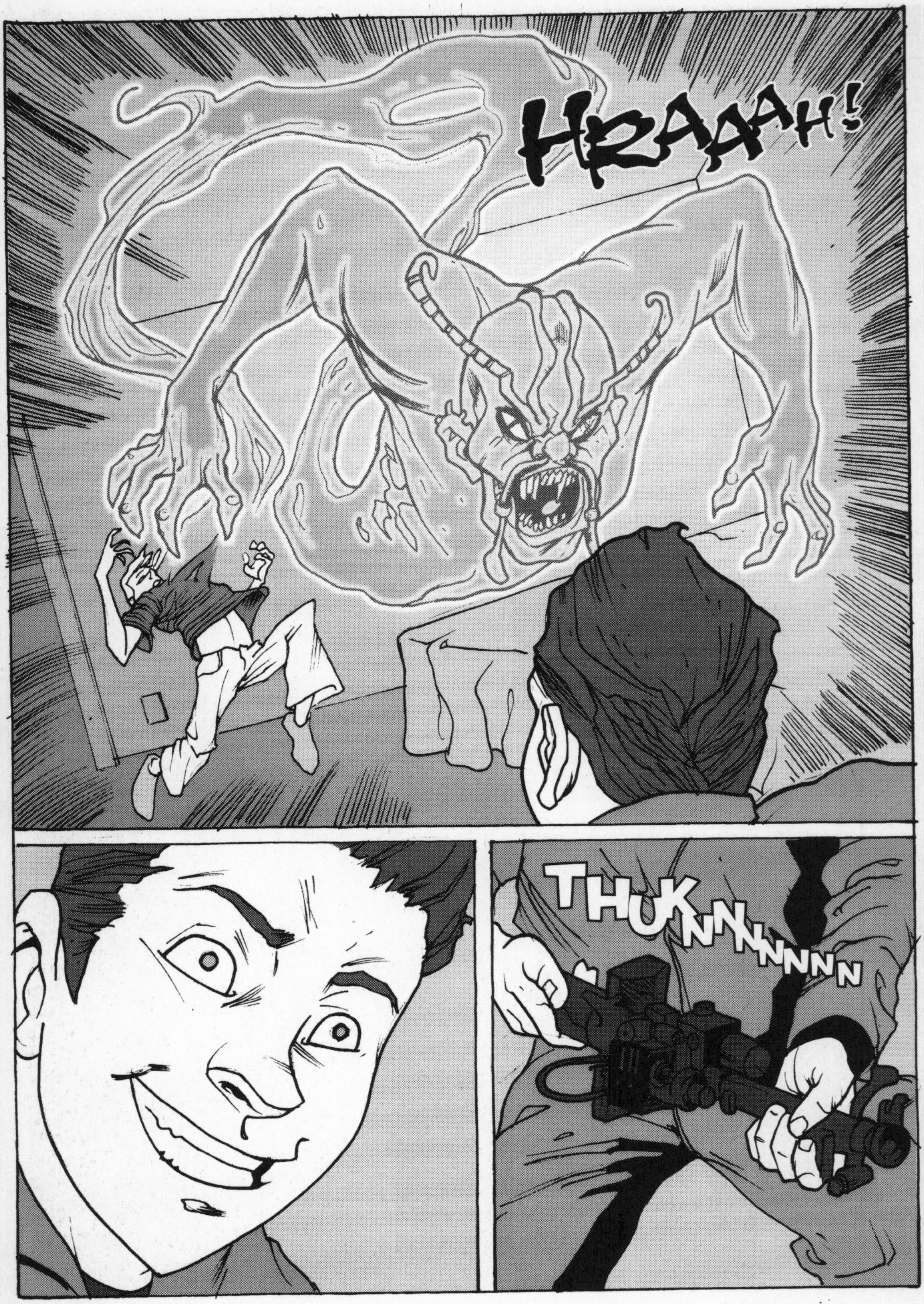
HRAAAH!
THUKNNNNNNNN

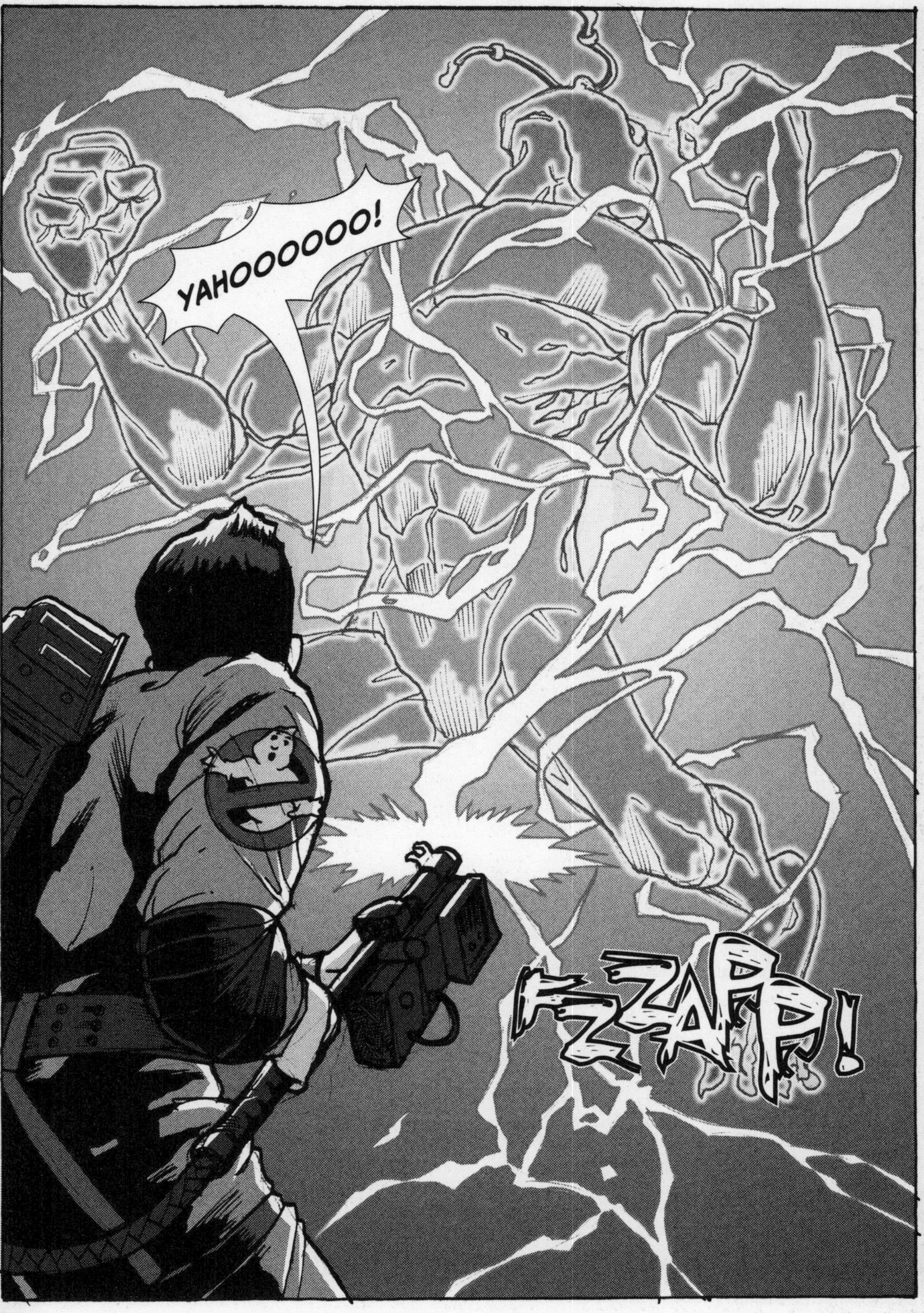
YAHOOOOOOO!
FZZAPP!

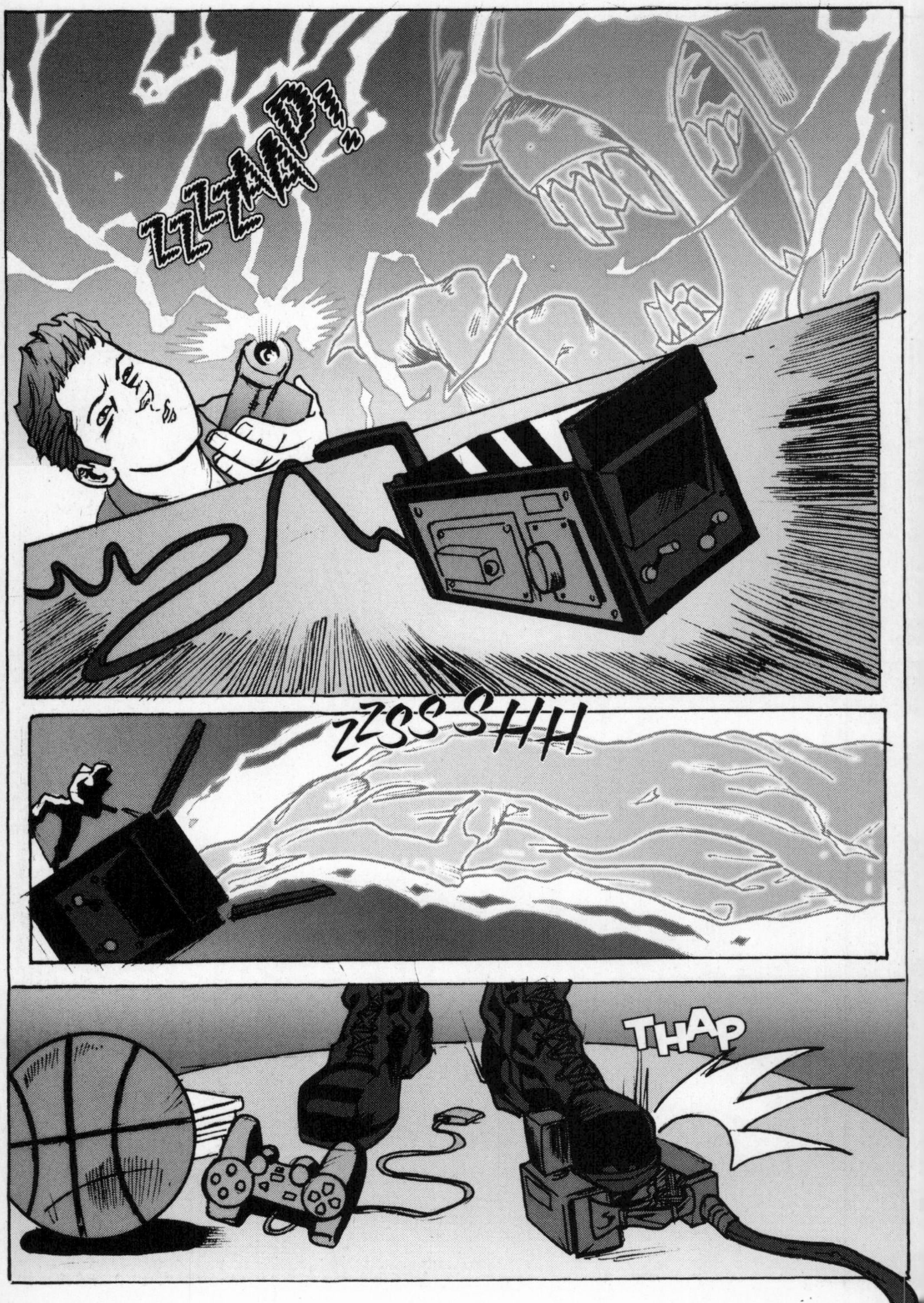
ZZZZAP!
ZZSSSHH
THAP

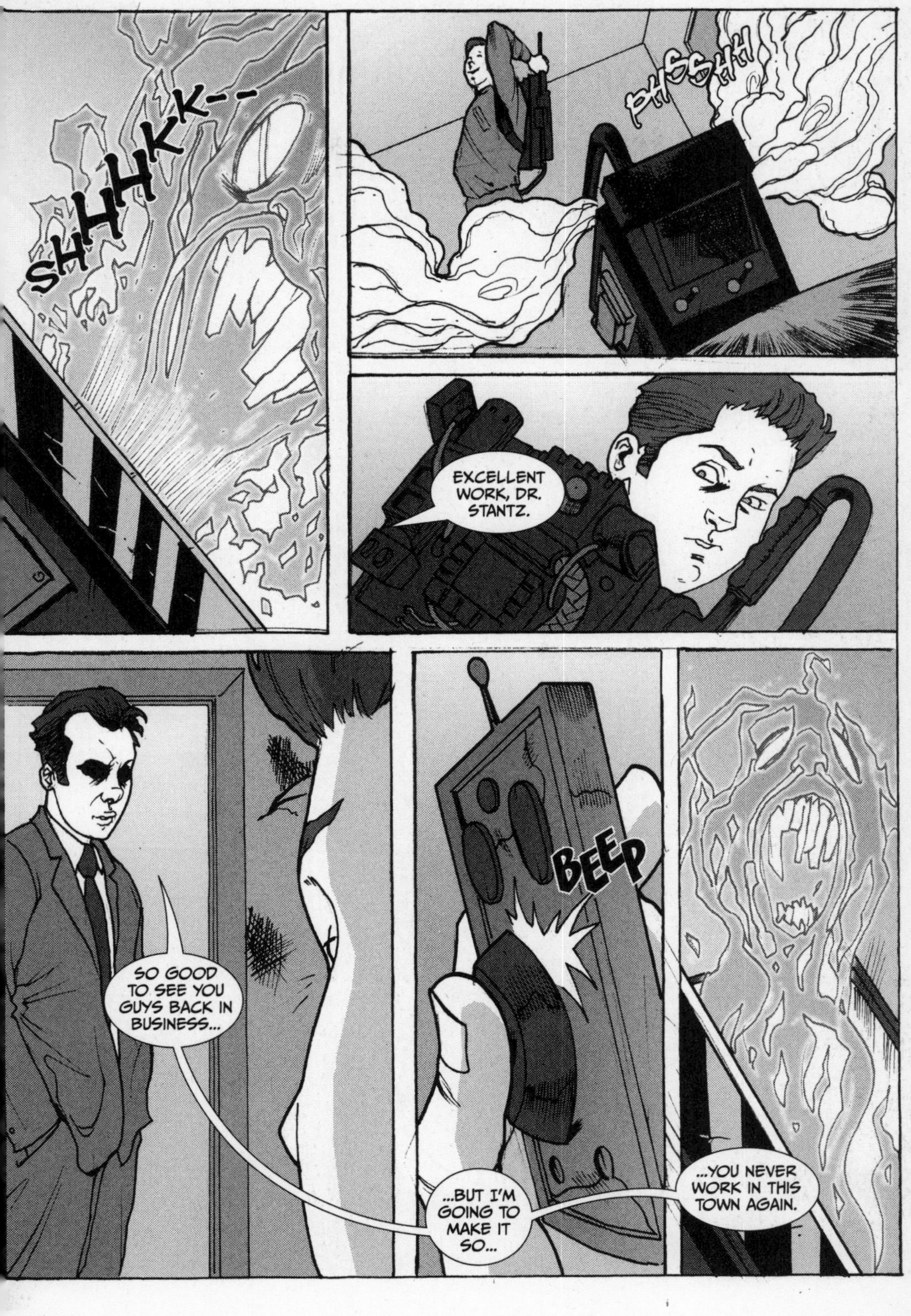
SHHHKK--
PHSSHH
EXCELLENT WORK, DR. STANTZ.
SO GOOD TO SEE YOU GUYS BACK IN BUSINESS...
...BUT I'M GOING TO MAKE IT SO...
...YOU NEVER WORK IN THIS TOWN AGAIN.
BEEP

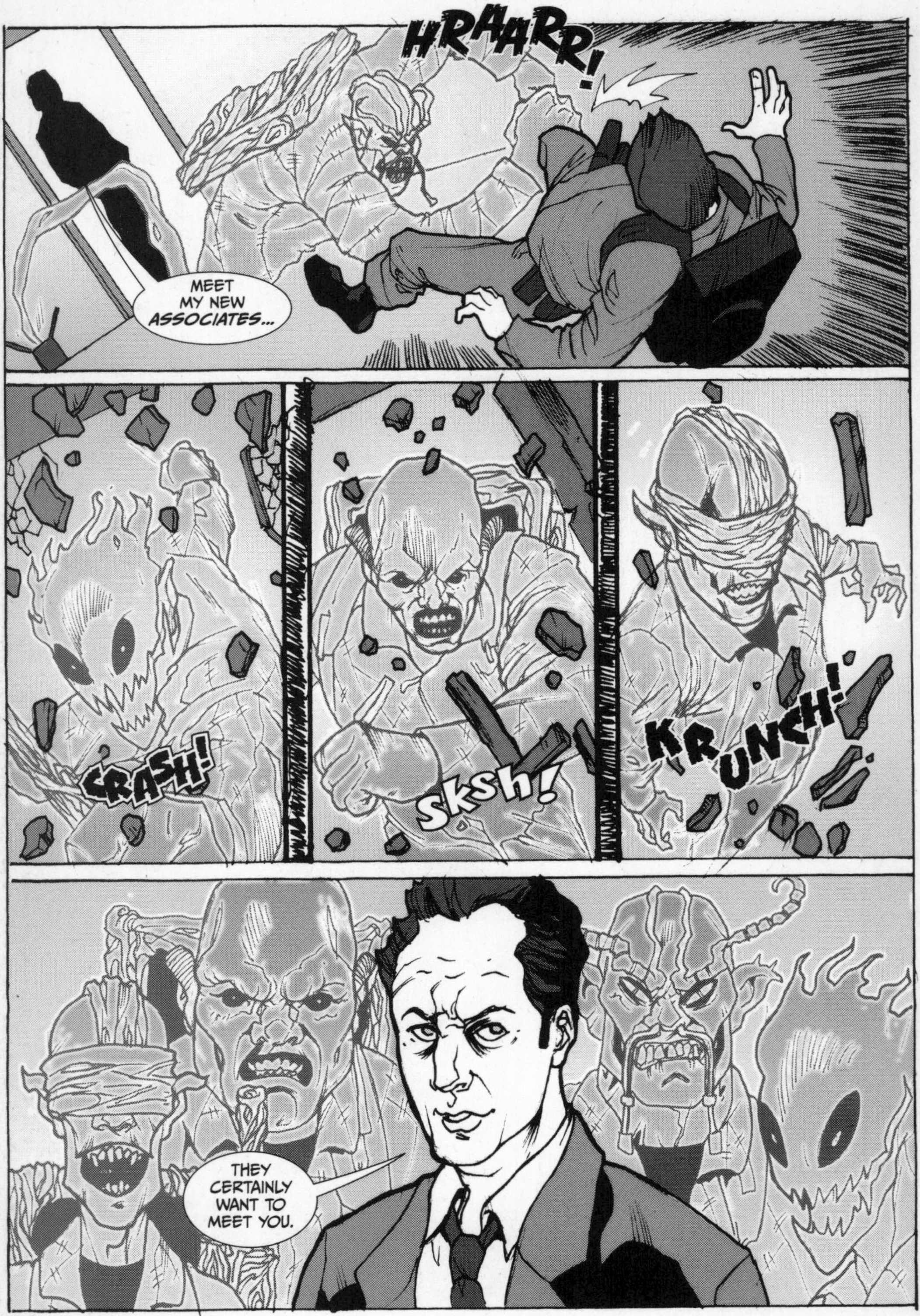
HRAARR!
MEET MY NEW ASSOCIATES...
CRASH!
SKSH!
KRUNCH!
THEY CERTAINLY WANT TO MEET YOU.

# GHOSTBUSTERS™

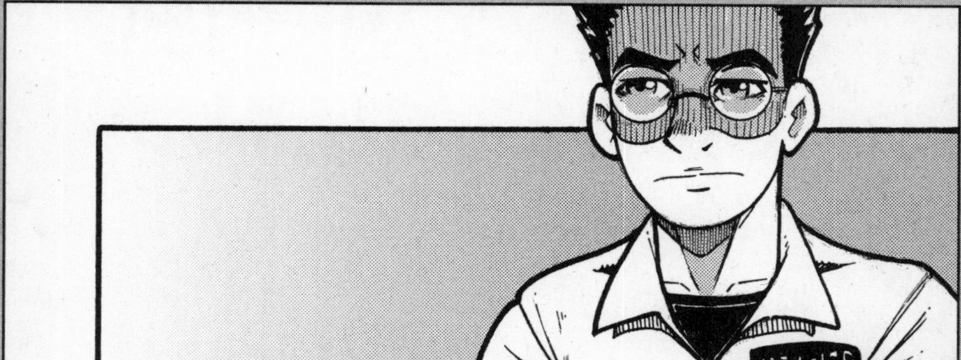

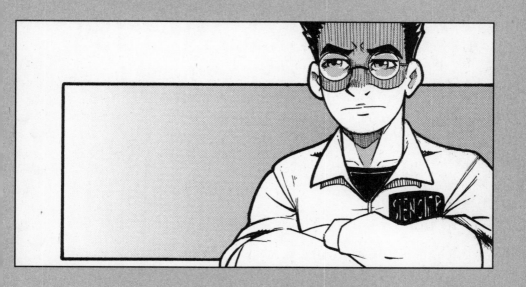

# CHAPTER IV

## JUST YOUR TYPICAL CLASS 1 CONFINED INFESTATION

STORY BY
NATHAN JOHNSON

ART BY
MICHAEL SHELFER

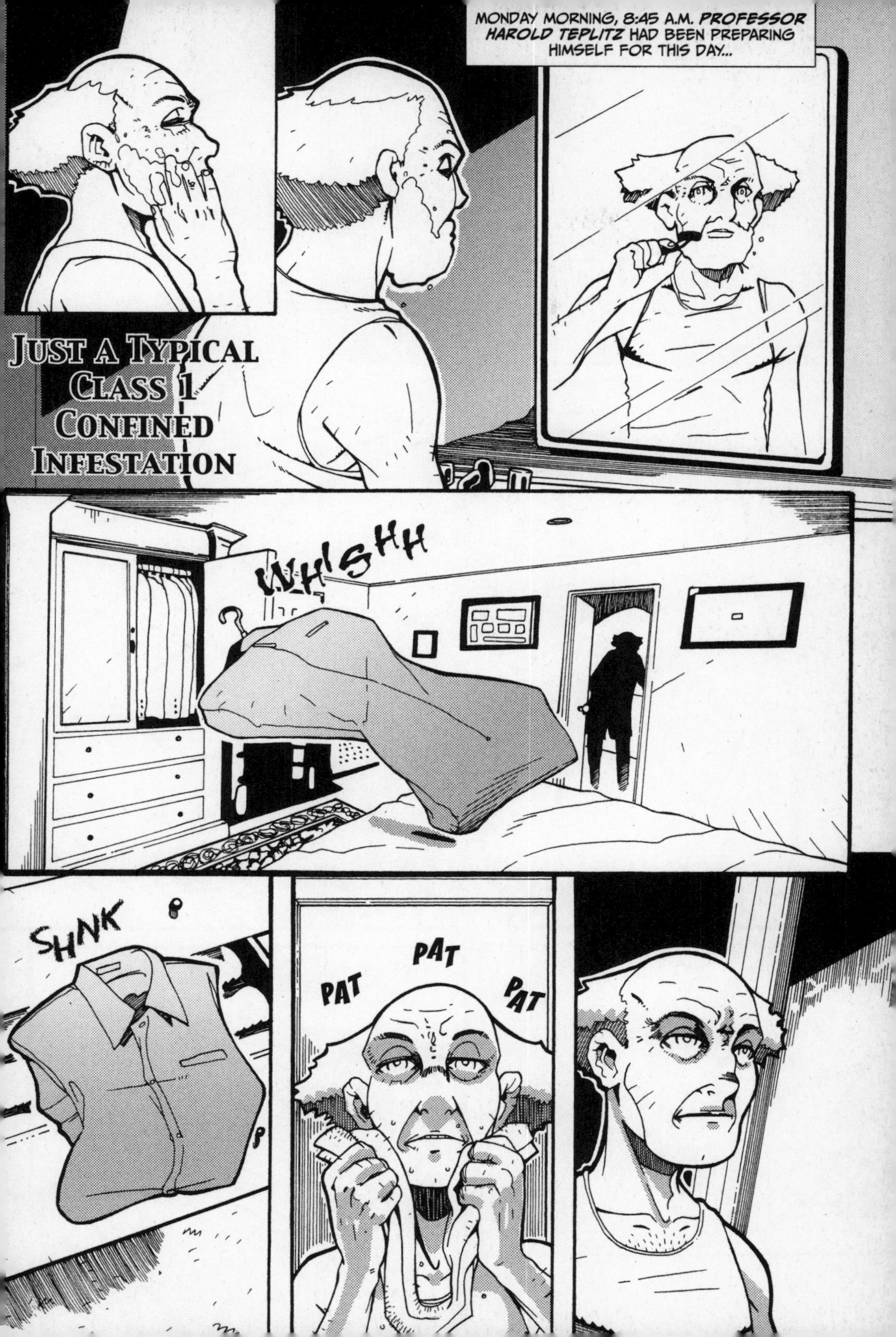

MONDAY MORNING, 8:45 A.M. *PROFESSOR HAROLD TEPLITZ* HAD BEEN PREPARING HIMSELF FOR THIS DAY...
JUST A TYPICAL CLASS 1 CONFINED INFESTATION
WHISHH
SHNK
PAT
PAT
PAT

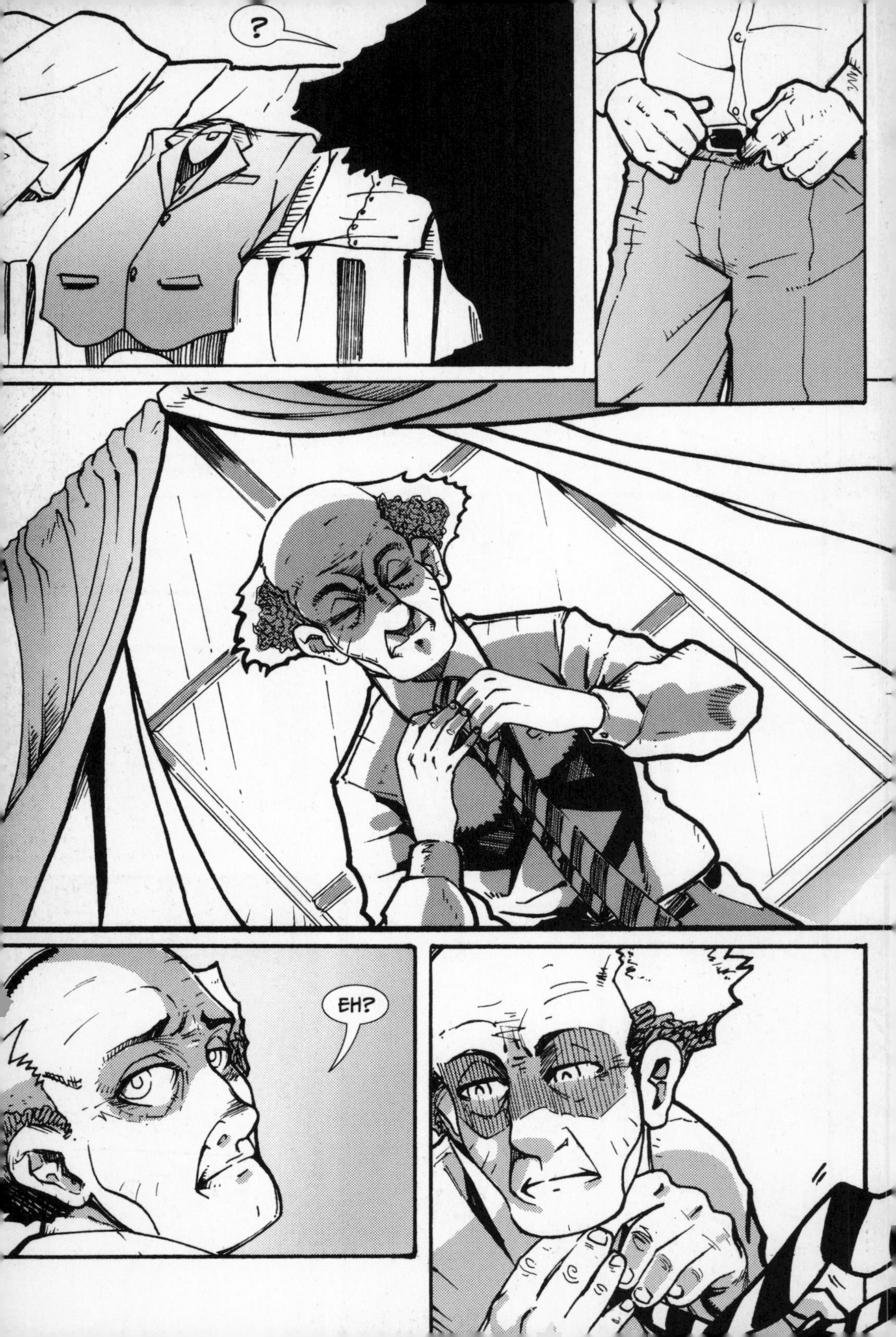
?
EH?

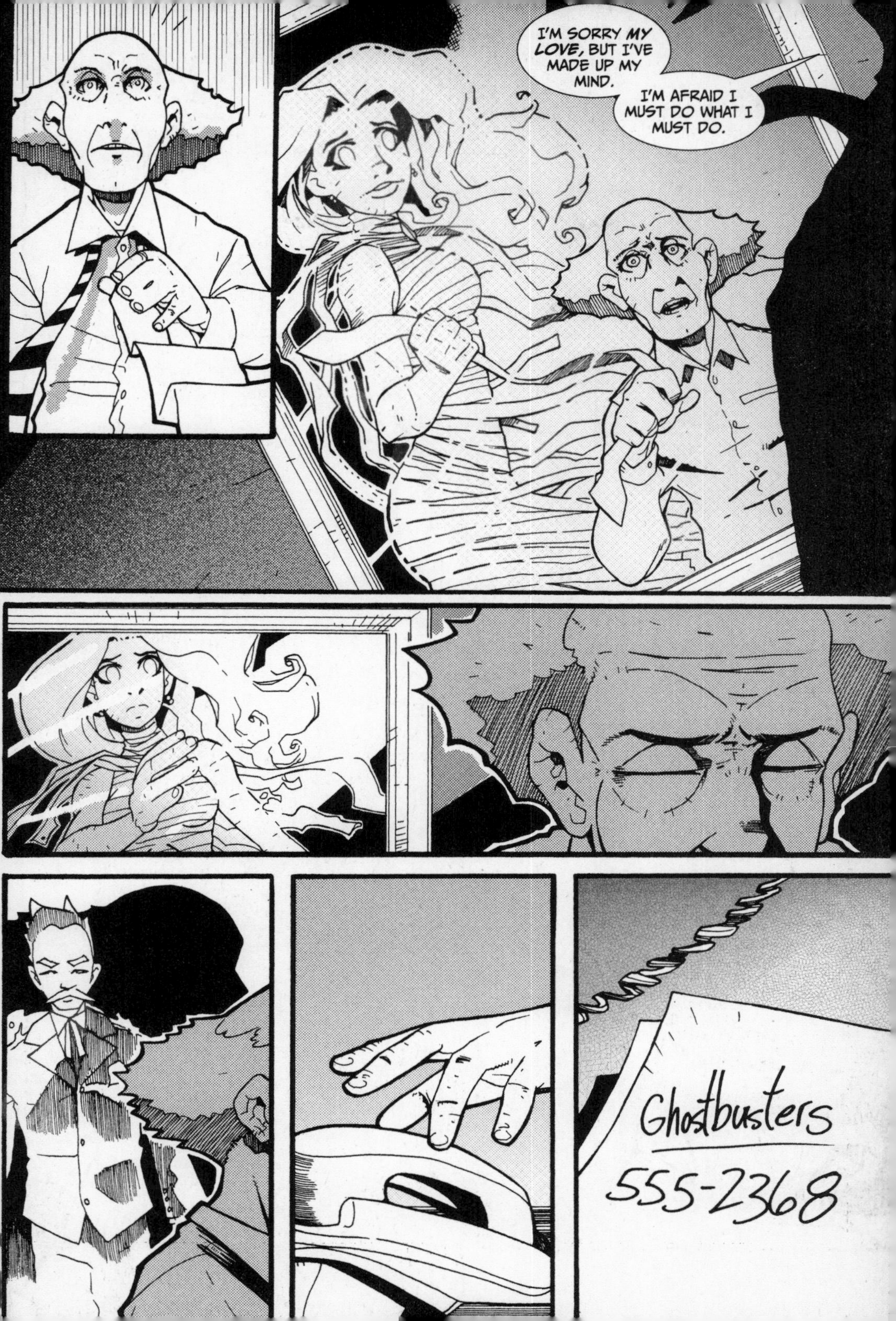
I'M SORRY MY LOVE, BUT I'VE MADE UP MY MIND.
I'M AFRAID I MUST DO WHAT I MUST DO.
Ghostbusters
555-2368

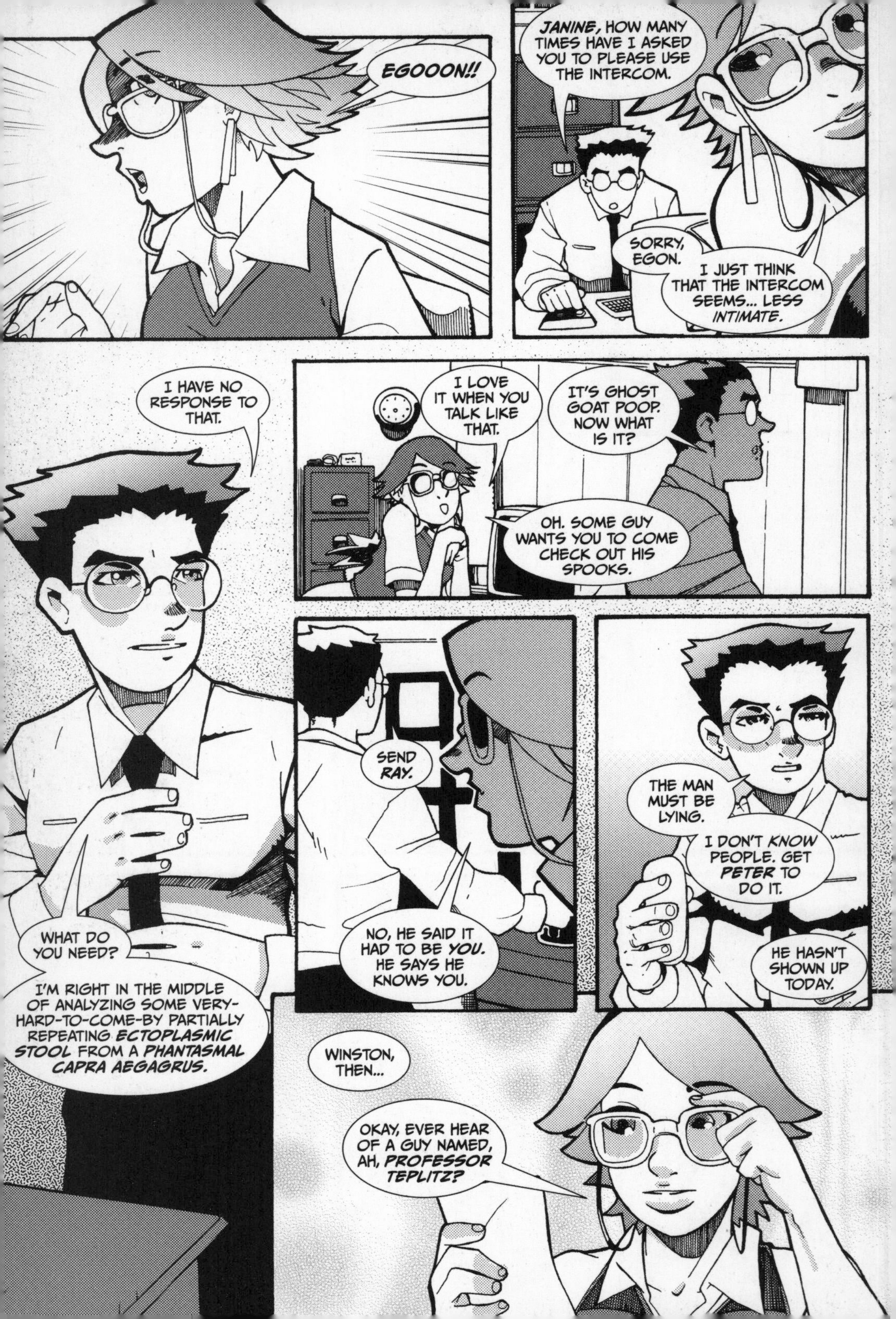
EGOOON!!
JANINE, HOW MANY TIMES HAVE I ASKED YOU TO PLEASE USE THE INTERCOM.
SORRY, EGON.
I JUST THINK THAT THE INTERCOM SEEMS... LESS INTIMATE.
I HAVE NO RESPONSE TO THAT.
WHAT DO YOU NEED?
I'M RIGHT IN THE MIDDLE OF ANALYZING SOME VERY-HARD-TO-COME-BY PARTIALLY REPEATING ECTOPLASMIC STOOL FROM A PHANTASMAL CAPRA AEGAGRUS.
I LOVE IT WHEN YOU TALK LIKE THAT.
IT'S GHOST GOAT POOP. NOW WHAT IS IT?
OH. SOME GUY WANTS YOU TO COME CHECK OUT HIS SPOOKS.
SEND RAY.
NO, HE SAID IT HAD TO BE YOU. HE SAYS HE KNOWS YOU.
THE MAN MUST BE LYING.
I DON'T KNOW PEOPLE. GET PETER TO DO IT.
HE HASN'T SHOWN UP TODAY.
WINSTON, THEN...
OKAY, EVER HEAR OF A GUY NAMED, AH, PROFESSOR TEPLITZ?

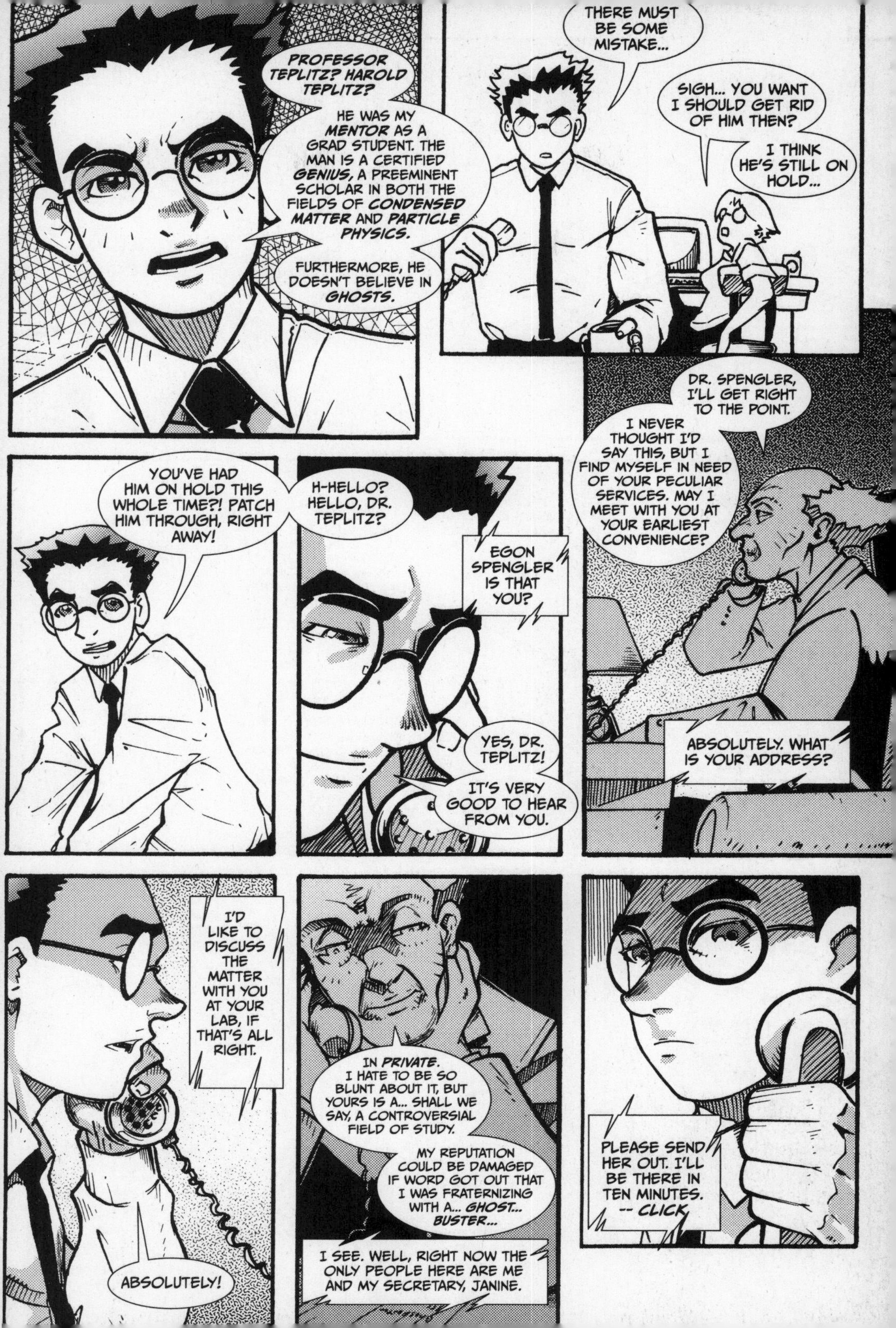
PROFESSOR TEPLITZ? HAROLD TEPLITZ?
HE WAS MY MENTOR AS A GRAD STUDENT. THE MAN IS A CERTIFIED GENIUS, A PREEMINENT SCHOLAR IN BOTH THE FIELDS OF CONDENSED MATTER AND PARTICLE PHYSICS.
FURTHERMORE, HE DOESN'T BELIEVE IN GHOSTS.
THERE MUST BE SOME MISTAKE...
SIGH... YOU WANT I SHOULD GET RID OF HIM THEN?
I THINK HE'S STILL ON HOLD...
YOU'VE HAD HIM ON HOLD THIS WHOLE TIME?! PATCH HIM THROUGH, RIGHT AWAY!
H-HELLO? HELLO, DR. TEPLITZ?
EGON SPENGLER IS THAT YOU?
YES, DR. TEPLITZ!
IT'S VERY GOOD TO HEAR FROM YOU.
DR. SPENGLER, I'LL GET RIGHT TO THE POINT.
I NEVER THOUGHT I'D SAY THIS, BUT I FIND MYSELF IN NEED OF YOUR PECULIAR SERVICES. MAY I MEET WITH YOU AT YOUR EARLIEST CONVENIENCE?
ABSOLUTELY. WHAT IS YOUR ADDRESS?
I'D LIKE TO DISCUSS THE MATTER WITH YOU AT YOUR LAB, IF THAT'S ALL RIGHT.
ABSOLUTELY!
IN PRIVATE. I HATE TO BE SO BLUNT ABOUT IT, BUT YOURS IS A... SHALL WE SAY, A CONTROVERSIAL FIELD OF STUDY.
MY REPUTATION COULD BE DAMAGED IF WORD GOT OUT THAT I WAS FRATERNIZING WITH A... GHOST... BUSTER...
I SEE. WELL, RIGHT NOW THE ONLY PEOPLE HERE ARE ME AND MY SECRETARY, JANINE.
PLEASE SEND HER OUT. I'LL BE THERE IN TEN MINUTES. -- CLICK

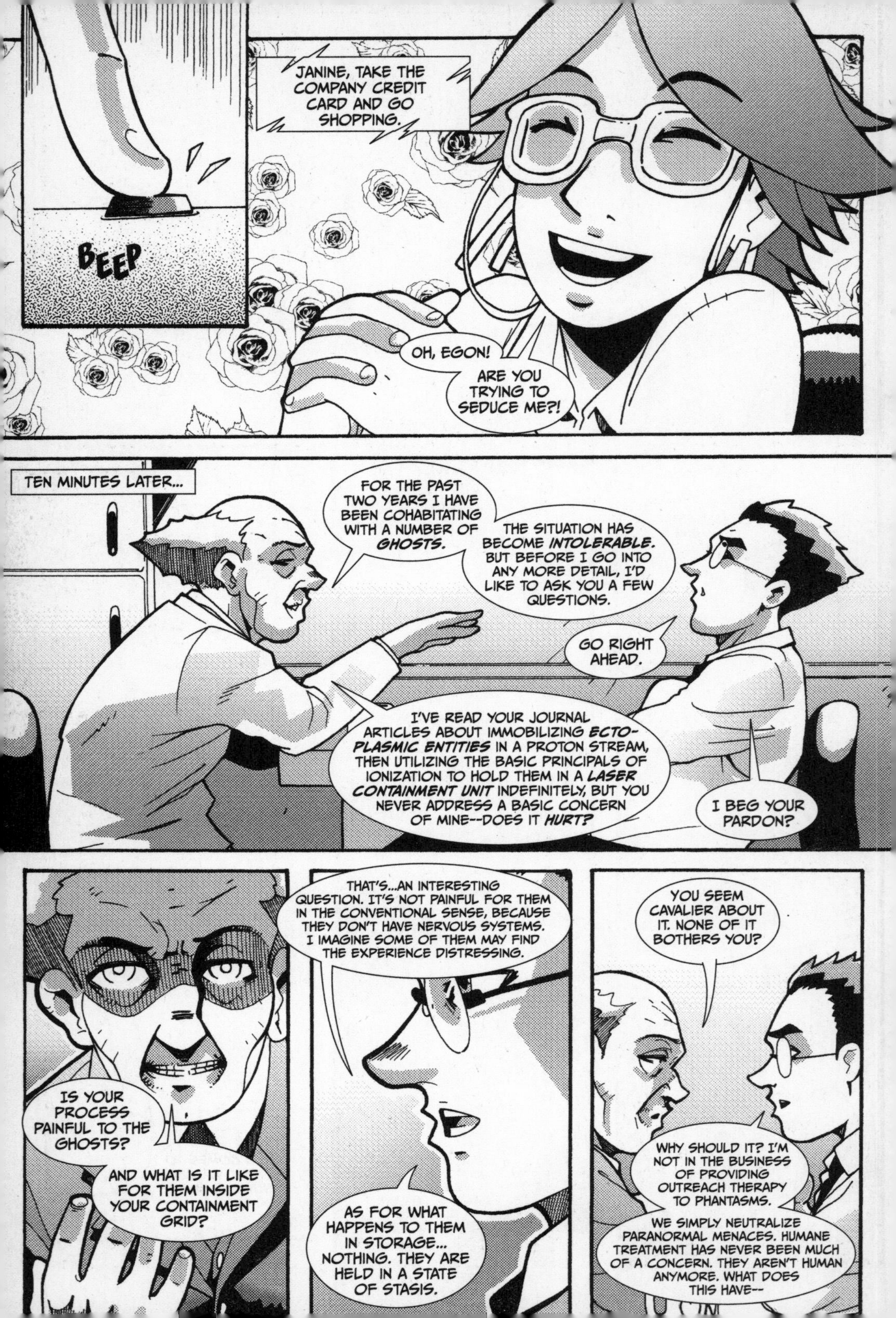

JANINE, TAKE THE COMPANY CREDIT CARD AND GO SHOPPING.
BEEP
OH, EGON!
ARE YOU TRYING TO SEDUCE ME?!
TEN MINUTES LATER...
FOR THE PAST TWO YEARS I HAVE BEEN COHABITATING WITH A NUMBER OF GHOSTS.
THE SITUATION HAS BECOME INTOLERABLE. BUT BEFORE I GO INTO ANY MORE DETAIL, I'D LIKE TO ASK YOU A FEW QUESTIONS.
GO RIGHT AHEAD.
I'VE READ YOUR JOURNAL ARTICLES ABOUT IMMOBILIZING ECTO-PLASMIC ENTITIES IN A PROTON STREAM, THEN UTILIZING THE BASIC PRINCIPALS OF IONIZATION TO HOLD THEM IN A LASER CONTAINMENT UNIT INDEFINITELY, BUT YOU NEVER ADDRESS A BASIC CONCERN OF MINE--DOES IT HURT?
I BEG YOUR PARDON?
IS YOUR PROCESS PAINFUL TO THE GHOSTS?
AND WHAT IS IT LIKE FOR THEM INSIDE YOUR CONTAINMENT GRID?
THAT'S...AN INTERESTING QUESTION. IT'S NOT PAINFUL FOR THEM IN THE CONVENTIONAL SENSE, BECAUSE THEY DON'T HAVE NERVOUS SYSTEMS. I IMAGINE SOME OF THEM MAY FIND THE EXPERIENCE DISTRESSING.
AS FOR WHAT HAPPENS TO THEM IN STORAGE... NOTHING. THEY ARE HELD IN A STATE OF STASIS.
YOU SEEM CAVALIER ABOUT IT. NONE OF IT BOTHERS YOU?
WHY SHOULD IT? I'M NOT IN THE BUSINESS OF PROVIDING OUTREACH THERAPY TO PHANTASMS.
WE SIMPLY NEUTRALIZE PARANORMAL MENACES. HUMANE TREATMENT HAS NEVER BEEN MUCH OF A CONCERN. THEY AREN'T HUMAN ANYMORE. WHAT DOES THIS HAVE--

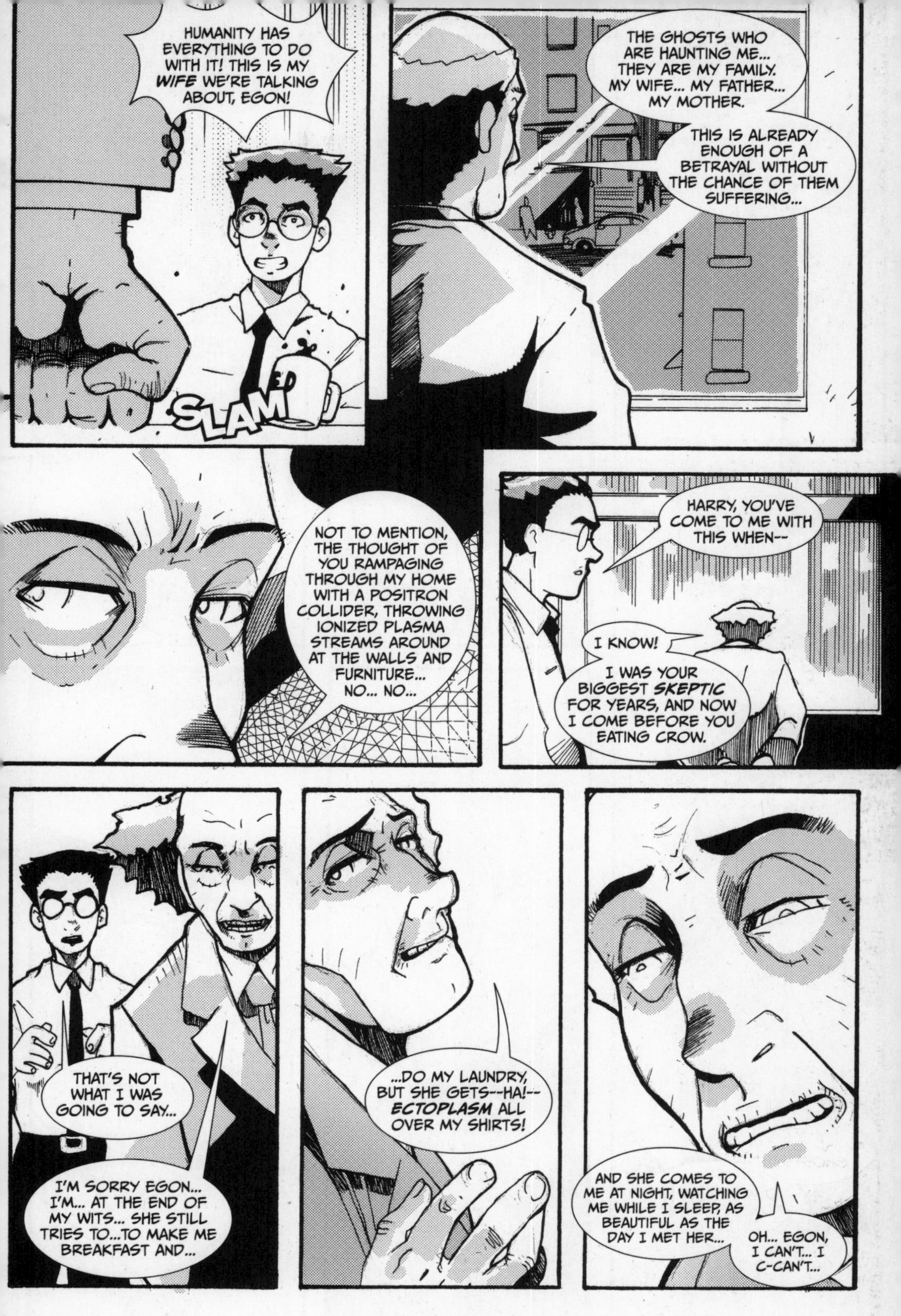
HUMANITY HAS EVERYTHING TO DO WITH IT! THIS IS MY WIFE WE'RE TALKING ABOUT, EGON!
SLAM
THE GHOSTS WHO ARE HAUNTING ME... THEY ARE MY FAMILY. MY WIFE... MY FATHER... MY MOTHER.
THIS IS ALREADY ENOUGH OF A BETRAYAL WITHOUT THE CHANCE OF THEM SUFFERING...
NOT TO MENTION, THE THOUGHT OF YOU RAMPAGING THROUGH MY HOME WITH A POSITRON COLLIDER, THROWING IONIZED PLASMA STREAMS AROUND AT THE WALLS AND FURNITURE... NO... NO...
HARRY, YOU'VE COME TO ME WITH THIS WHEN--
I KNOW!
I WAS YOUR BIGGEST SKEPTIC FOR YEARS, AND NOW I COME BEFORE YOU EATING CROW.
THAT'S NOT WHAT I WAS GOING TO SAY...
I'M SORRY EGON... I'M... AT THE END OF MY WITS... SHE STILL TRIES TO...TO MAKE ME BREAKFAST AND...
...DO MY LAUNDRY, BUT SHE GETS--HA!--ECTOPLASM ALL OVER MY SHIRTS!
AND SHE COMES TO ME AT NIGHT, WATCHING ME WHILE I SLEEP, AS BEAUTIFUL AS THE DAY I MET HER...
OH... EGON, I CAN'T... I C-CAN'T...

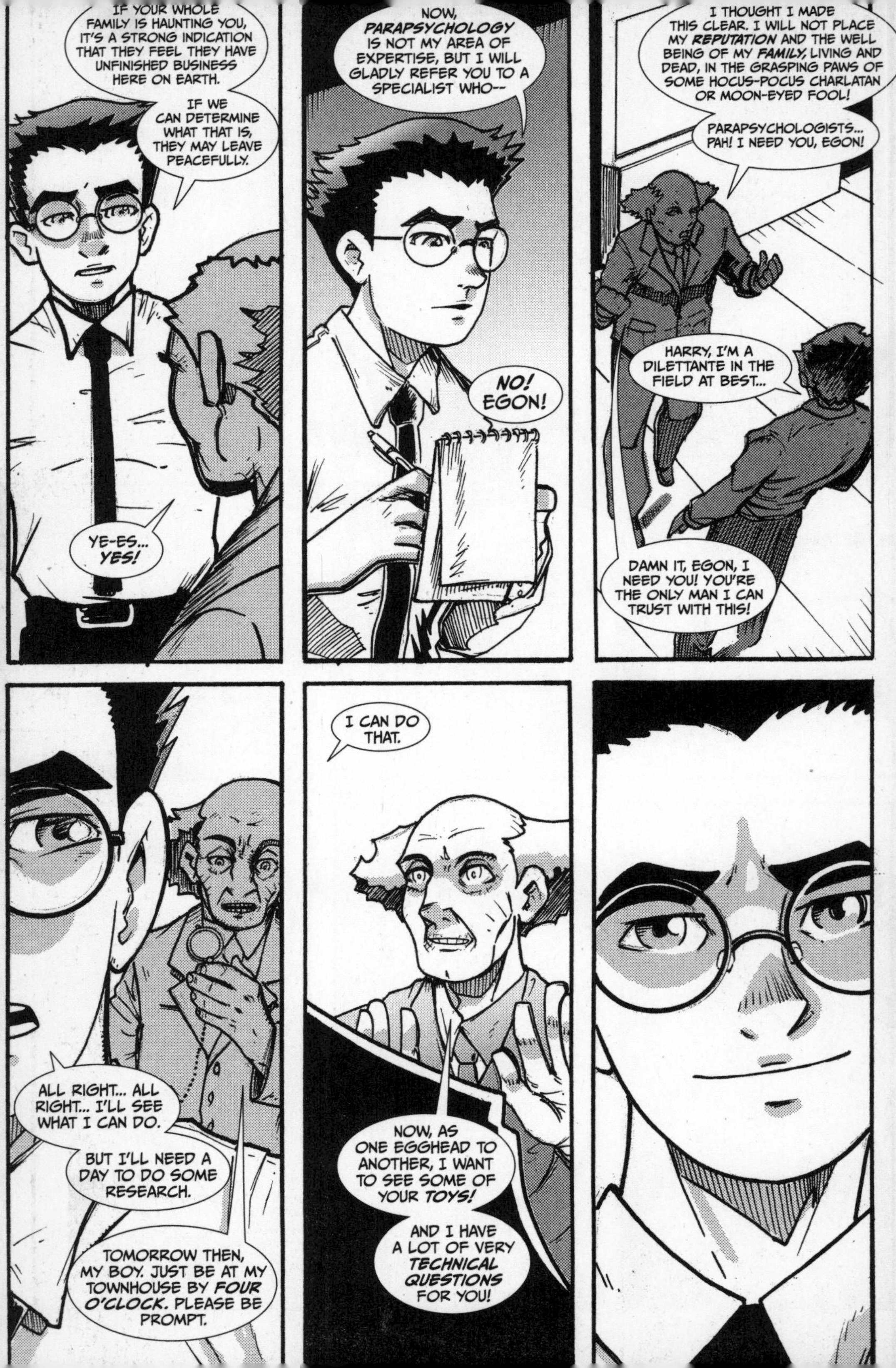
IF YOUR WHOLE FAMILY IS HAUNTING YOU, IT'S A STRONG INDICATION THAT THEY FEEL THEY HAVE UNFINISHED BUSINESS HERE ON EARTH.
IF WE CAN DETERMINE WHAT THAT IS, THEY MAY LEAVE PEACEFULLY.
YE-ES... YES!
NOW, PARAPSYCHOLOGY IS NOT MY AREA OF EXPERTISE, BUT I WILL GLADLY REFER YOU TO A SPECIALIST WHO--
NO! EGON!
I THOUGHT I MADE THIS CLEAR. I WILL NOT PLACE MY REPUTATION AND THE WELL BEING OF MY FAMILY, LIVING AND DEAD, IN THE GRASPING PAWS OF SOME HOCUS-POCUS CHARLATAN OR MOON-EYED FOOL!
PARAPSYCHOLOGISTS... PAH! I NEED YOU, EGON!
HARRY, I'M A DILETTANTE IN THE FIELD AT BEST...
DAMN IT, EGON, I NEED YOU! YOU'RE THE ONLY MAN I CAN TRUST WITH THIS!
ALL RIGHT... ALL RIGHT... I'LL SEE WHAT I CAN DO.
BUT I'LL NEED A DAY TO DO SOME RESEARCH.
TOMORROW THEN, MY BOY. JUST BE AT MY TOWNHOUSE BY FOUR O'CLOCK. PLEASE BE PROMPT.
I CAN DO THAT.
NOW, AS ONE EGGHEAD TO ANOTHER, I WANT TO SEE SOME OF YOUR TOYS!
AND I HAVE A LOT OF VERY TECHNICAL QUESTIONS FOR YOU!

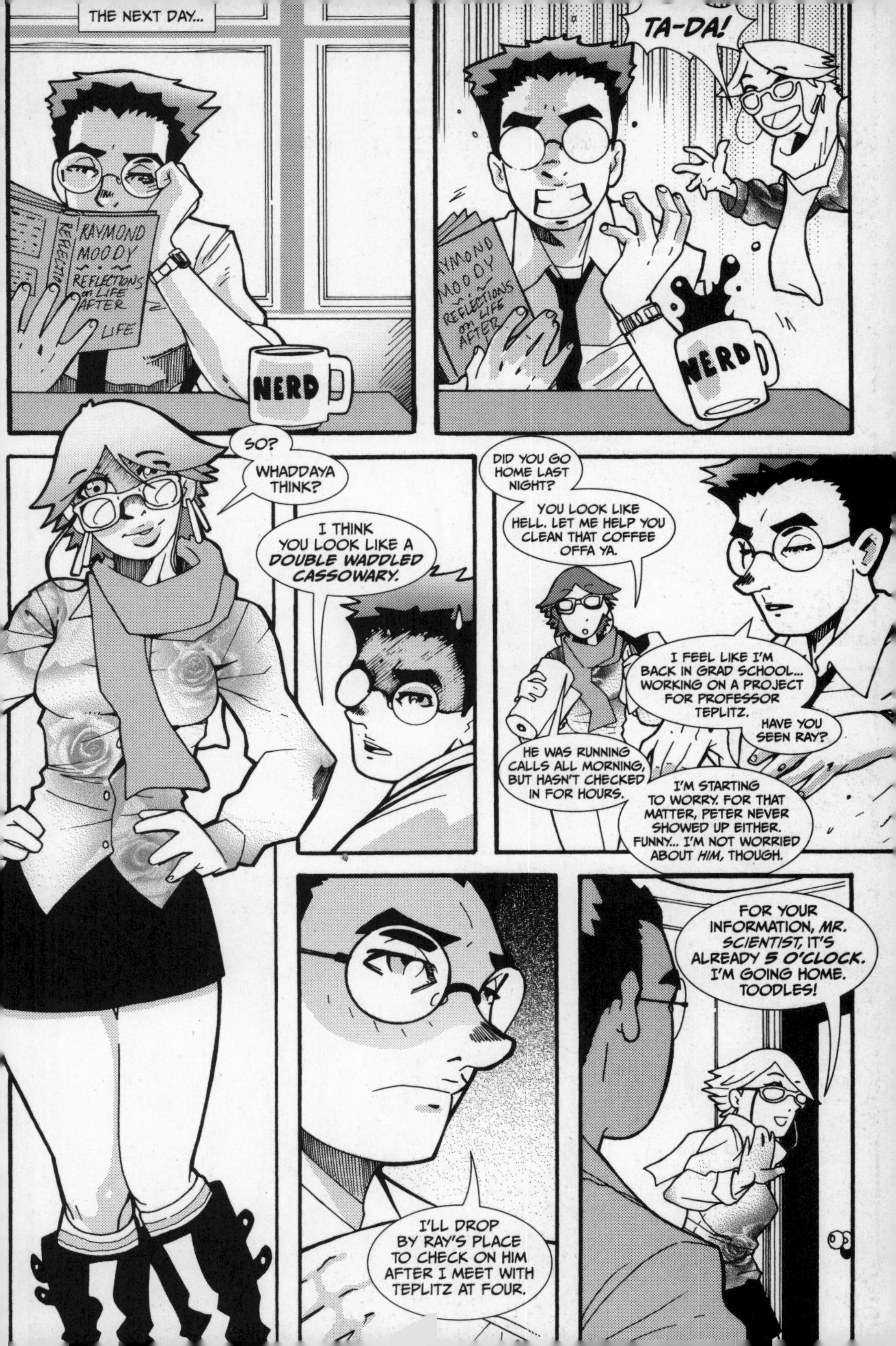
THE NEXT DAY...
RAYMOND MOODY
REFLECTIONS on LIFE AFTER LIFE
NERD
TA-DA!
RAYMOND MOODY
REFLECTIONS on LIFE AFTER
NERD
SO?
WHADDAYA THINK?
I THINK YOU LOOK LIKE A DOUBLE WADDLED CASSOWARY.
DID YOU GO HOME LAST NIGHT?
YOU LOOK LIKE HELL. LET ME HELP YOU CLEAN THAT COFFEE OFFA YA.
I FEEL LIKE I'M BACK IN GRAD SCHOOL... WORKING ON A PROJECT FOR PROFESSOR TEPLITZ.
HAVE YOU SEEN RAY?
HE WAS RUNNING CALLS ALL MORNING, BUT HASN'T CHECKED IN FOR HOURS.
I'M STARTING TO WORRY. FOR THAT MATTER, PETER NEVER SHOWED UP EITHER. FUNNY... I'M NOT WORRIED ABOUT HIM, THOUGH.
I'LL DROP BY RAY'S PLACE TO CHECK ON HIM AFTER I MEET WITH TEPLITZ AT FOUR.
FOR YOUR INFORMATION, MR. SCIENTIST, IT'S ALREADY 5 O'CLOCK. I'M GOING HOME. TOODLES!

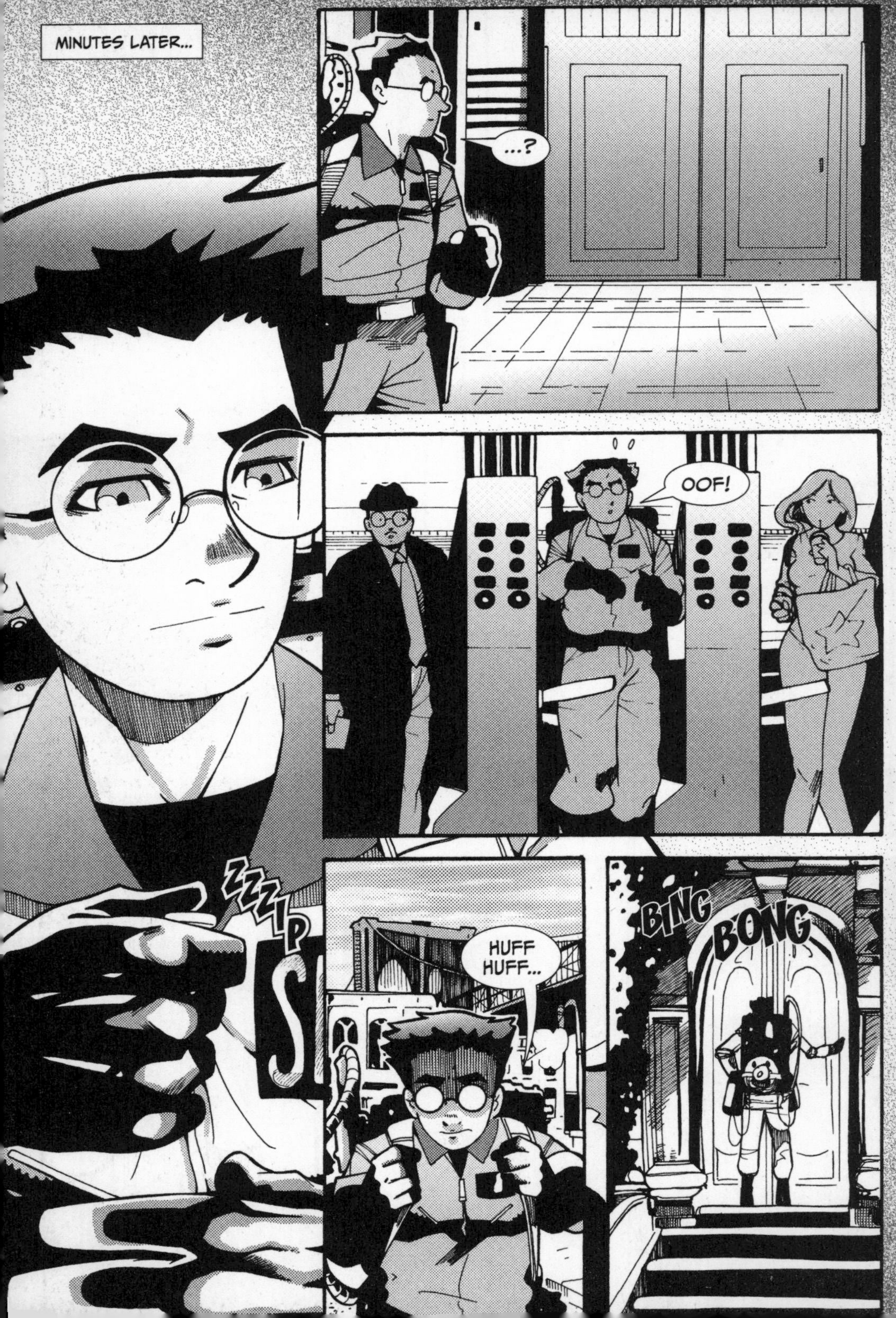
MINUTES LATER...
...?
OOF!
ZZZIP
HUFF HUFF...
BING
BONG

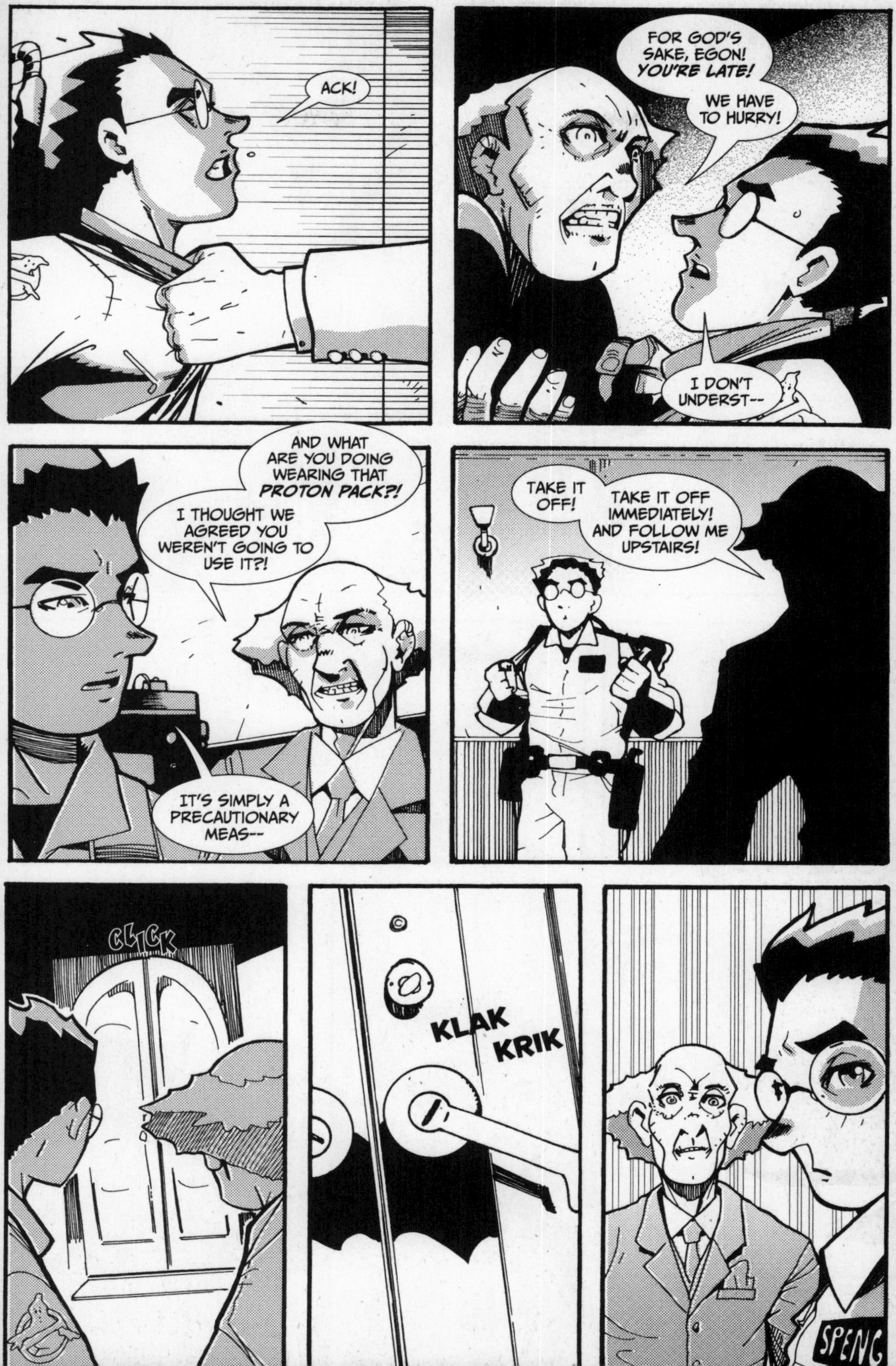
ACK!
FOR GOD'S SAKE, EGON! *YOU'RE LATE!*
WE HAVE TO HURRY!
I DON'T UNDERST--
AND WHAT ARE YOU DOING WEARING THAT *PROTON PACK?!*
I THOUGHT WE AGREED YOU WEREN'T GOING TO USE IT?!
IT'S SIMPLY A PRECAUTIONARY MEAS--
TAKE IT OFF!
TAKE IT OFF IMMEDIATELY! AND FOLLOW ME UPSTAIRS!
CLICK
KLAK
KRIK
SPENG

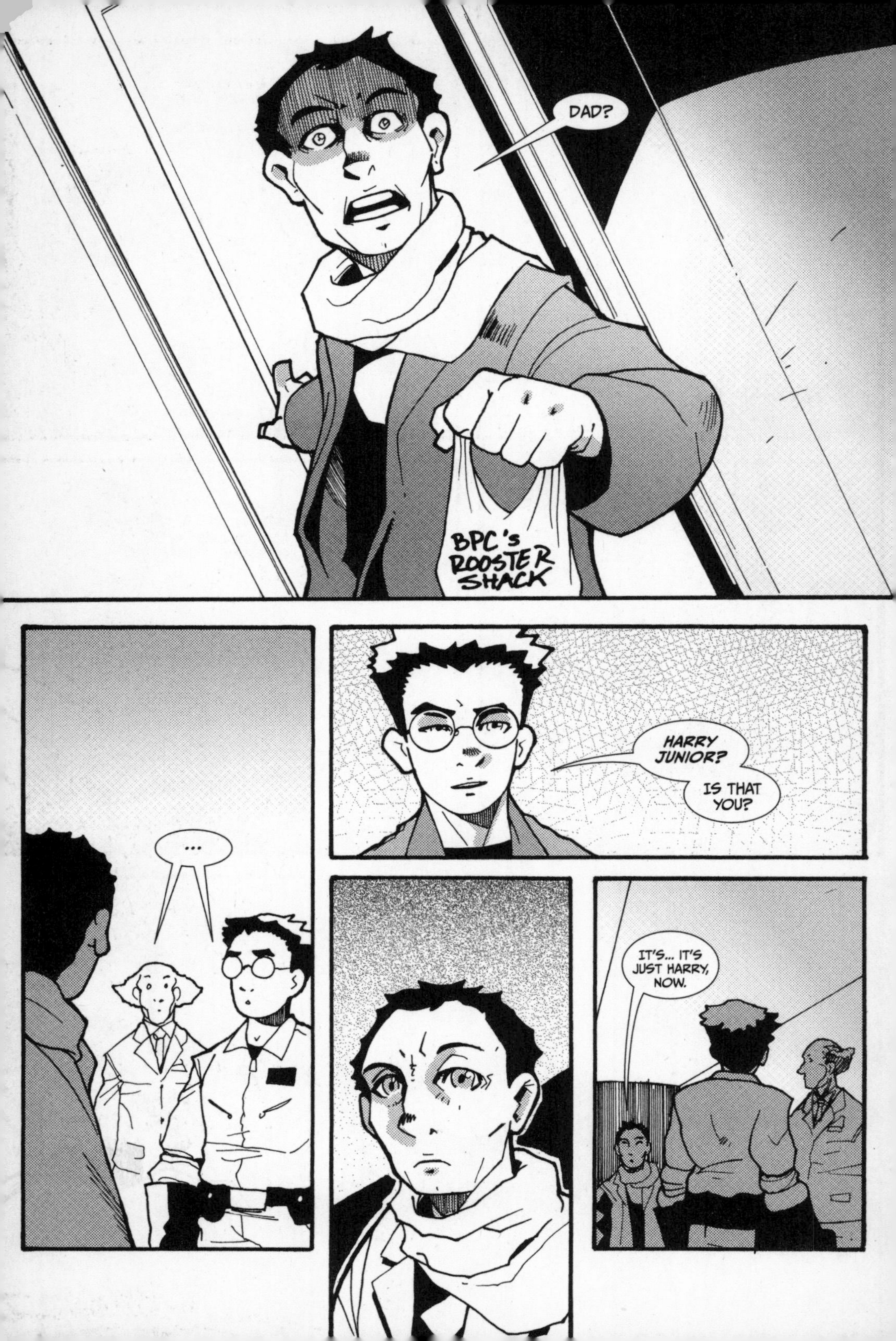
DAD?
BPC's ROOSTER SHACK
HARRY JUNIOR?
IS THAT YOU?
...
IT'S... IT'S JUST HARRY, NOW.

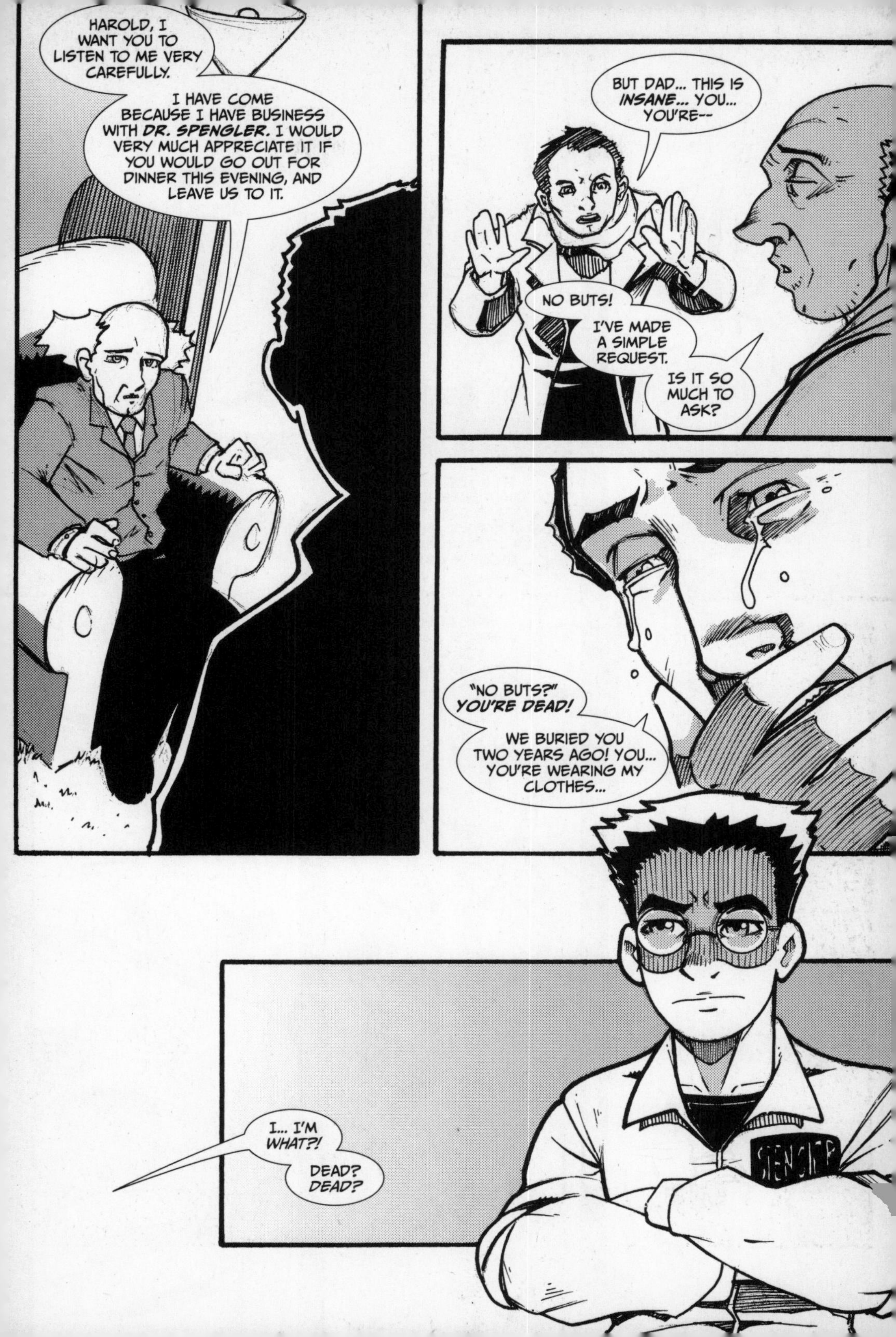
HAROLD, I WANT YOU TO LISTEN TO ME VERY CAREFULLY.
I HAVE COME BECAUSE I HAVE BUSINESS WITH DR. SPENGLER. I WOULD VERY MUCH APPRECIATE IT IF YOU WOULD GO OUT FOR DINNER THIS EVENING, AND LEAVE US TO IT.
BUT DAD... THIS IS INSANE... YOU... YOU'RE--
NO BUTS!
I'VE MADE A SIMPLE REQUEST.
IS IT SO MUCH TO ASK?
"NO BUTS?" YOU'RE DEAD!
WE BURIED YOU TWO YEARS AGO! YOU... YOU'RE WEARING MY CLOTHES...
I... I'M WHAT?!
DEAD? DEAD?

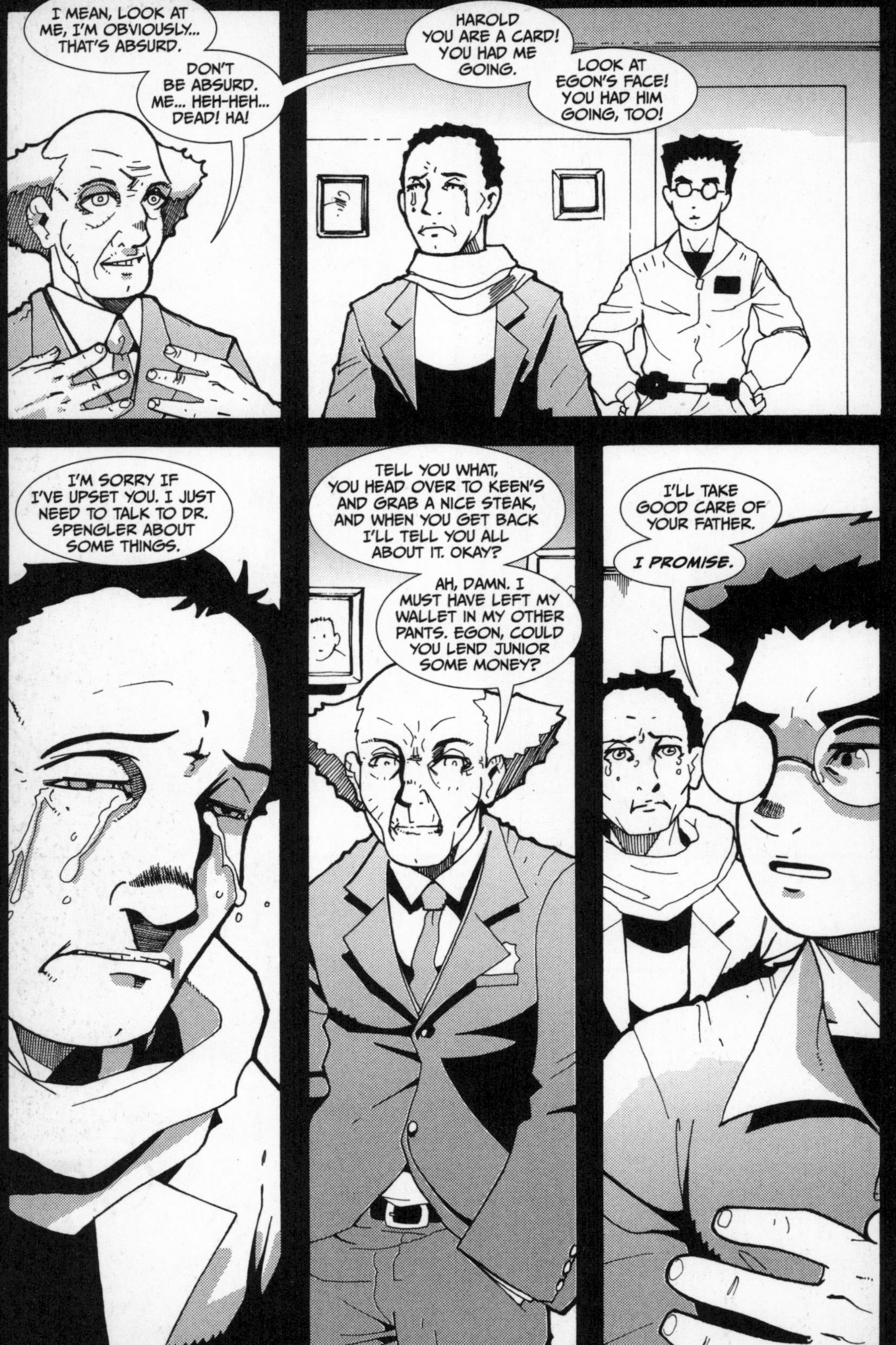
I MEAN, LOOK AT ME, I'M OBVIOUSLY... THAT'S ABSURD.
DON'T BE ABSURD. ME... HEH-HEH... DEAD! HA!
HAROLD YOU ARE A CARD! YOU HAD ME GOING.
LOOK AT EGON'S FACE! YOU HAD HIM GOING, TOO!
I'M SORRY IF I'VE UPSET YOU. I JUST NEED TO TALK TO DR. SPENGLER ABOUT SOME THINGS.
TELL YOU WHAT, YOU HEAD OVER TO KEEN'S AND GRAB A NICE STEAK, AND WHEN YOU GET BACK I'LL TELL YOU ALL ABOUT IT. OKAY?
AH, DAMN. I MUST HAVE LEFT MY WALLET IN MY OTHER PANTS. EGON, COULD YOU LEND JUNIOR SOME MONEY?
I'LL TAKE GOOD CARE OF YOUR FATHER.
I PROMISE.

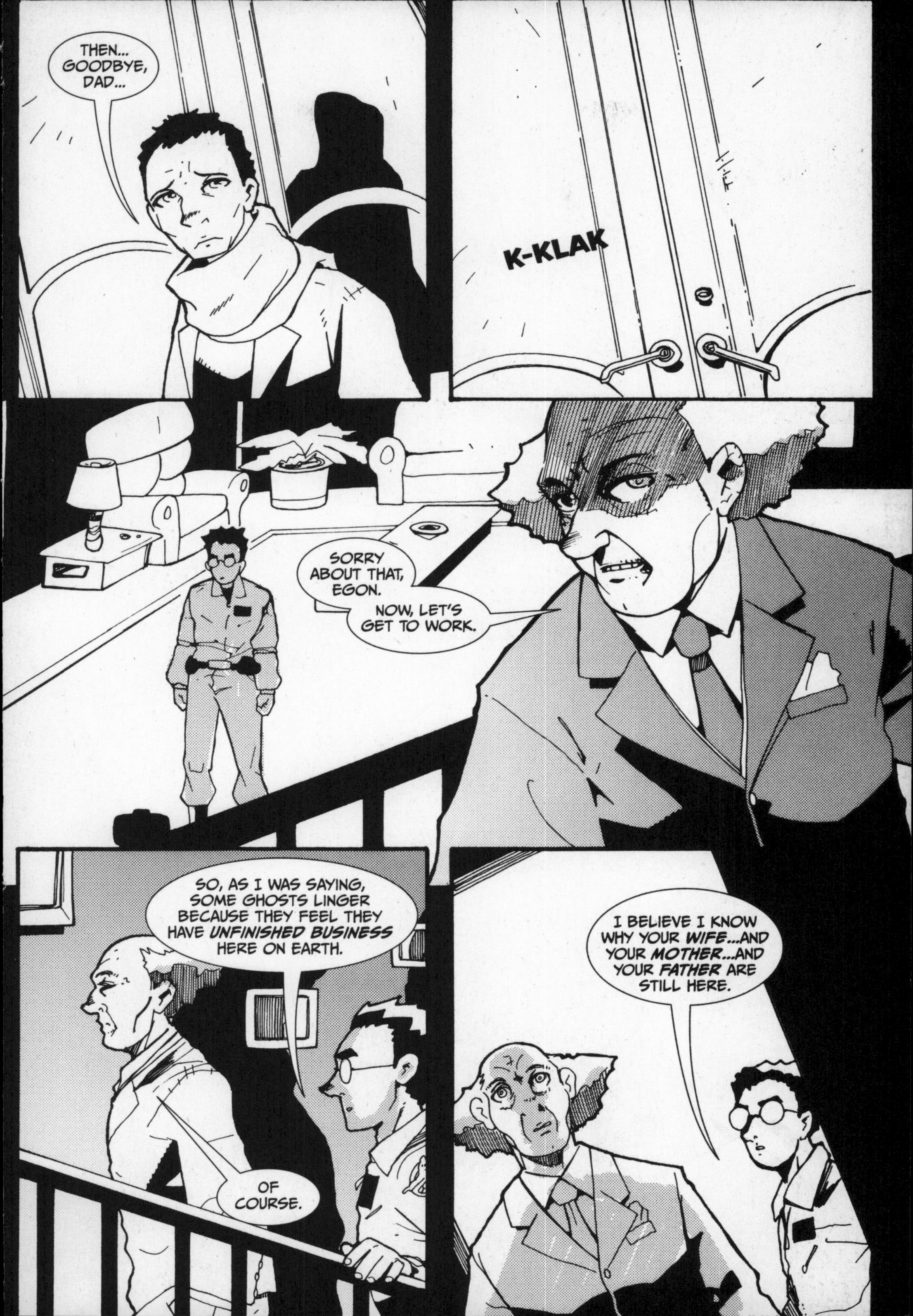
THEN... GOODBYE, DAD...
K-KLAK
SORRY ABOUT THAT, EGON.
NOW, LET'S GET TO WORK.
SO, AS I WAS SAYING, SOME GHOSTS LINGER BECAUSE THEY FEEL THEY HAVE *UNFINISHED BUSINESS* HERE ON EARTH.
OF COURSE.
I BELIEVE I KNOW WHY YOUR *WIFE*...AND YOUR *MOTHER*...AND YOUR *FATHER* ARE STILL HERE.

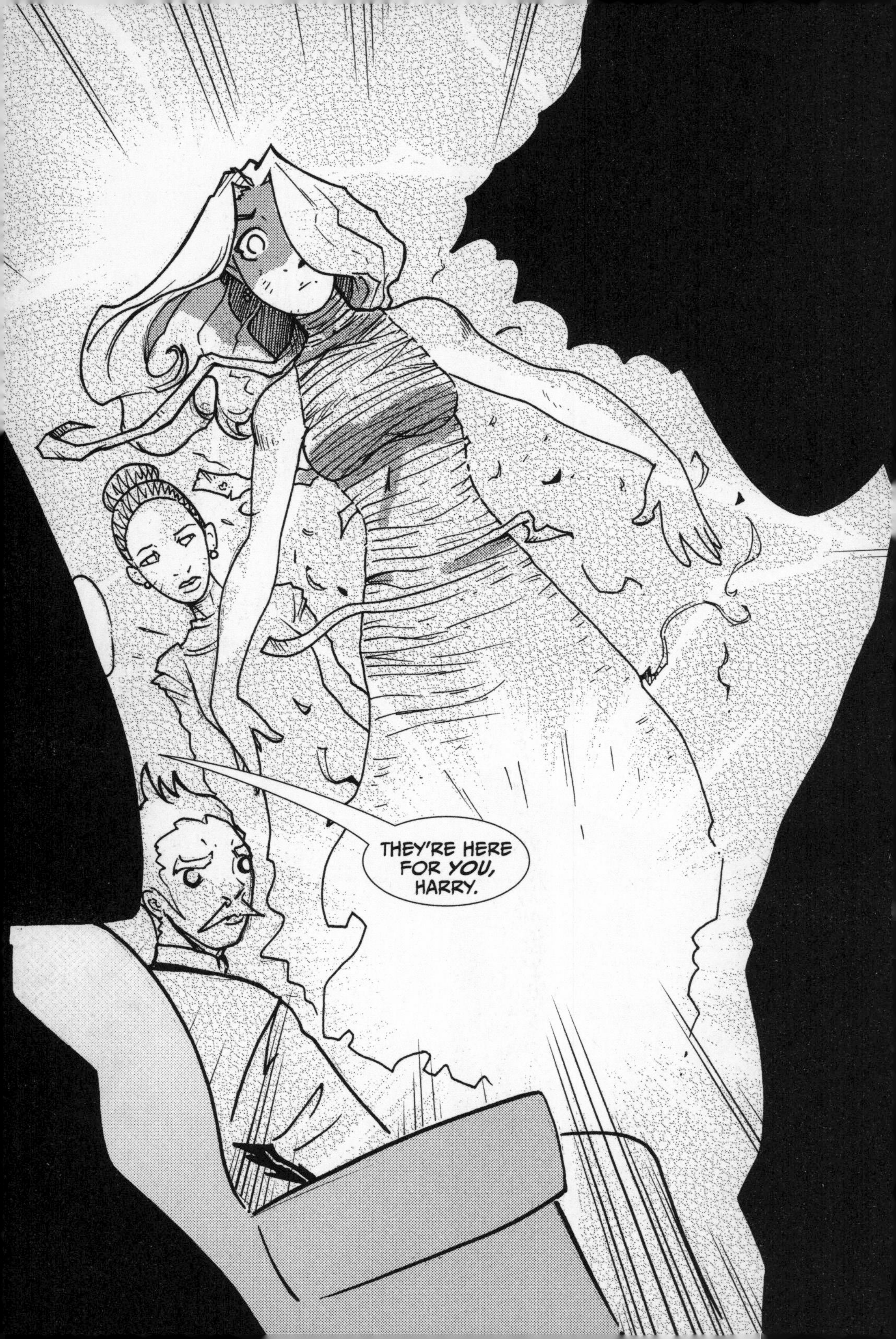
THEY'RE HERE FOR *YOU*, HARRY.

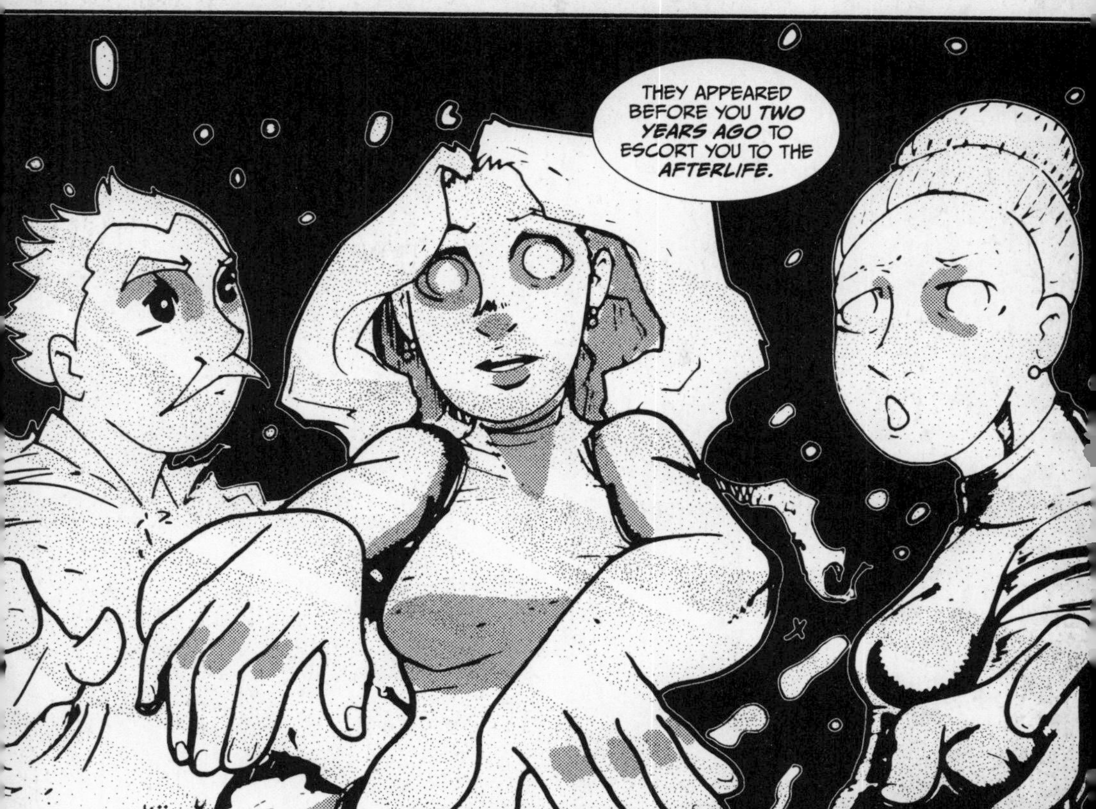
THEY APPEARED BEFORE YOU *TWO YEARS AGO* TO ESCORT YOU TO THE *AFTERLIFE.*

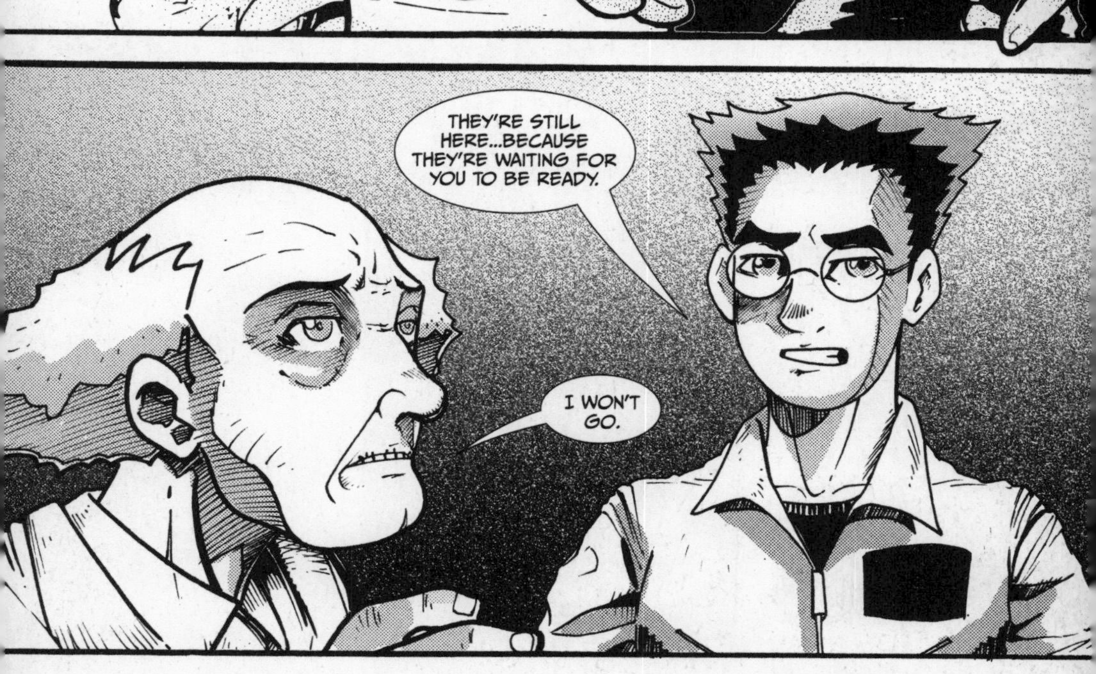
THEY'RE STILL HERE...BECAUSE THEY'RE WAITING FOR YOU TO BE READY.
I WON'T GO.

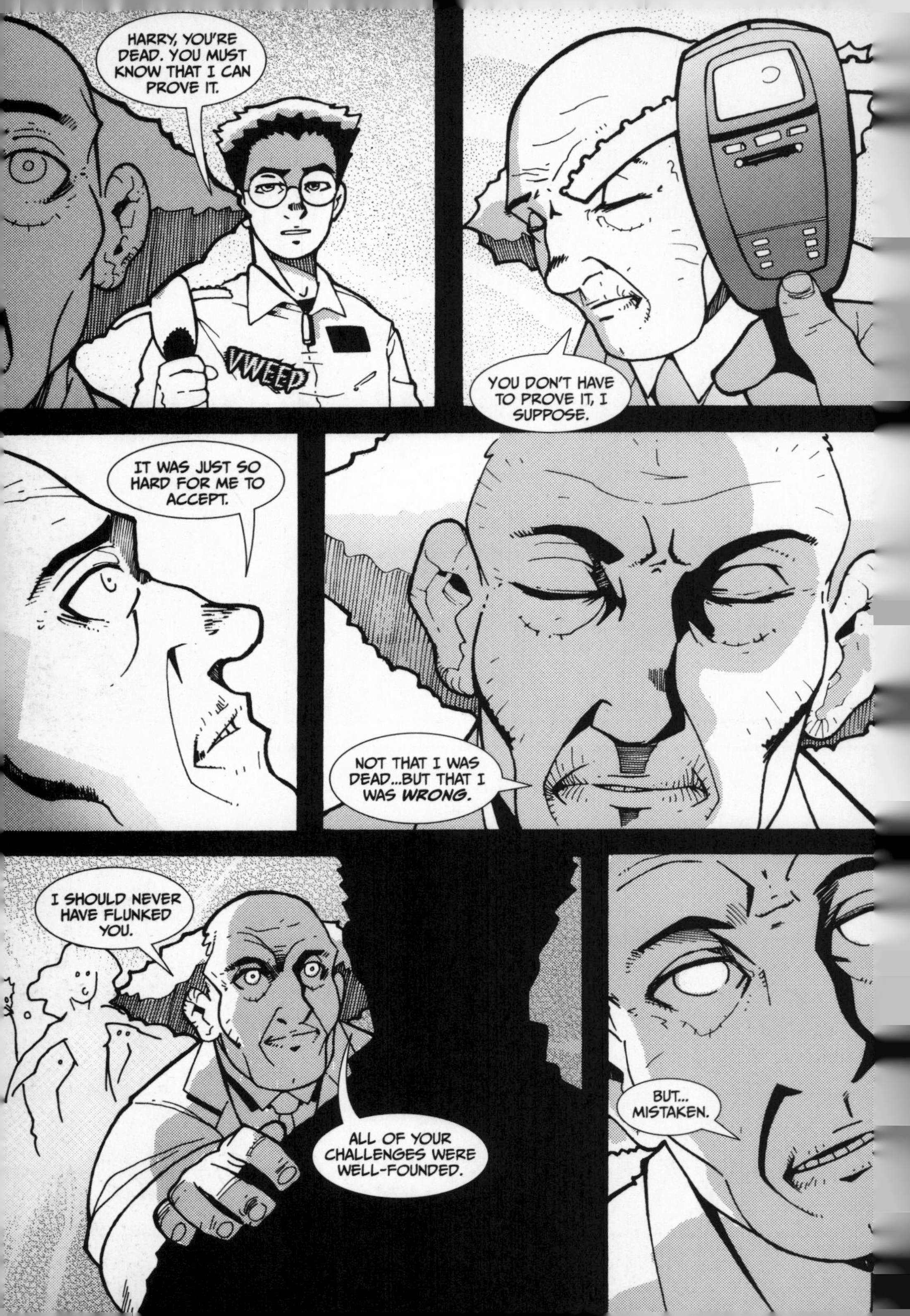
HARRY, YOU'RE DEAD. YOU MUST KNOW THAT I CAN PROVE IT.
VWEEP
YOU DON'T HAVE TO PROVE IT, I SUPPOSE.
IT WAS JUST SO HARD FOR ME TO ACCEPT.
NOT THAT I WAS DEAD...BUT THAT I WAS *WRONG.*
I SHOULD NEVER HAVE FLUNKED YOU.
ALL OF YOUR CHALLENGES WERE WELL-FOUNDED.
BUT... MISTAKEN.

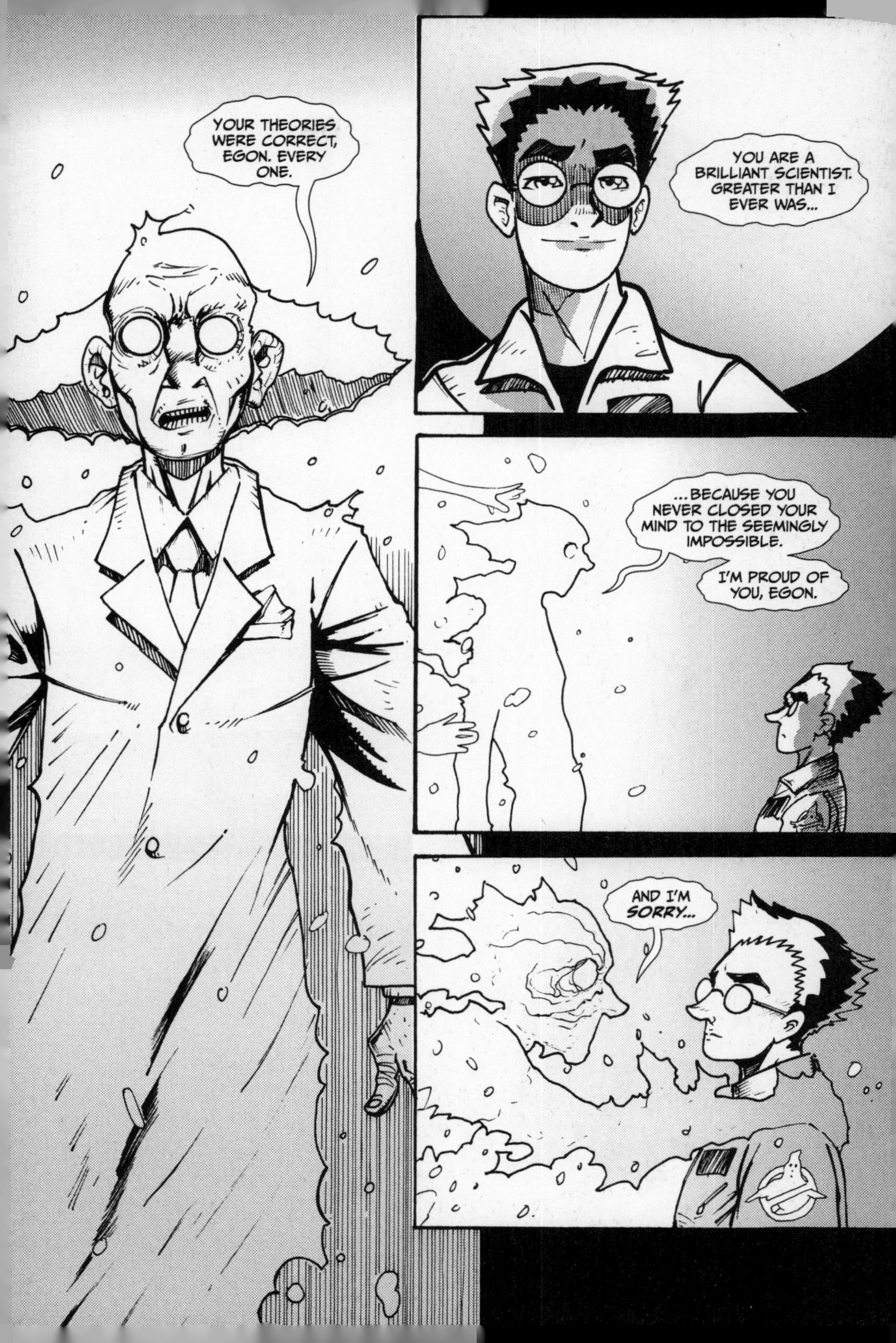

YOUR THEORIES WERE CORRECT, EGON. EVERY ONE.
YOU ARE A BRILLIANT SCIENTIST. GREATER THAN I EVER WAS...
...BECAUSE YOU NEVER CLOSED YOUR MIND TO THE SEEMINGLY IMPOSSIBLE.
I'M PROUD OF YOU, EGON.
AND I'M SORRY...

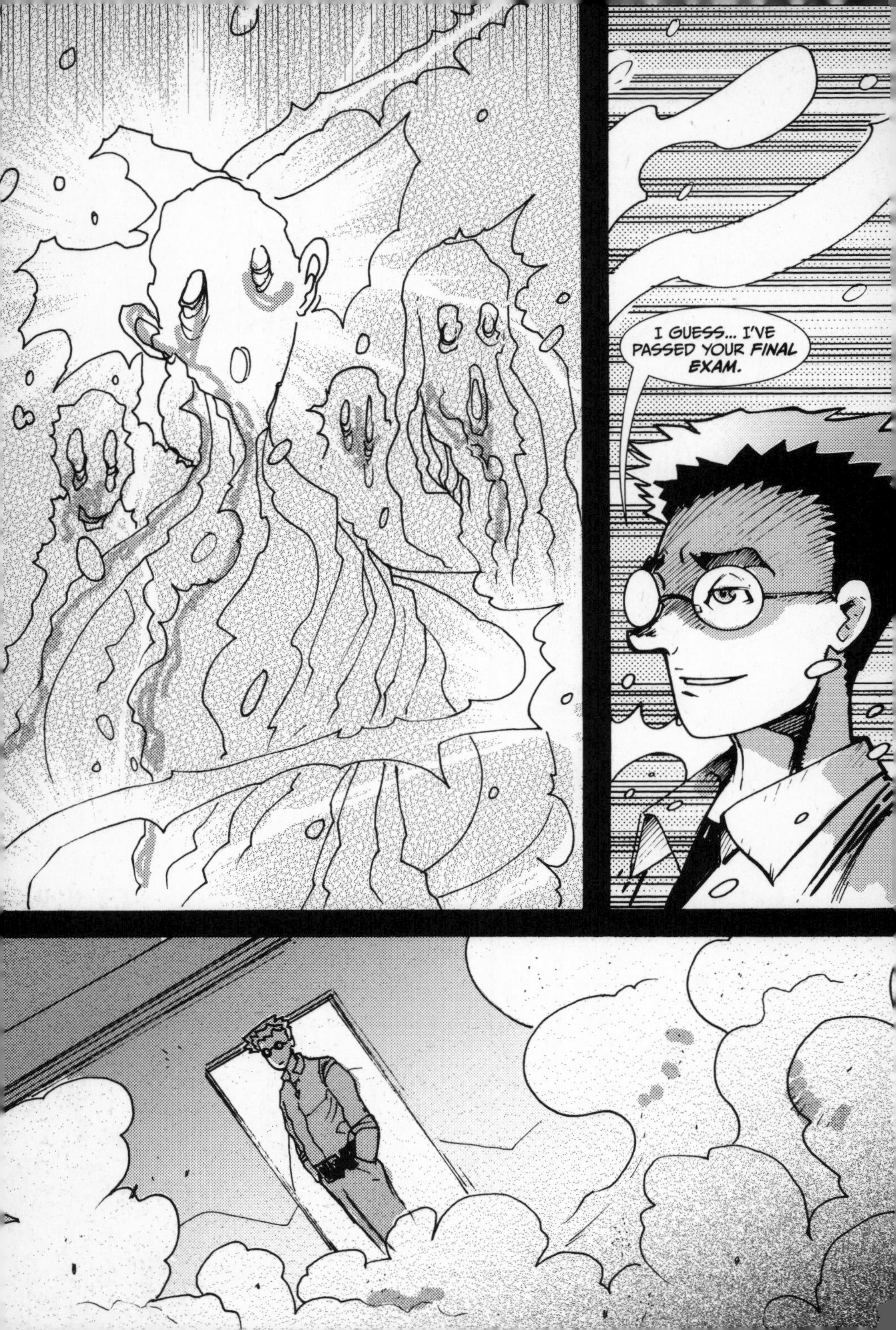
I GUESS... I'VE PASSED YOUR FINAL EXAM.

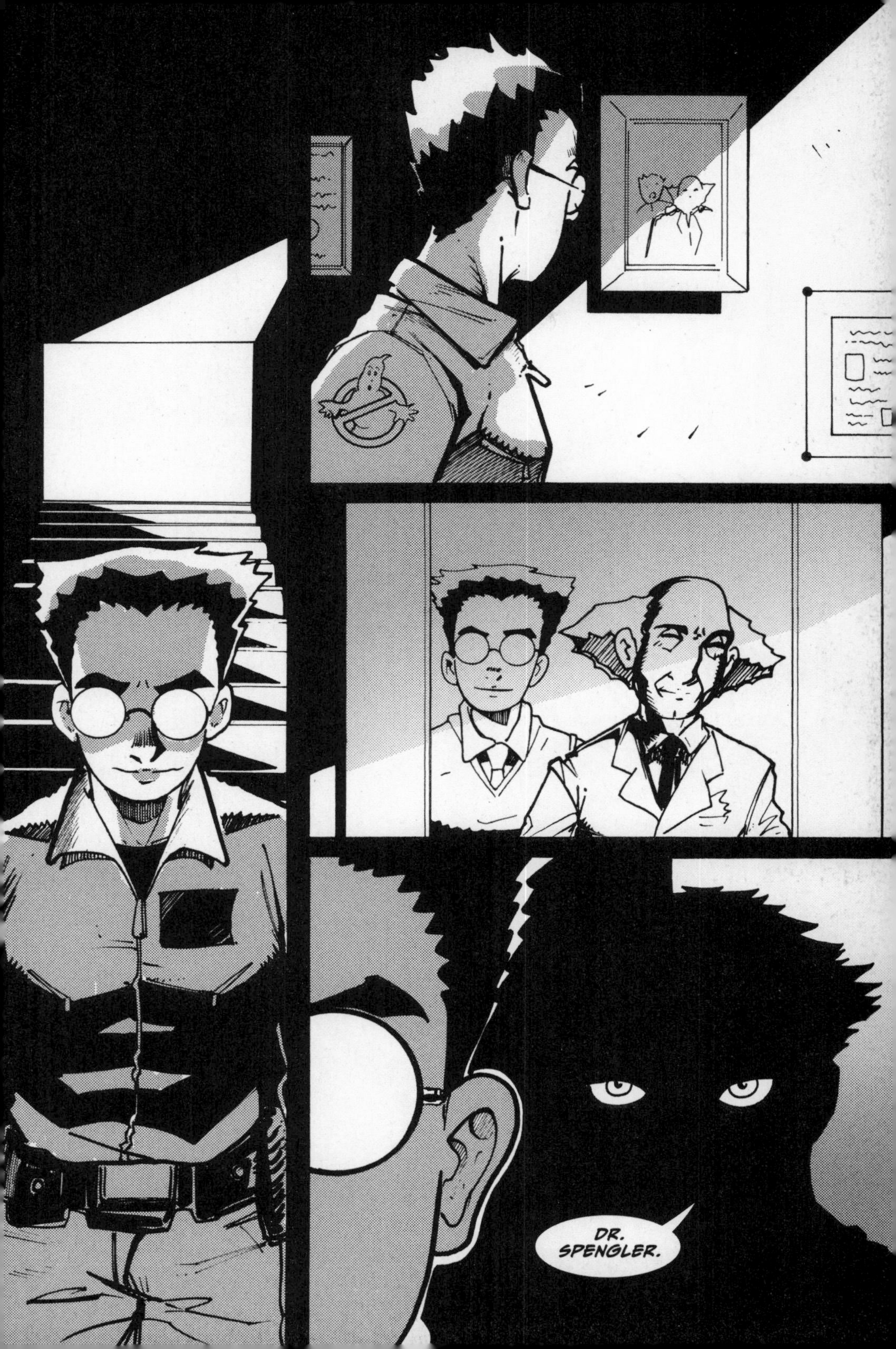
DR. SPENGLER.

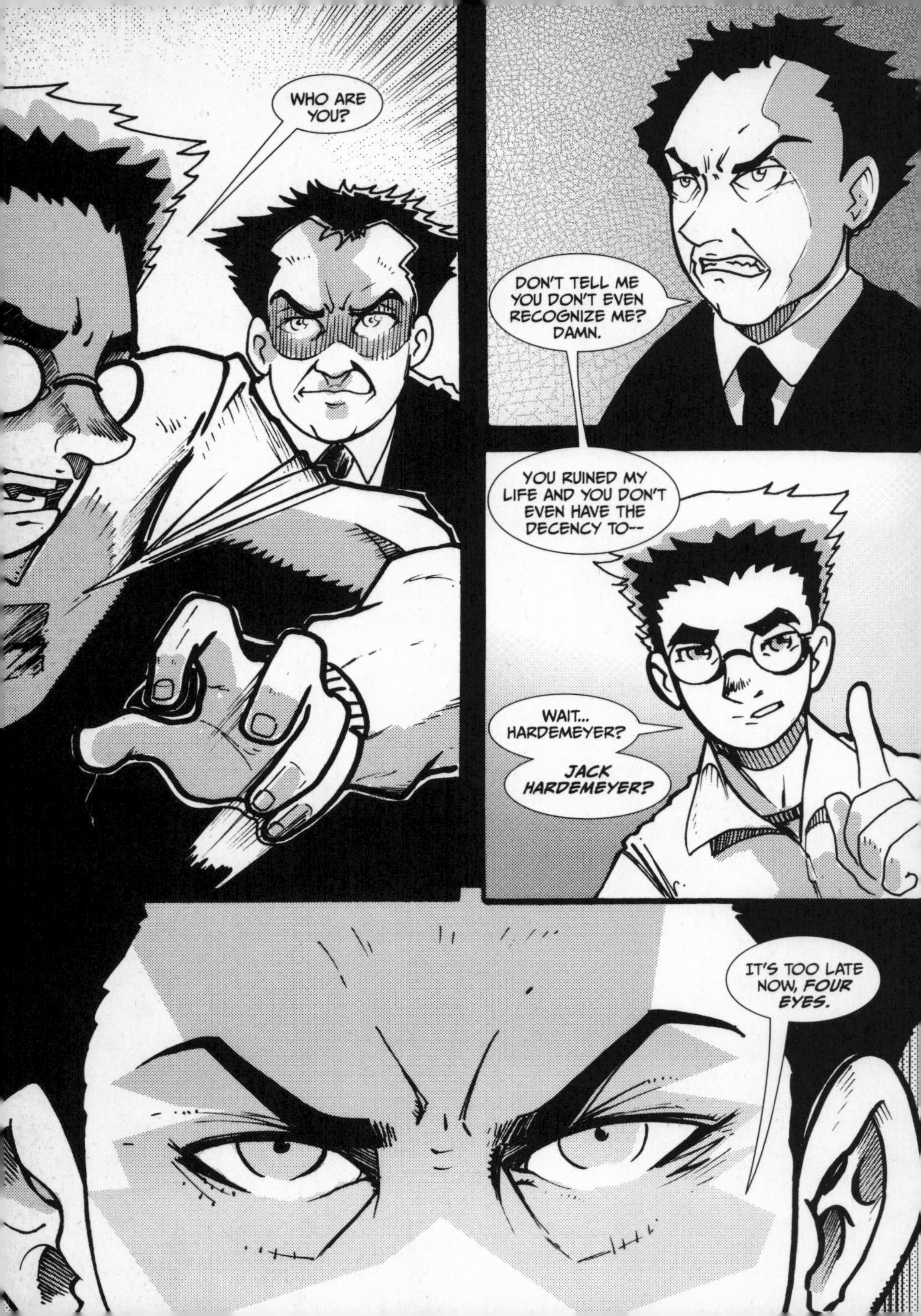
WHO ARE YOU?
DON'T TELL ME YOU DON'T EVEN RECOGNIZE ME? DAMN.
YOU RUINED MY LIFE AND YOU DON'T EVEN HAVE THE DECENCY TO--
WAIT... HARDEMEYER?
JACK HARDEMEYER?
IT'S TOO LATE NOW, FOUR EYES.

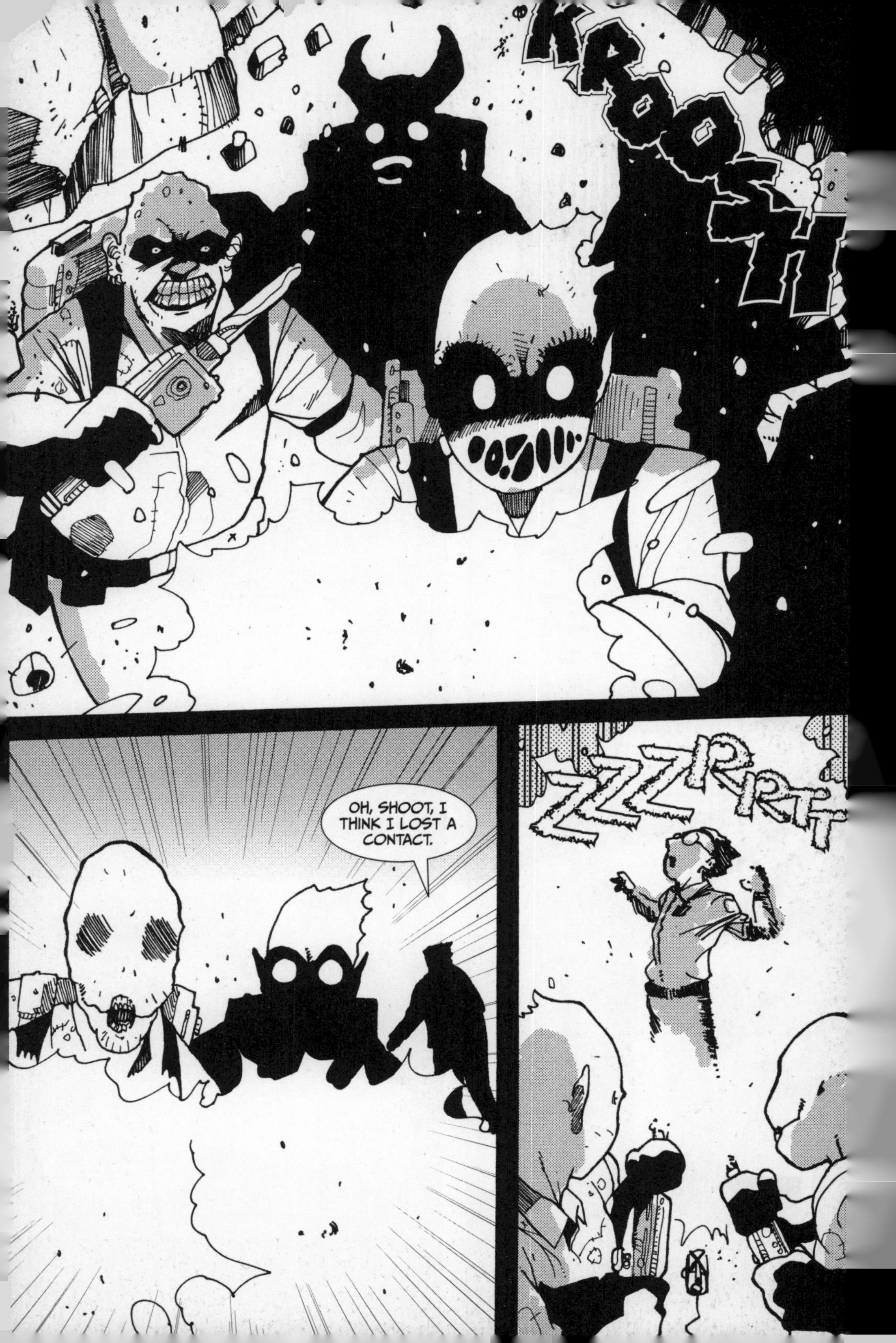
KROOSH
OH, SHOOT, I THINK I LOST A CONTACT.
ZZZRRRT

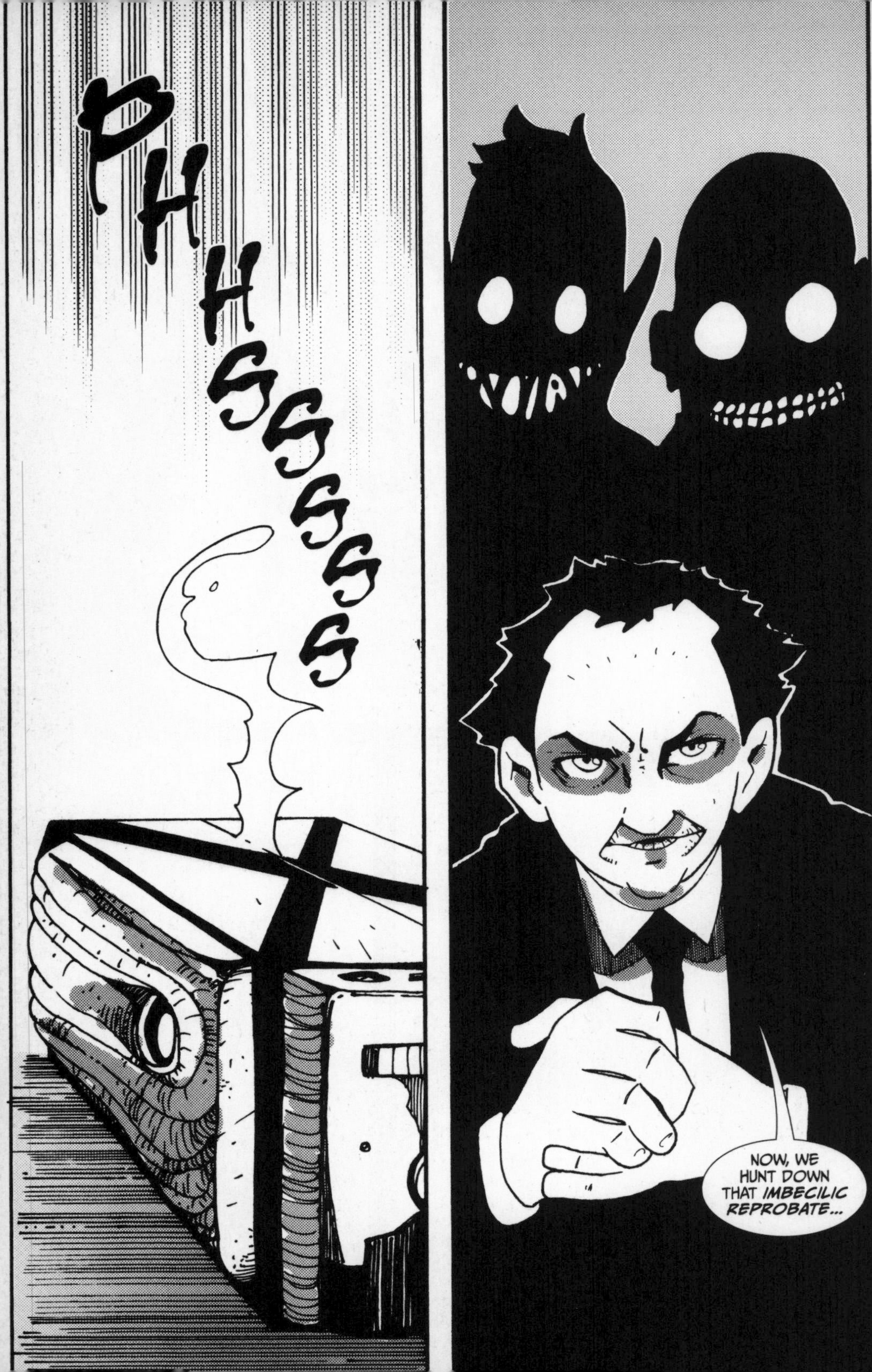
PHHSSSSSSS
NOW, WE HUNT DOWN THAT *IMBECILIC* REPROBATE...

# GHOSTBUSTERS™

# CHAPTER V

# GHOST BUSTED

### STORY BY
### NATHAN JOHNSON

### ART BY
### MICHAEL SHELFER

### INKS & TONES BY
### MAXIMO V. LORENZO

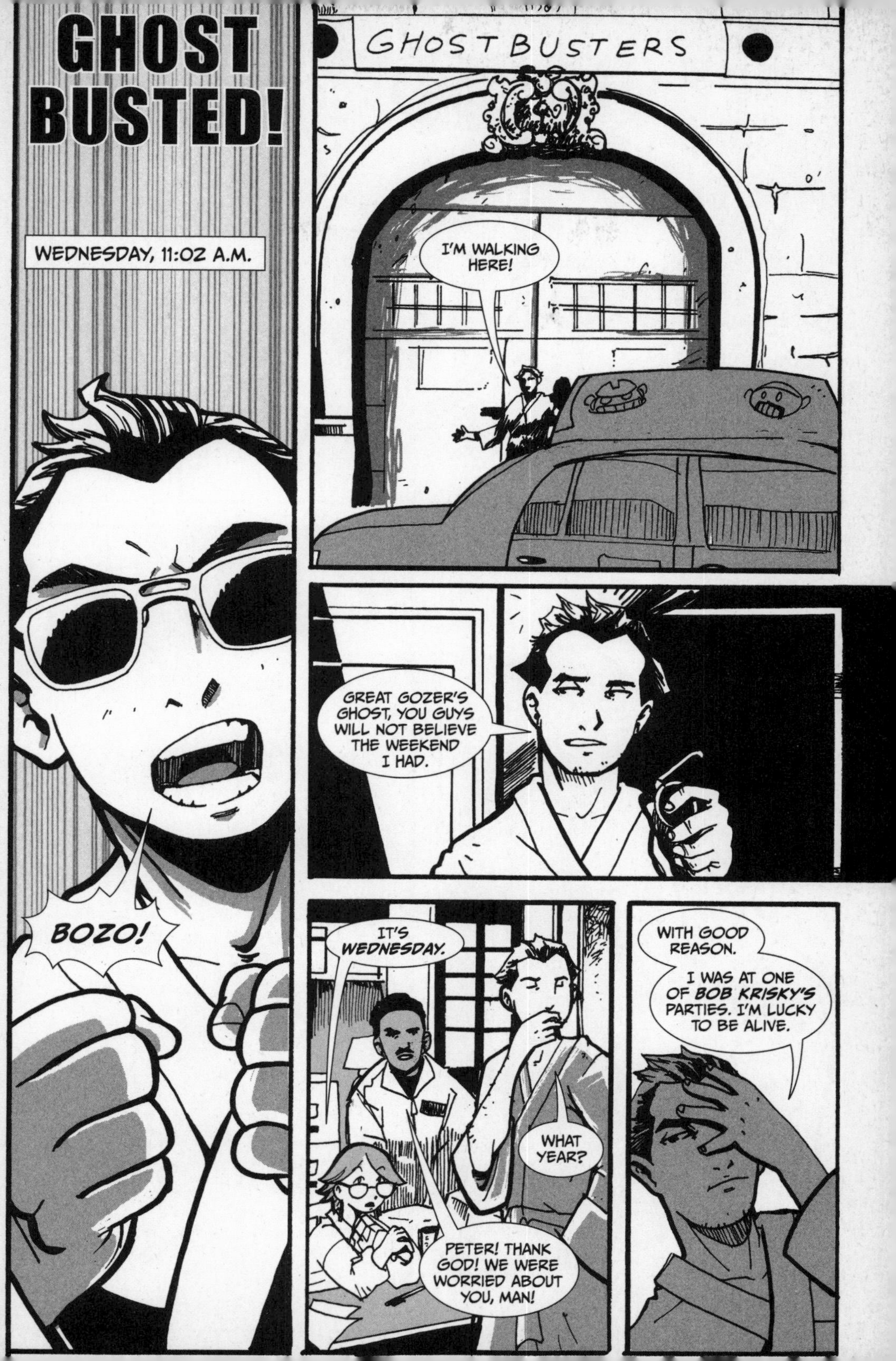
GHOST BUSTED!
WEDNESDAY, 11:02 A.M.
BOZO!
GHOSTBUSTERS
I'M WALKING HERE!
GREAT GOZER'S GHOST, YOU GUYS WILL NOT BELIEVE THE WEEKEND I HAD.
PETER! THANK GOD! WE WERE WORRIED ABOUT YOU, MAN!
IT'S WEDNESDAY.
WHAT YEAR?
WITH GOOD REASON.
I WAS AT ONE OF BOB KRISKY'S PARTIES. I'M LUCKY TO BE ALIVE.

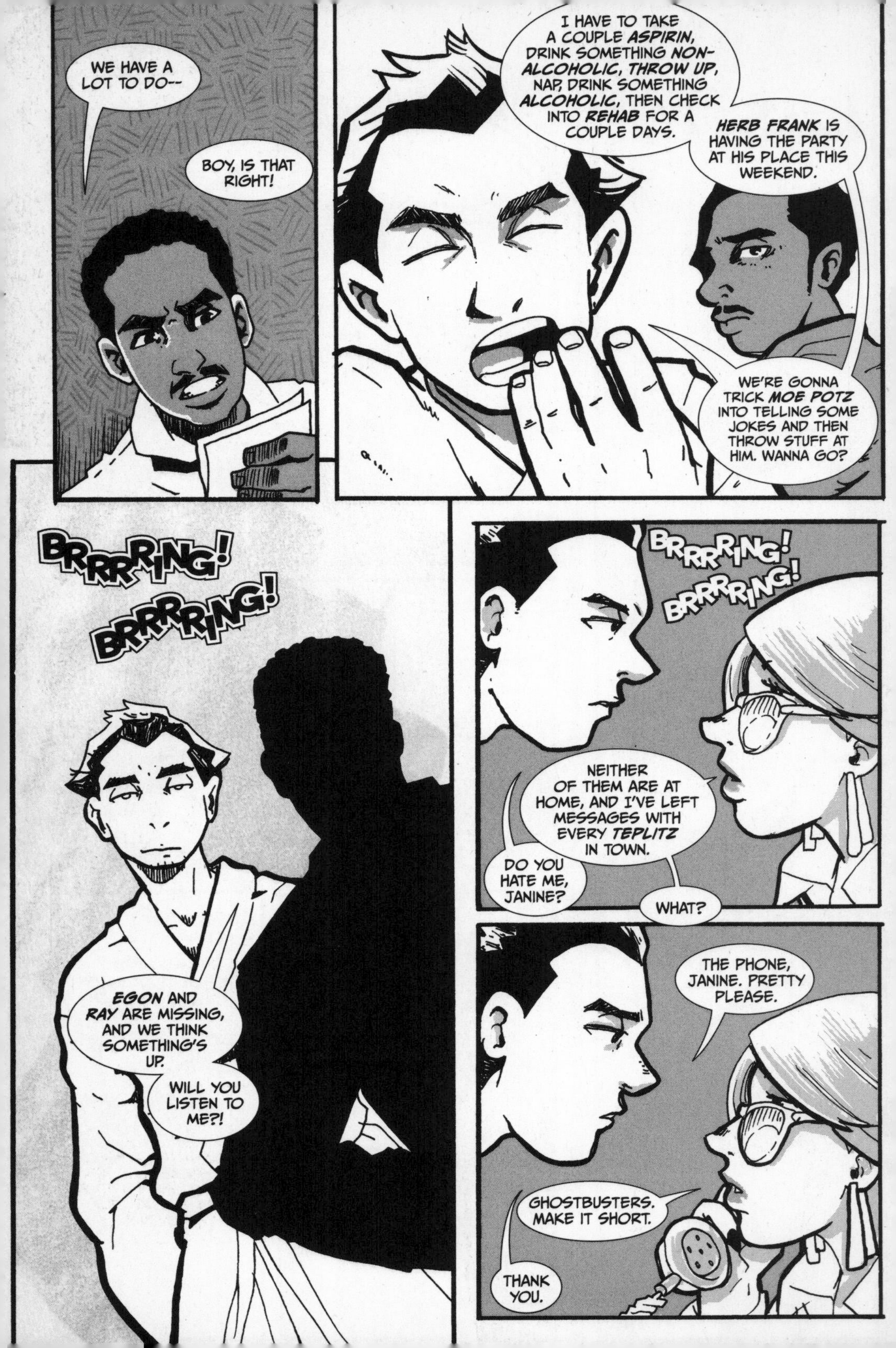
WE HAVE A LOT TO DO--
BOY, IS THAT RIGHT!
I HAVE TO TAKE A COUPLE ASPIRIN, DRINK SOMETHING NON-ALCOHOLIC, THROW UP, NAP, DRINK SOMETHING ALCOHOLIC, THEN CHECK INTO REHAB FOR A COUPLE DAYS.
HERB FRANK IS HAVING THE PARTY AT HIS PLACE THIS WEEKEND.
WE'RE GONNA TRICK MOE POTZ INTO TELLING SOME JOKES AND THEN THROW STUFF AT HIM. WANNA GO?
BRRRRING!
BRRRRING!
EGON AND RAY ARE MISSING, AND WE THINK SOMETHING'S UP.
WILL YOU LISTEN TO ME?!
BRRRRING!
BRRRRING!
NEITHER OF THEM ARE AT HOME, AND I'VE LEFT MESSAGES WITH EVERY TEPLITZ IN TOWN.
DO YOU HATE ME, JANINE?
WHAT?
THE PHONE, JANINE. PRETTY PLEASE.
GHOSTBUSTERS. MAKE IT SHORT.
THANK YOU.

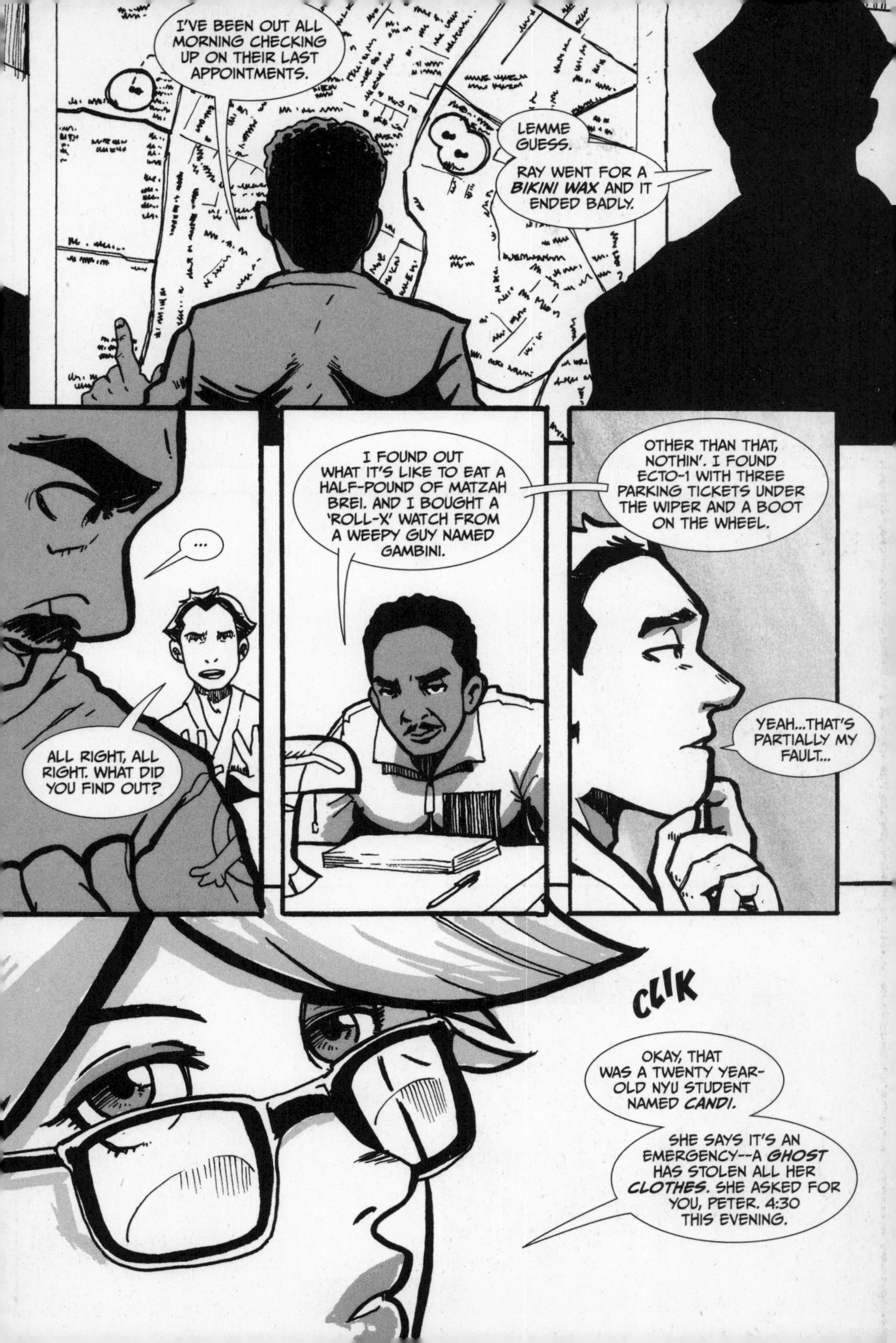

I'VE BEEN OUT ALL MORNING CHECKING UP ON THEIR LAST APPOINTMENTS.
LEMME GUESS.
RAY WENT FOR A BIKINI WAX AND IT ENDED BADLY.
...
ALL RIGHT, ALL RIGHT. WHAT DID YOU FIND OUT?
I FOUND OUT WHAT IT'S LIKE TO EAT A HALF-POUND OF MATZAH BREI. AND I BOUGHT A 'ROLL-X' WATCH FROM A WEEPY GUY NAMED GAMBINI.
OTHER THAN THAT, NOTHIN'. I FOUND ECTO-1 WITH THREE PARKING TICKETS UNDER THE WIPER AND A BOOT ON THE WHEEL.
YEAH...THAT'S PARTIALLY MY FAULT...
CLIK
OKAY, THAT WAS A TWENTY YEAR-OLD NYU STUDENT NAMED CANDI.
SHE SAYS IT'S AN EMERGENCY--A GHOST HAS STOLEN ALL HER CLOTHES. SHE ASKED FOR YOU, PETER. 4:30 THIS EVENING.

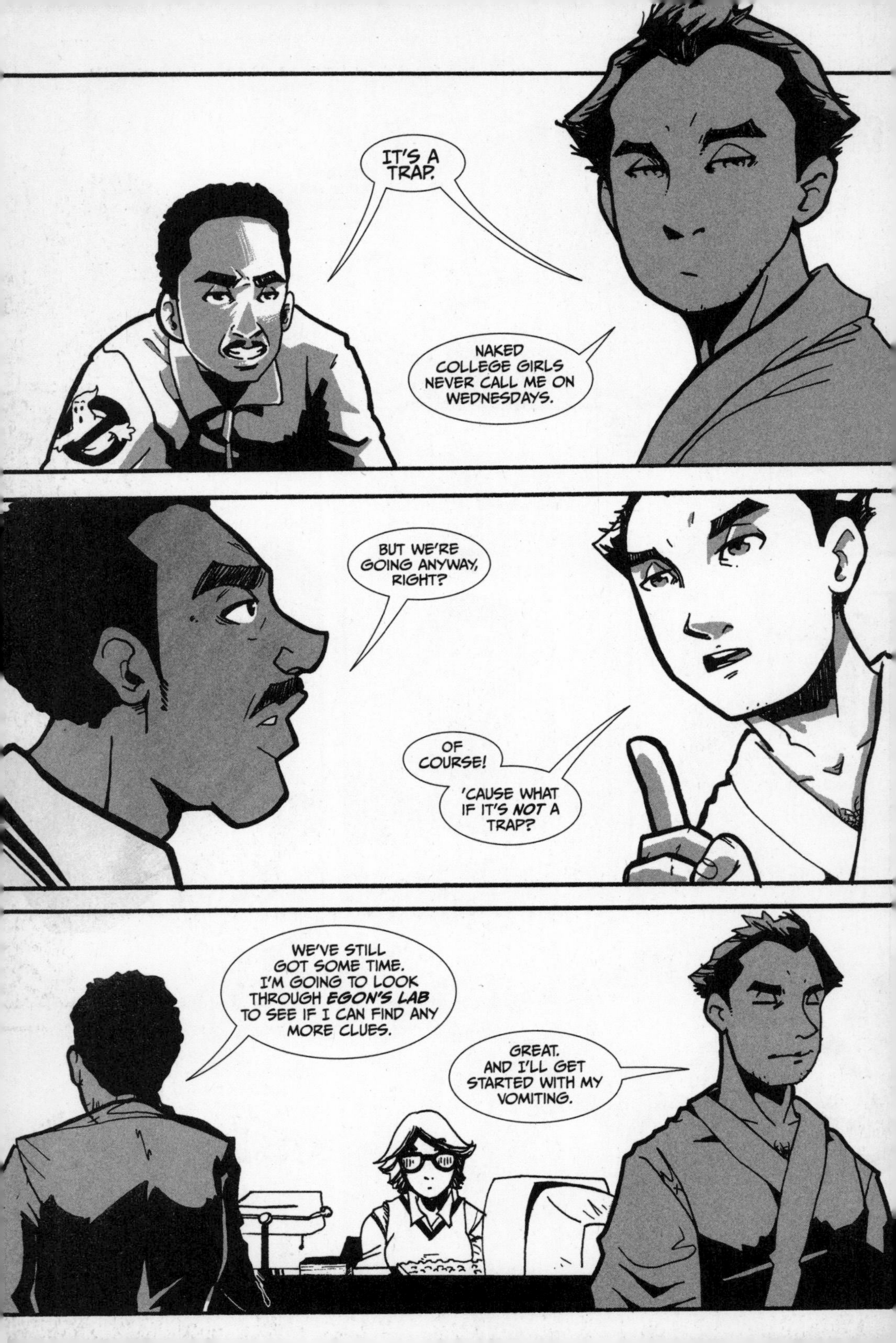
IT'S A TRAP.
NAKED COLLEGE GIRLS NEVER CALL ME ON WEDNESDAYS.
BUT WE'RE GOING ANYWAY, RIGHT?
OF COURSE!
'CAUSE WHAT IF IT'S *NOT* A TRAP?
WE'VE STILL GOT SOME TIME. I'M GOING TO LOOK THROUGH ***EGON'S LAB*** TO SEE IF I CAN FIND ANY MORE CLUES.
GREAT. AND I'LL GET STARTED WITH MY VOMITING.

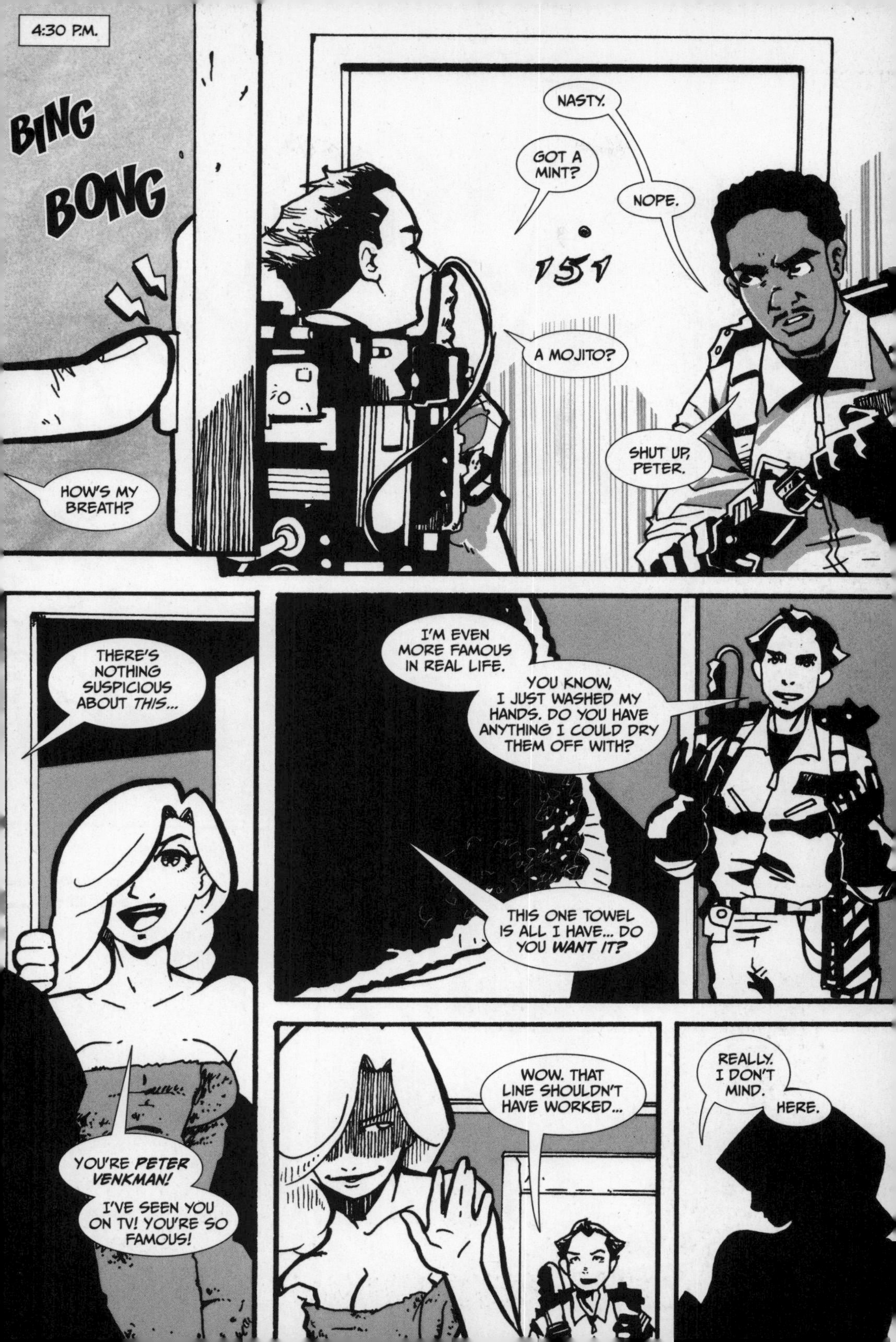
4:30 P.M.
BING
BONG
HOW'S MY BREATH?
NASTY.
GOT A MINT?
NOPE.
A MOJITO?
SHUT UP, PETER.
THERE'S NOTHING SUSPICIOUS ABOUT *THIS*...
YOU'RE *PETER VENKMAN!*
I'VE SEEN YOU ON TV! YOU'RE SO FAMOUS!
I'M EVEN MORE FAMOUS IN REAL LIFE.
YOU KNOW, I JUST WASHED MY HANDS. DO YOU HAVE ANYTHING I COULD DRY THEM OFF WITH?
THIS ONE TOWEL IS ALL I HAVE... DO YOU ***WANT IT?***
WOW. THAT LINE SHOULDN'T HAVE WORKED...
REALLY. I DON'T MIND.
HERE.

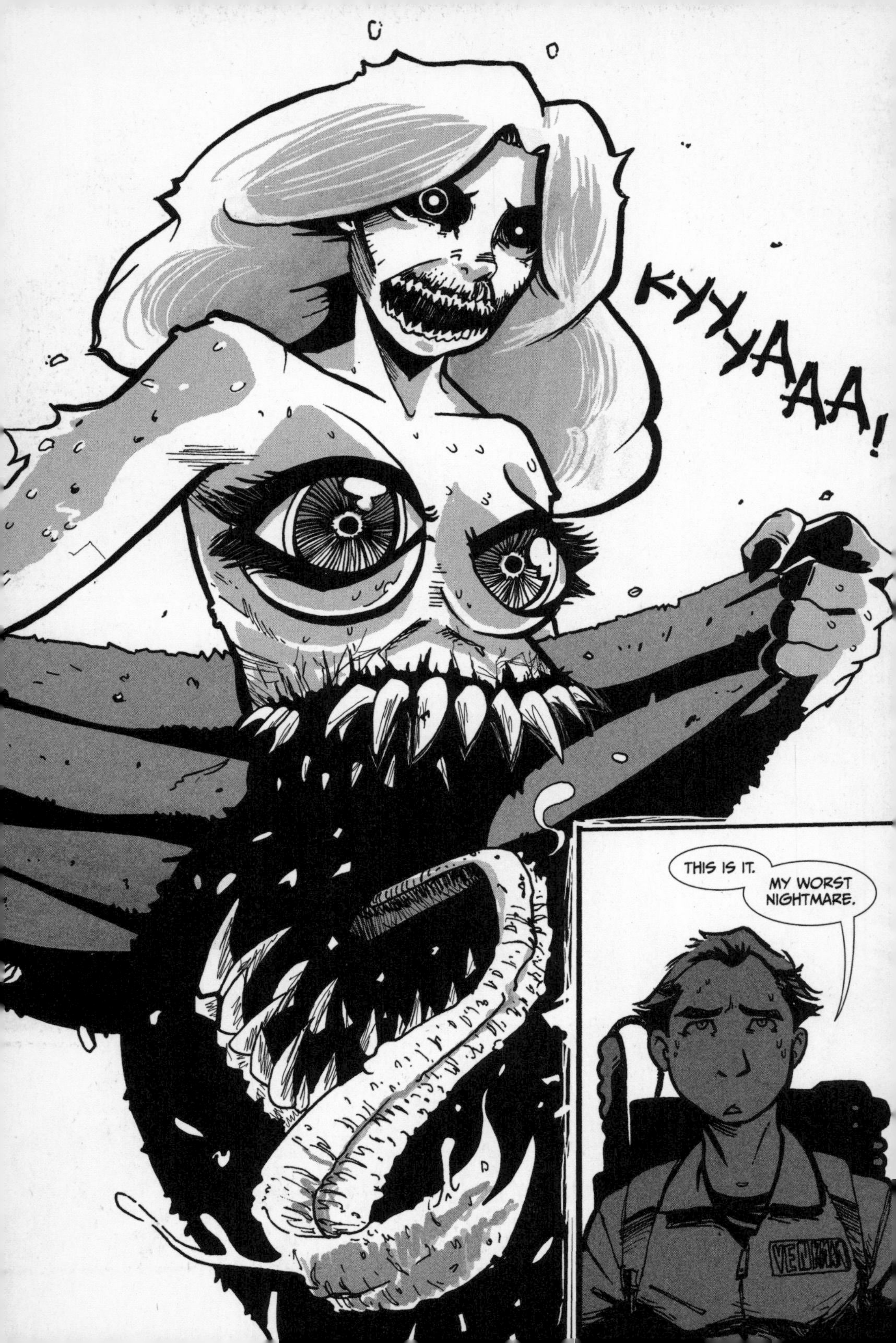
KYYYAAAA!
THIS IS IT.
MY WORST NIGHTMARE.
VENKMAN

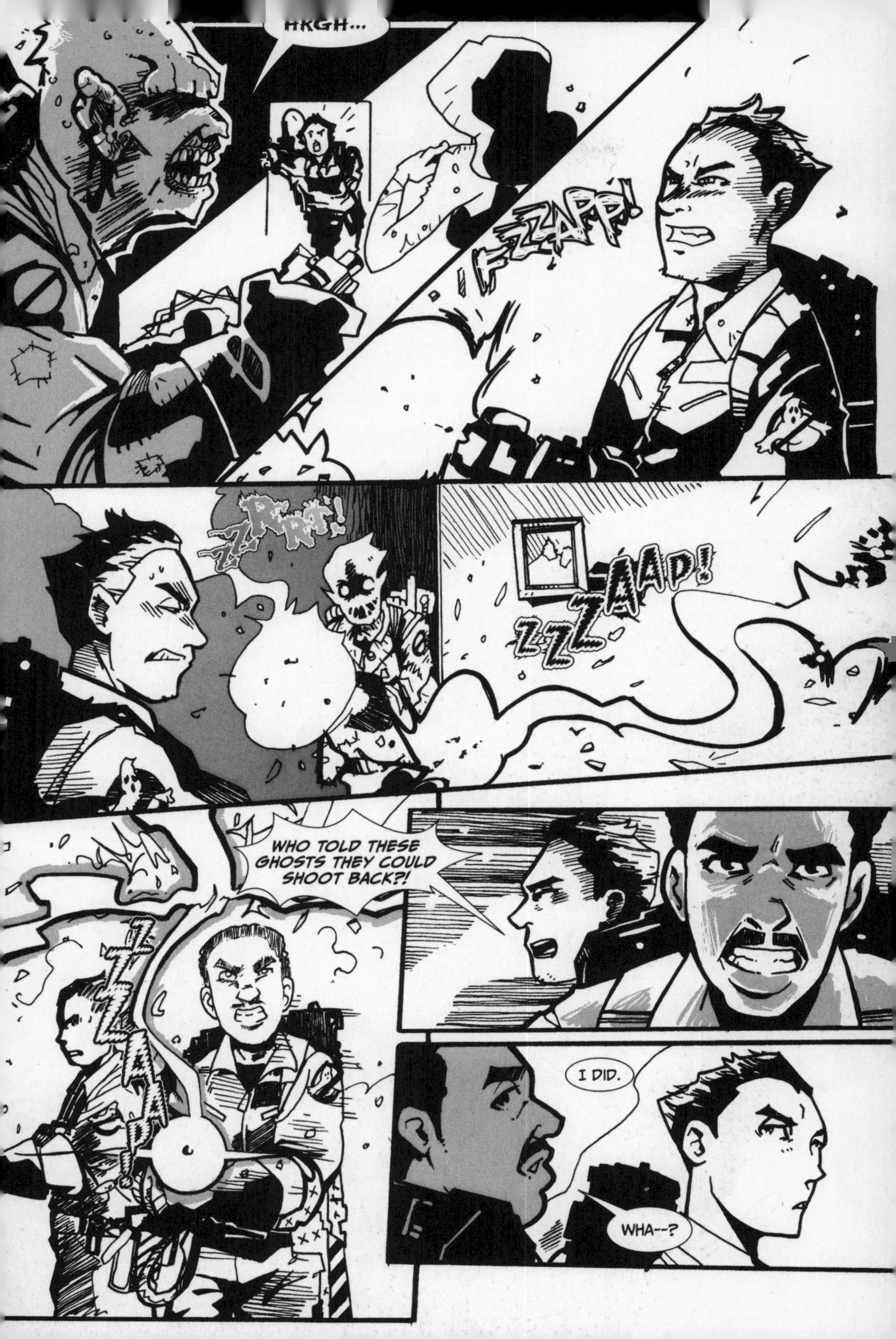
HRGH...
FZZAPP!
ZZ-RRT!
ZZZAAP!
WHO TOLD THESE GHOSTS THEY COULD SHOOT BACK?!
I DID.
WHA--?

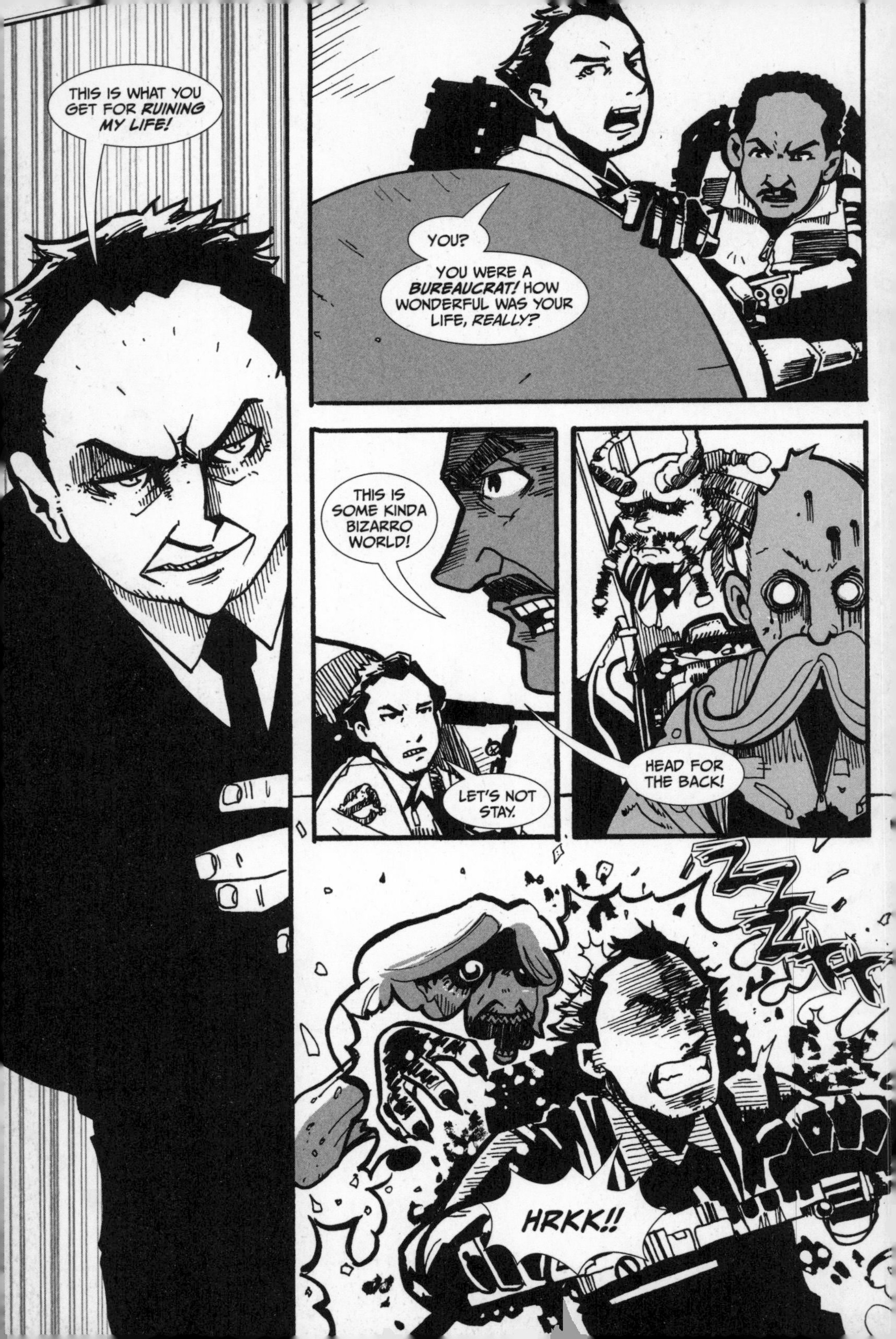
THIS IS WHAT YOU GET FOR RUINING MY LIFE!
YOU?
YOU WERE A BUREAUCRAT! HOW WONDERFUL WAS YOUR LIFE, REALLY?
THIS IS SOME KINDA BIZARRO WORLD!
LET'S NOT STAY.
HEAD FOR THE BACK!
HRKK!!

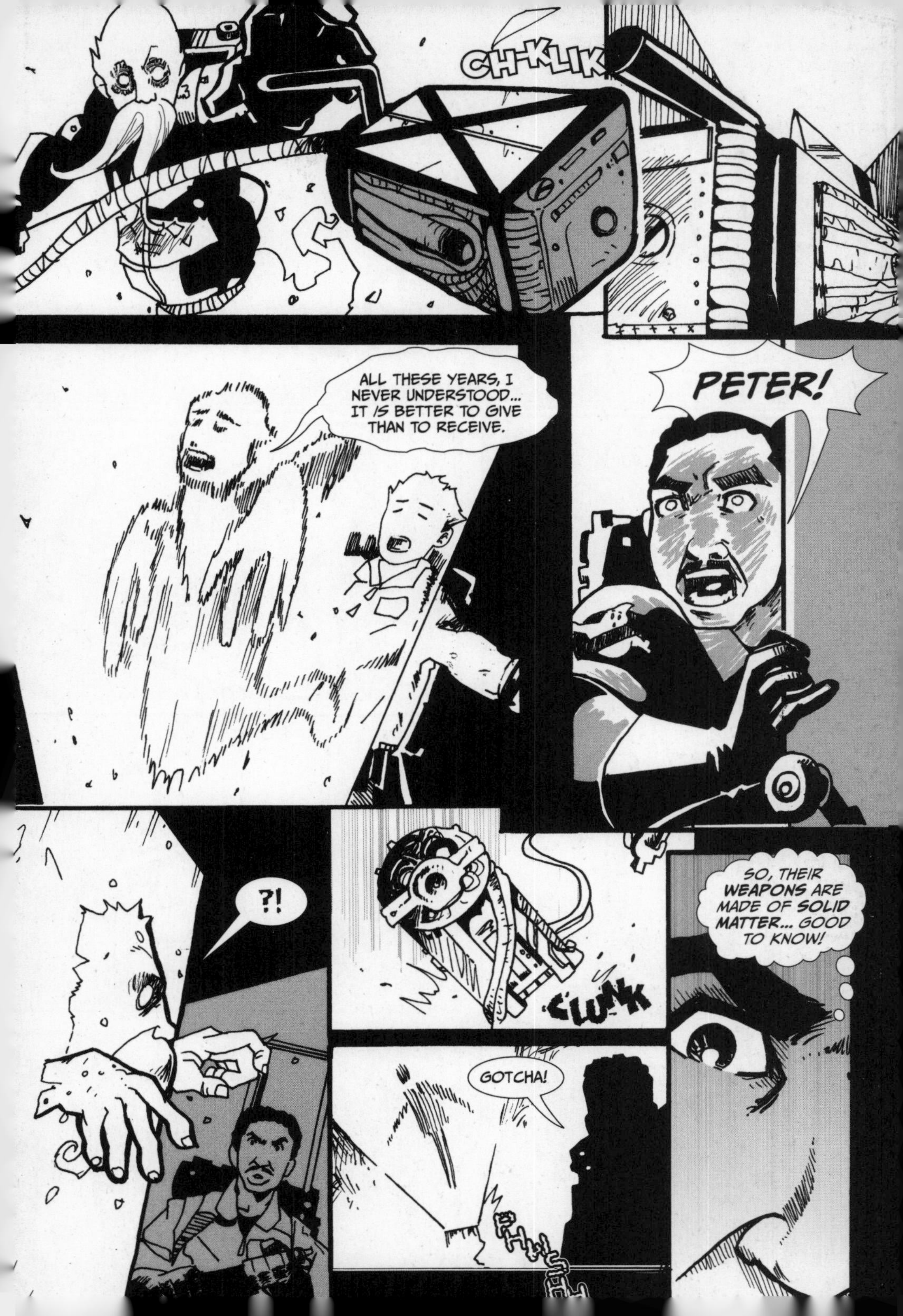
CH-KLIK
ALL THESE YEARS, I NEVER UNDERSTOOD... IT IS BETTER TO GIVE THAN TO RECEIVE.
PETER!
?!
CLUNK
SO, THEIR WEAPONS ARE MADE OF SOLID MATTER... GOOD TO KNOW!
GOTCHA!

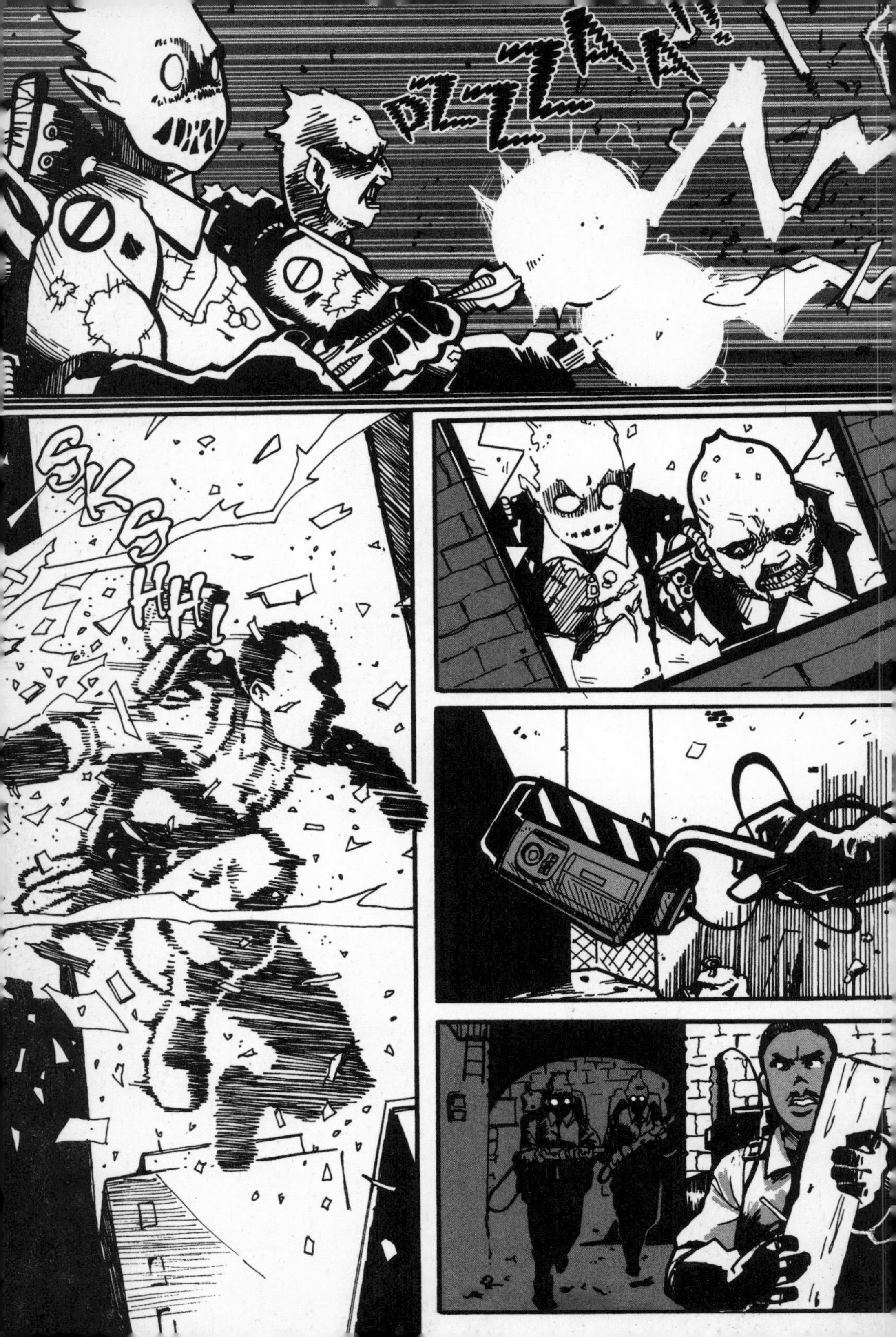
DZZZAA!
SKSHH!

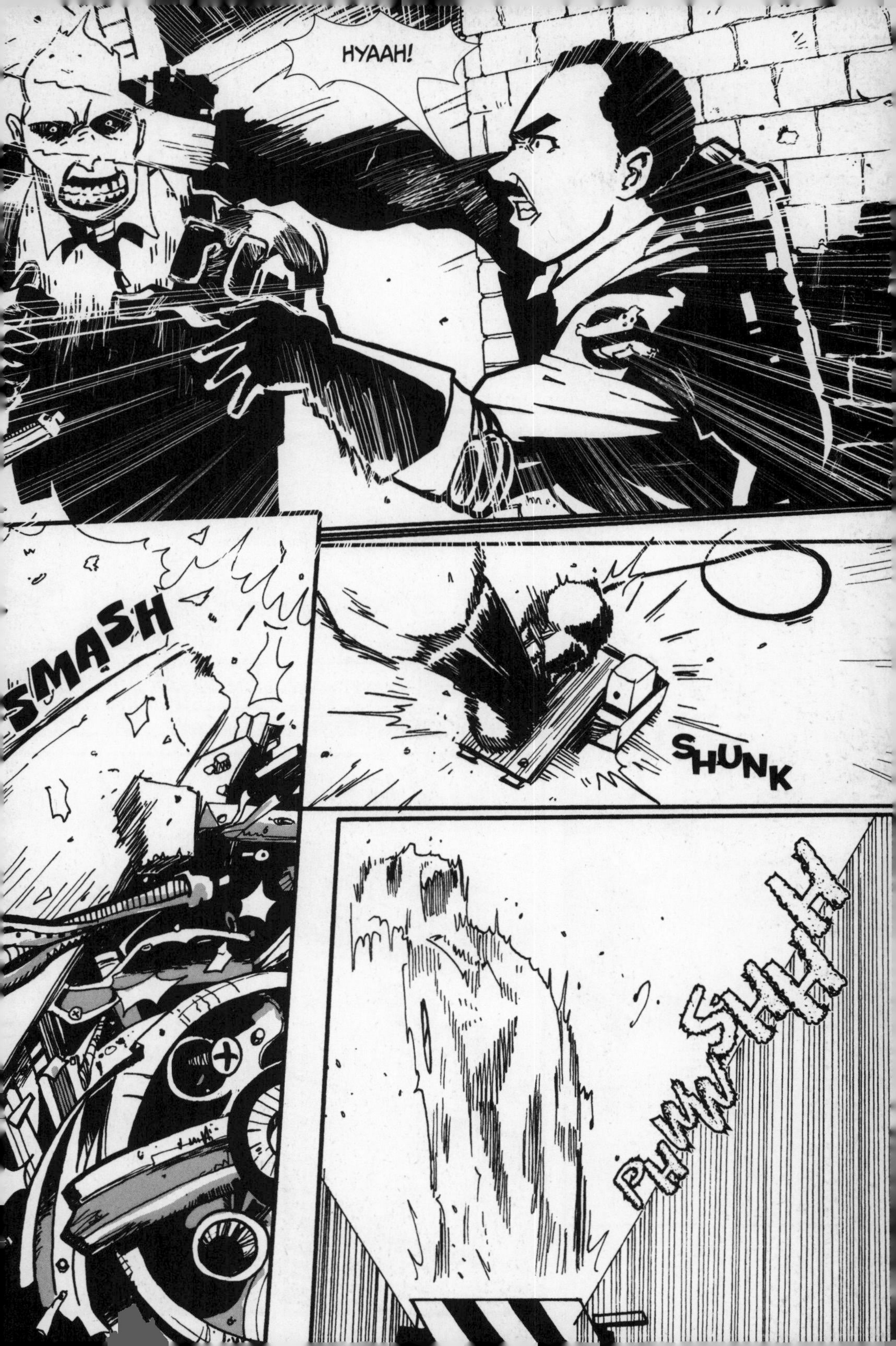
HYAAH!
SMASH
SHUNK
PHWWSHHH

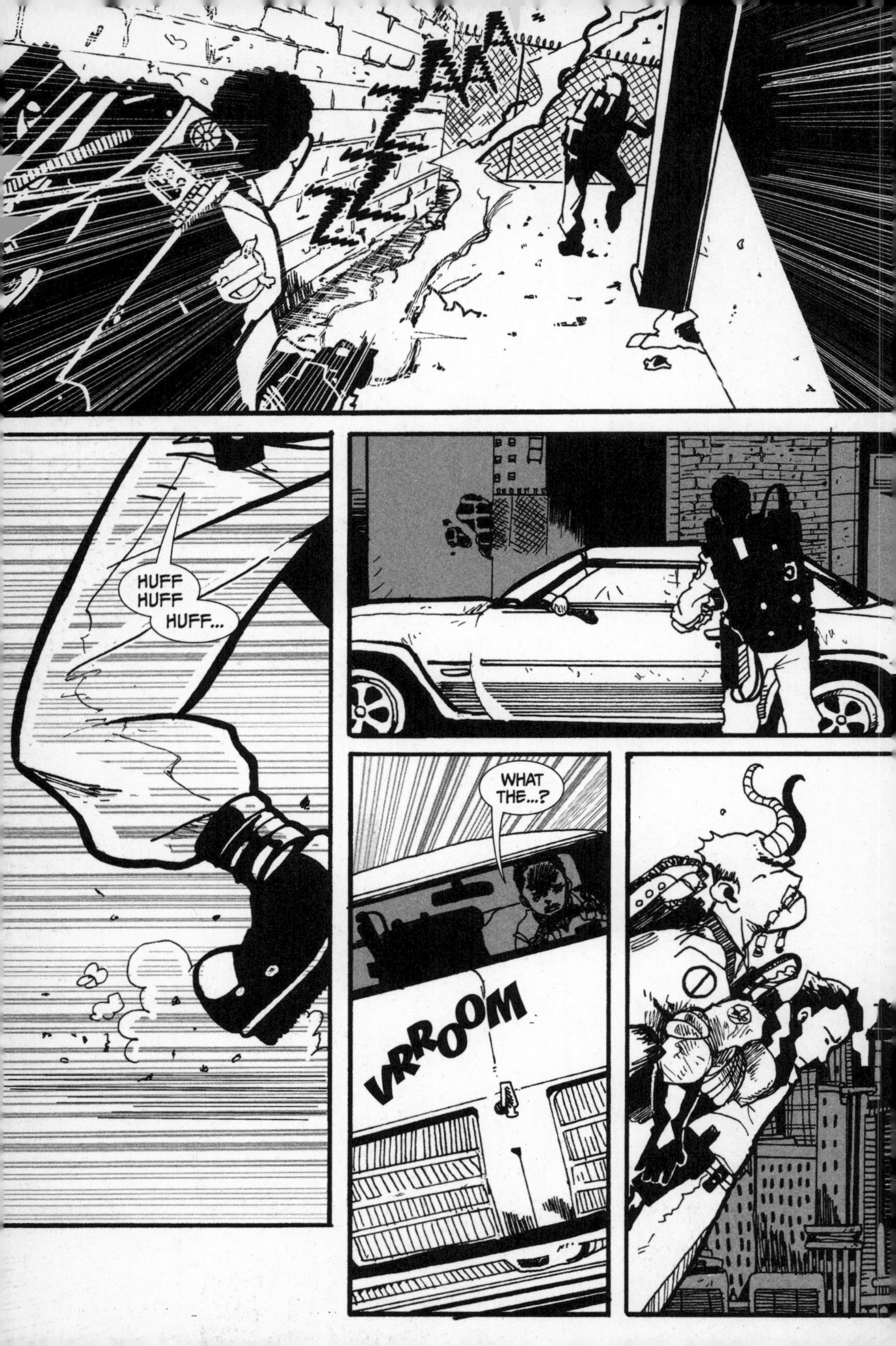
HUFF
HUFF
HUFF...
WHAT THE...?
VRROOM

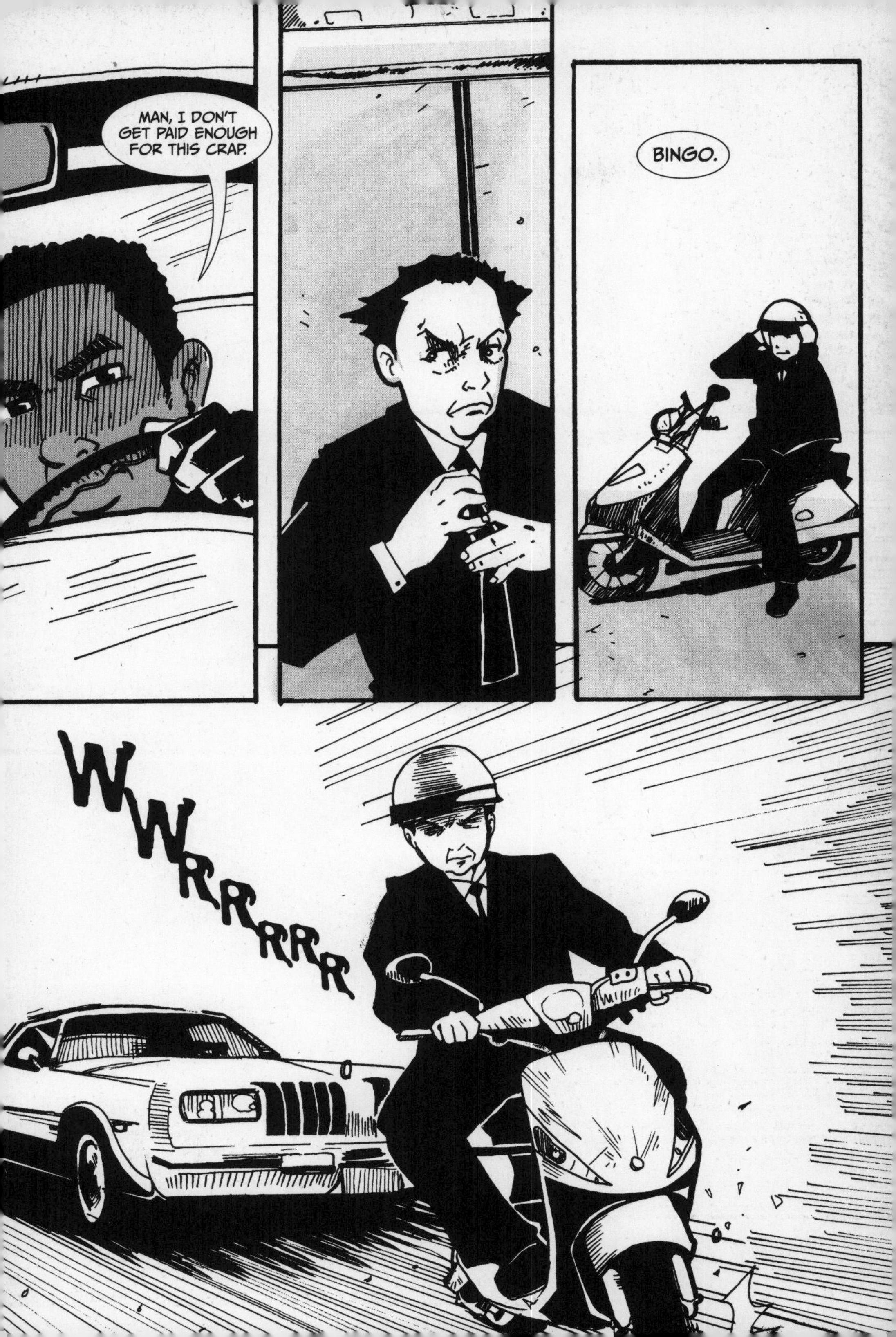
MAN, I DON'T GET PAID ENOUGH FOR THIS CRAP.
BINGO.
WWRRRRRR

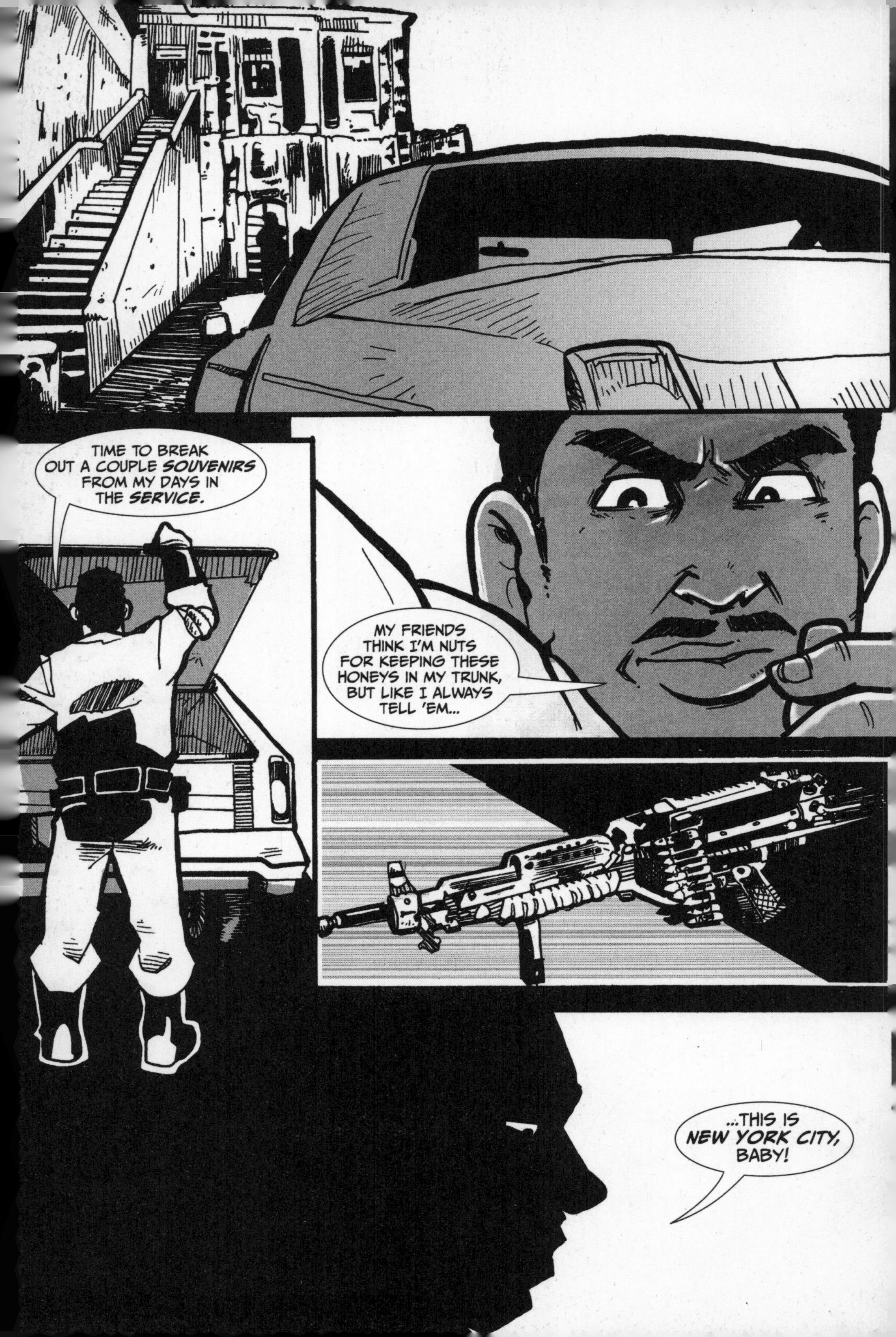
TIME TO BREAK OUT A COUPLE SOUVENIRS FROM MY DAYS IN THE SERVICE.
MY FRIENDS THINK I'M NUTS FOR KEEPING THESE HONEYS IN MY TRUNK, BUT LIKE I ALWAYS TELL 'EM...
...THIS IS NEW YORK CITY, BABY!

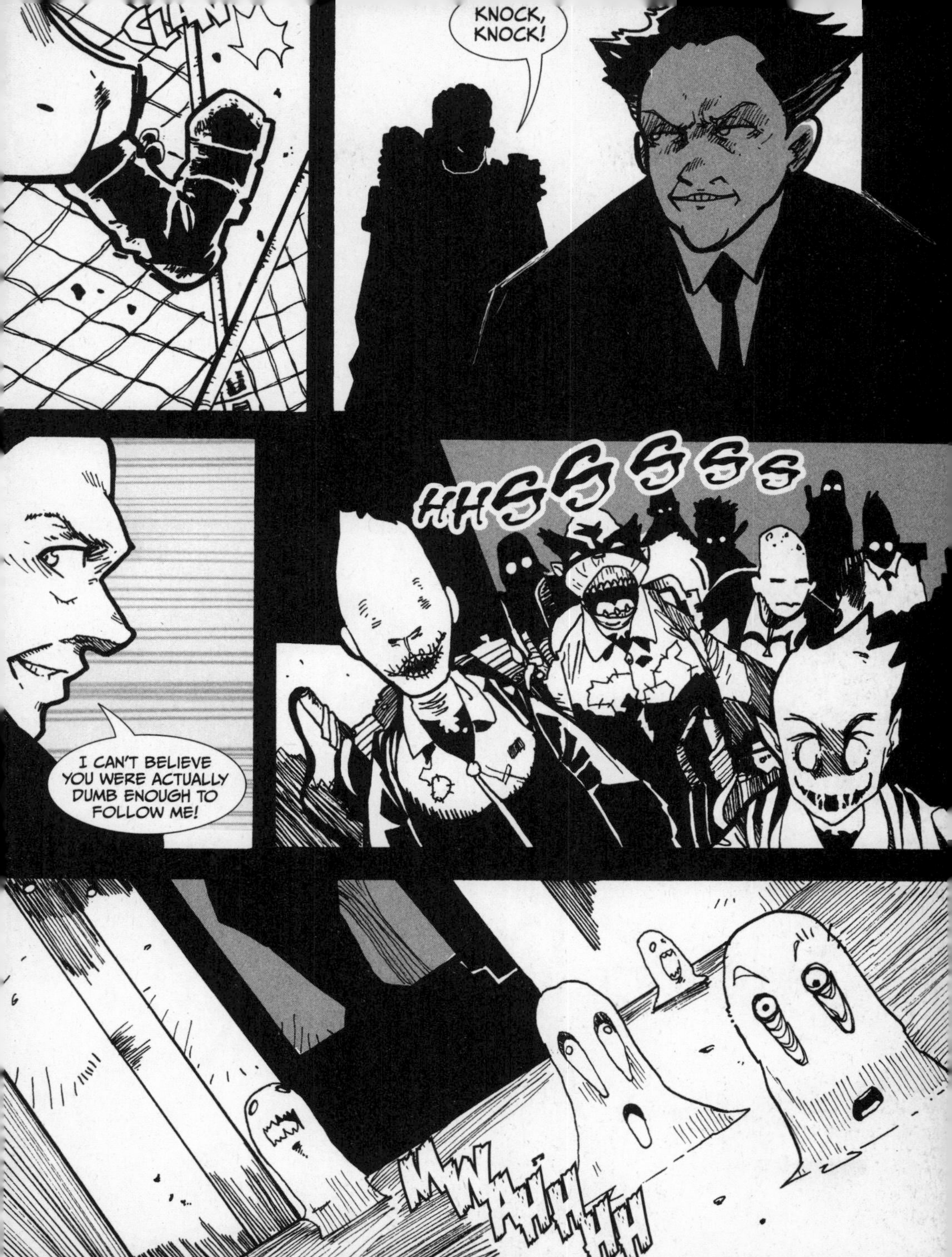
KNOCK, KNOCK!
I CAN'T BELIEVE YOU WERE ACTUALLY DUMB ENOUGH TO FOLLOW ME!
HHSSSSSS
MWAHHHHH

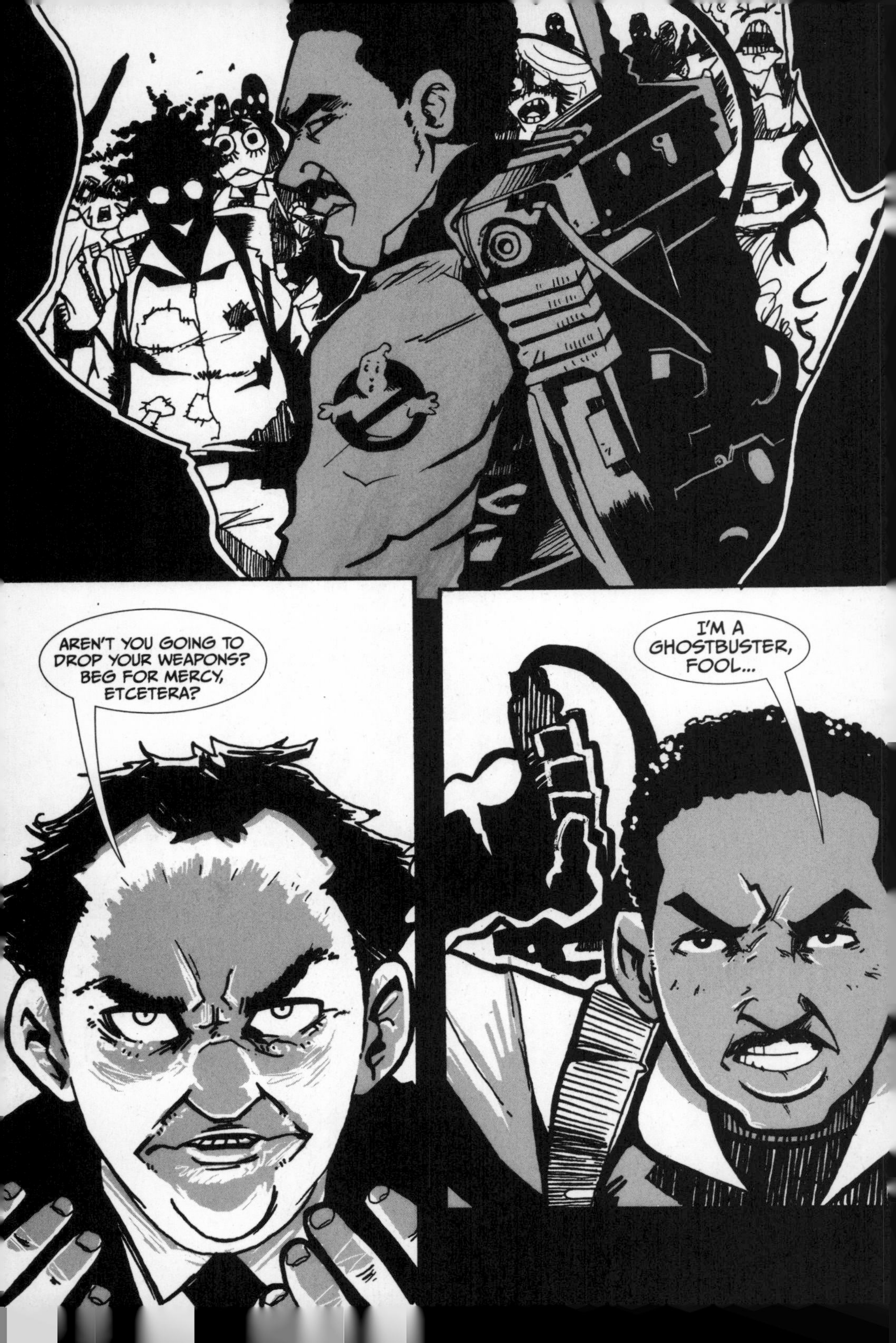
AREN'T YOU GOING TO DROP YOUR WEAPONS? BEG FOR MERCY, ETCETERA?
I'M A GHOSTBUSTER, FOOL...

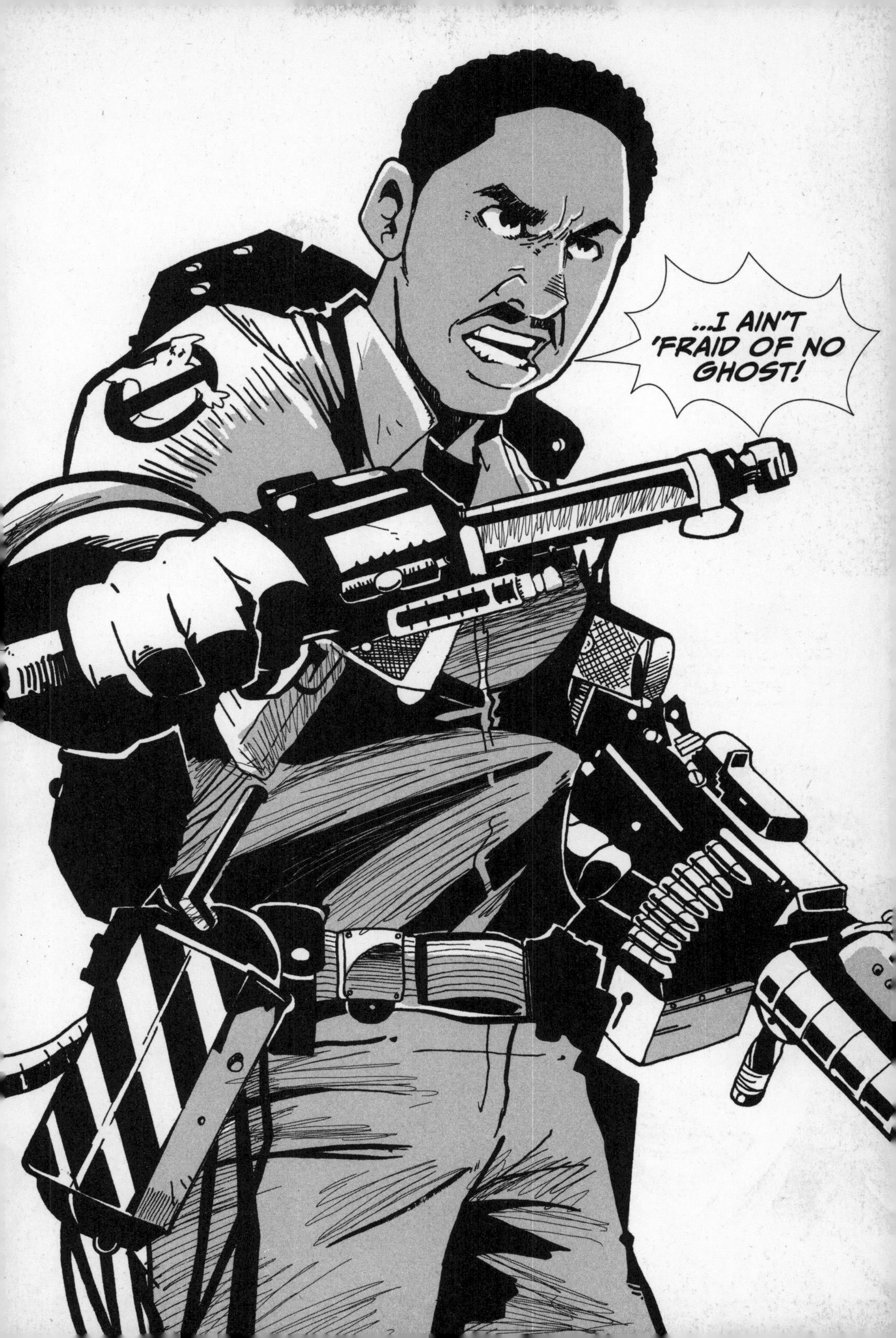
...I AIN'T 'FRAID OF NO GHOST!

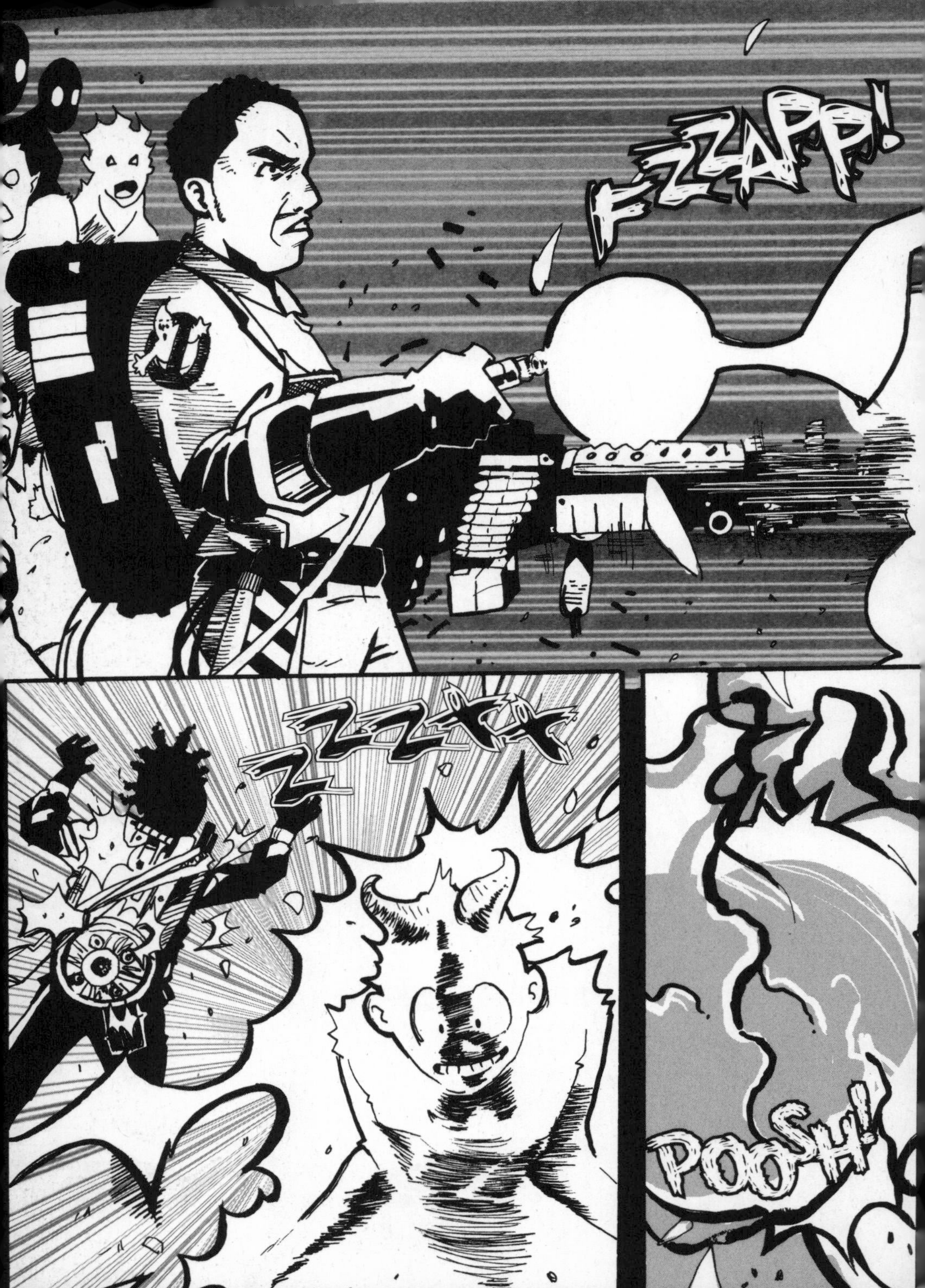
FZZAPP!
ZZZZKK
POOSH!

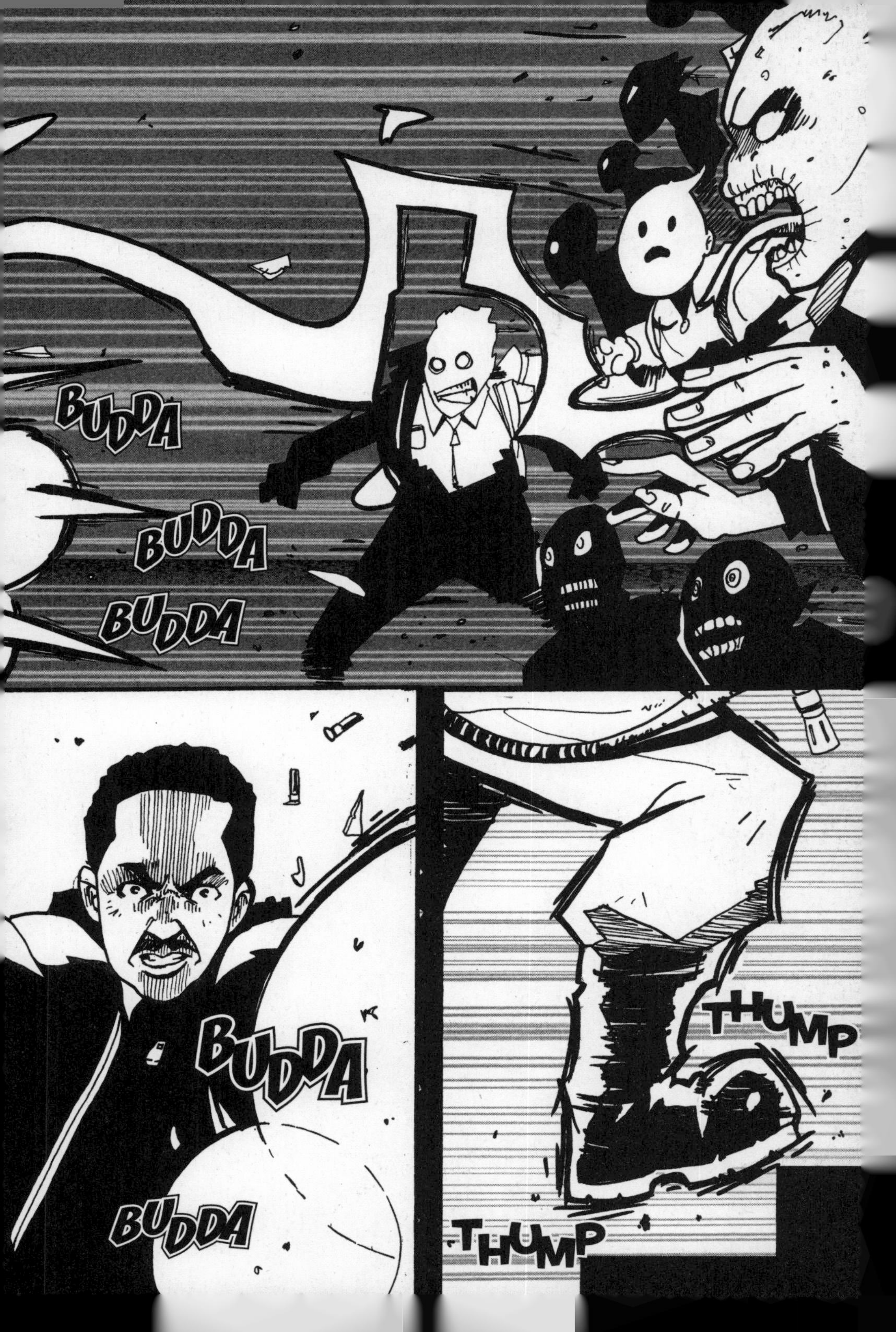
BUDDA
BUDDA
BUDDA
BUDDA
BUDDA
THUMP
THUMP

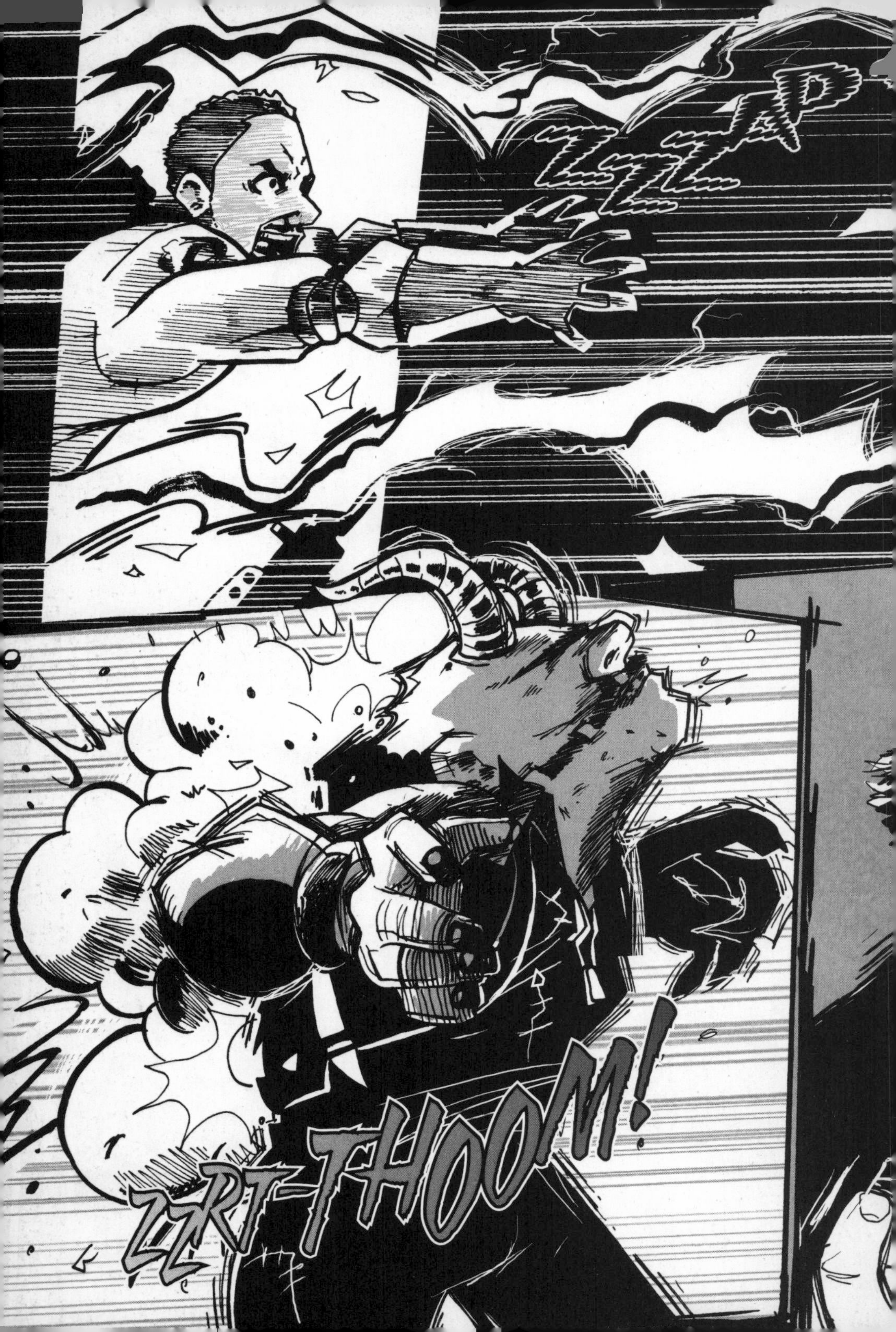
ZZZAP
ZZRT-THOOM!

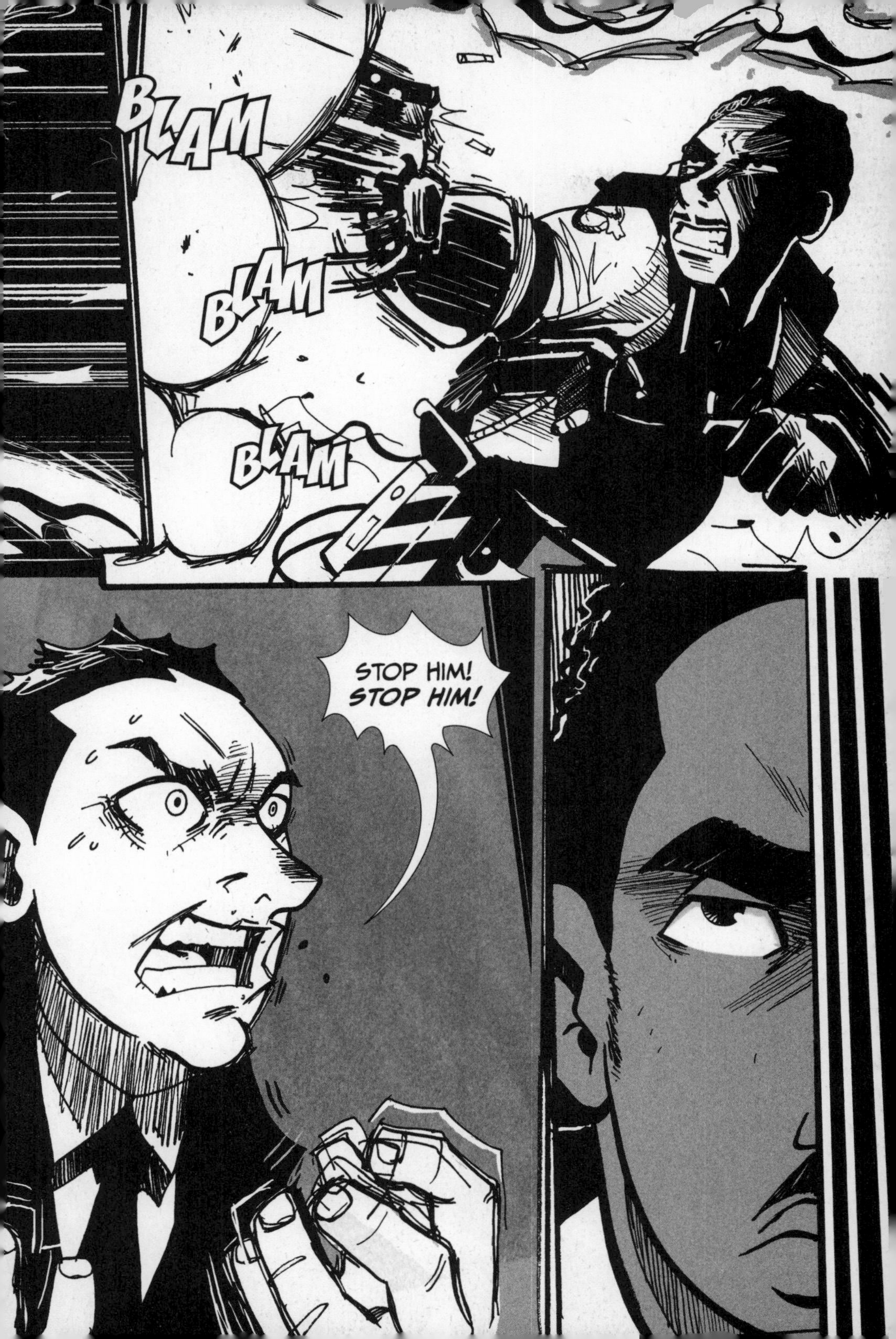
BLAM
BLAM
BLAM
STOP HIM! STOP HIM!

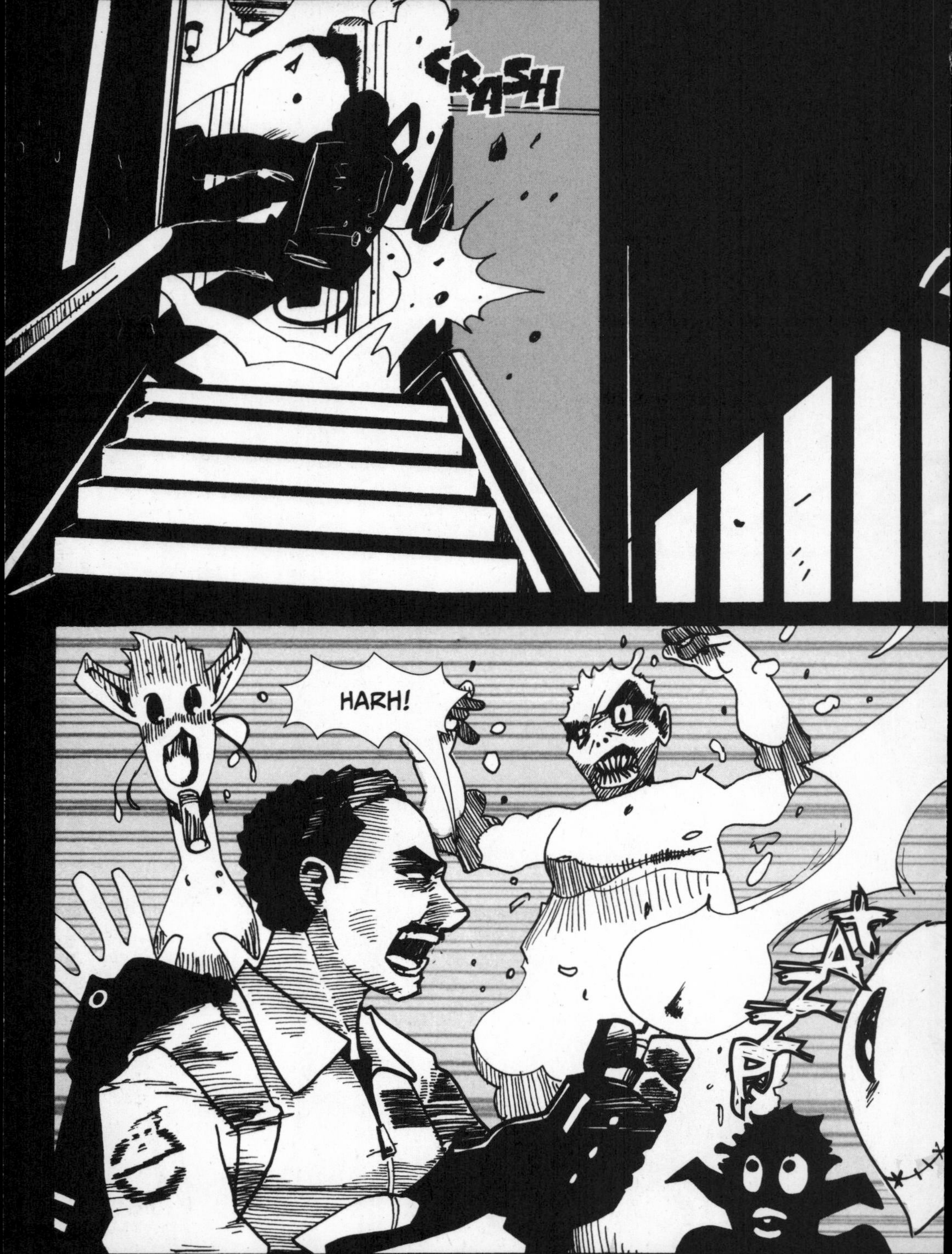
CRASH
HARH!
PZZAT

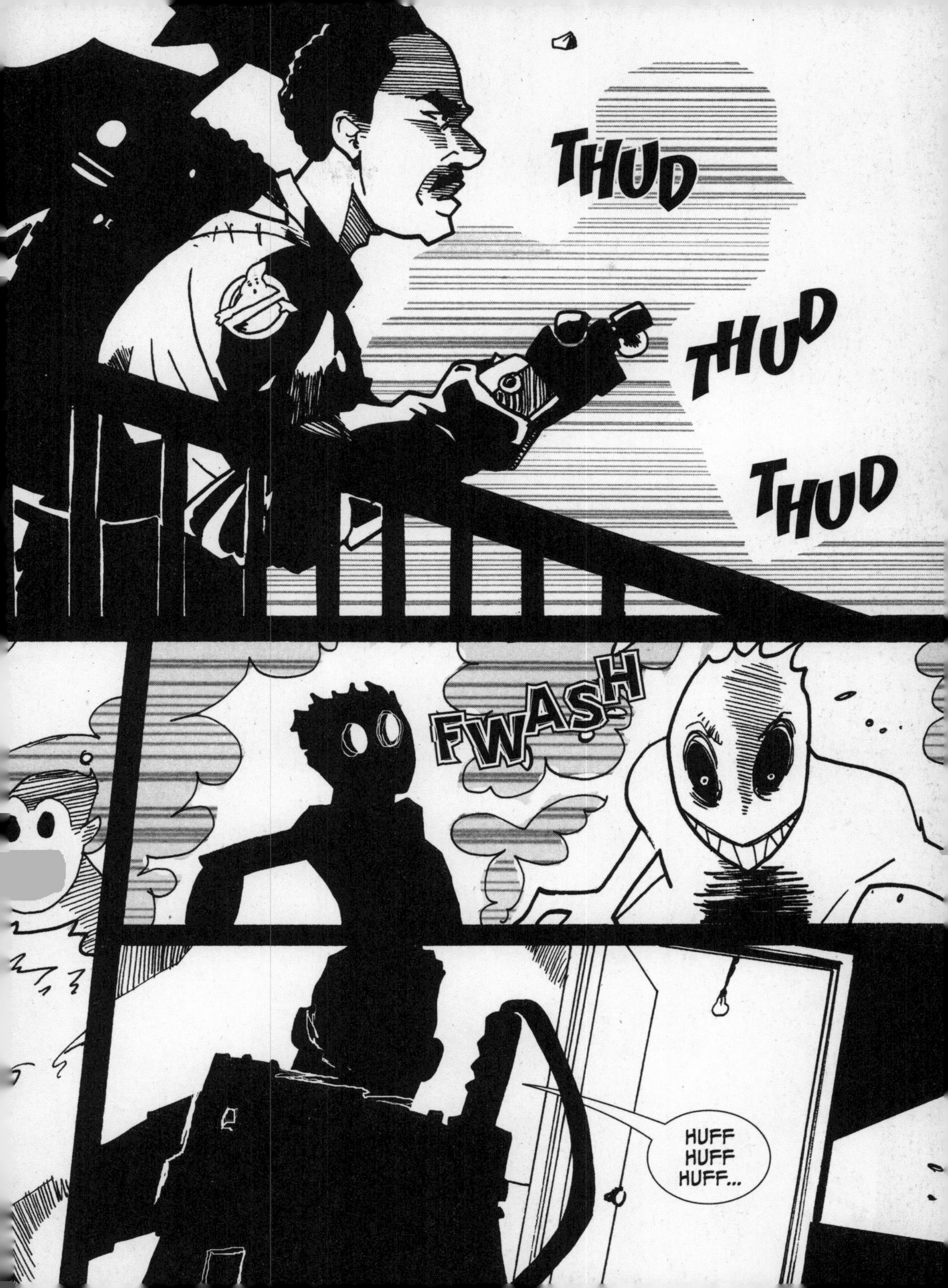
THUD
THUD
THUD
FWASH
HUFF HUFF HUFF...

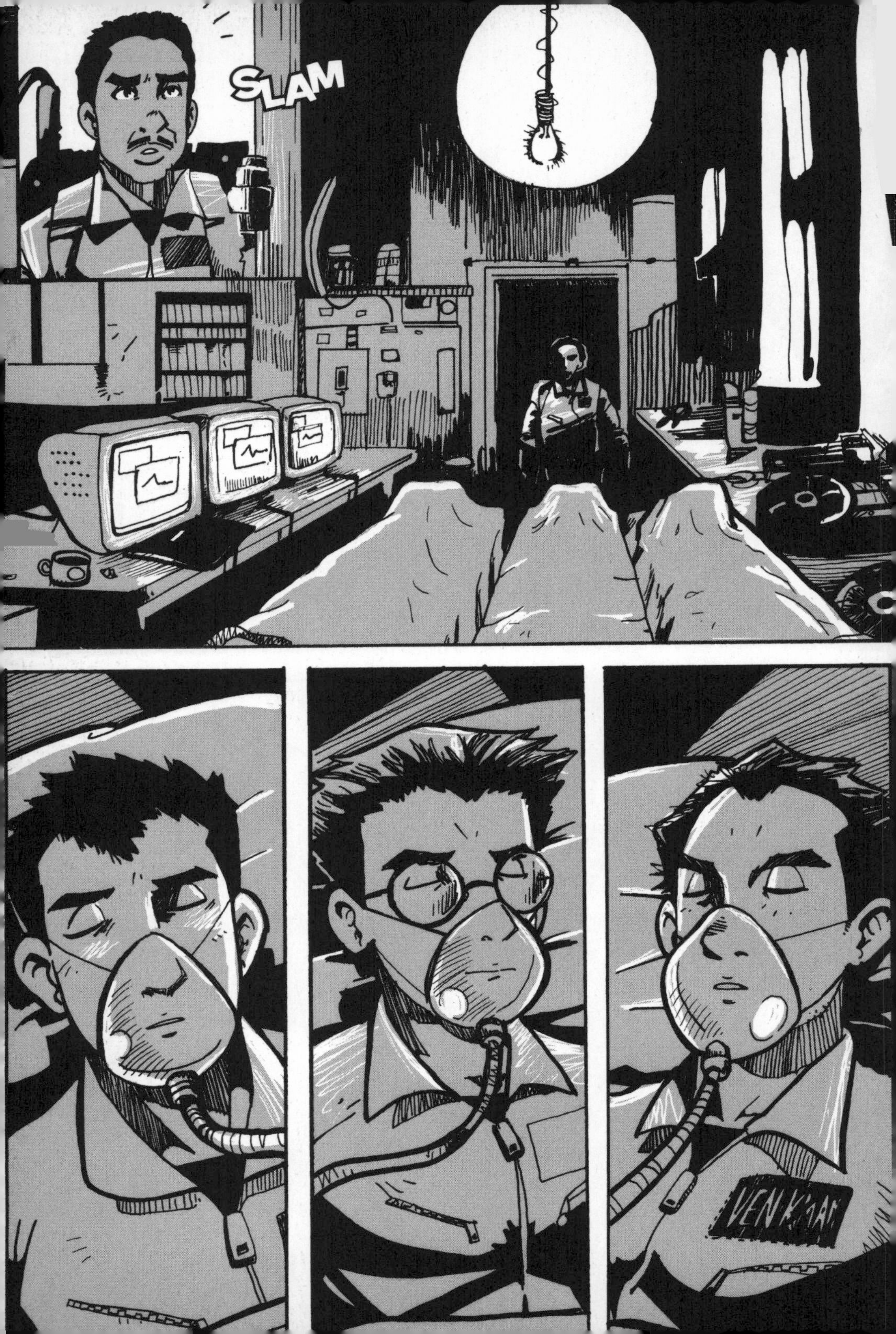
SLAM

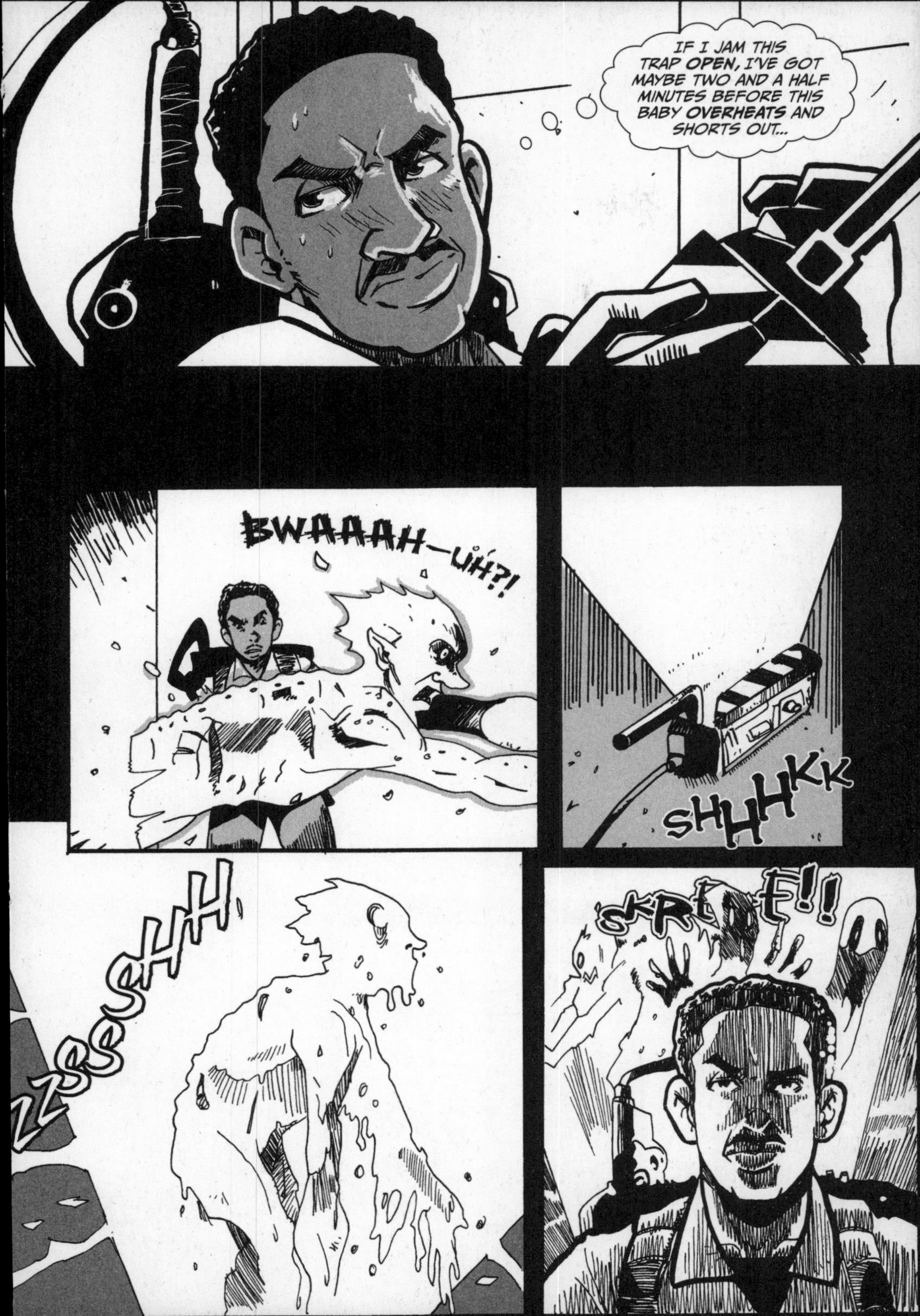
IF I JAM THIS TRAP OPEN, I'VE GOT MAYBE TWO AND A HALF MINUTES BEFORE THIS BABY OVERHEATS AND SHORTS OUT...
BWAAAH—UH?!
SHHHKK
ZZSSSSHH
SKREE!!

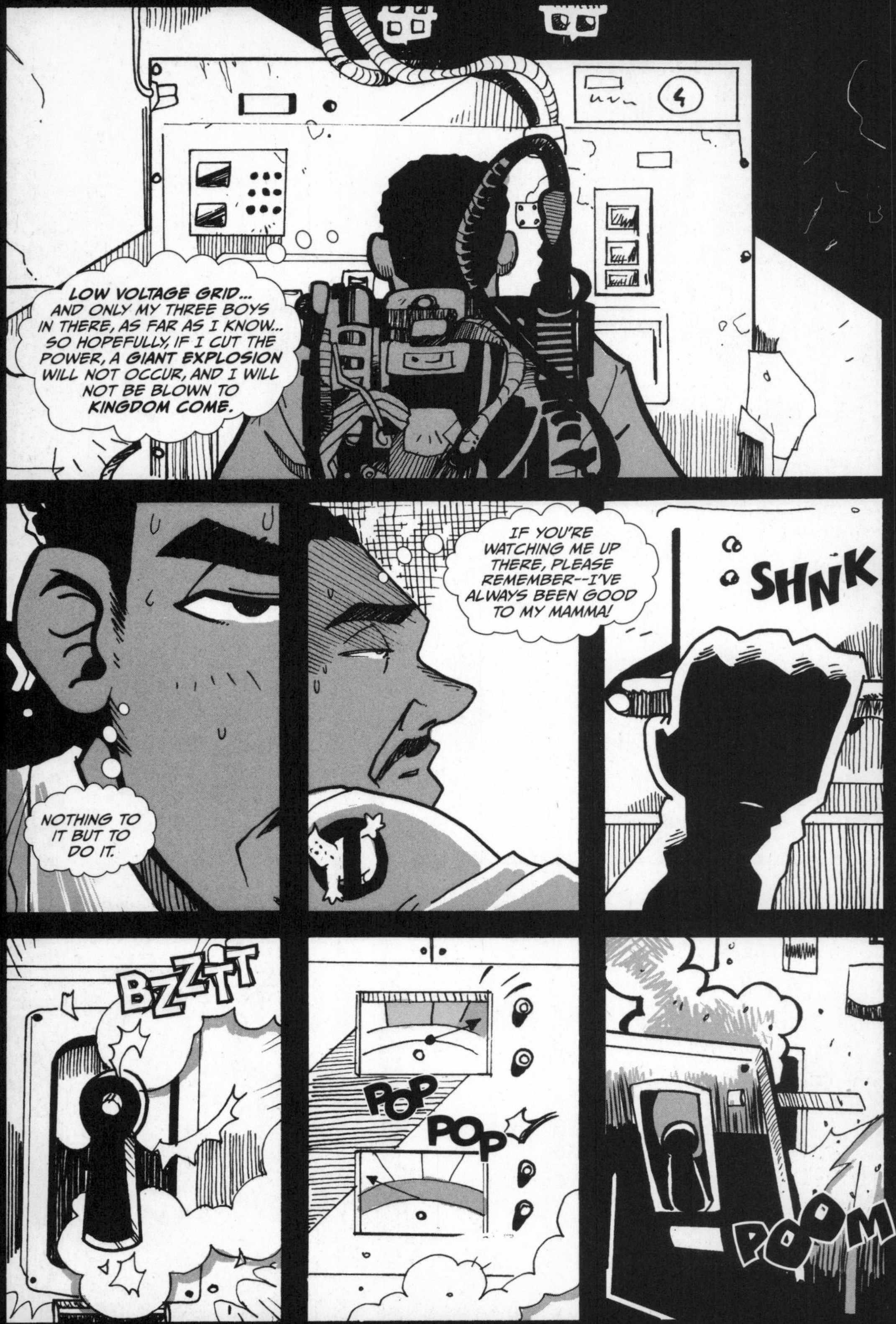
LOW VOLTAGE GRID... AND ONLY MY THREE BOYS IN THERE, AS FAR AS I KNOW... SO HOPEFULLY, IF I CUT THE POWER, A GIANT EXPLOSION WILL NOT OCCUR, AND I WILL NOT BE BLOWN TO KINGDOM COME.
NOTHING TO IT BUT TO DO IT.
IF YOU'RE WATCHING ME UP THERE, PLEASE REMEMBER--I'VE ALWAYS BEEN GOOD TO MY MAMMA!
SHNK
BZZTT
POP
POP
POOM

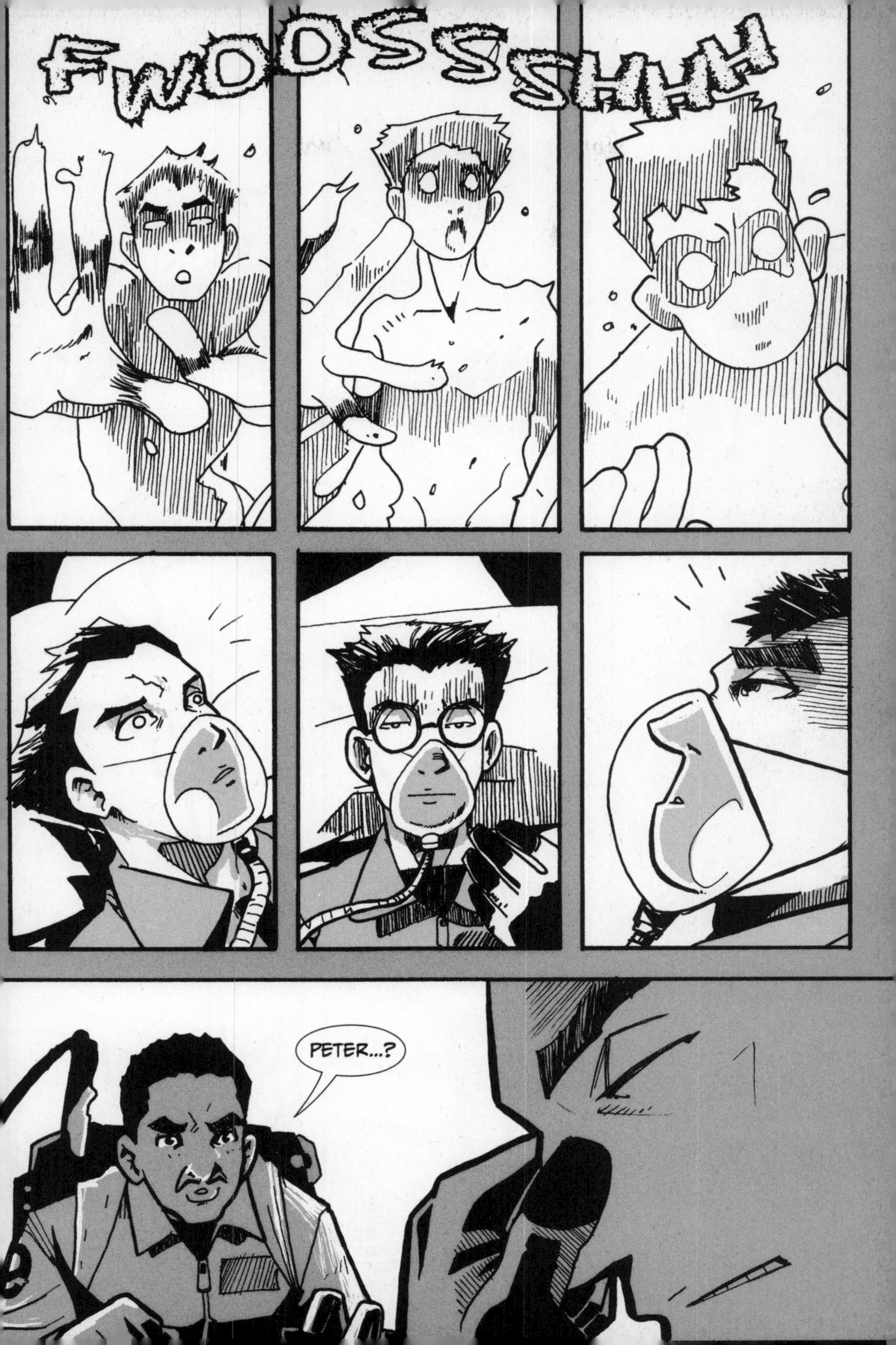
FWOOSSSHHH
PETER...?

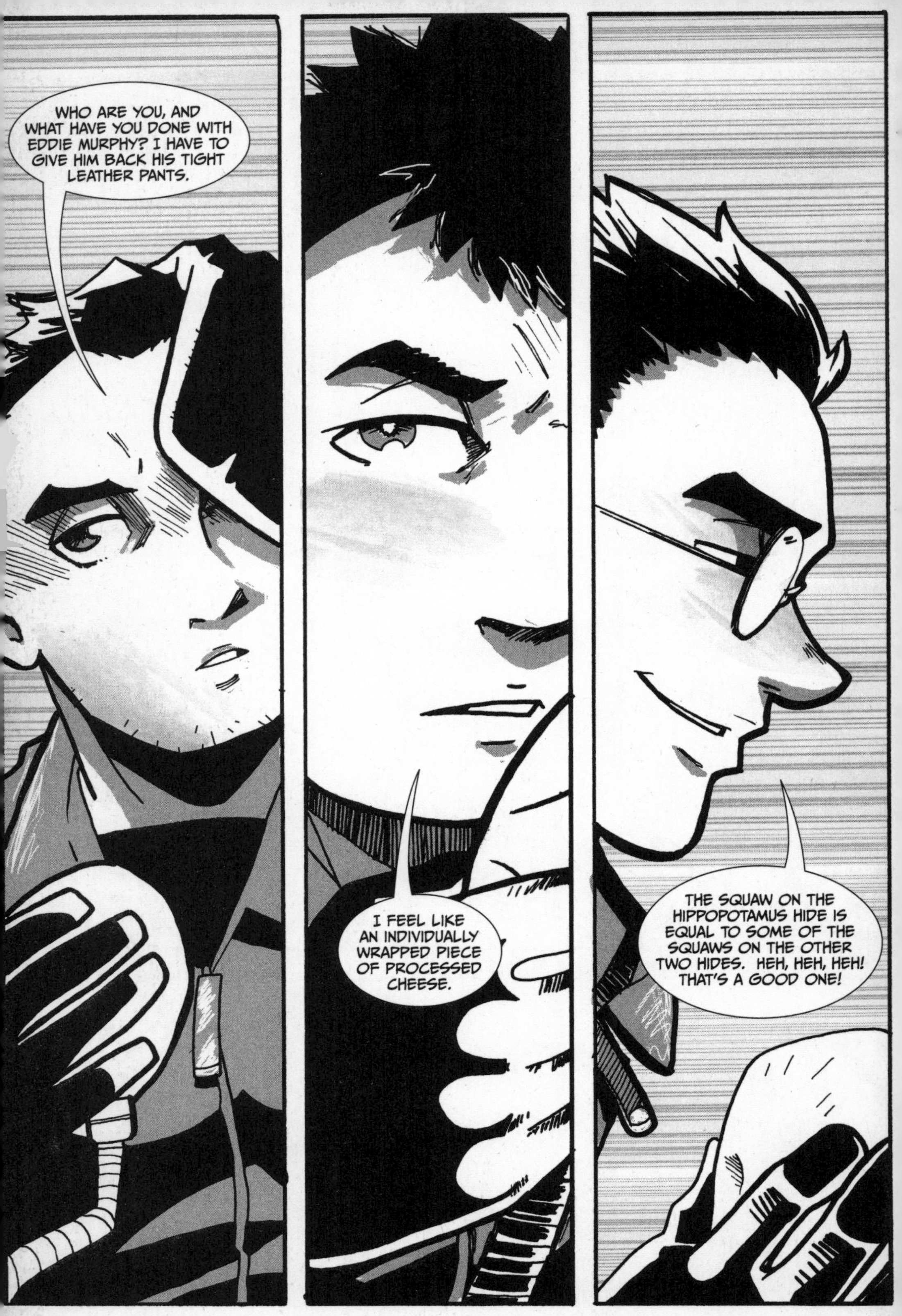
WHO ARE YOU, AND WHAT HAVE YOU DONE WITH EDDIE MURPHY? I HAVE TO GIVE HIM BACK HIS TIGHT LEATHER PANTS.
I FEEL LIKE AN INDIVIDUALLY WRAPPED PIECE OF PROCESSED CHEESE.
THE SQUAW ON THE HIPPOPOTAMUS HIDE IS EQUAL TO SOME OF THE SQUAWS ON THE OTHER TWO HIDES. HEH, HEH, HEH! THAT'S A GOOD ONE!

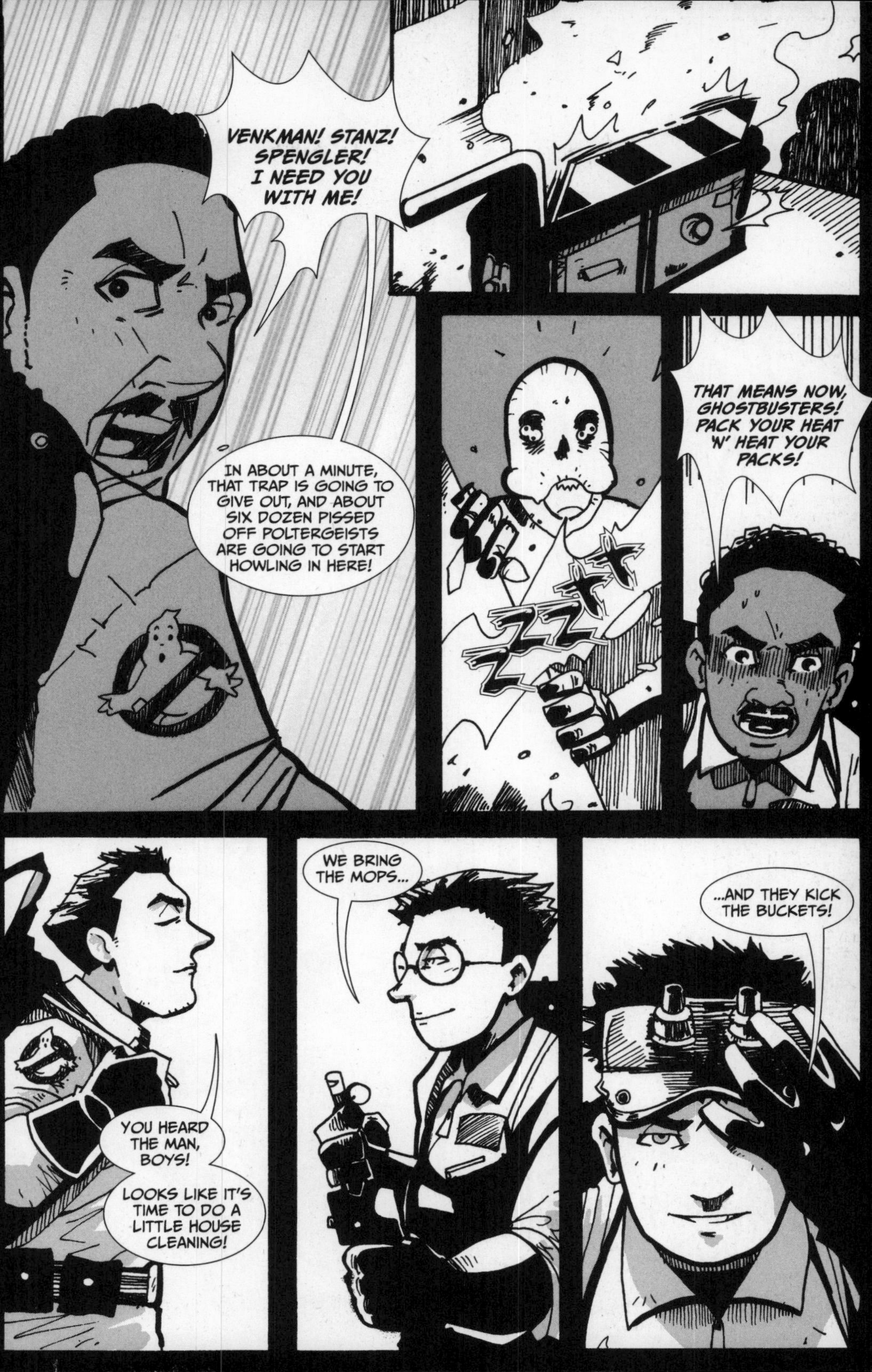
VENKMAN! STANZ! SPENGLER! I NEED YOU WITH ME!
IN ABOUT A MINUTE, THAT TRAP IS GOING TO GIVE OUT, AND ABOUT SIX DOZEN PISSED OFF POLTERGEISTS ARE GOING TO START HOWLING IN HERE!
THAT MEANS NOW, GHOSTBUSTERS! PACK YOUR HEAT 'N' HEAT YOUR PACKS!
YOU HEARD THE MAN, BOYS!
LOOKS LIKE IT'S TIME TO DO A LITTLE HOUSE CLEANING!
WE BRING THE MOPS...
...AND THEY KICK THE BUCKETS!

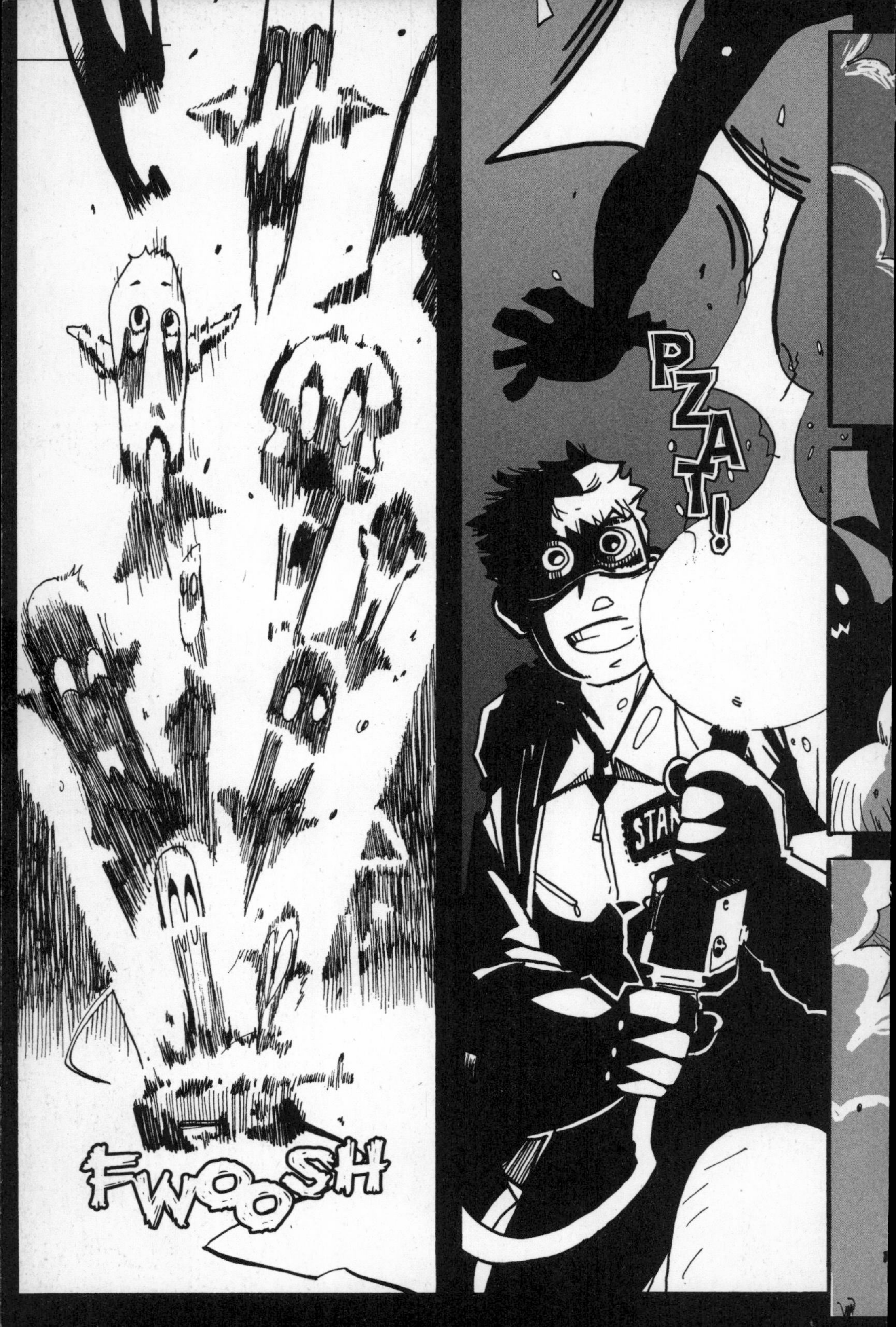
PZAT!
STAN
FWOOSH

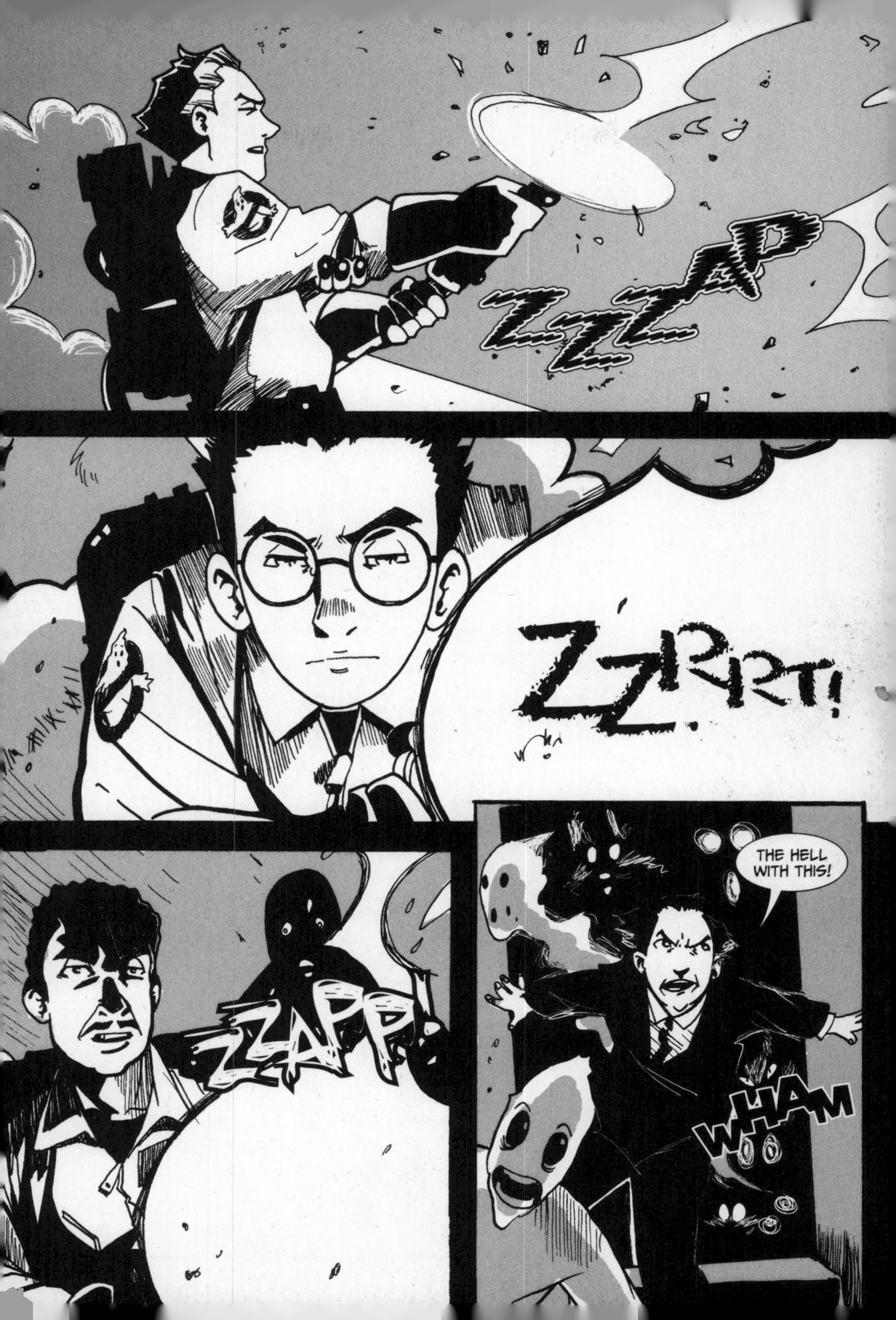
ZZZAP
ZZRRT!
ZZAPP!
THE HELL WITH THIS!
WHAM

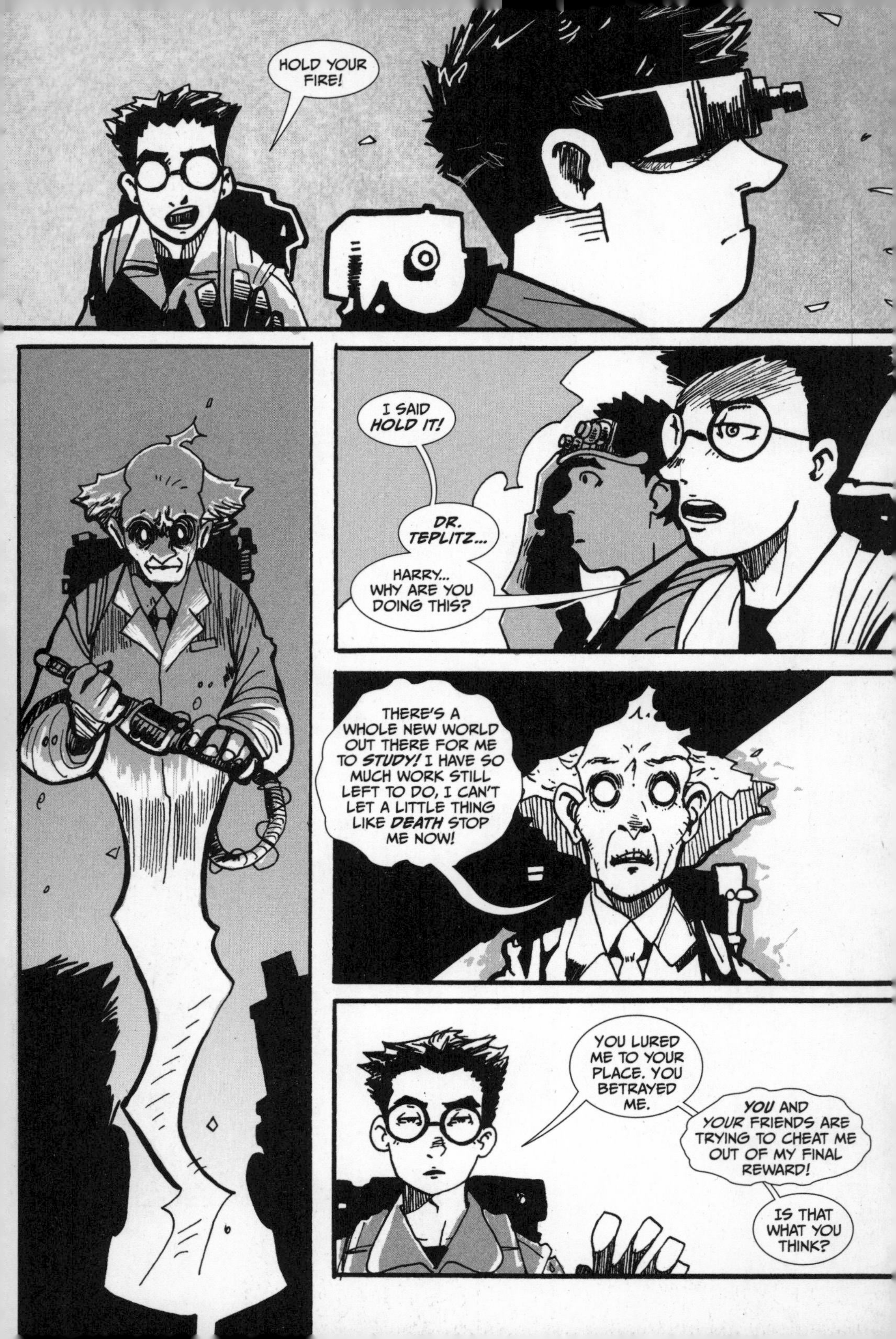
HOLD YOUR FIRE!
I SAID HOLD IT!
DR. TEPLITZ...
HARRY... WHY ARE YOU DOING THIS?
THERE'S A WHOLE NEW WORLD OUT THERE FOR ME TO STUDY! I HAVE SO MUCH WORK STILL LEFT TO DO, I CAN'T LET A LITTLE THING LIKE DEATH STOP ME NOW!
YOU LURED ME TO YOUR PLACE. YOU BETRAYED ME.
YOU AND YOUR FRIENDS ARE TRYING TO CHEAT ME OUT OF MY FINAL REWARD!
IS THAT WHAT YOU THINK?

THERE ARE MANY LIKE ME, DR. SPENGLER, WHO WANT TO ENJOY OUR AFTERLIVES *HERE ON EARTH*, THANK YOU VERY MUCH. SO, WHEN *MR. HARDEMEYER* MADE CONTACT WITH SOME OF MY ASSOCIATES, WE AGREED THAT YOU AND YOUR FRIENDS REALLY MUST BE STOPPED.

I ANALYZED THE *SCHEMATICS* HE PROVIDED US, AND FOUND THAT BY SIMPLY INVERTING SOME OF THE PROCESSES, WE COULD BUILD OUR OWN EQUIPMENT, WHICH WORKS ON THE LIVING. THE ELECTRON STREAMS WE USED ON YOU WORK MUCH THE WAY A MILD STUN GUN WOULD. THE TRAP I INVENTED STRIPS YOUR LIVING SOUL FROM YOUR BODY, LEAVING IT BEHIND IN A *COMATOSE STATE* WHILE YOUR ESSENCE IS HELD IN STASIS INDEFINITELY.

I HOPE YOU DIDN'T FIND IT *INHUMANE*. IT WASN'T PERSONAL. I LIKE YOU AND RESPECT YOU, BUT YOU LEFT

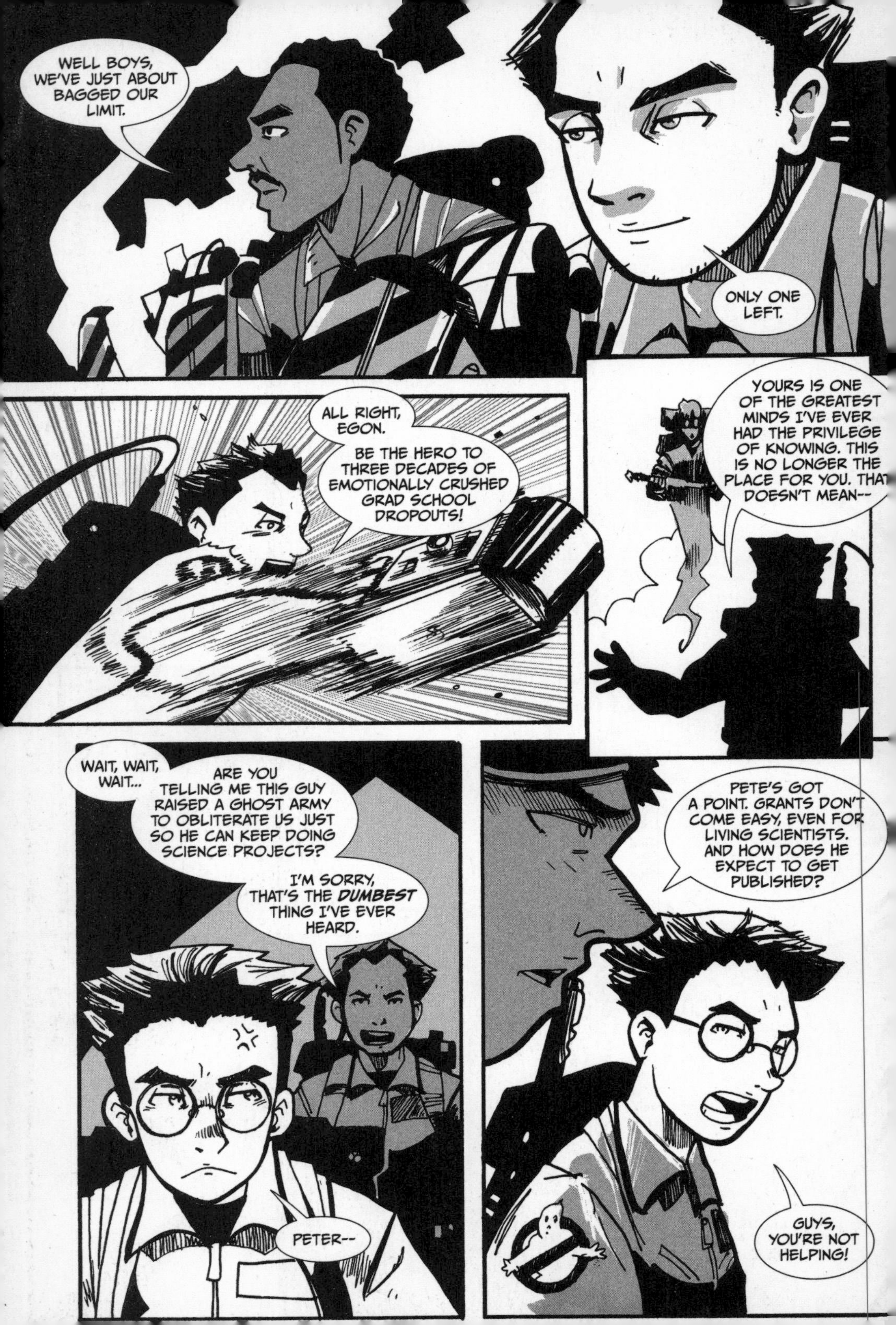

WELL BOYS, WE'VE JUST ABOUT BAGGED OUR LIMIT.
ONLY ONE LEFT.
ALL RIGHT, EGON.
BE THE HERO TO THREE DECADES OF EMOTIONALLY CRUSHED GRAD SCHOOL DROPOUTS!
YOURS IS ONE OF THE GREATEST MINDS I'VE EVER HAD THE PRIVILEGE OF KNOWING. THIS IS NO LONGER THE PLACE FOR YOU. THAT DOESN'T MEAN--
WAIT, WAIT, WAIT...
ARE YOU TELLING ME THIS GUY RAISED A GHOST ARMY TO OBLITERATE US JUST SO HE CAN KEEP DOING SCIENCE PROJECTS?
I'M SORRY, THAT'S THE *DUMBEST* THING I'VE EVER HEARD.
PETER--
PETE'S GOT A POINT. GRANTS DON'T COME EASY, EVEN FOR LIVING SCIENTISTS. AND HOW DOES HE EXPECT TO GET PUBLISHED?
GUYS, YOU'RE NOT HELPING!

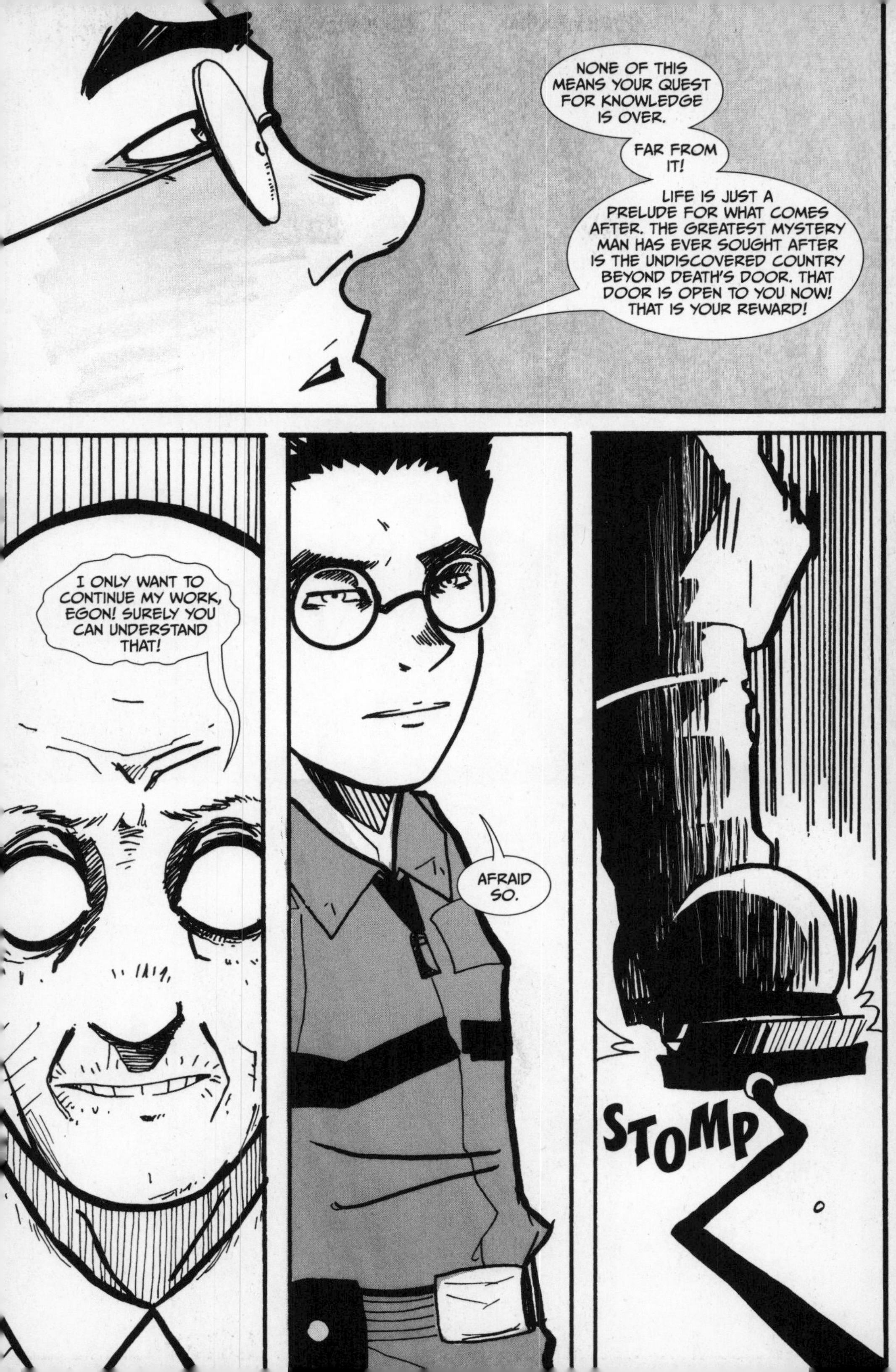
NONE OF THIS MEANS YOUR QUEST FOR KNOWLEDGE IS OVER.
FAR FROM IT!
LIFE IS JUST A PRELUDE FOR WHAT COMES AFTER. THE GREATEST MYSTERY MAN HAS EVER SOUGHT AFTER IS THE UNDISCOVERED COUNTRY BEYOND DEATH'S DOOR. THAT DOOR IS OPEN TO YOU NOW! THAT IS YOUR REWARD!
I ONLY WANT TO CONTINUE MY WORK, EGON! SURELY YOU CAN UNDERSTAND THAT!
AFRAID SO.
STOMP

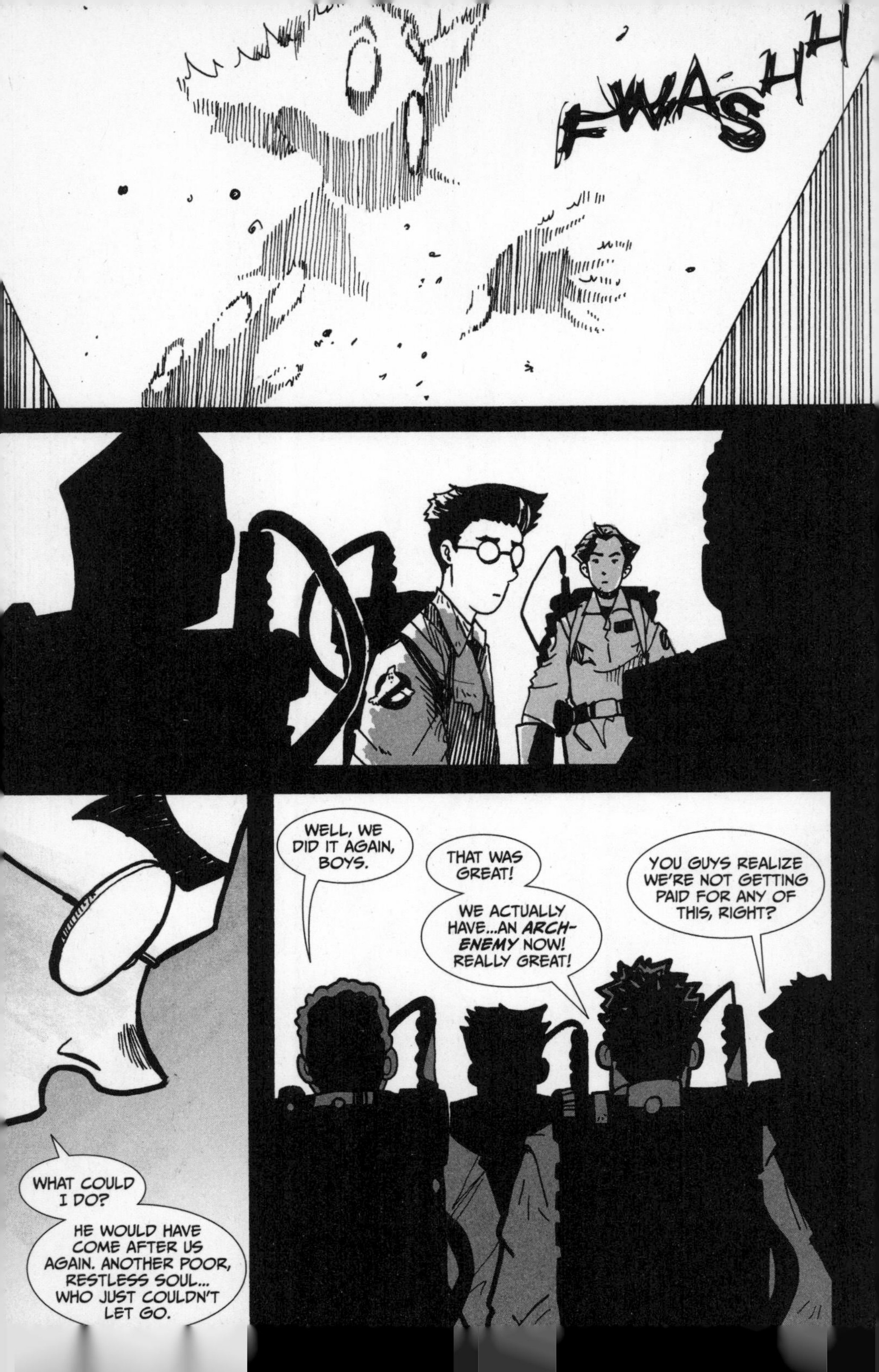
FWASHH
WHAT COULD I DO?
HE WOULD HAVE COME AFTER US AGAIN. ANOTHER POOR, RESTLESS SOUL... WHO JUST COULDN'T LET GO.
WELL, WE DID IT AGAIN, BOYS.
THAT WAS GREAT!
WE ACTUALLY HAVE...AN ARCH-ENEMY NOW! REALLY GREAT!
YOU GUYS REALIZE WE'RE NOT GETTING PAID FOR ANY OF THIS, RIGHT?

GHOSTBUSTERS™

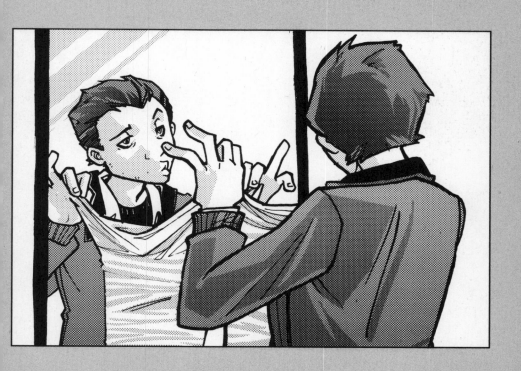

# CHAPTER VI

# THE DEVIL WEARS NADA

## STORY BY
## MATT YAMASHITA

## ART BY
## CHRISSY DELK

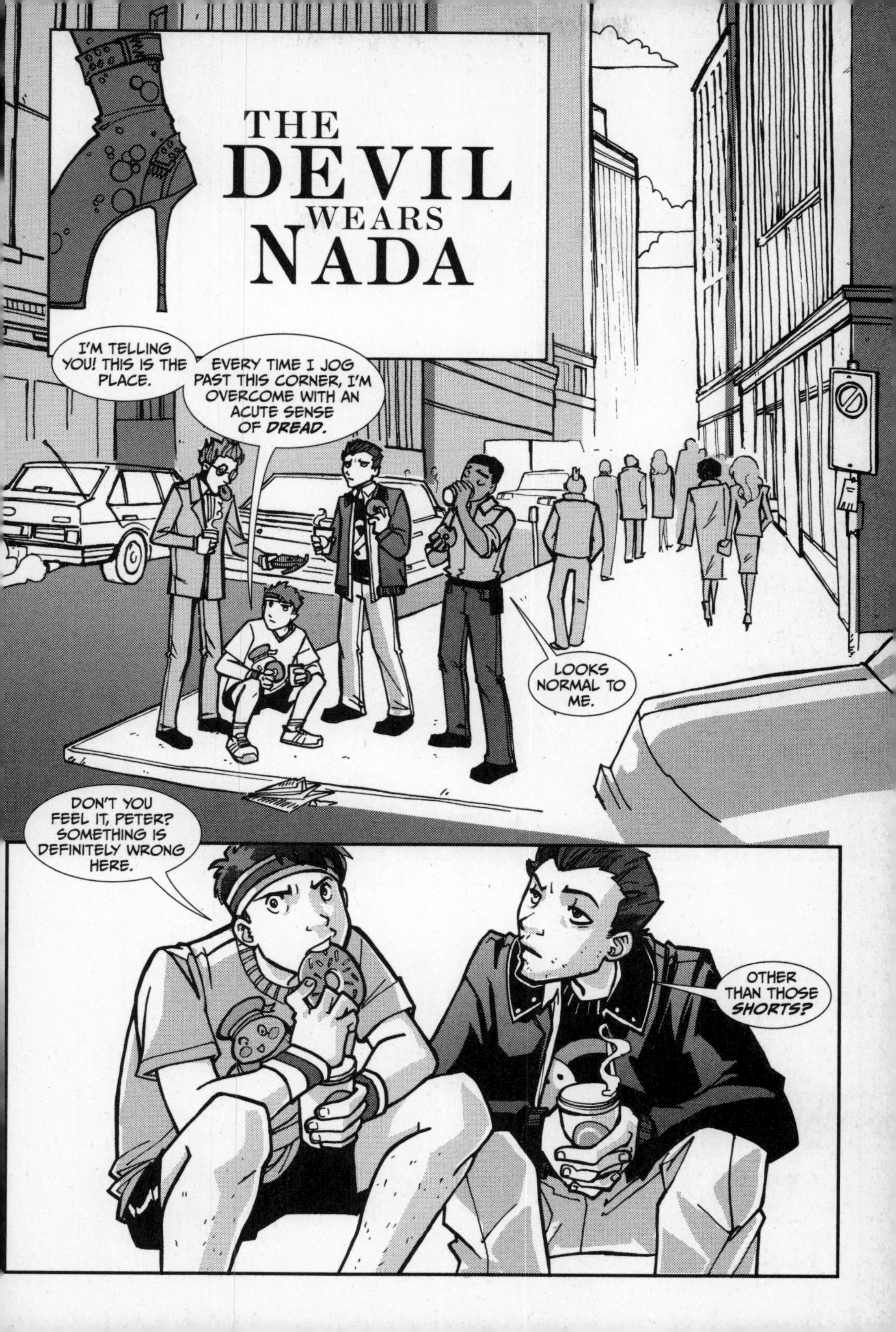
THE DEVIL WEARS NADA
I'M TELLING YOU! THIS IS THE PLACE.
EVERY TIME I JOG PAST THIS CORNER, I'M OVERCOME WITH AN ACUTE SENSE OF DREAD.
LOOKS NORMAL TO ME.
DON'T YOU FEEL IT, PETER? SOMETHING IS DEFINITELY WRONG HERE.
OTHER THAN THOSE SHORTS?

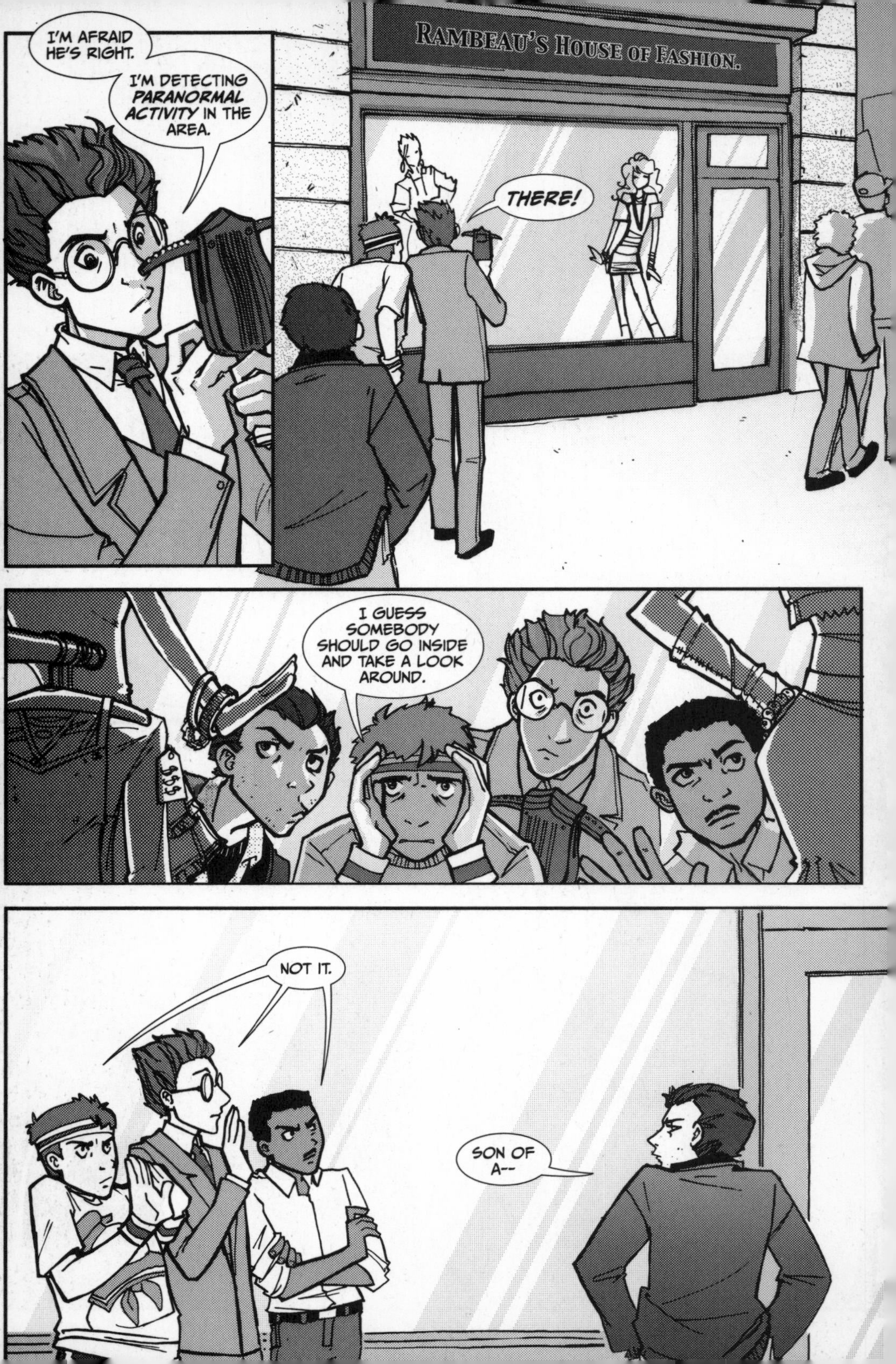
I'M AFRAID HE'S RIGHT.
I'M DETECTING PARANORMAL ACTIVITY IN THE AREA.
RAMBEAU'S HOUSE OF FASHION.
THERE!
I GUESS SOMEBODY SHOULD GO INSIDE AND TAKE A LOOK AROUND.
NOT IT.
SON OF A--

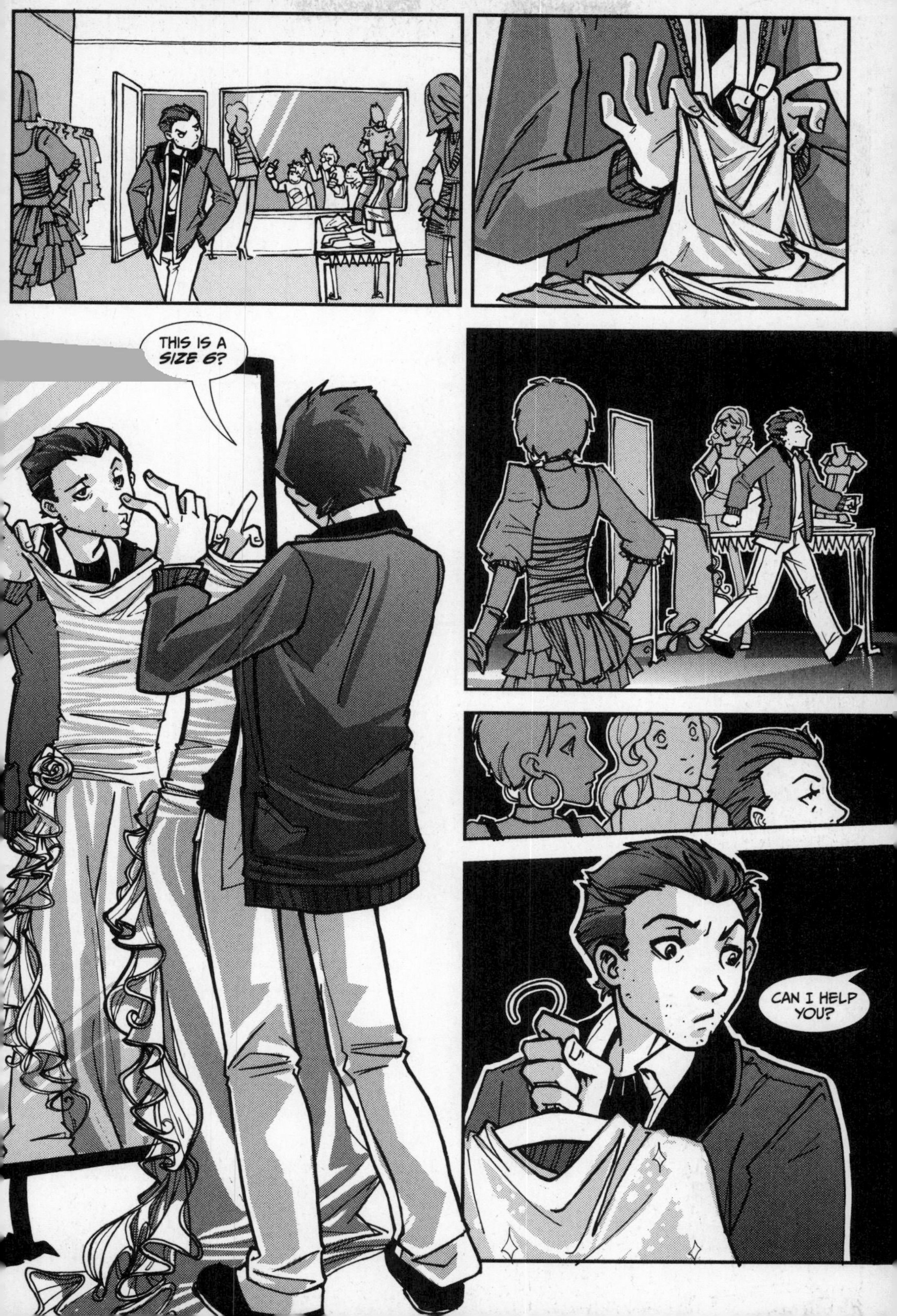
THIS IS A SIZE 6?
CAN I HELP YOU?

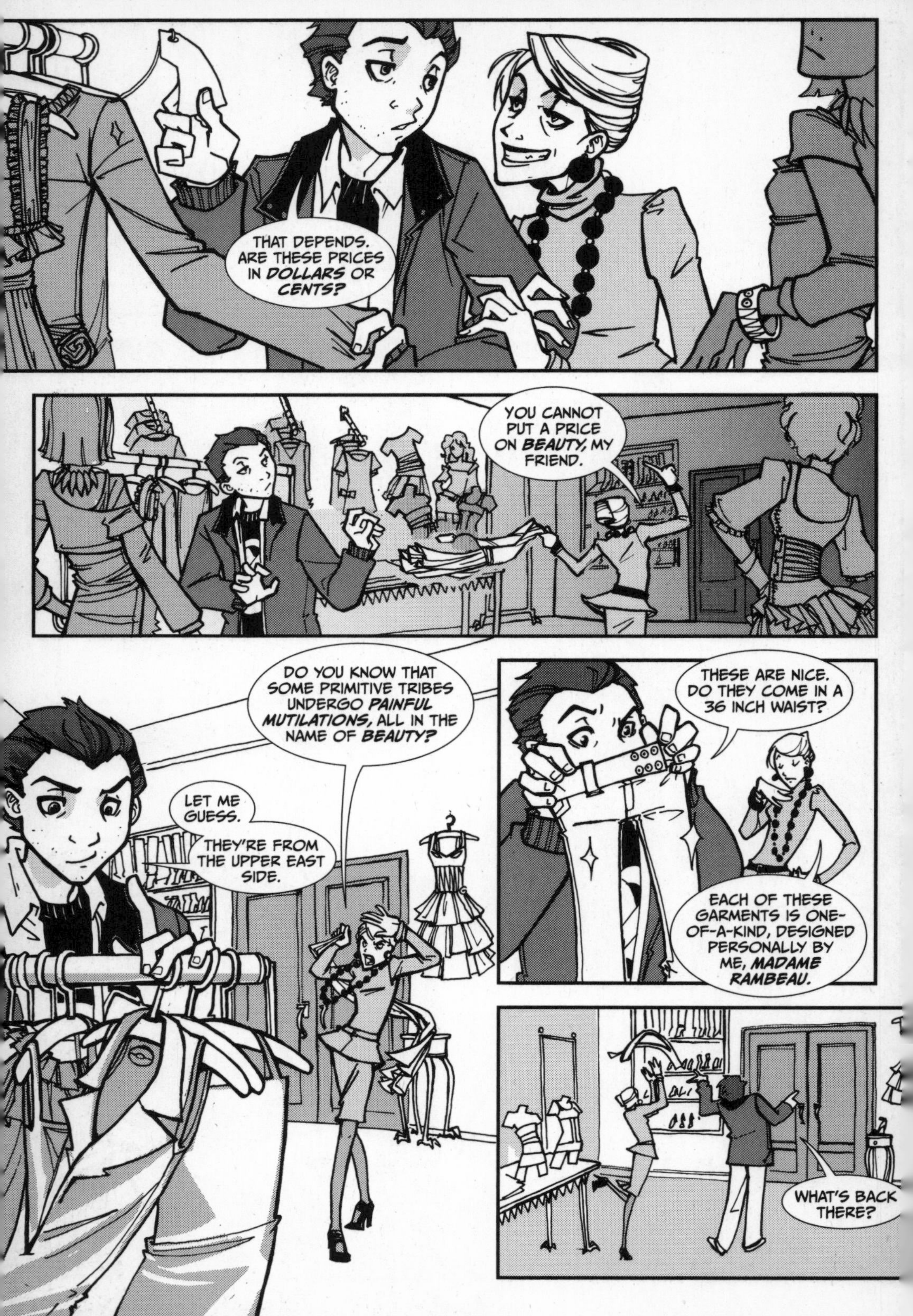
THAT DEPENDS. ARE THESE PRICES IN DOLLARS OR CENTS?
YOU CANNOT PUT A PRICE ON BEAUTY, MY FRIEND.
DO YOU KNOW THAT SOME PRIMITIVE TRIBES UNDERGO PAINFUL MUTILATIONS, ALL IN THE NAME OF BEAUTY?
LET ME GUESS.
THEY'RE FROM THE UPPER EAST SIDE.
THESE ARE NICE. DO THEY COME IN A 36 INCH WAIST?
EACH OF THESE GARMENTS IS ONE-OF-A-KIND, DESIGNED PERSONALLY BY ME, MADAME RAMBEAU.
WHAT'S BACK THERE?

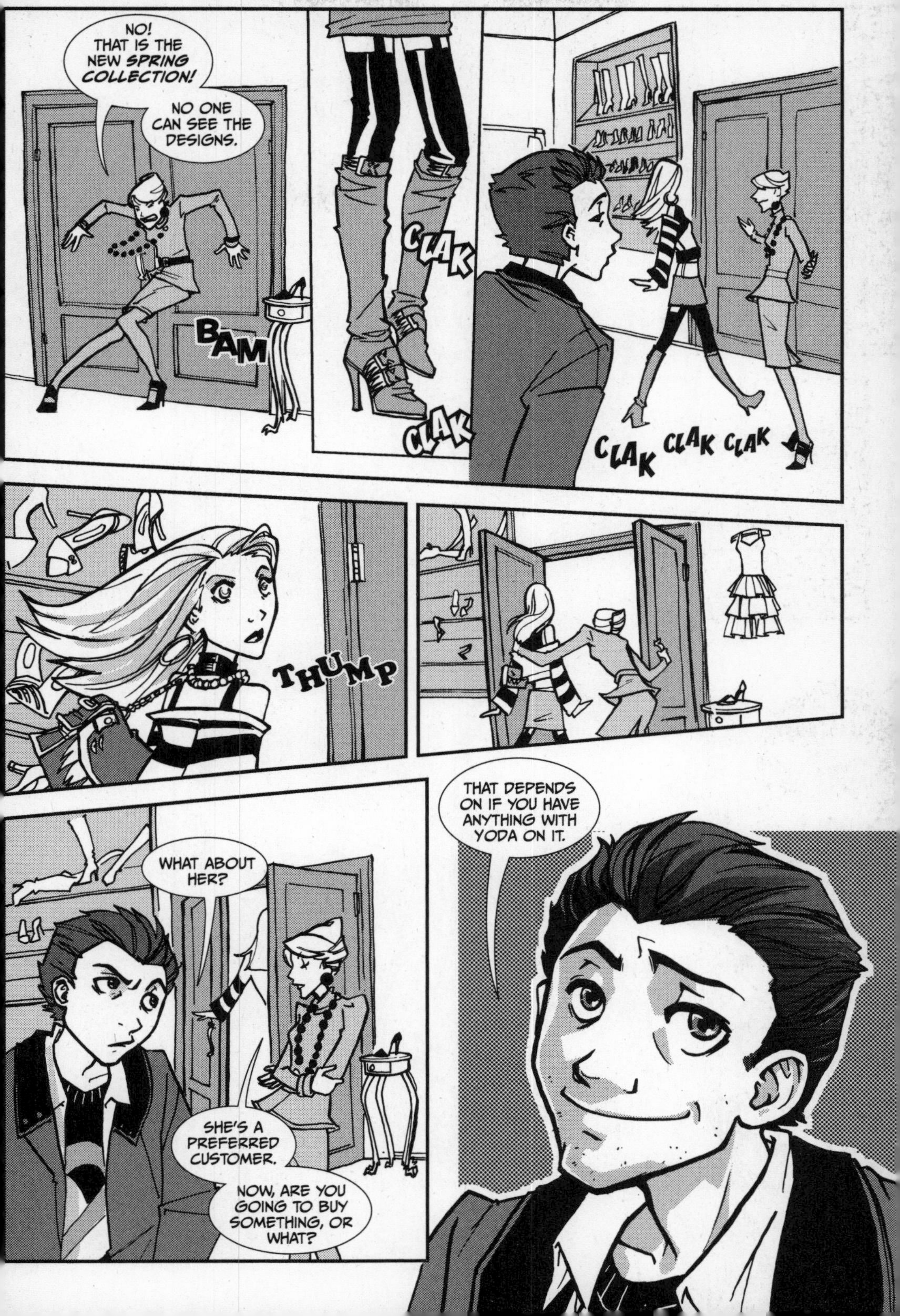
NO! THAT IS THE NEW SPRING COLLECTION!
NO ONE CAN SEE THE DESIGNS.
BAM
CLAK
CLAK
CLAK CLAK CLAK
THUMP
WHAT ABOUT HER?
SHE'S A PREFERRED CUSTOMER.
NOW, ARE YOU GOING TO BUY SOMETHING, OR WHAT?
THAT DEPENDS ON IF YOU HAVE ANYTHING WITH YODA ON IT.

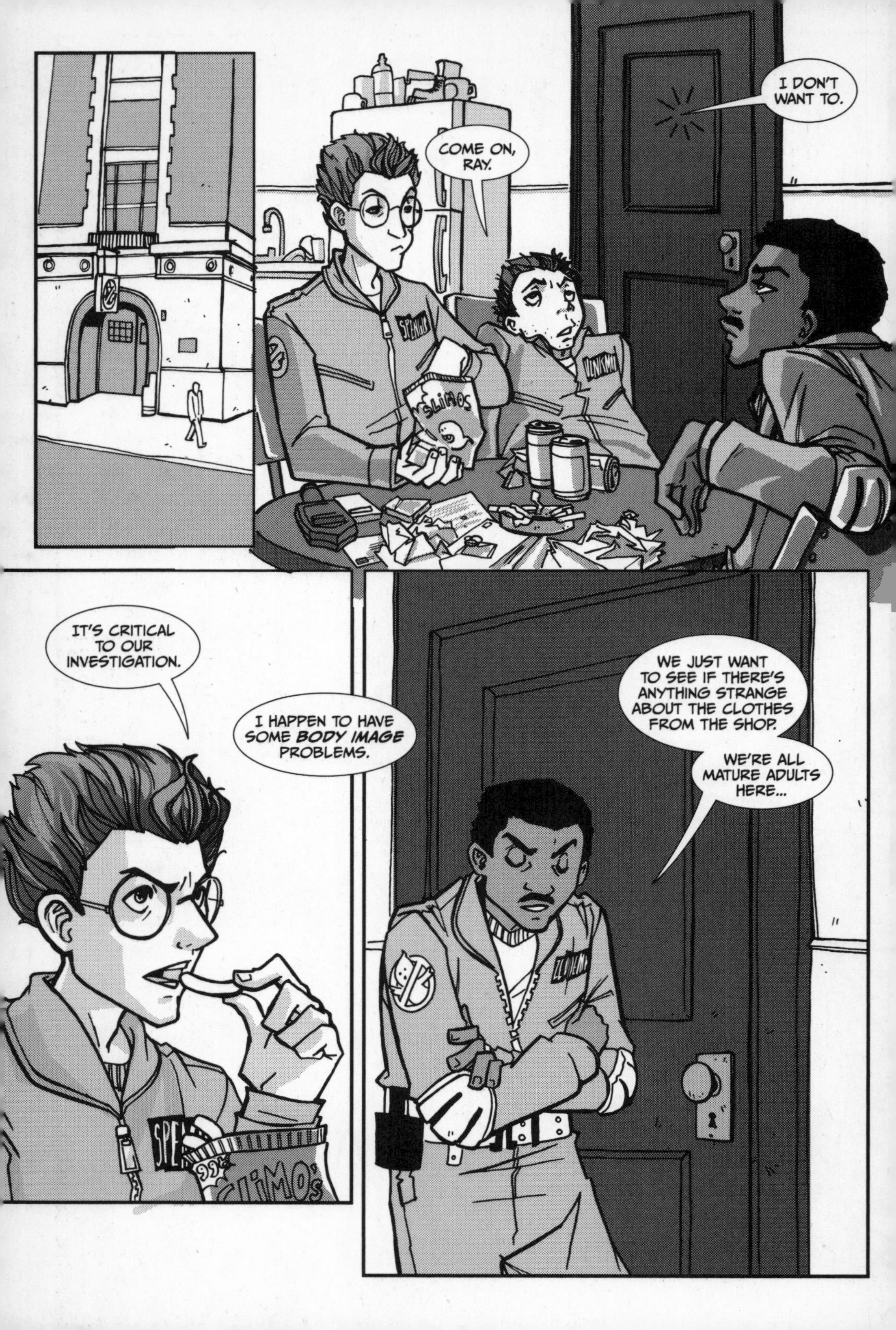
COME ON, RAY.
I DON'T WANT TO.
IT'S CRITICAL TO OUR INVESTIGATION.
I HAPPEN TO HAVE SOME BODY IMAGE PROBLEMS.
WE JUST WANT TO SEE IF THERE'S ANYTHING STRANGE ABOUT THE CLOTHES FROM THE SHOP.
WE'RE ALL MATURE ADULTS HERE...

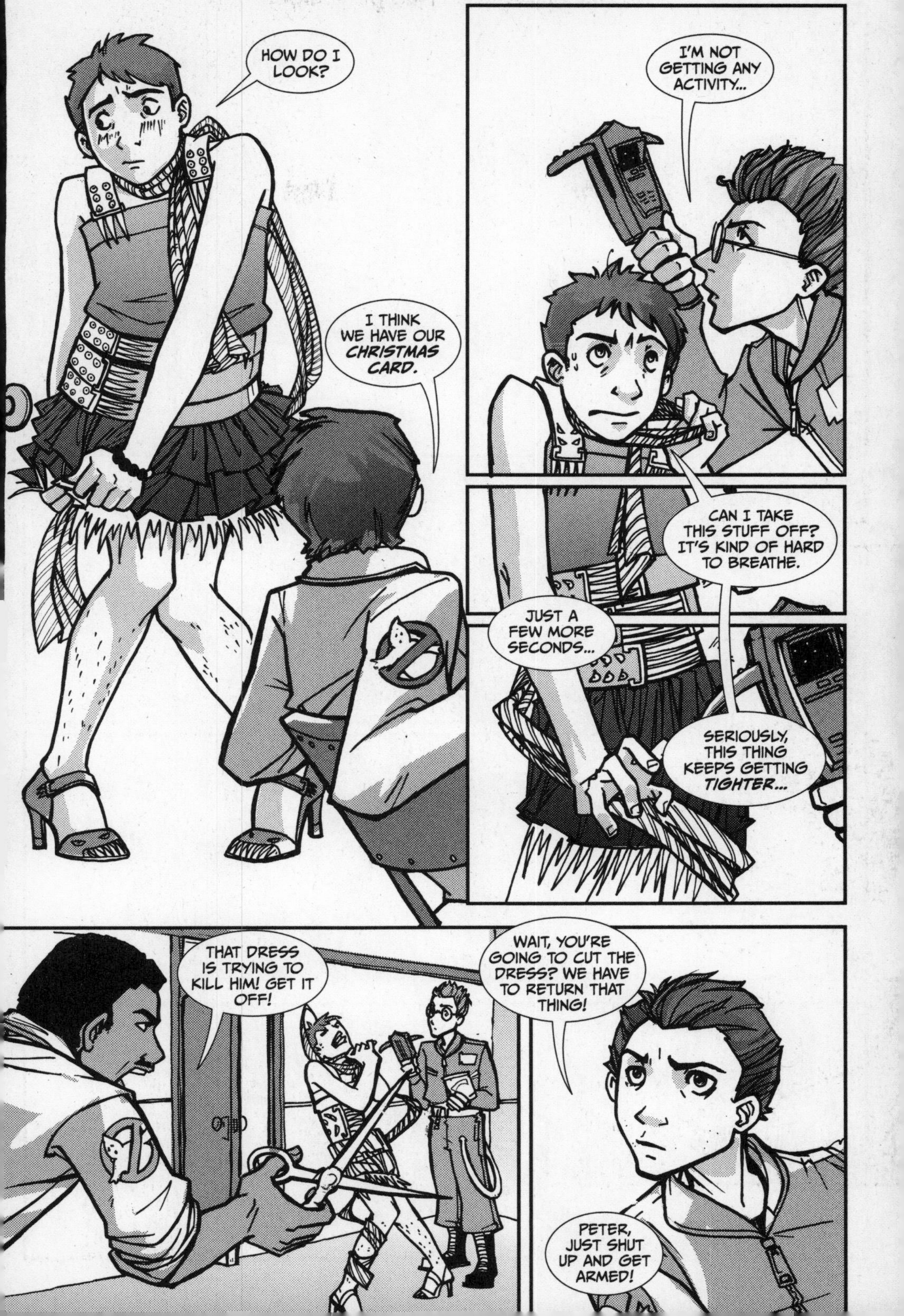
HOW DO I LOOK?
I THINK WE HAVE OUR *CHRISTMAS CARD.*
I'M NOT GETTING ANY ACTIVITY...
CAN I TAKE THIS STUFF OFF? IT'S KIND OF HARD TO BREATHE.
JUST A FEW MORE SECONDS...
SERIOUSLY, THIS THING KEEPS GETTING *TIGHTER...*
THAT DRESS IS TRYING TO KILL HIM! GET IT OFF!
WAIT, YOU'RE GOING TO CUT THE DRESS? WE HAVE TO RETURN THAT THING!
PETER, JUST SHUT UP AND GET ARMED!

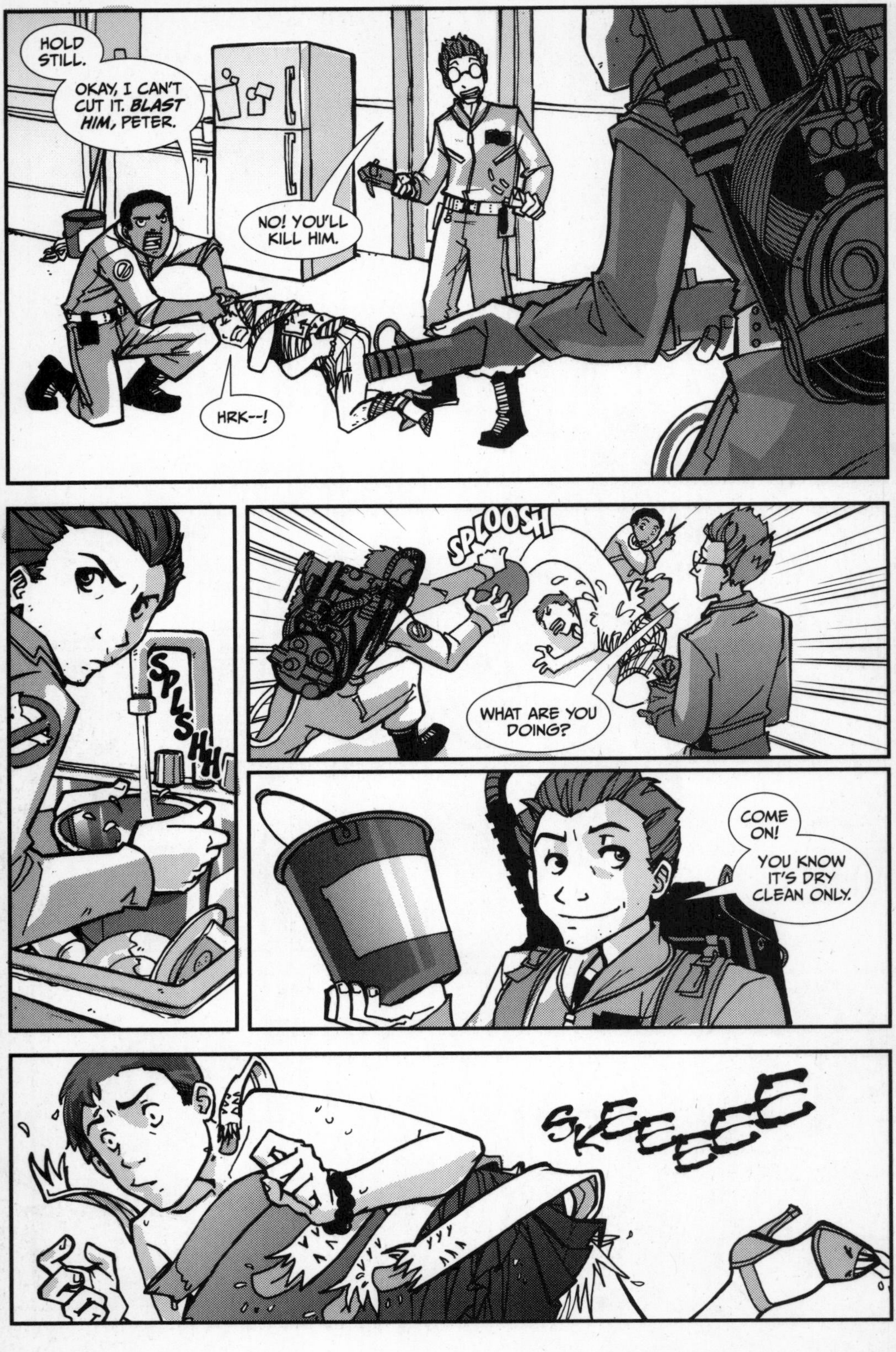
HOLD STILL.
OKAY, I CAN'T CUT IT. *BLAST HIM*, PETER.
NO! YOU'LL KILL HIM.
HRK--!
SPLSHH
SPLOOSH
WHAT ARE YOU DOING?
COME ON!
YOU KNOW IT'S DRY CLEAN ONLY.
SKEEEEEEE

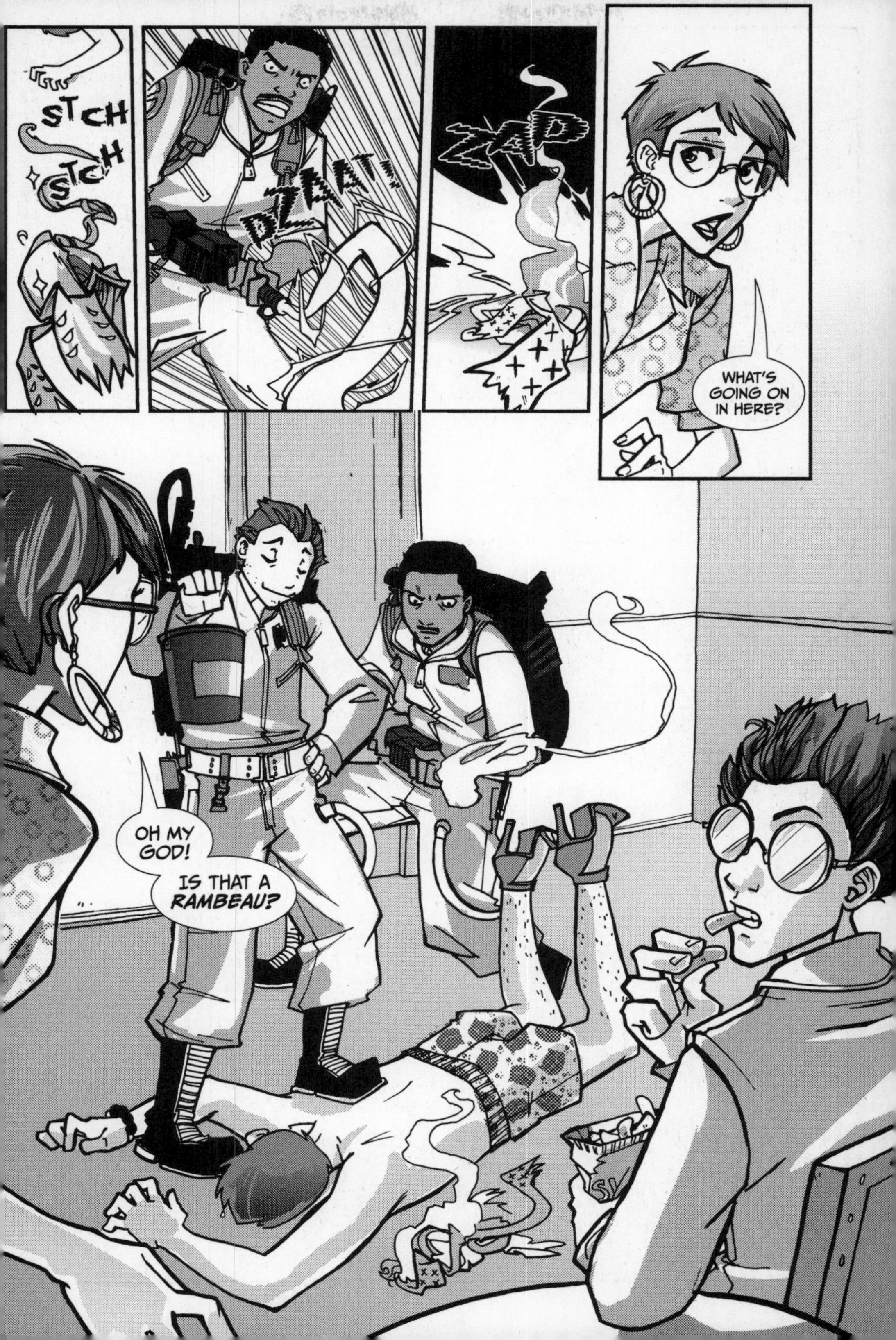
STCH
STCH
DZAAT!
ZAP
WHAT'S GOING ON IN HERE?
OH MY GOD!
IS THAT A *RAMBEAU?*

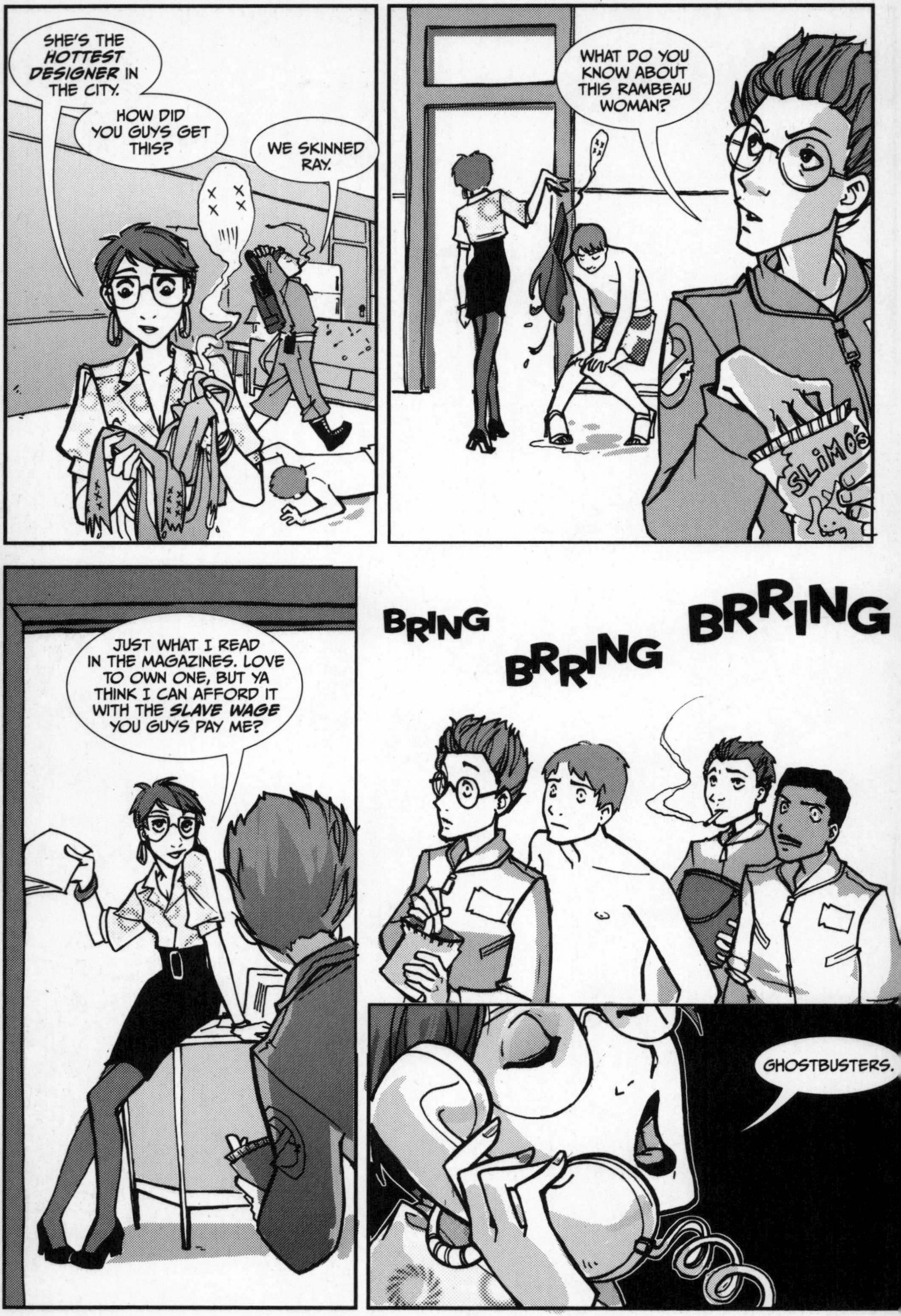
SHE'S THE HOTTEST DESIGNER IN THE CITY.
HOW DID YOU GUYS GET THIS?
WE SKINNED RAY.
WHAT DO YOU KNOW ABOUT THIS RAMBEAU WOMAN?
SLIMO'S
JUST WHAT I READ IN THE MAGAZINES. LOVE TO OWN ONE, BUT YA THINK I CAN AFFORD IT WITH THE SLAVE WAGE YOU GUYS PAY ME?
BRING
BRRING
BRRING
GHOSTBUSTERS.

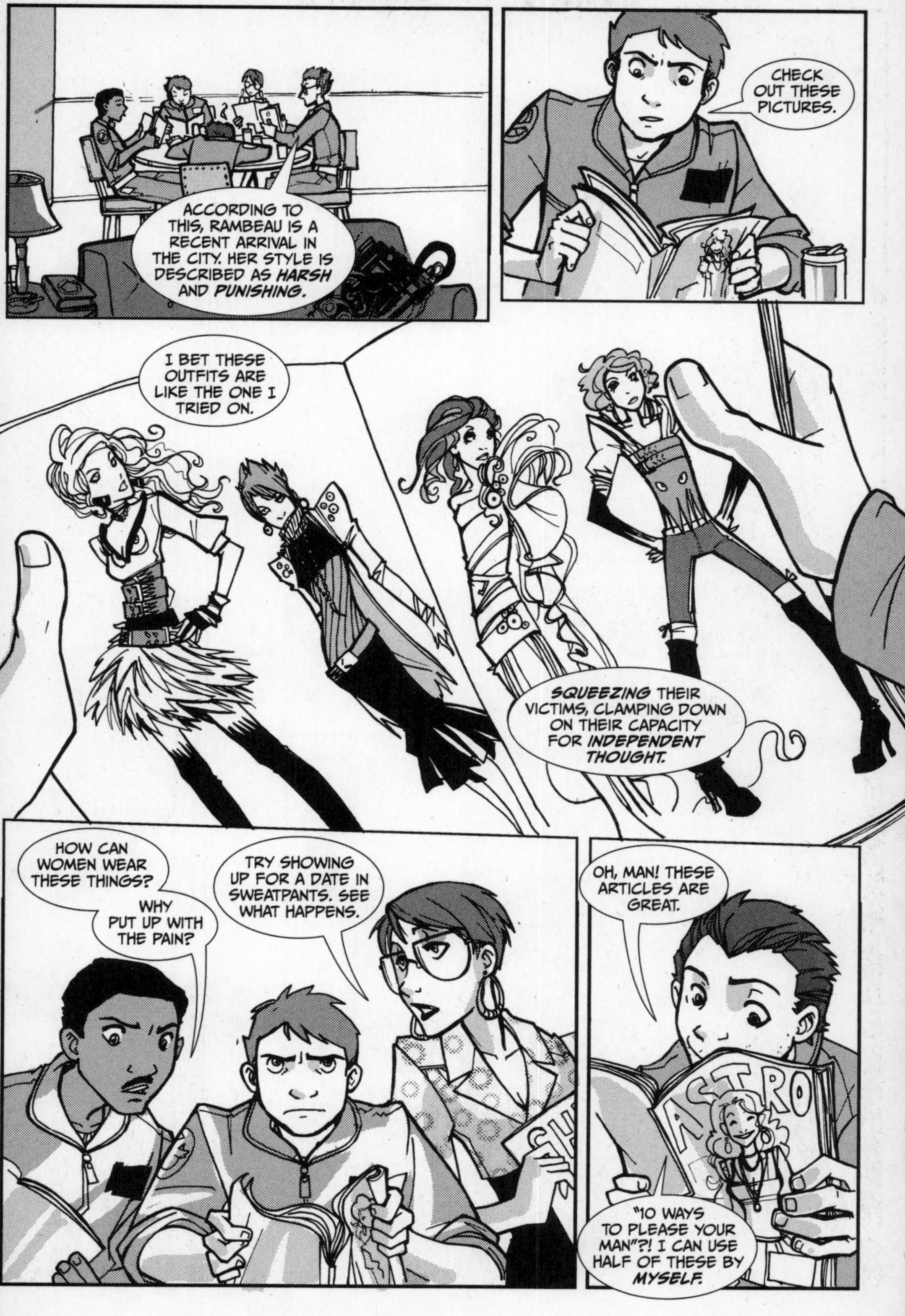
ACCORDING TO THIS, RAMBEAU IS A RECENT ARRIVAL IN THE CITY. HER STYLE IS DESCRIBED AS *HARSH* AND *PUNISHING*.
CHECK OUT THESE PICTURES.
I BET THESE OUTFITS ARE LIKE THE ONE I TRIED ON.
*SQUEEZING* THEIR VICTIMS, CLAMPING DOWN ON THEIR CAPACITY FOR *INDEPENDENT THOUGHT.*
HOW CAN WOMEN WEAR THESE THINGS?
WHY PUT UP WITH THE PAIN?
TRY SHOWING UP FOR A DATE IN SWEATPANTS. SEE WHAT HAPPENS.
OH, MAN! THESE ARTICLES ARE GREAT.
ASTRO
"10 WAYS TO PLEASE YOUR MAN"?! I CAN USE HALF OF THESE BY *MYSELF*.

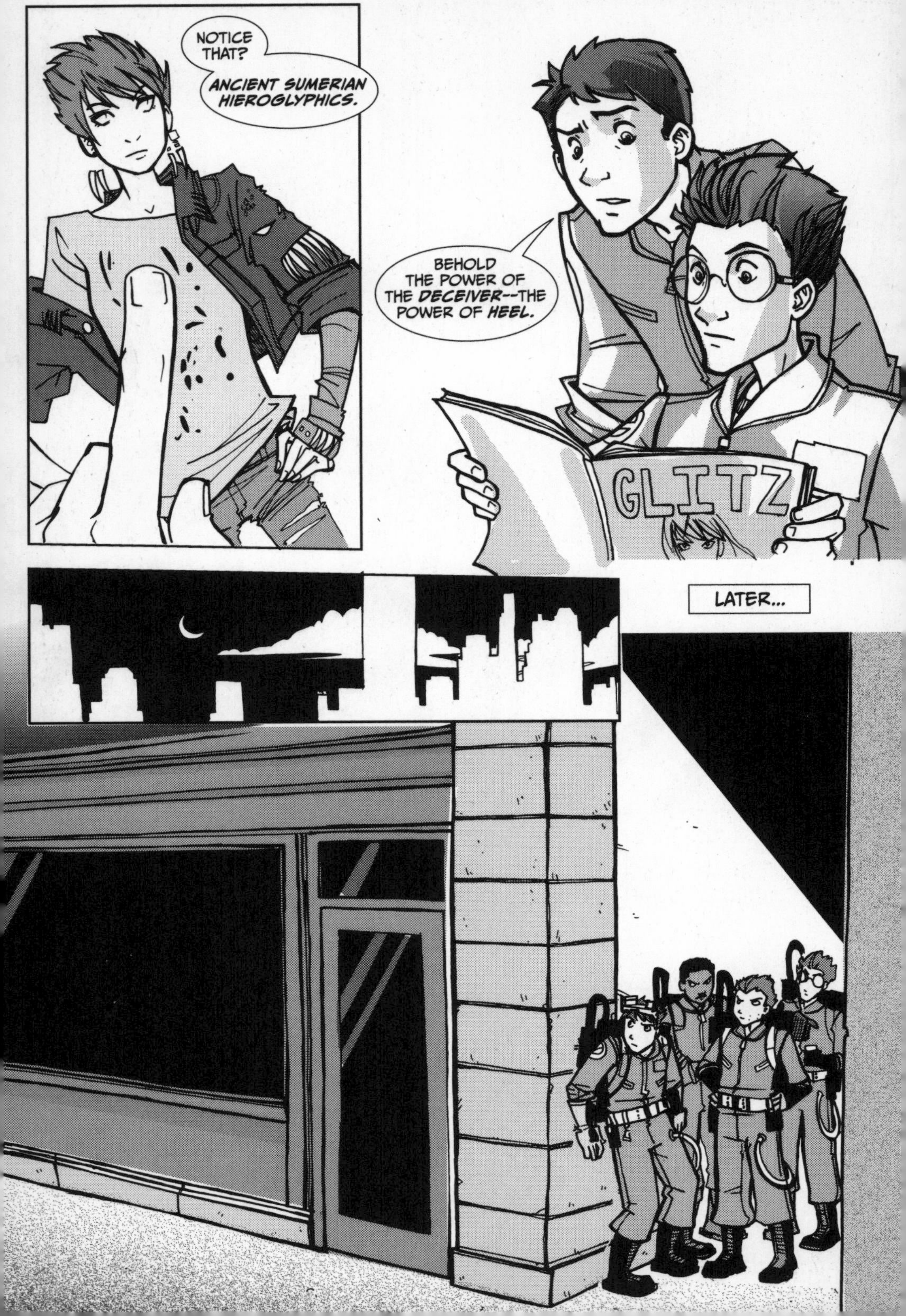

NOTICE THAT?
ANCIENT SUMERIAN HIEROGLYPHICS.
BEHOLD THE POWER OF THE DECEIVER--THE POWER OF HEEL.
GLITZ
LATER...

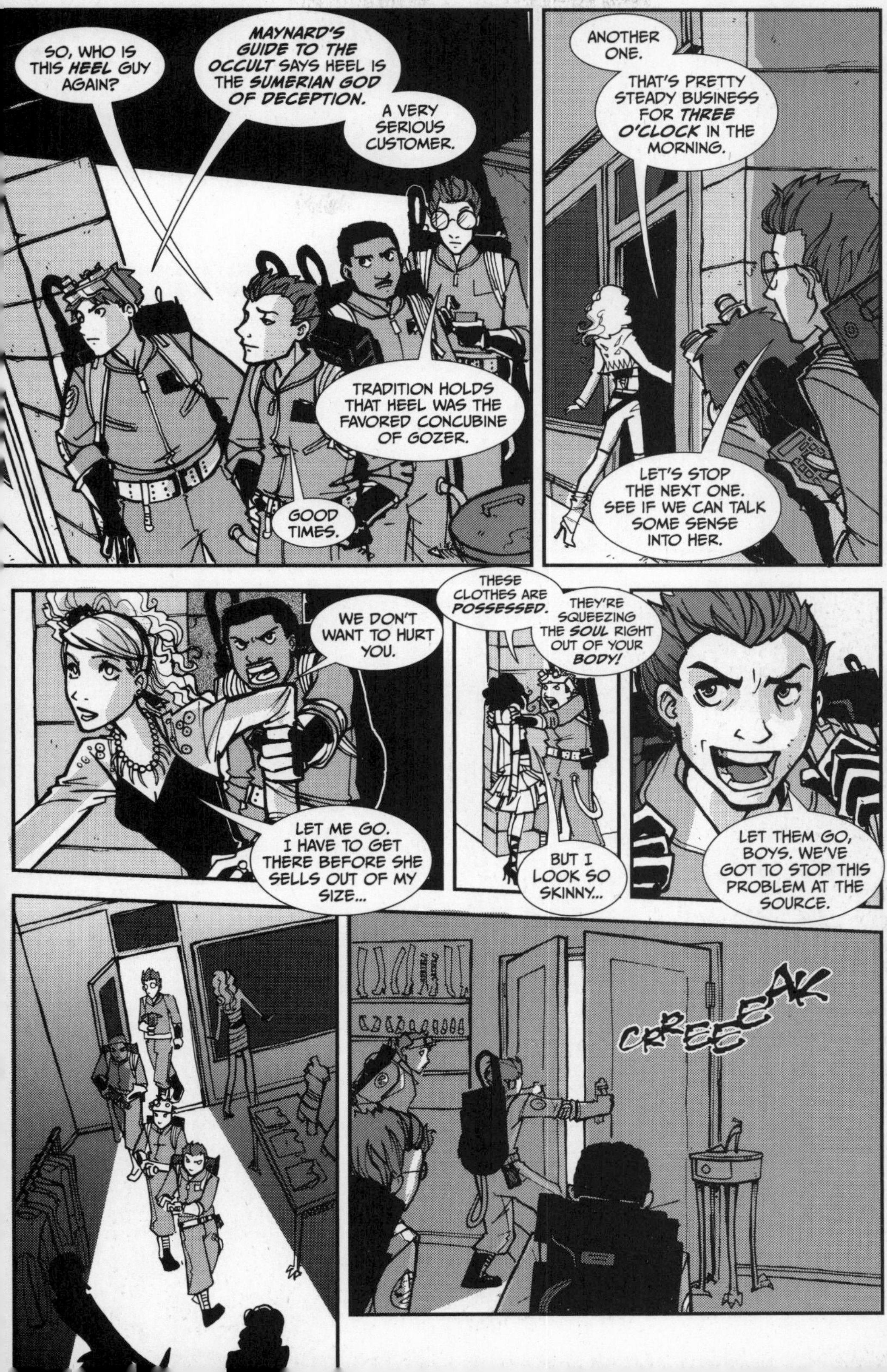
SO, WHO IS THIS HEEL GUY AGAIN?
MAYNARD'S GUIDE TO THE OCCULT SAYS HEEL IS THE SUMERIAN GOD OF DECEPTION.
A VERY SERIOUS CUSTOMER.
TRADITION HOLDS THAT HEEL WAS THE FAVORED CONCUBINE OF GOZER.
GOOD TIMES.
ANOTHER ONE.
THAT'S PRETTY STEADY BUSINESS FOR THREE O'CLOCK IN THE MORNING.
LET'S STOP THE NEXT ONE. SEE IF WE CAN TALK SOME SENSE INTO HER.
WE DON'T WANT TO HURT YOU.
LET ME GO. I HAVE TO GET THERE BEFORE SHE SELLS OUT OF MY SIZE...
THESE CLOTHES ARE POSSESSED.
THEY'RE SQUEEZING THE SOUL RIGHT OUT OF YOUR BODY!
BUT I LOOK SO SKINNY...
LET THEM GO, BOYS. WE'VE GOT TO STOP THIS PROBLEM AT THE SOURCE.
CRREEEAK

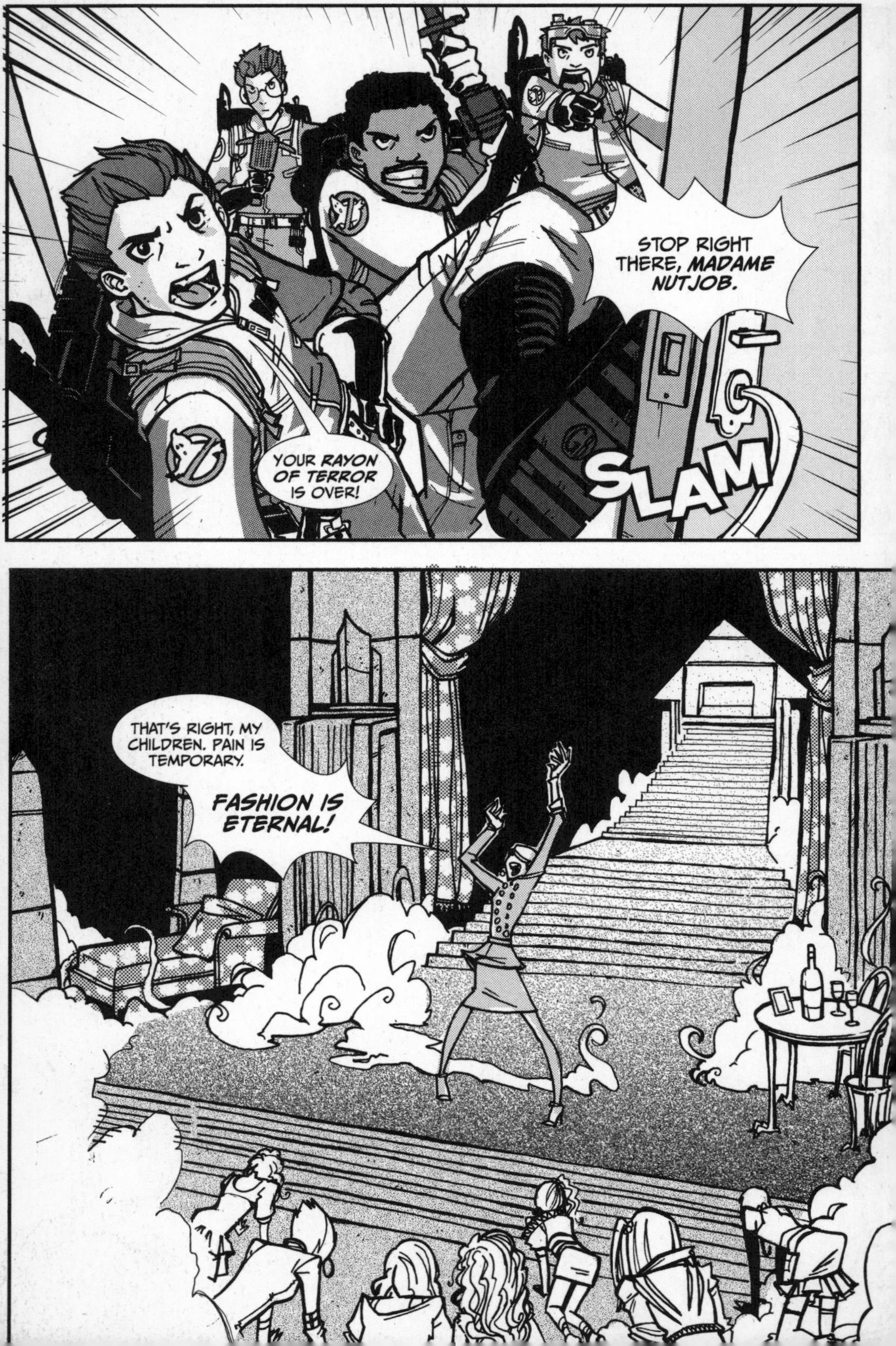
STOP RIGHT THERE, MADAME NUTJOB.
YOUR RAYON OF TERROR IS OVER!
SLAM
THAT'S RIGHT, MY CHILDREN. PAIN IS TEMPORARY.
FASHION IS ETERNAL!

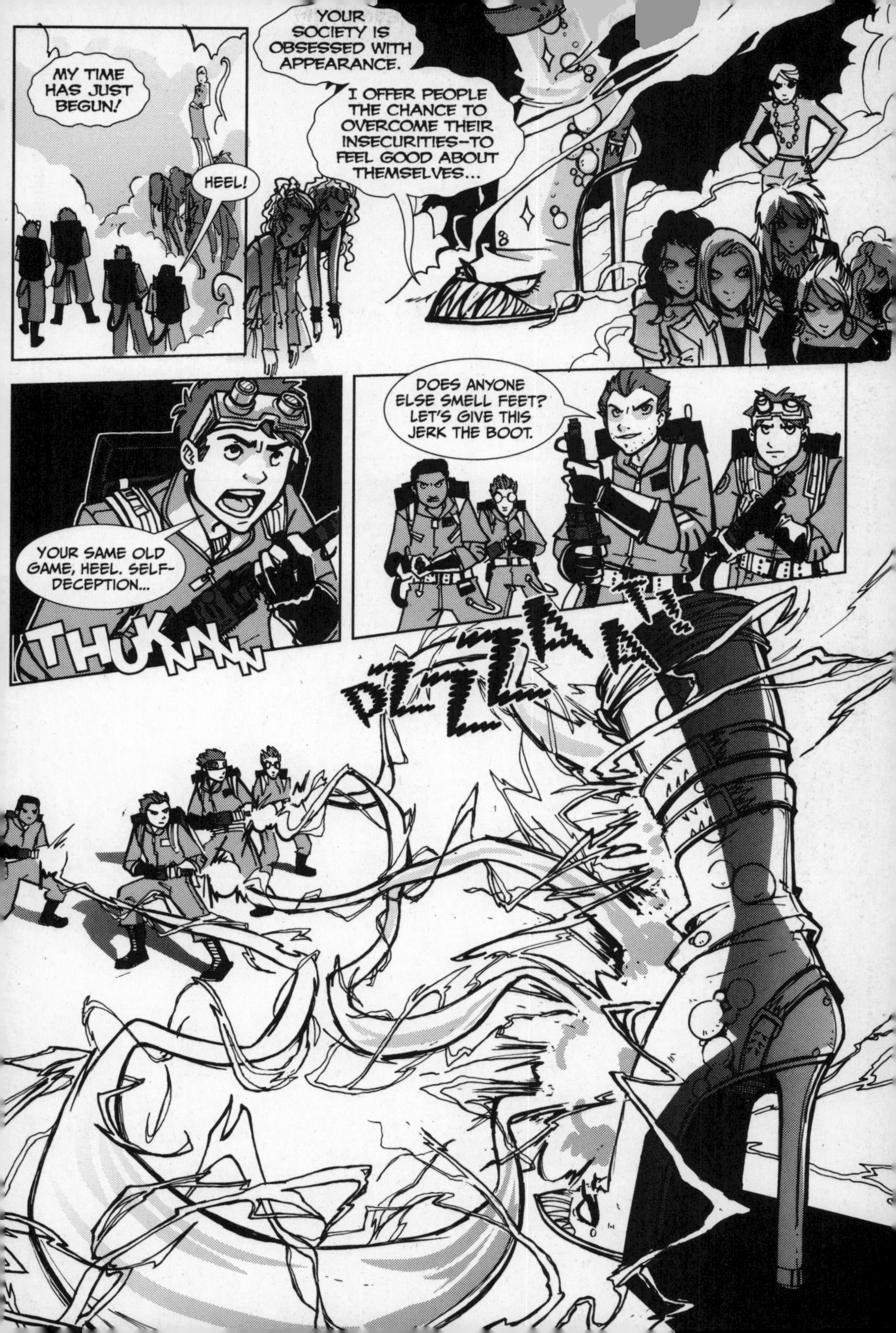
MY TIME HAS JUST BEGUN!
HEEL!
YOUR SOCIETY IS OBSESSED WITH APPEARANCE.
I OFFER PEOPLE THE CHANCE TO OVERCOME THEIR INSECURITIES—TO FEEL GOOD ABOUT THEMSELVES...
YOUR SAME OLD GAME, HEEL. SELF-DECEPTION...
THUKNNNN
DOES ANYONE ELSE SMELL FEET? LET'S GIVE THIS JERK THE BOOT.
DZZZAAK!

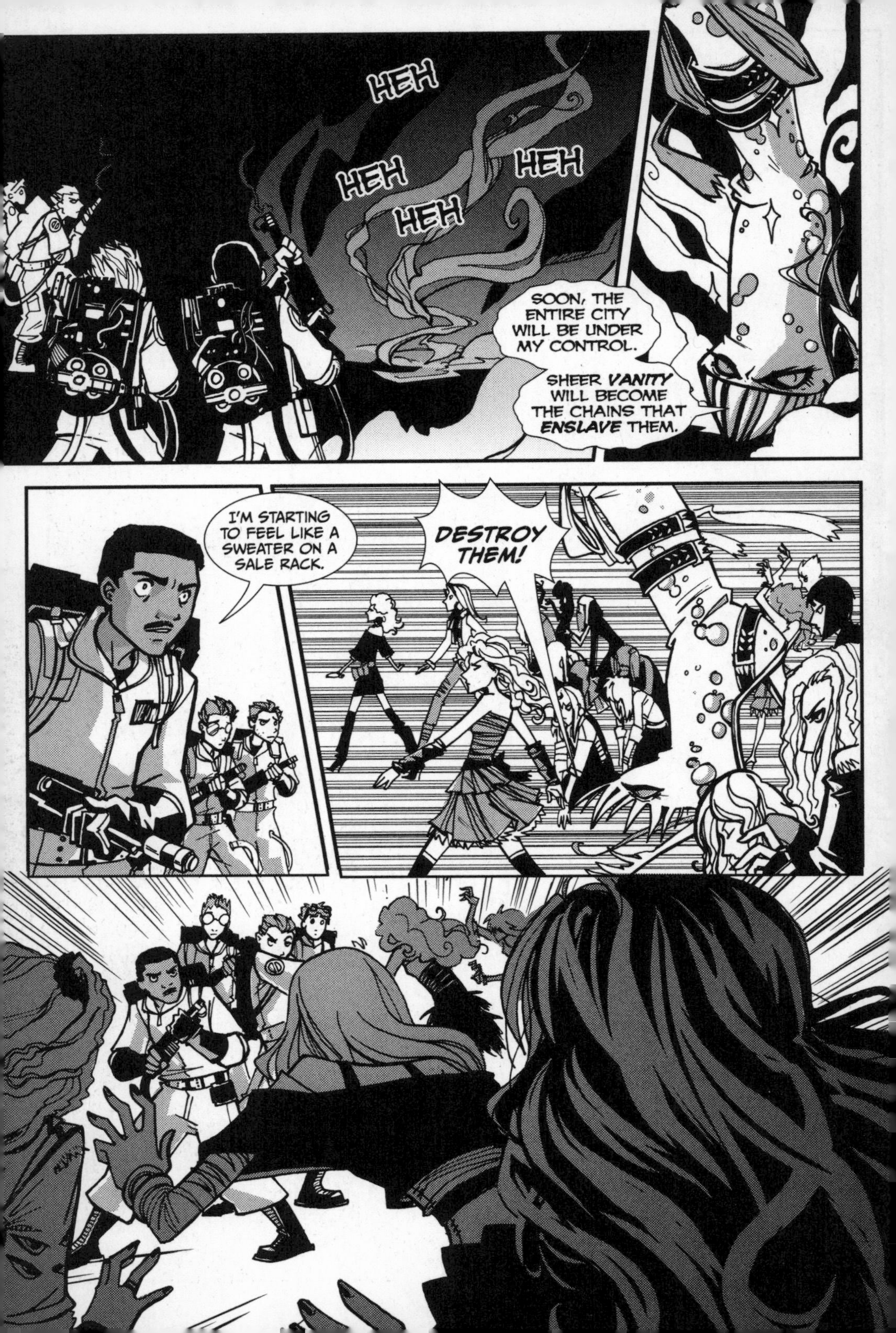
HEH
HEH
HEH
HEH
SOON, THE ENTIRE CITY WILL BE UNDER MY CONTROL.
SHEER *VANITY* WILL BECOME THE CHAINS THAT *ENSLAVE* THEM.
I'M STARTING TO FEEL LIKE A SWEATER ON A SALE RACK.
*DESTROY THEM!*

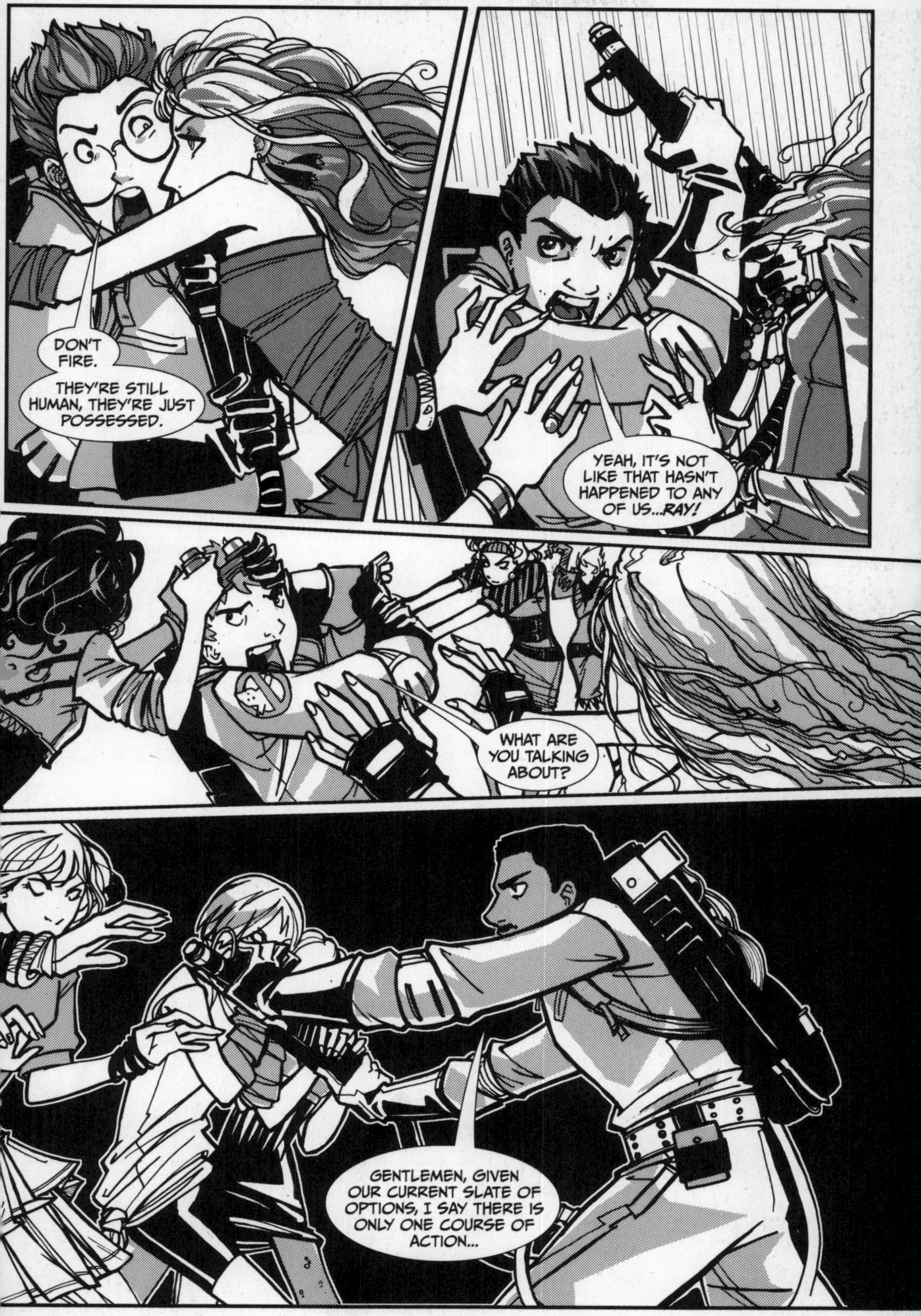
DON'T FIRE.
THEY'RE STILL HUMAN, THEY'RE JUST POSSESSED.
YEAH, IT'S NOT LIKE THAT HASN'T HAPPENED TO ANY OF US...*RAY!*
WHAT ARE YOU TALKING ABOUT?
GENTLEMEN, GIVEN OUR CURRENT SLATE OF OPTIONS, I SAY THERE IS ONLY ONE COURSE OF ACTION...

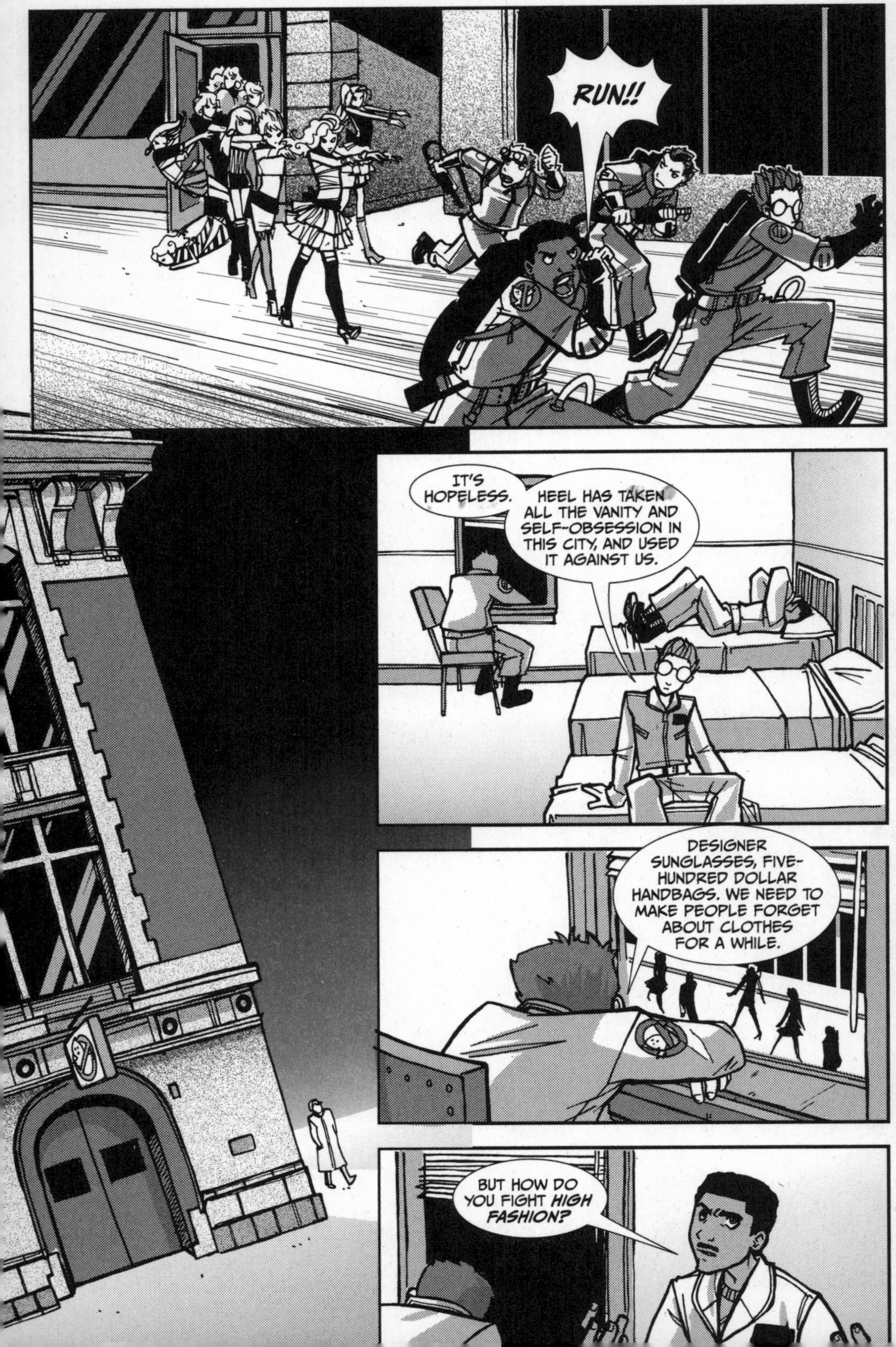
RUN!!
IT'S HOPELESS.
HEEL HAS TAKEN ALL THE VANITY AND SELF-OBSESSION IN THIS CITY, AND USED IT AGAINST US.
DESIGNER SUNGLASSES, FIVE-HUNDRED DOLLAR HANDBAGS. WE NEED TO MAKE PEOPLE FORGET ABOUT CLOTHES FOR A WHILE.
BUT HOW DO YOU FIGHT HIGH FASHION?

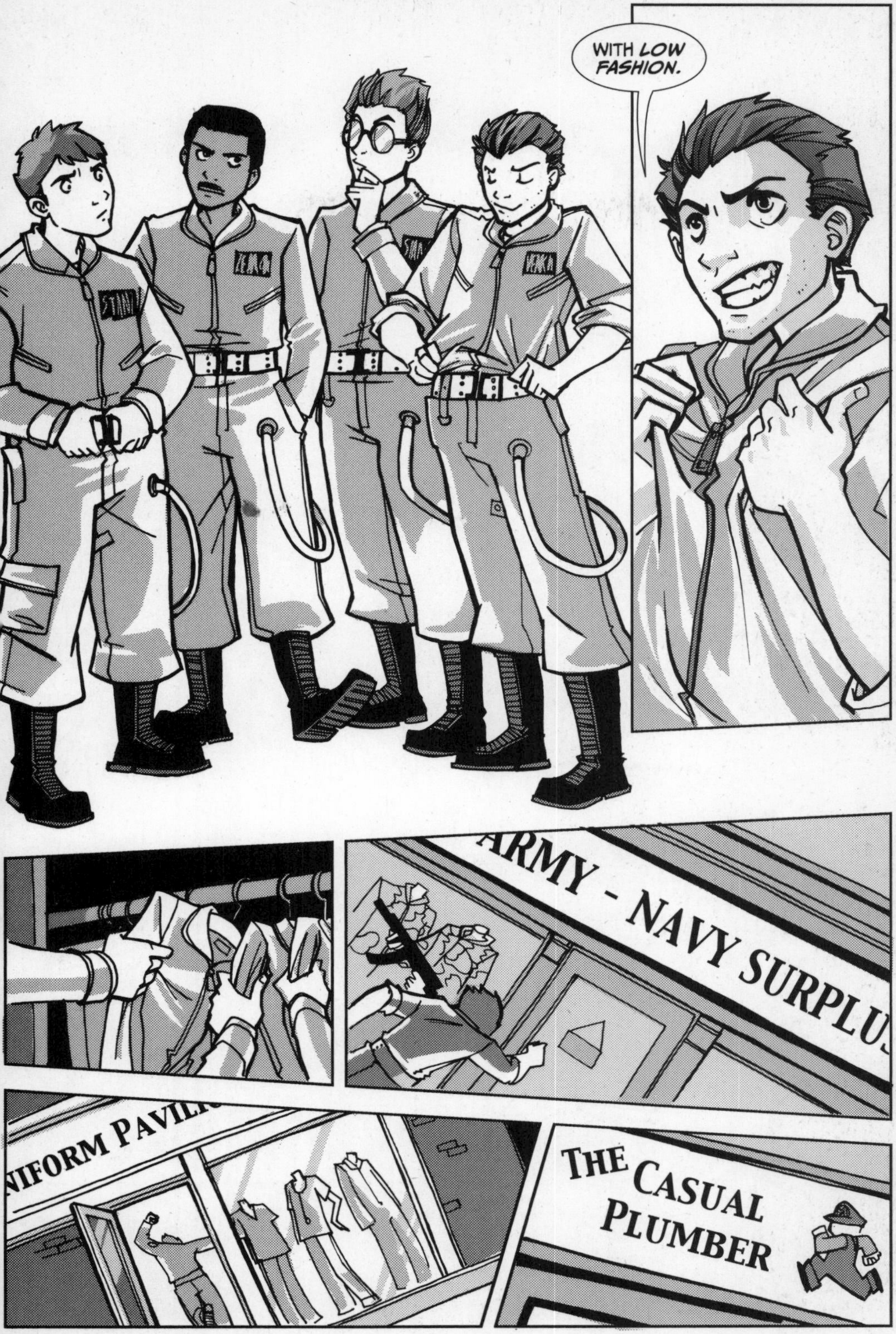
WITH LOW FASHION.
ARMY - NAVY SURPLU
NIFORM PAVIL
THE CASUAL PLUMBER

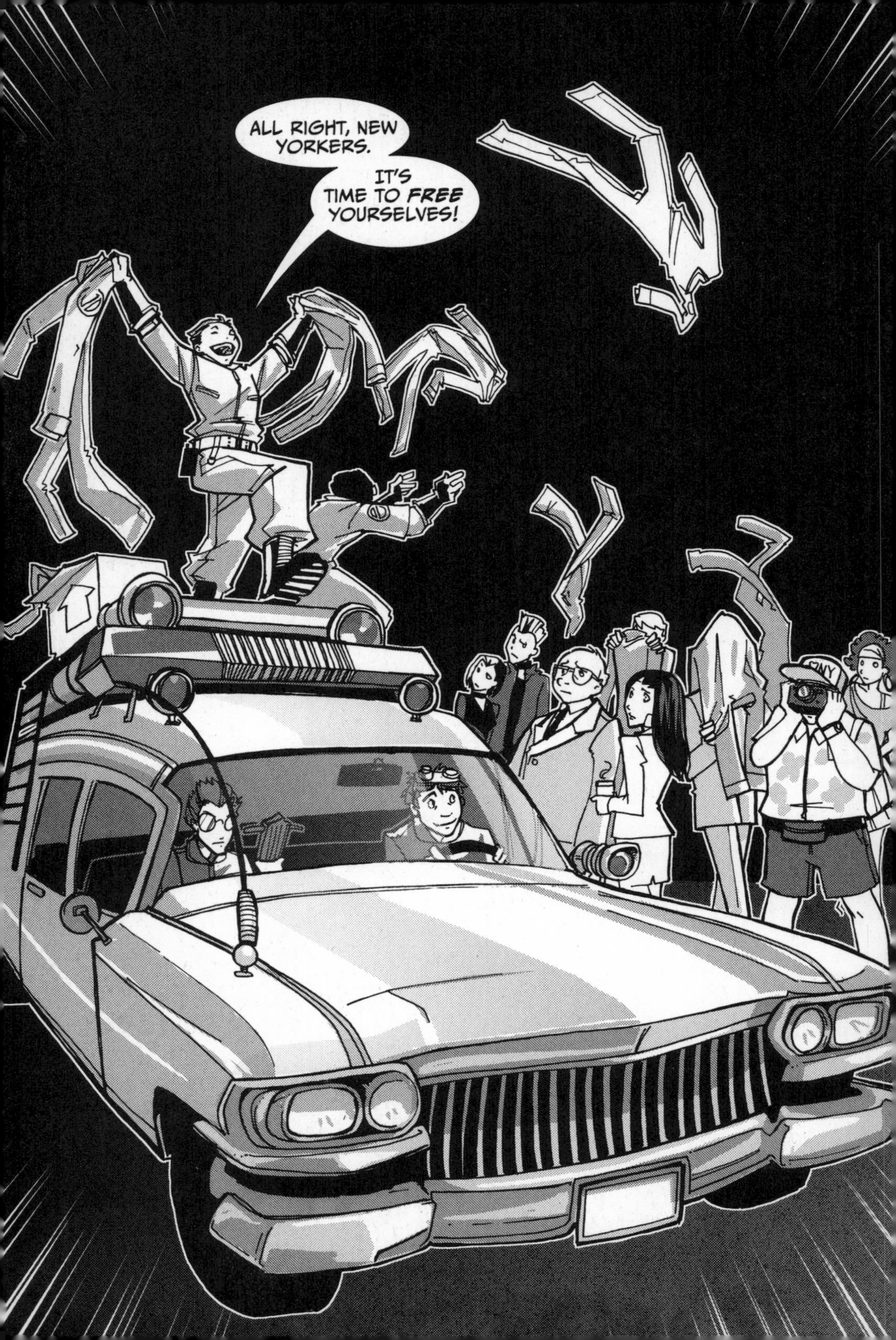
ALL RIGHT, NEW YORKERS.
IT'S TIME TO **FREE** YOURSELVES!
NY

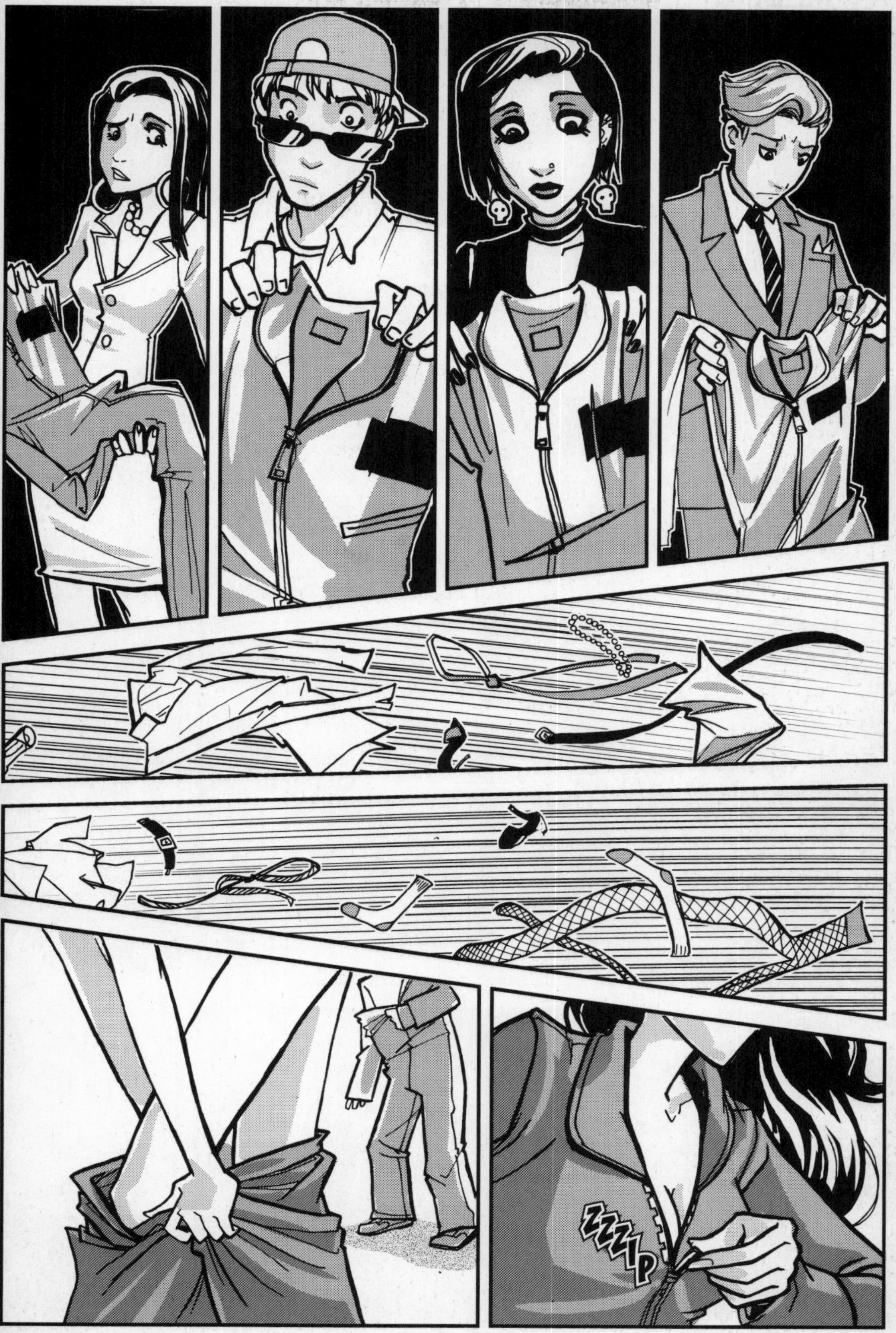
ZZZIP

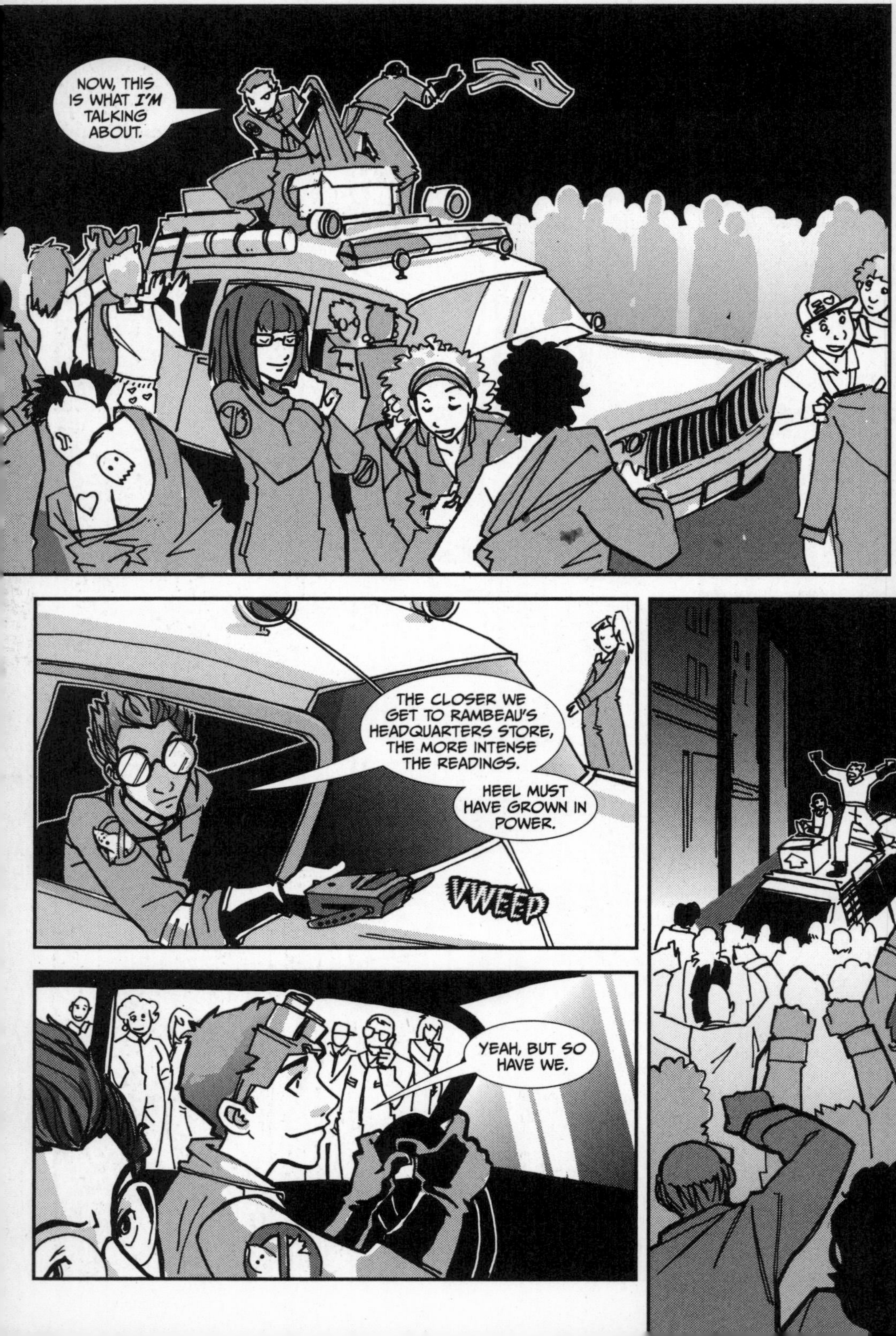
NOW, THIS IS WHAT *I'M* TALKING ABOUT.
THE CLOSER WE GET TO RAMBEAU'S HEADQUARTERS STORE, THE MORE INTENSE THE READINGS.
HEEL MUST HAVE GROWN IN POWER.
VWEEP
YEAH, BUT SO HAVE WE.

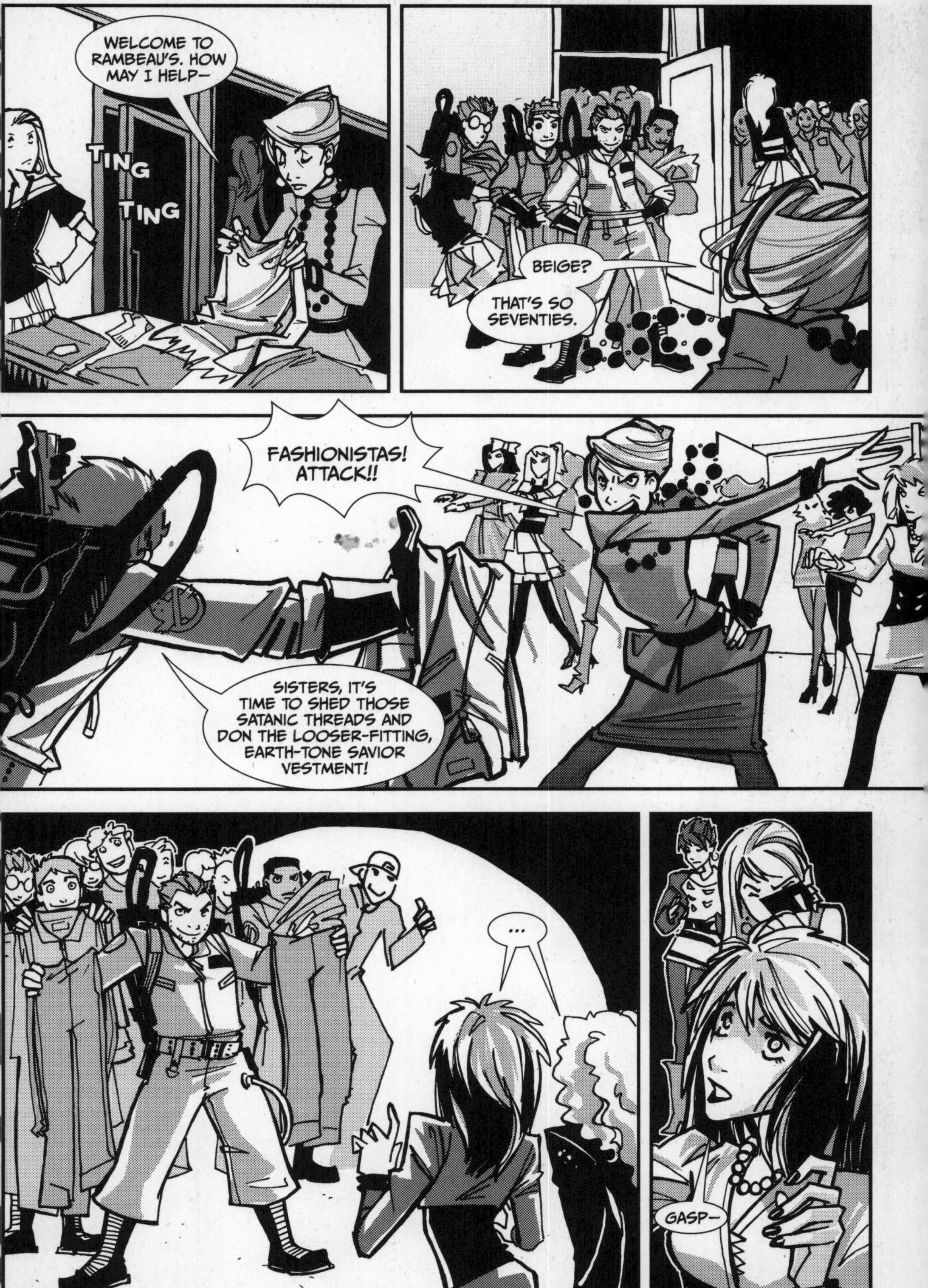
WELCOME TO RAMBEAU'S. HOW MAY I HELP—
TING
TING
BEIGE?
THAT'S SO SEVENTIES.
FASHIONISTAS! ATTACK!!
SISTERS, IT'S TIME TO SHED THOSE SATANIC THREADS AND DON THE LOOSER-FITTING, EARTH-TONE SAVIOR VESTMENT!
...
GASP—

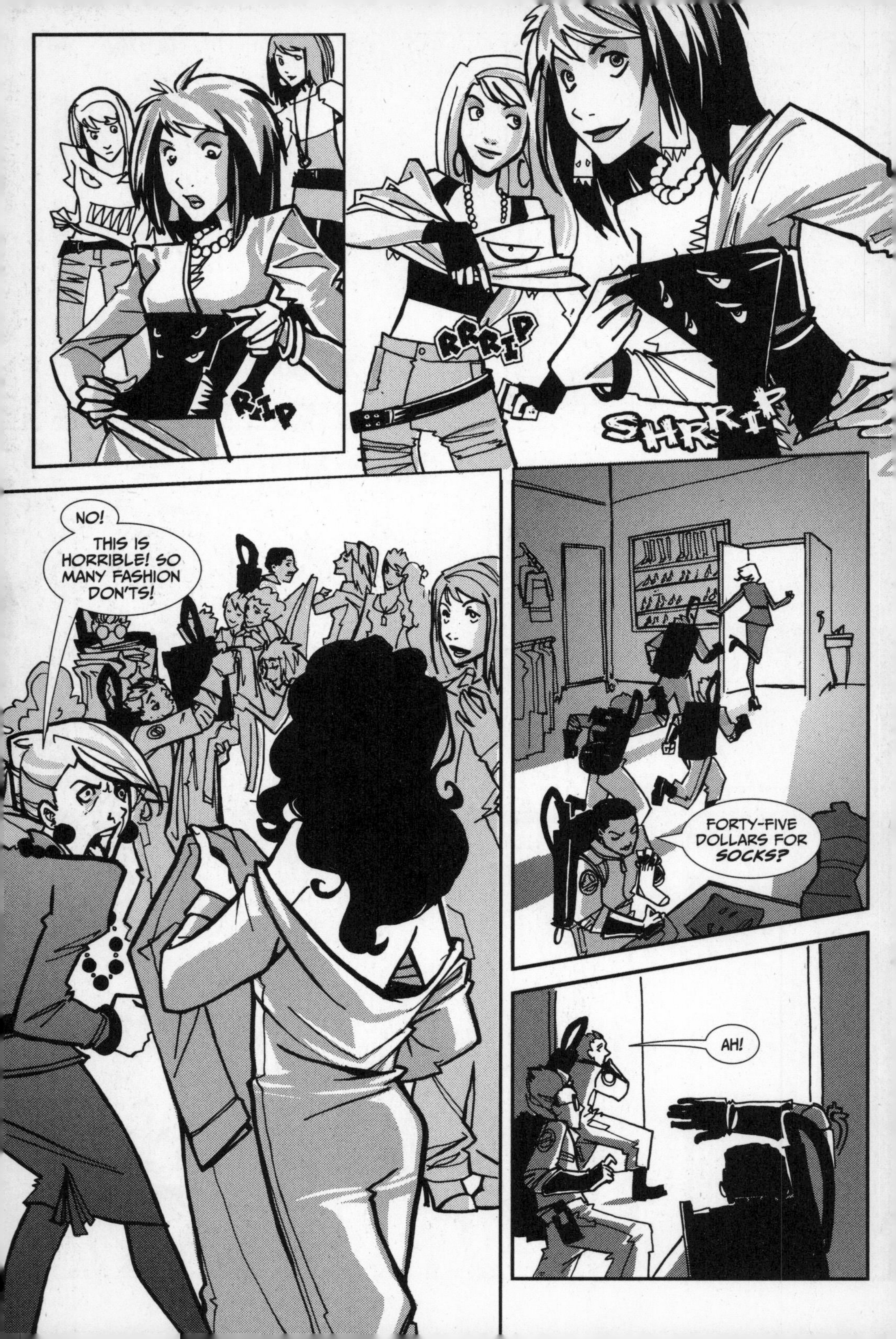
RIP
RRRIP
SHRRIP
NO!
THIS IS HORRIBLE! SO MANY FASHION DON'TS!
FORTY-FIVE DOLLARS FOR SOCKS?
AH!

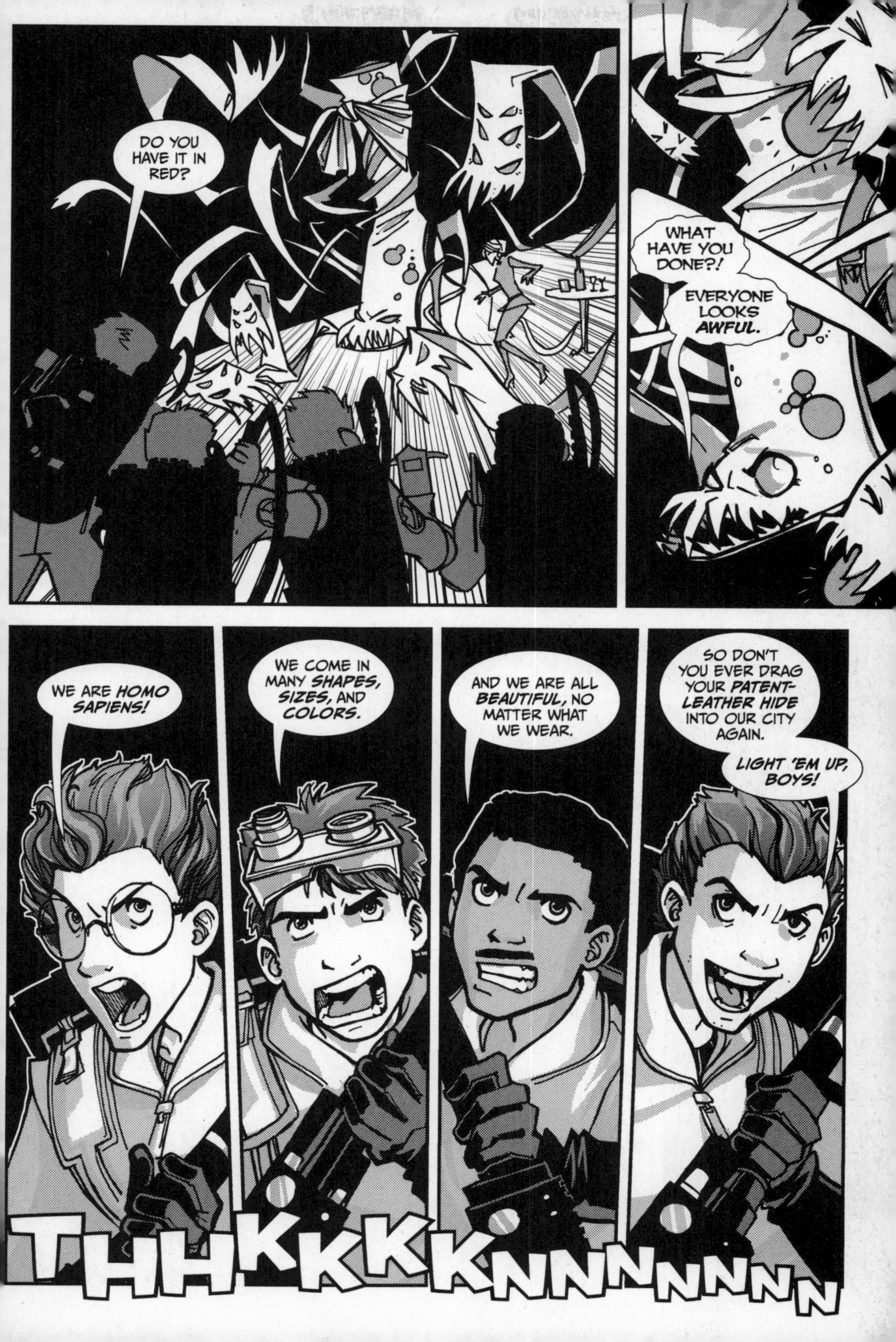
DO YOU HAVE IT IN RED?
WHAT HAVE YOU DONE?!
EVERYONE LOOKS AWFUL.
WE ARE HOMO SAPIENS!
WE COME IN MANY SHAPES, SIZES, AND COLORS.
AND WE ARE ALL BEAUTIFUL, NO MATTER WHAT WE WEAR.
SO DON'T YOU EVER DRAG YOUR PATENT-LEATHER HIDE INTO OUR CITY AGAIN.
LIGHT 'EM UP, BOYS!
THHKKKNNNNNNNN

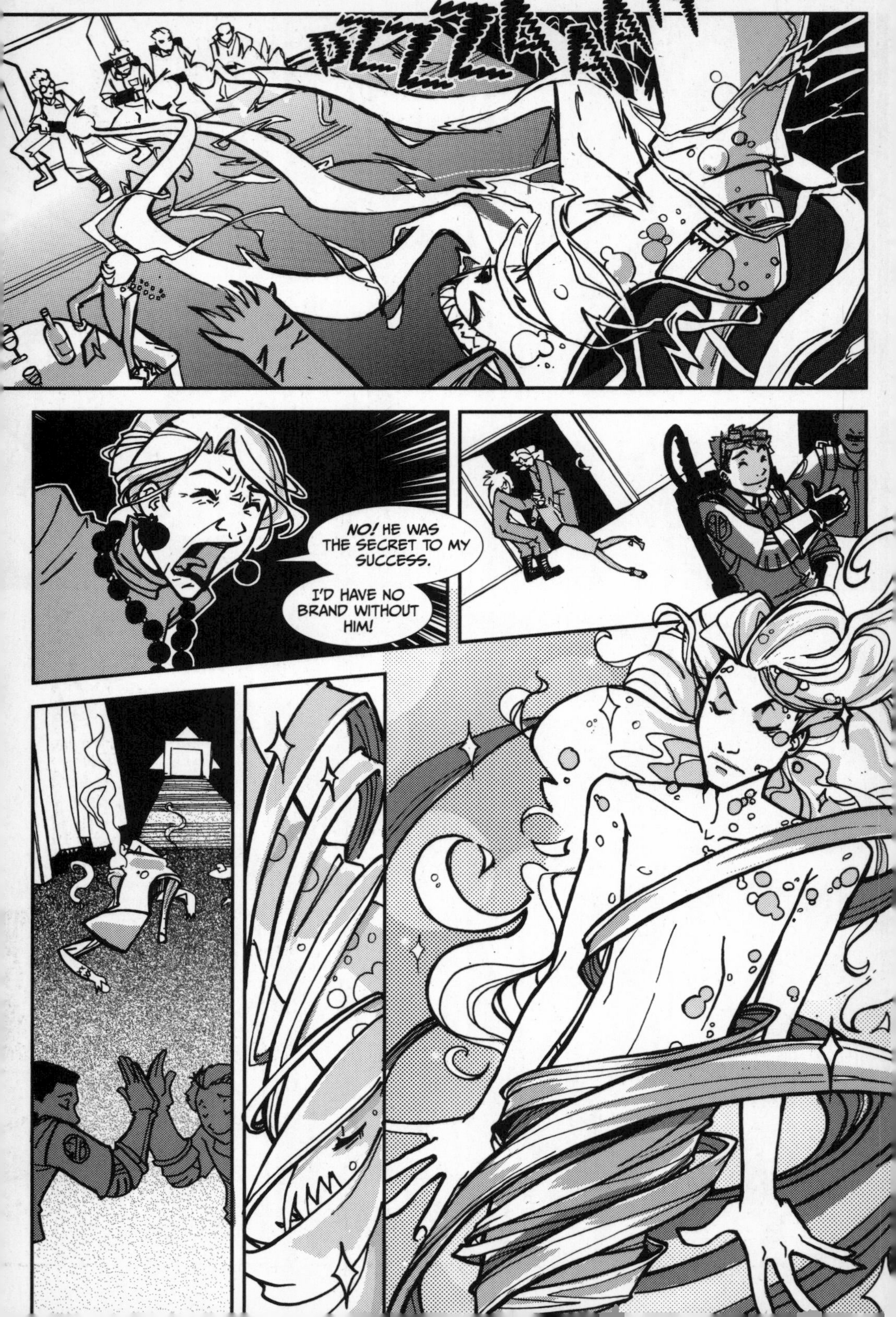
PZZZAAAT
NO! HE WAS THE SECRET TO MY SUCCESS.
I'D HAVE NO BRAND WITHOUT HIM!

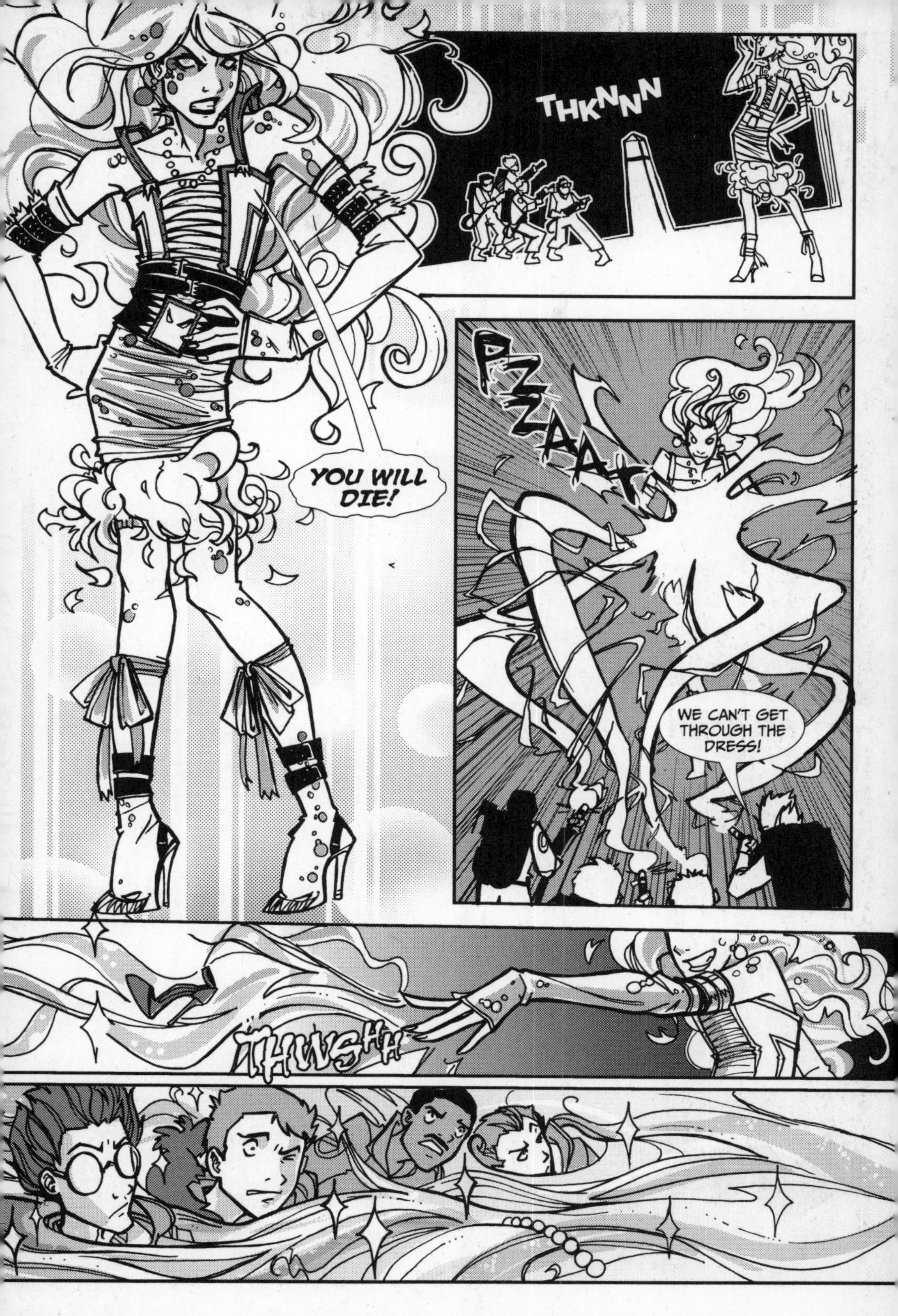
YOU WILL DIE!
THKNNN
PZZAAAX
WE CAN'T GET THROUGH THE DRESS!
THWSHH

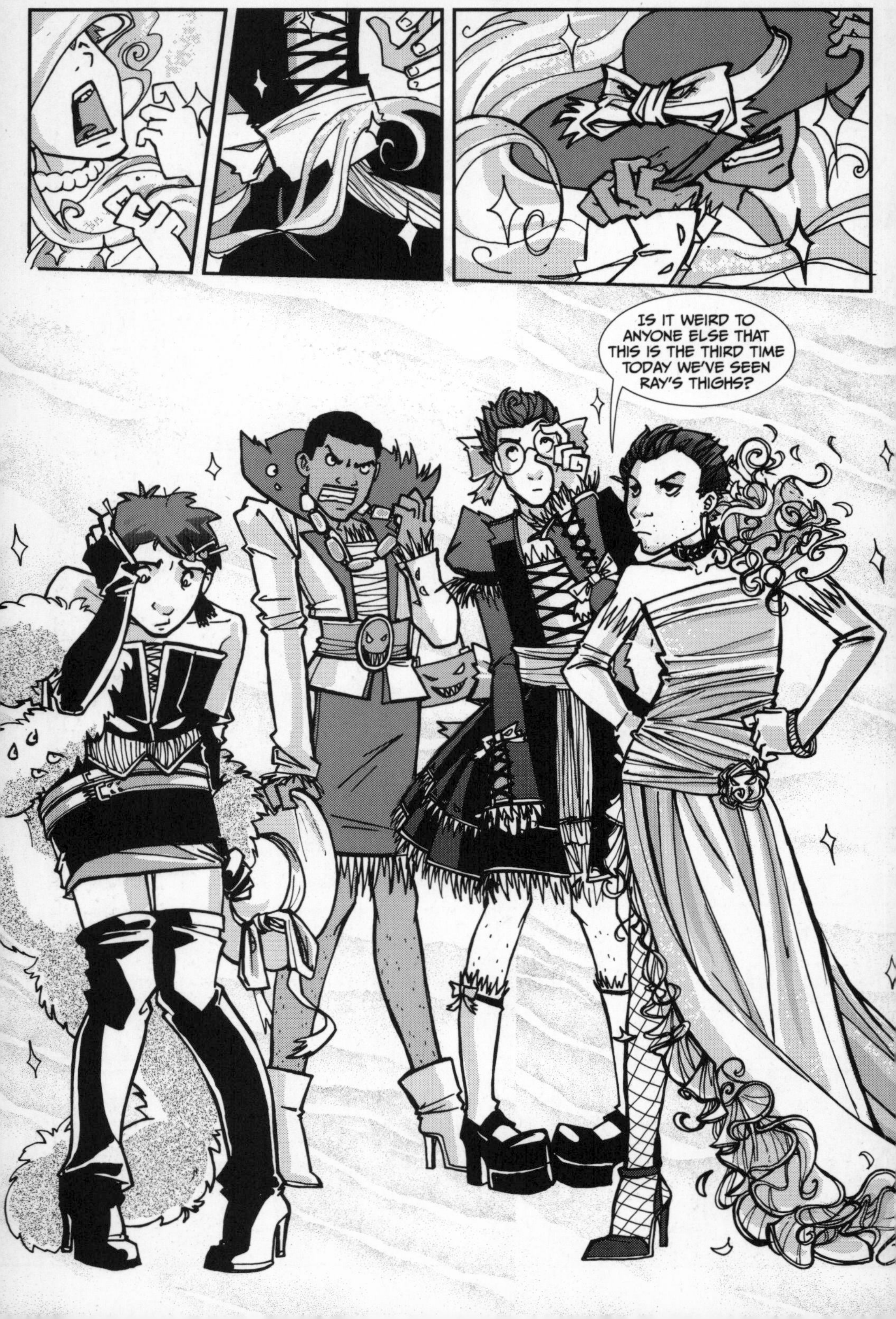
IS IT WEIRD TO ANYONE ELSE THAT THIS IS THE THIRD TIME TODAY WE'VE SEEN RAY'S THIGHS?

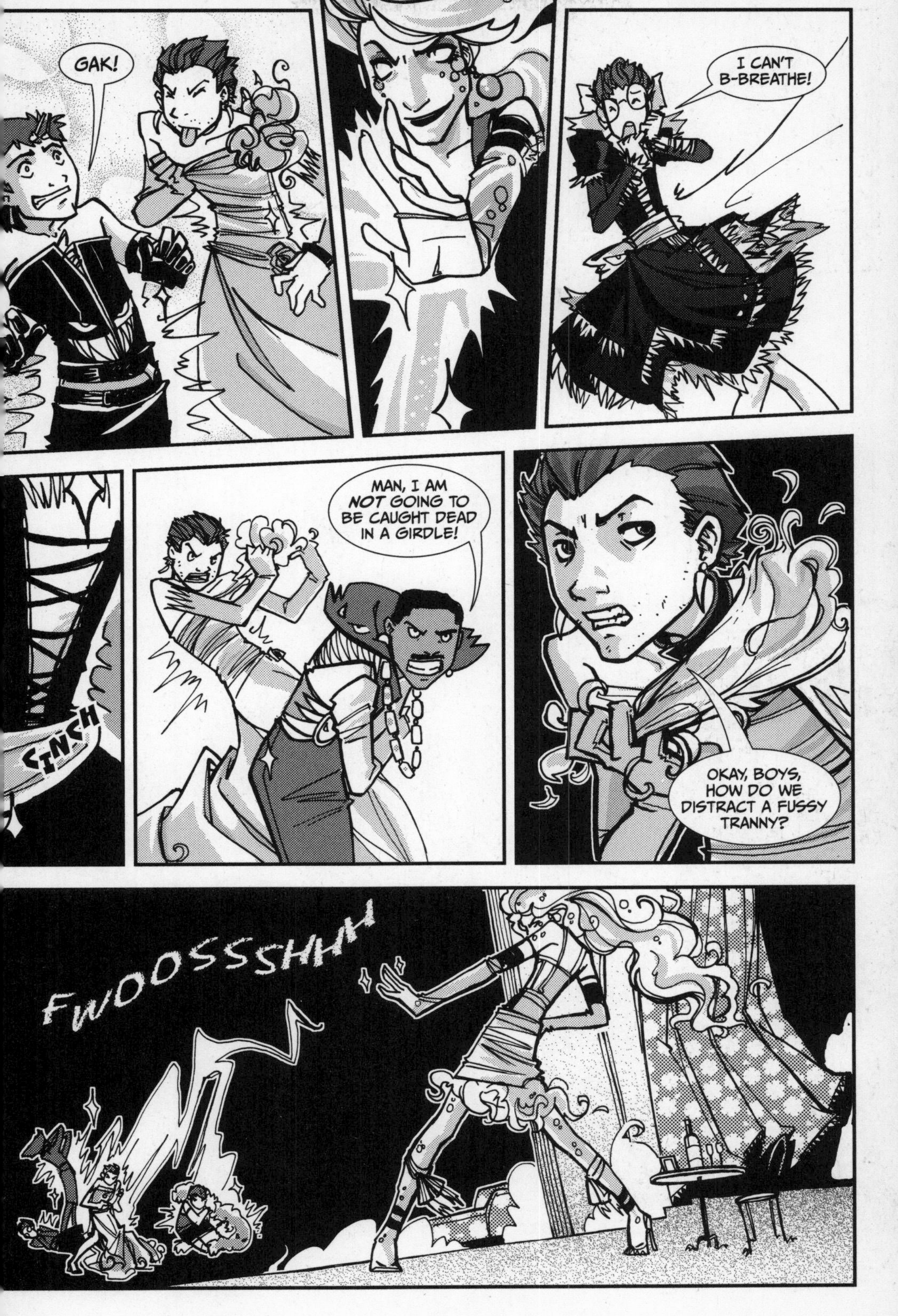
GAK!
I CAN'T B-BREATHE!
CINCH
MAN, I AM *NOT* GOING TO BE CAUGHT DEAD IN A GIRDLE!
OKAY, BOYS, HOW DO WE DISTRACT A FUSSY TRANNY?
FWOOSSSHHH

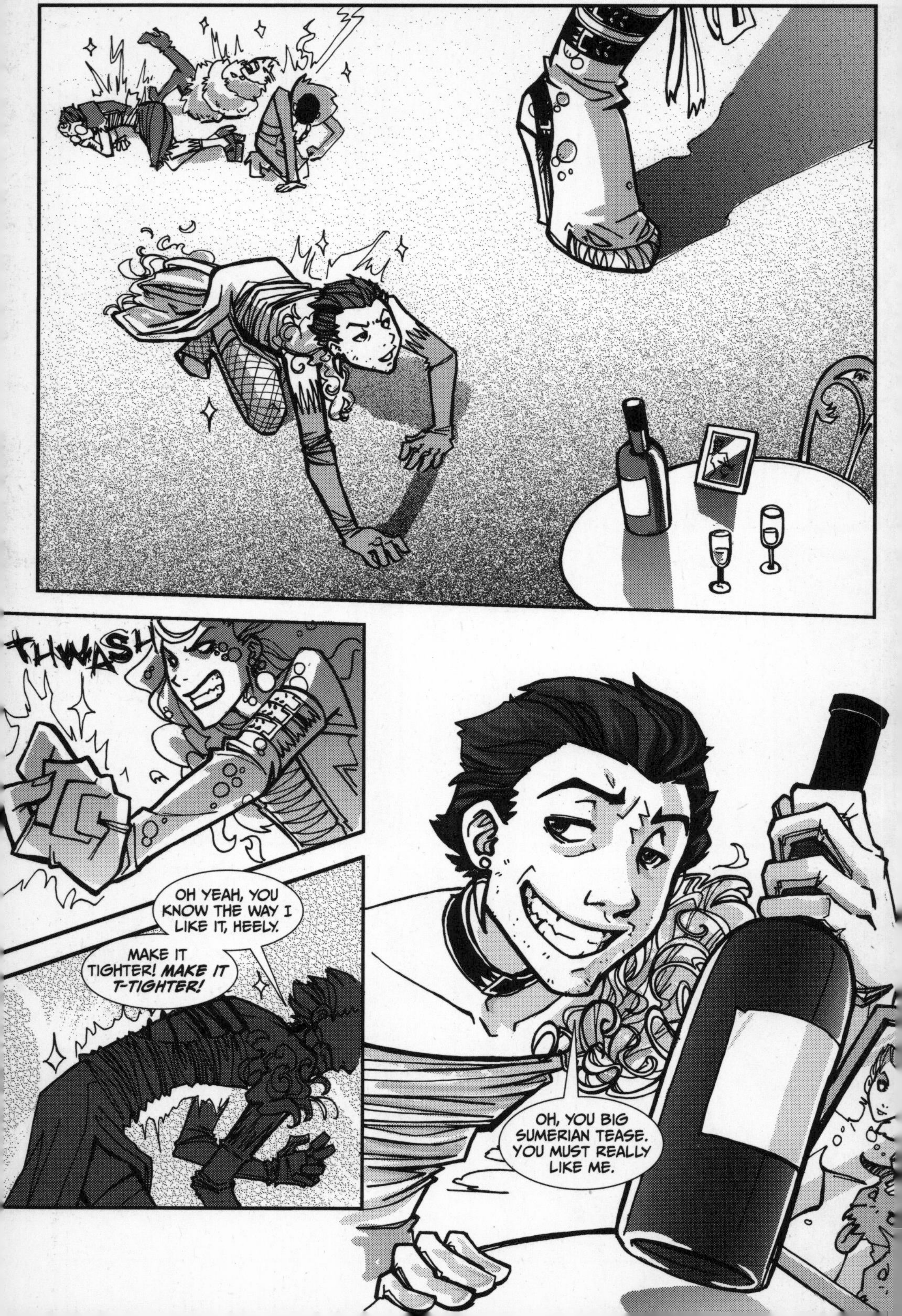
THWASH
OH YEAH, YOU KNOW THE WAY I LIKE IT, HEELY.
MAKE IT TIGHTER! *MAKE IT T-TIGHTER!*
OH, YOU BIG SUMERIAN TEASE. YOU MUST REALLY LIKE ME.

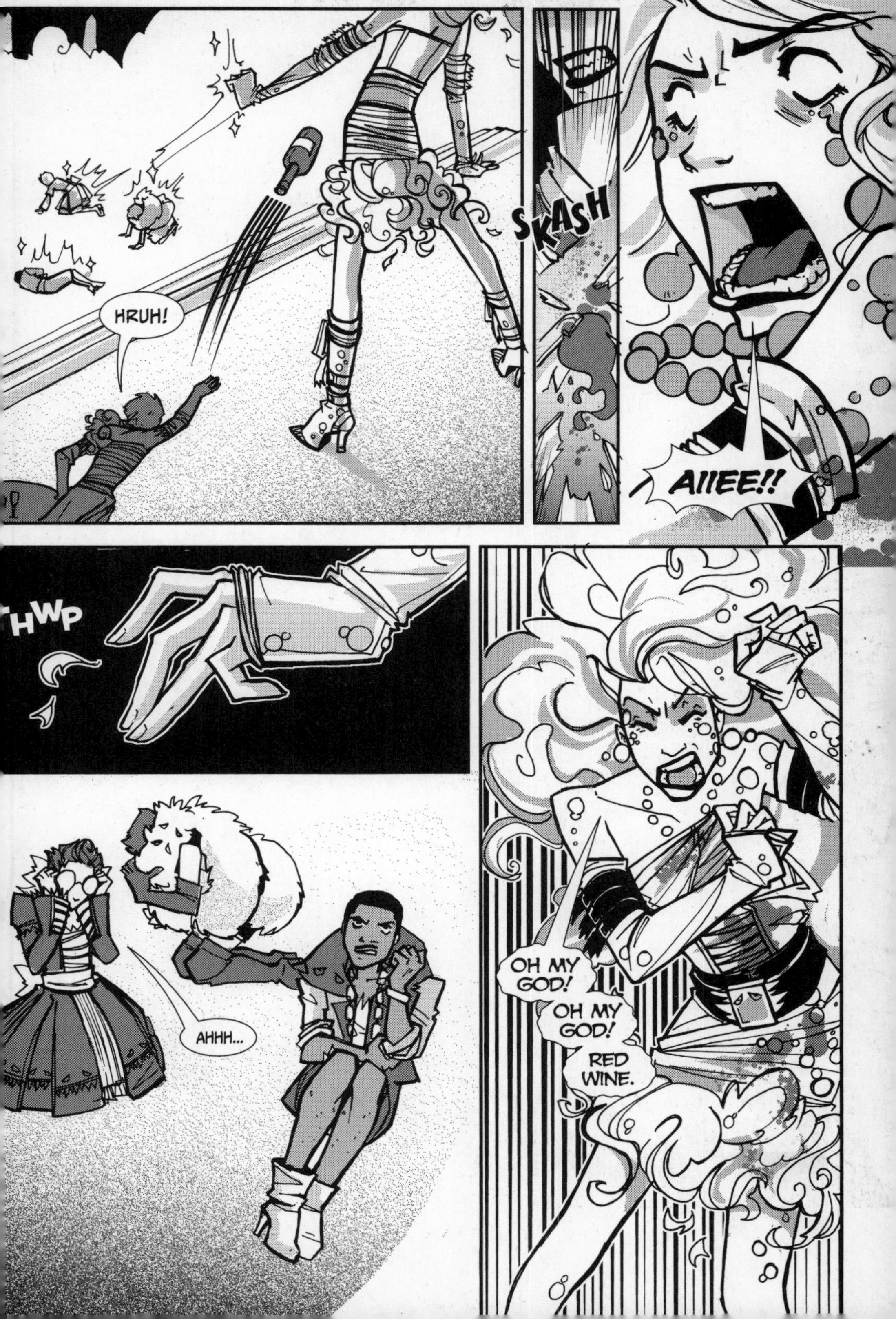
HRUH!
SKASH
AIIEE!!
THWP
OH MY GOD!
OH MY GOD!
RED WINE.
AHHH...

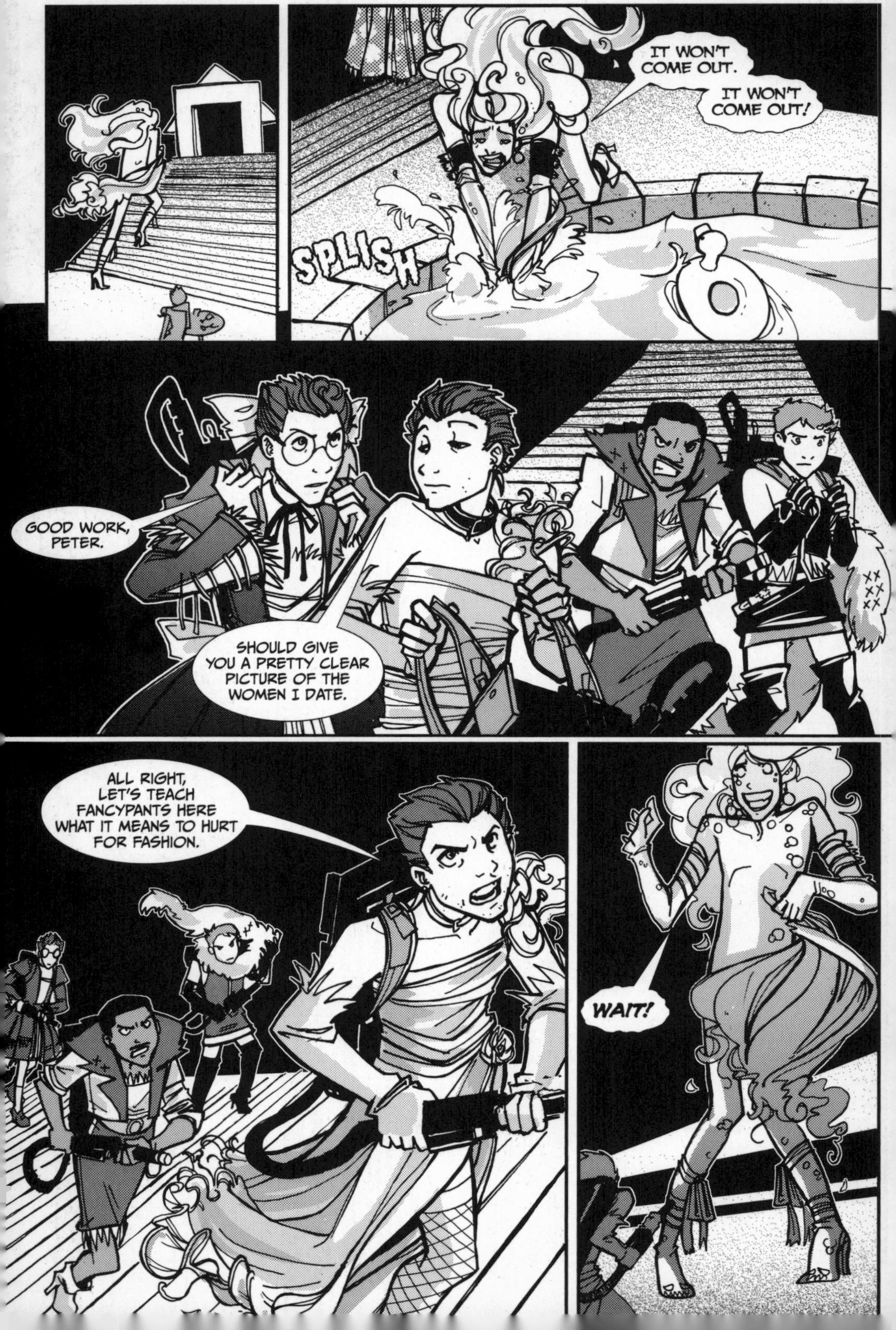
IT WON'T COME OUT.
IT WON'T COME OUT!
SPLISH
GOOD WORK, PETER.
SHOULD GIVE YOU A PRETTY CLEAR PICTURE OF THE WOMEN I DATE.
ALL RIGHT, LET'S TEACH FANCYPANTS HERE WHAT IT MEANS TO HURT FOR FASHION.
WAIT!

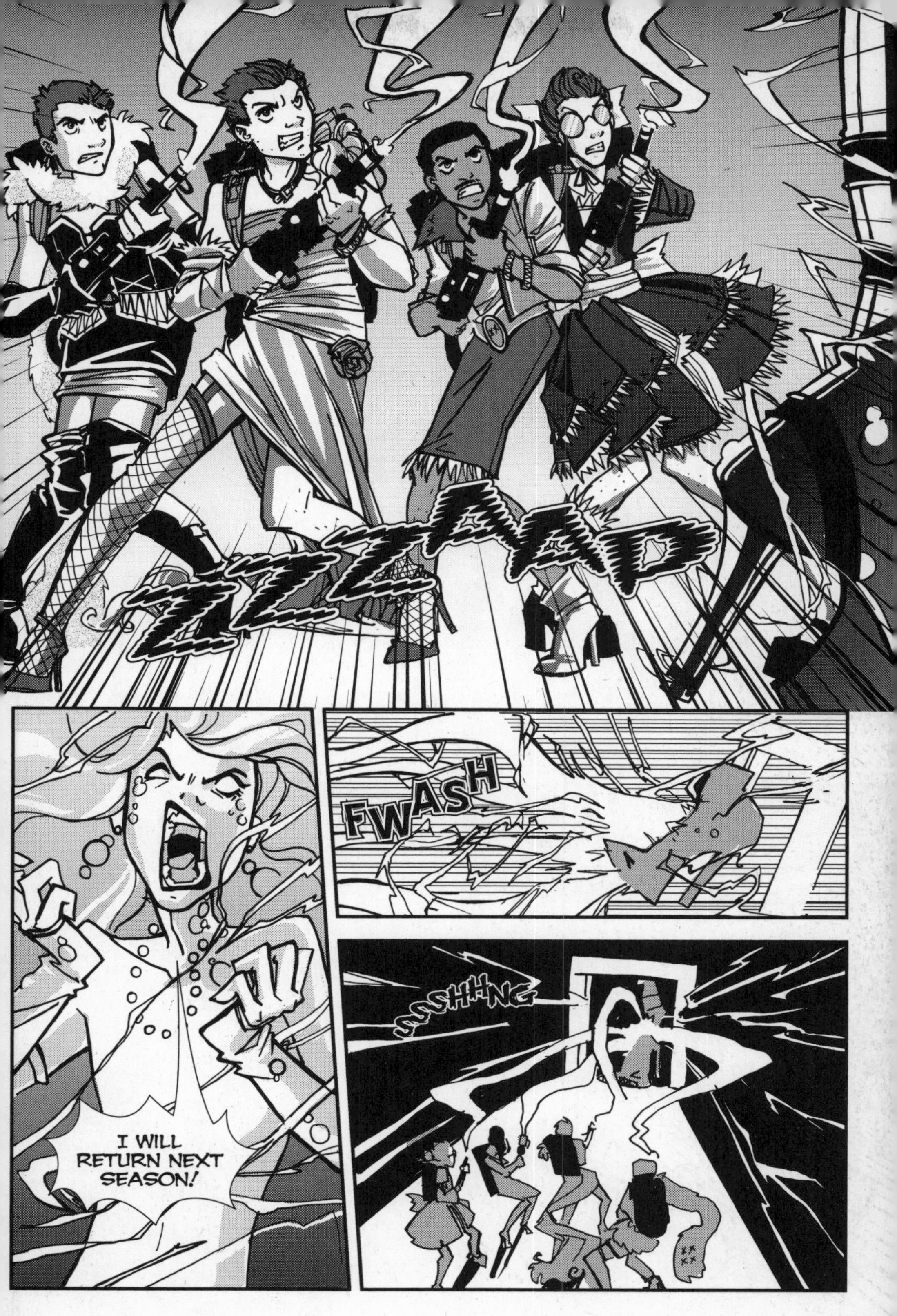
ZZZAAAP
I WILL RETURN NEXT SEASON!
FWASH
SSSSHHHNG

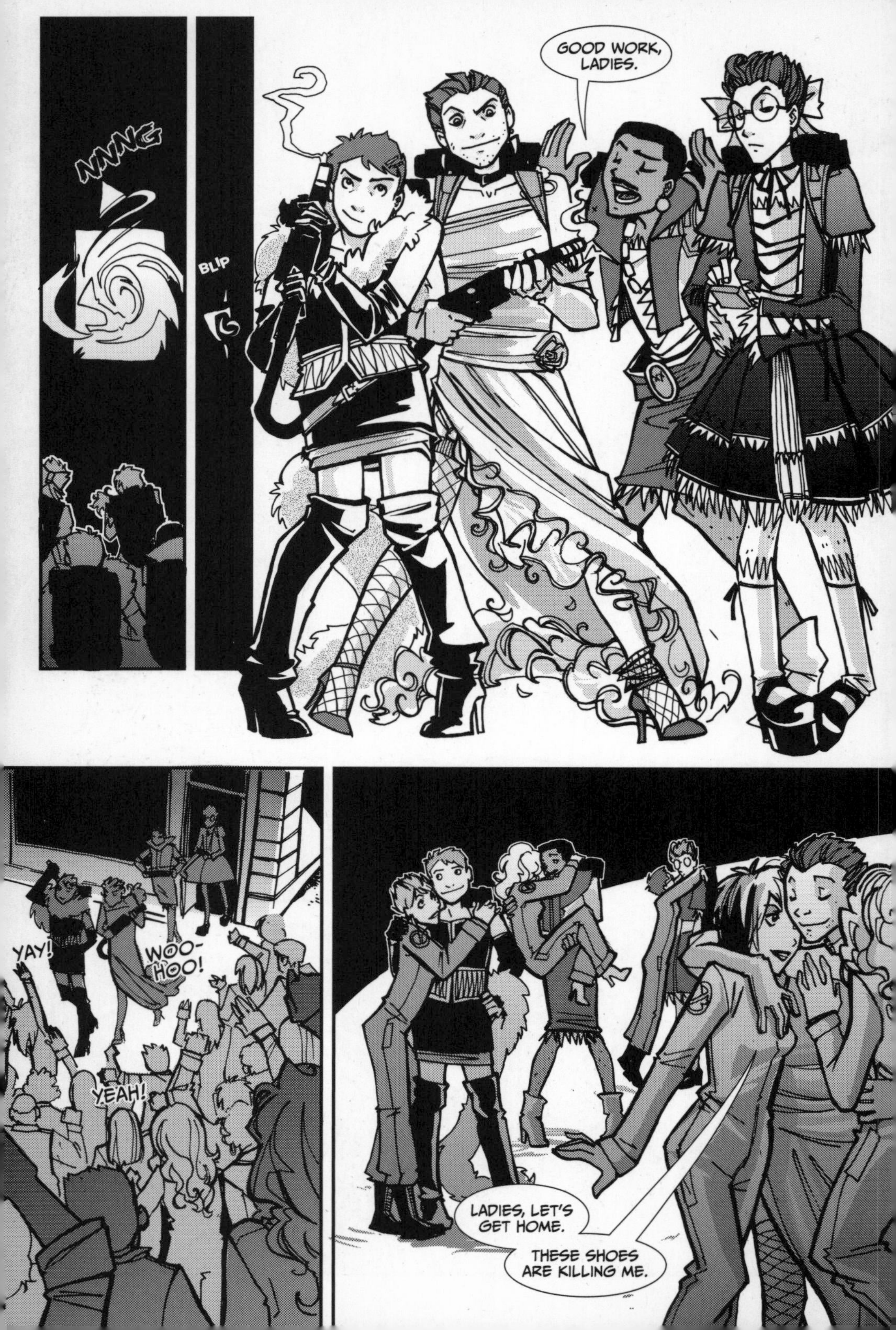
NNNG
BLIP
GOOD WORK, LADIES.
YAY!
WOO-HOO!
YEAH!
LADIES, LET'S GET HOME.
THESE SHOES ARE KILLING ME.

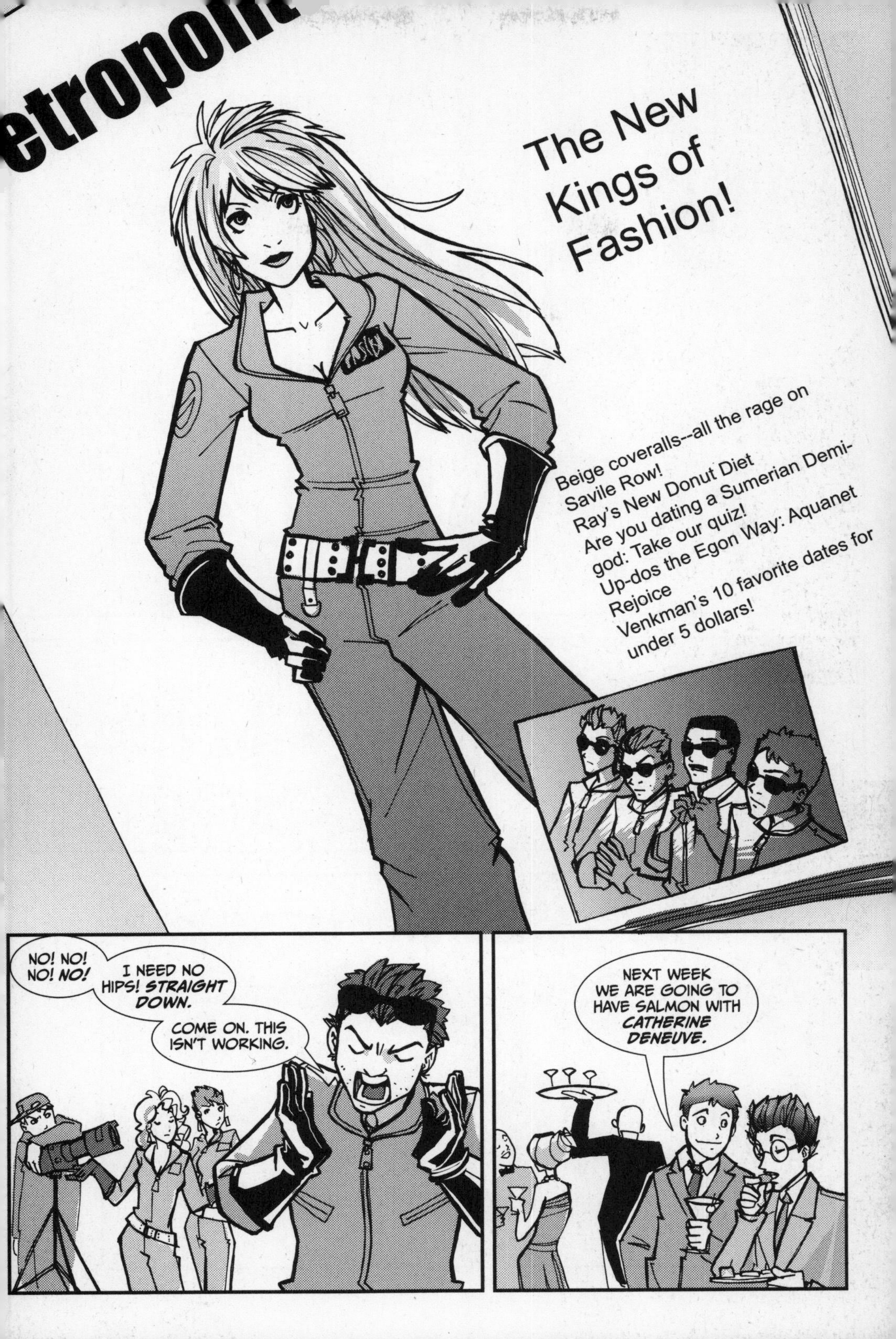
etropoli
The New Kings of Fashion!
Beige coveralls--all the rage on Savile Row!
Ray's New Donut Diet
Are you dating a Sumerian Demi-god: Take our quiz!
Up-dos the Egon Way: Aquanet Rejoice
Venkman's 10 favorite dates for under 5 dollars!
NO! NO! NO! NO!
I NEED NO HIPS! STRAIGHT DOWN.
COME ON. THIS ISN'T WORKING.
NEXT WEEK WE ARE GOING TO HAVE SALMON WITH CATHERINE DENEUVE.

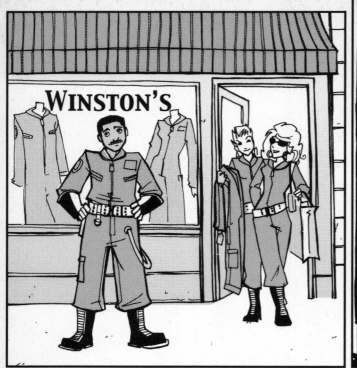

WINSTON'S

ACTUALLY, NOT HALF BAD.

GHOSTBUSTERS. WHAT DO YOU WANT?

SPLIT PEA?

AGAIN?

MOTHERS OF MERCY SOUP KITCHEN

END

# GHOSTBUSTERS™

THE END?

I WOULDN'T BET ON IT, BUB!
YOU KNOW WHO TO CALL...

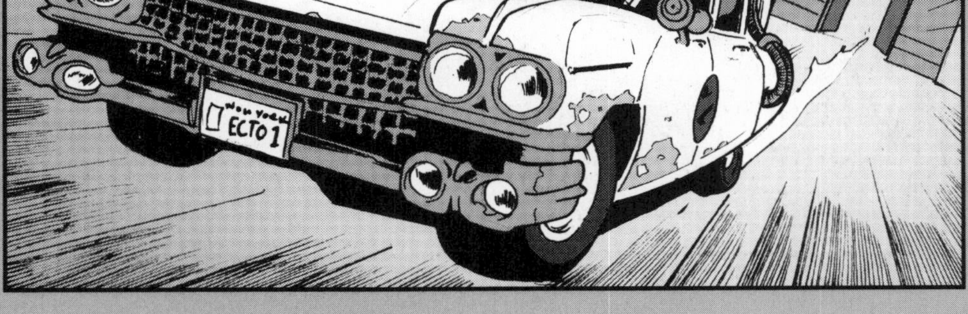
New York
ECTO 1

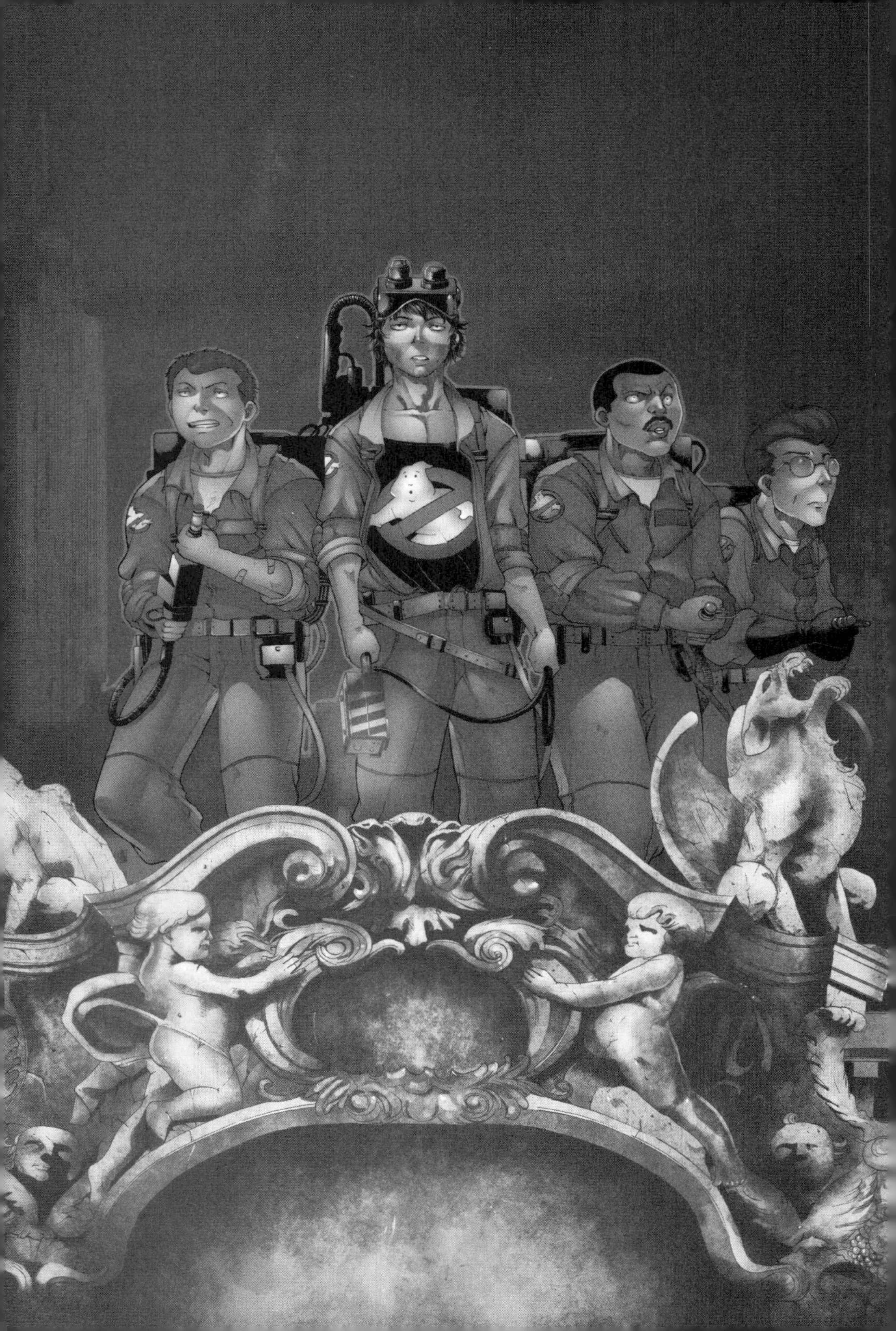

# Ghostbusters Auxiliary

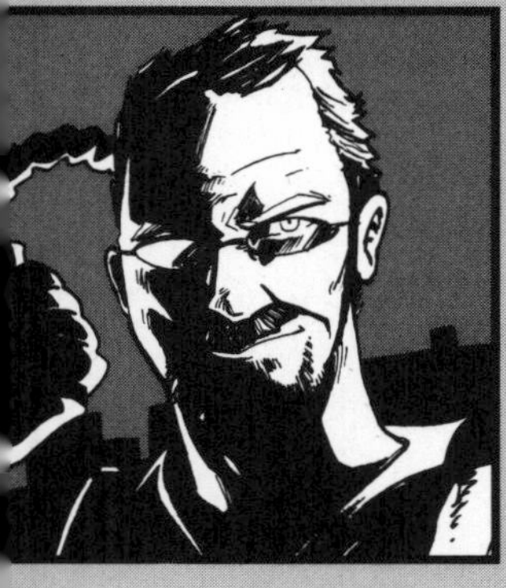

## NATHAN JOHNSON - WRITER

A NATIVE OF BELL BUCKLE, TN, NATHAN G. JOHNSON FIRST CAME TO LOS ANGELES TO STUDY THEATER AS AN UNDERGRAD AT UCLA. HE NOW MAKES HIS LIVING AS A BLUE-COLLAR ACTOR, HUSTLING FOR COMMERCIALS, VOICE-OVER WORK, BIT TV PARTS AND THE OCCASIONAL CHEAP FLICK. THE TITLE HE IS MOST PROUD OF, OTHER THAN *GHOSTBUSTERS,* IS *STRAWBERRY MARSHMALLOW.* NATHAN LIVES HAPPILY IN MONTEREY HILLS WITH HIS CHARMING WIFE, YUKI AND THEIR FREAKING SUPER-CUTE BABY, ALICE.

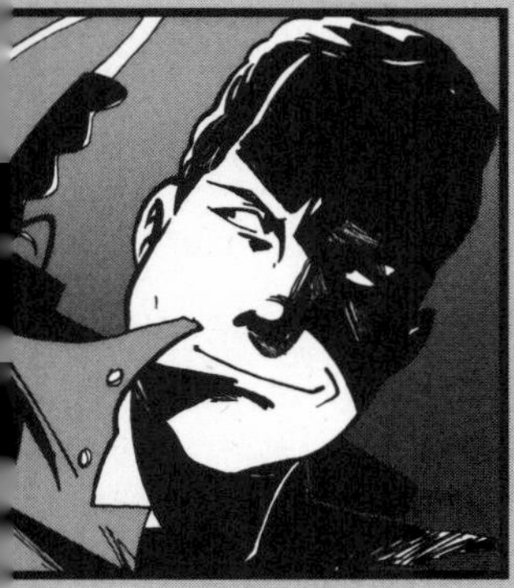

## MATT YAMASHITA - WRITER

MATT YAMASHITA LIVES IN LOS ANGELES WITH HIS WIFE AND DOG. IN ADDITION TO THE ADAPTATIONS OF *LUPIN III* AND *SATISFACTION GUARANTEED* FOR TOKYOPOP, MATT HAS PUBLISHED SHORT FICTION, TWO PLAYS, AND COUNTLESS PERSONAL MANIFESTOS. HE WOULD LIKE TO THANK THE ARTISTS, EDITORS, AND, OF COURSE, THE GHOST OF LUIS REYES FOR THEIR WORK ON THIS PROJECT.

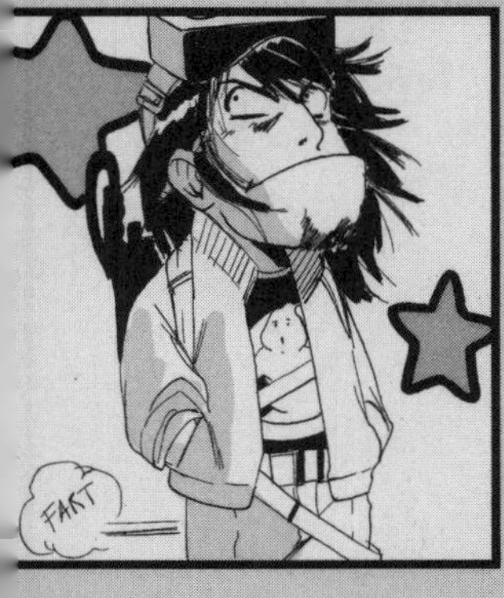
FART

## HANS "HANZO" STEINBACH - COVER ARTIST

HANS STEINBACH IS THE CREATOR OF *A MIDNIGHT OPERA* AND *POISON CANDY,* BOTH PUBLISHED BY TOKYOPOP. HANS' ELEGANT ART STYLE IS HEAVILY INFLUENCED BY YEARS OF TRAVELING WITH HIS FAMILY. HE HAS LIVED IN SYRIA, LEBANON, GERMANY, FRANCE, CANADA, TURKEY AND THE U.S., BUT YOU CAN FIND HIM ONLINE AT: WWW.TOKYOPOP.COM/A_MIDNIGHT_OPERA AND WWW.TOKYOPOP.COM/POISON_CANDY.

# Ghostbusters Auxiliary

## CHRISSY DELK - ARTIST

CHRISSY DELK GREW UP OUTSIDE OF DENVER, COLORADO AND EVENTUALLY MIGRATED TO THE SOUTH FOR A DEGREE IN COMICS. NOW, UNLEASHED UPON THE WORLD, SHE'S DRAWN INSTALLMENTS FOR THE *STAR TREK: THE NEXT GENERATION* ANTHOLOGY AND, OF COURSE, THIS *GHOSTBUSTERS* MANGA, BOTH FROM TOKYOPOP. SHE CURRENTLY RESIDES IN THE LOS ANGELES AREA WITH HER HOARD OF BOOKS AND PLANTS. MORE OF HER WORK AND PROJECTS ARE AVAILABLE AT HTTP://CHRISSYDELK.DEVIANTART. COM AND HTTP://CHRISSYDELK.COM

## MAXIMO V. LORENZO - ARTIST

BORN IN VENEZUELA THEN RAISED IN VIRGINIA, MAXIMO MOVED TO NJ TO FINISH HIS STUDIES AT THE JOE KUBERT SCHOOL OF COMICS AND CARTOONING. HE CURRENTLY WORKS ON COMICS, COMMISSIONS, CARICATURES, CONCEPT ART, AND ANYTHING ELSE HE CAN GET HIS HANDS ON. HE ENJOYS A WIDE VARIETY OF ART AND COMICS FROM AROUND THE WORLD, AND ALSO ENJOYS APPLYING THE MANY VARIETIES OF STYLES FOR HIMSELF. YOU CAN SEE MORE ABOUT HIM AND HIS PROJECTS AT HTTP://SPEEDKING.DEVIANTART. COM AND HTTP://8BITMAXIMO.COM

# Ghostbusters Auxiliary

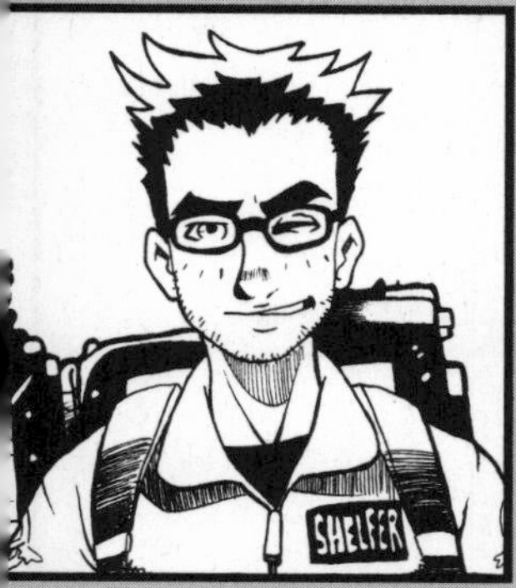
SHELFER

## MICHAEL SHELFER – ARTIST

AFTER WINNING RSOM 5'S PEOPLES CHOICE AWARD, MICHAEL SHELFER HAS GONE ON TO ILLUSTRATE A VARIETY OF GRAPHIC NOVELS AND MANGA, INCLUDING *DEAD ALREADY* FOR SEVEN SEAS ENTERTAINMENT AND *PRIVATE SCHOOL* FOR TOKYOPOP. HE WAS ALSO A CONTRIBUTING ARTIST FOR *STAR TREK* THE MANGA VOL. 1. IN HIS FREE TIME HE ENJOYS....WELL, HE HAS NO FREE TIME. MICHAEL WAS LAST SEEN ATOP THE SUMMIT OF MT. FUGI TRYING DESPERATELY TO GET HIS "CHI" ON.

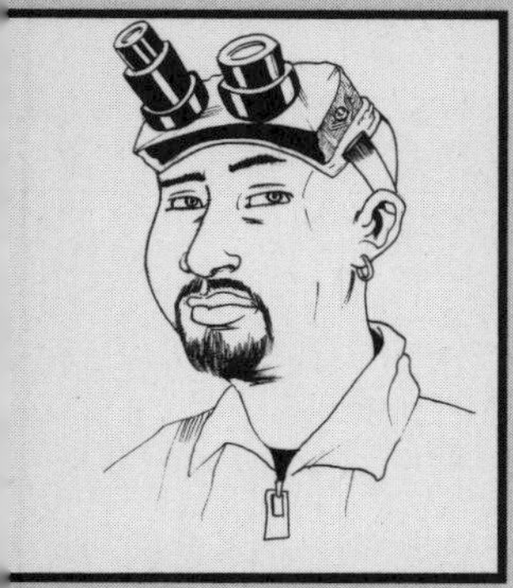

## NATE WATSON – ARTIST

NATE WATSON GREW UP IN THE DESERT OASIS KNOWN AS EL PASO IN THE STATE OF TEXAS. AFTER A STINT IN THE MILITARY, HE SETTLED IN SAN FRANCISCO, WHERE HE DRAWS FUNNY BOOKS AND TENDS TO HIS MULTIPLE OFFSPRING. HE HAS WORKED FOR ZENESCOPE ENTERTAINMENT, BOOM! STUDIOS AND ON TOKYOPOP'S THIRD INSTALLMENT OF *THE STAR TREK: TOS* MANGA.

# Early Design Sketches

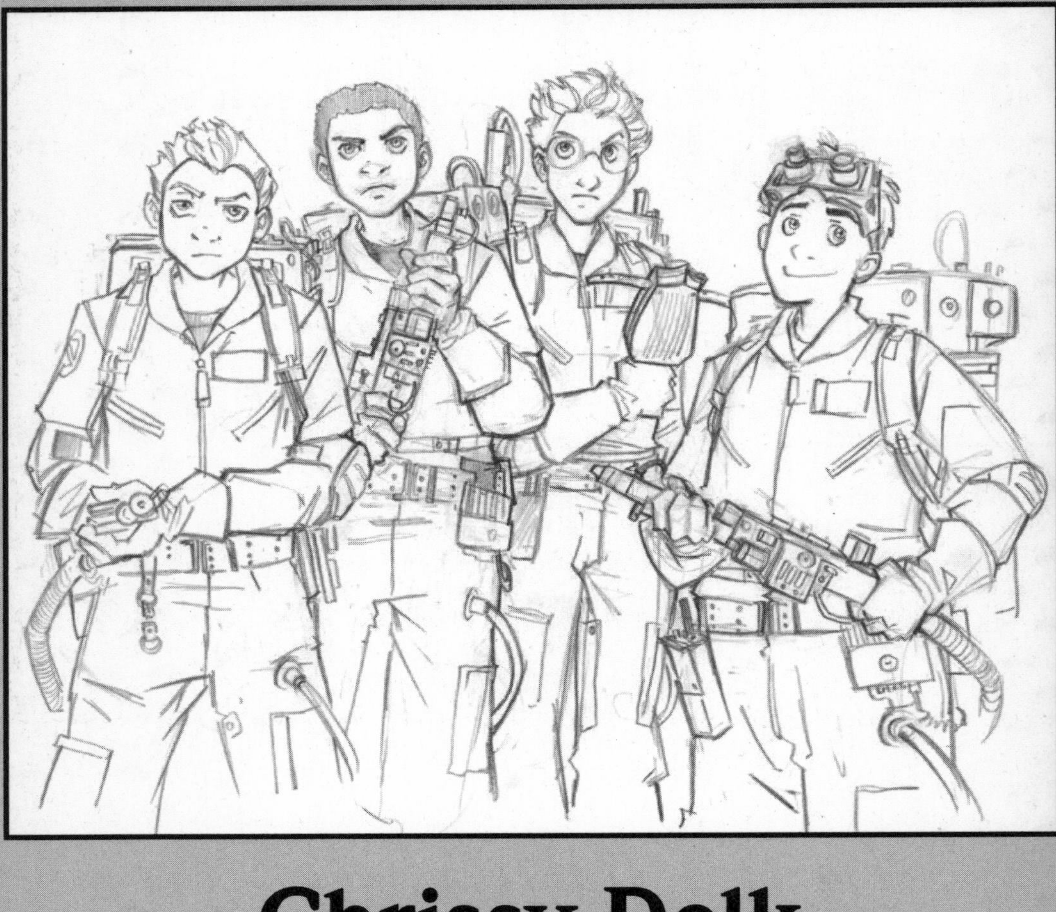

# Chrissy Delk

# Early Design Sketches

# Maximo V. Lorenzo

# Early Design Sketches

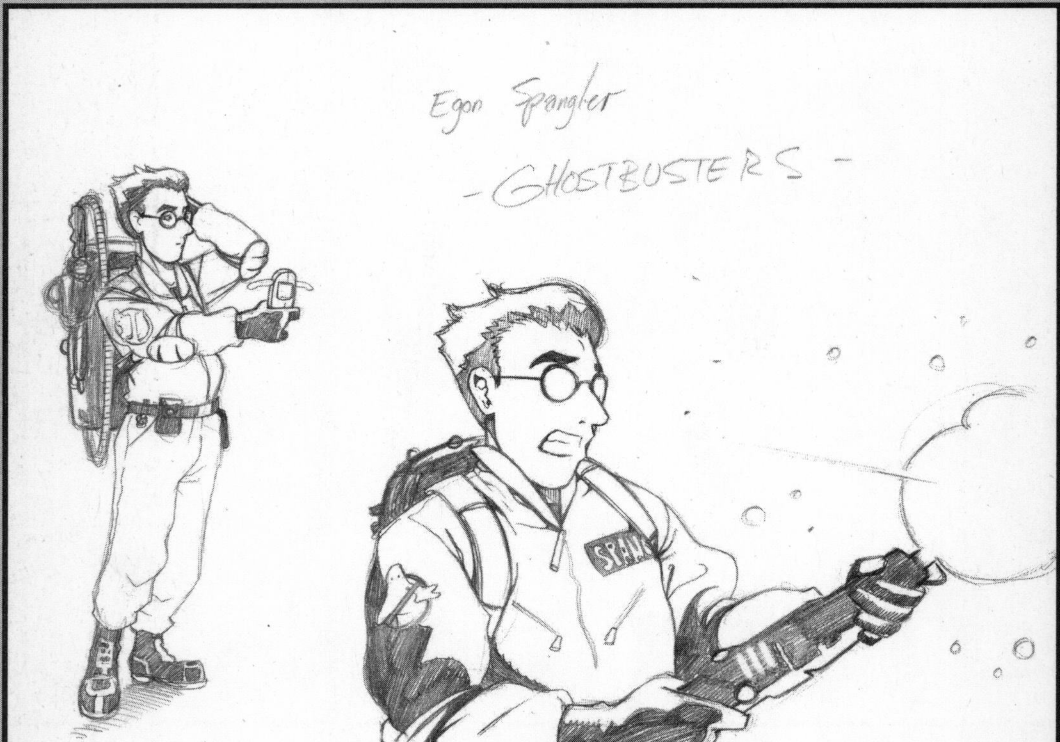

Egon Spangler
- GHOSTBUSTERS -
Shelfer -08


# Michael Shelfer

# Early Design Sketches

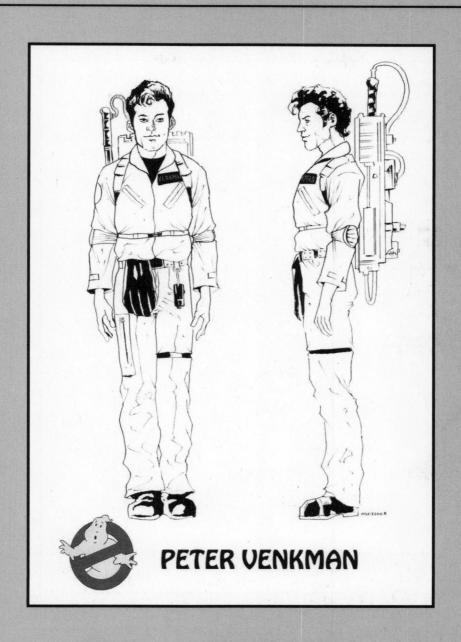

PETER VENKMAN

# Nate Watson

# Early Design Sketches

## Hans Steinbach

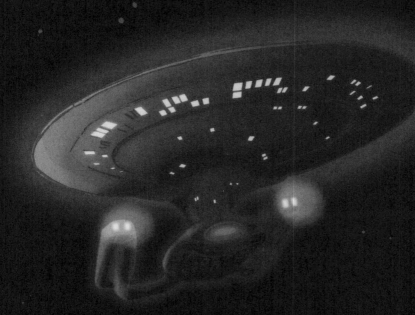